THE CORPORATION IN NEW JERSEY

STUDIES IN ECONOMIC HISTORY

PUBLISHED IN COÖPERATION WITH THE COMMITTEE
ON RESEARCH IN ECONOMIC HISTORY
SOCIAL SCIENCE RESEARCH COUNCIL

THE CORPORATION IN NEW JERSEY

BUSINESS AND POLITICS 1791–1875

JOHN W. CADMAN, JR.

HARVARD UNIVERSITY PRESS
CAMBRIDGE, MASSACHUSETTS
1949

PRINTED IN THE UNITED STATES OF AMERICA

LONDON : GEOFFREY CUMBERLEGE
OXFORD UNIVERSITY PRESS

TO

MY FATHER AND MOTHER

Foreword

STUDENTS of American economic development have for decades felt a special annoyance at one particular aspect of our constitutional and legal evolution, that which left the chartering of business corporations chiefly in the hands of the several states. English experience with the corporate form has had its Scott, Dubois, and Hunt, who together have surveyed the whole story. The study of equivalent developments in France or Canada has appeared even more feasible than the study of developments in England — although unhappily neither survey has been carried through. But the spectacle of forty-eight jurisdictions seems to have palsied the efforts of American students in examination of American corporations.

For the United States, the literature respecting corporation history has indeed been meagre, despite the large amount of research that in recent decades has gone into an examination of American economic development. Joseph S. Davis' excellent study of the eighteenth-century beginnings — with the delectably modest title, "Essays in the Earlier History of American Corporations" — has stood out as an example of careful inquiry. But few indeed have ventured to go further, even into the experience of individual states.

The Committee on Research in Economic History, accordingly, displayed no peculiar sagacity in fixing upon the "later" development of American corporations as one of the important neglected areas in our economic history. (At that time it was unaware of the work that G. Heberton Evans, Jr., had already begun and that subsequently resulted in his path-breaking statistical volume, *Business Incorporations in the United States, 1800–1943*. Even with this valuable contribution, much remained to be done.) Unfortunately, the Committee's offers to assist in explorations within the field evoked little response. Possibly other topics appeared more manageable to doctoral or even more mature students. Possibly such men hesitated from lack of a model by which to mold their own inquiries in this relatively unexplored area.

Quite obviously, then, the Committee could welcome with enthusiasm the submission by Dr. Cadman of his manuscript upon the New Jersey business corporation which he had prepared at Princeton at the suggestion of Professor Stanley E. Howard. Here was a careful, thorough study relative to a state particularly significant for corporation history. Here was a model by which other inquiries could be organized. And here was also an important contribution to American economic history. The Committee, therefore, takes pleasure in offering Dr. Cadman's study to the world of scholars.

August 5, 1949

ARTHUR H. COLE
Chairman, Committee on Research in Economic History

Preface

IN SPITE of the immense importance that business corporations have attained among present-day economic institutions, there is a notable lack of exact knowledge about many aspects of the early history of the business corporation in the United States that should be of interest to the student of the American economy. The small amount of attention paid to the early development of the business corporation in this country has frequently been commented upon by students of economic history. A little over a decade ago, for example, Edwin M. Dodd, Jr., made the following statement:

> Already important by 1830, the business corporation has to-day become the outstanding fact in our economic organization. Yet its early history remains obscure. The legal side of that history is contained in a multitude of special acts of incorporation, a wilderness as yet largely unexplored. Although much has been written about the economic history of the United States, the failure of economists to devote much attention to the early corporation laws has prevented them from dealing adequately with the effect of these laws on business development.[1]

A similar observation was made by Charles C. Abbott:

> Oddly enough there is little precise or accurate knowledge of many of the aspects of the growth of the business corporation which are of particular interest to the economist. We know from common knowledge of the great multiplication of business corporations in the last hundred and fifty years, of the increase in their size, the number of their employees and stockholders, of their spread from industry to industry, of the importance of corporation and franchise taxes to the individual states and, more recently, the reliance of the federal government upon corporation income taxes. But in spite of the material

[1] E. M. Dodd, Jr., "The First Half Century of Statutory Regulation of Business Coporations in Massachusetts," *Harvard Legal Essays*, pp. 69–70.

available for the investigation of subjects of this sort few such studies have been undertaken. Only here and there can opinion and general observation be substantiated by statistical or factual proof.[2]

The essays of Joseph S. Davis dealing with eighteenth century corporations are still the most important single contribution to our knowledge of the pre-twentieth century history of the American business corporation. These essays were published over thirty years ago.[3] Since that time, Edwin M. Dodd, Jr., has published an essay that sets forth the principal facts about the history of business corporations in Massachusetts before 1830,[4] Joseph G. Blandi has investigated certain aspects of the development of business corporations in Maryland between 1783 and 1852,[5] Louis Hartz has presented many significant facts about Pennsylvania's corporation policy up to 1860,[6] William C. Kessler has published a statistical study of the corporate charters granted in the New England States from 1800 to 1875,[7] and George H. Evans, Jr., has made a very valuable contribution by compiling and analyzing the statistics of business incorporations for a number of states.[8] Systematic studies of the history of the business corporation in many important jurisdictions, however, are still lacking. Moreover, very little attention has been given to the period between 1850 and 1875, years of great industrial expansion in the United States. The development of general incorporation laws in the United States during the nineteenth century has also been virtually neglected as a subject of investigation.

It is with a view to adding further illumination to this dark corner of economic history that the present study of the early development of the business corporation in New Jersey has been undertaken. For a variety of reasons, New Jersey was selected

[2] C. C. Abbott, *The Rise of the Business Corporation*, pp. 45–46.

[3] J. S. Davis, *Essays in the Earlier History of American Corporations.*

[4] Dodd, pp. 65–132.

[5] J. G. Blandi, *Maryland Business Corporations: 1783–1852.*

[6] Louis Hartz, *Economic Policy and Democratic Thought: Pennsylvania, 1776–1860.*

[7] W. C. Kessler, "Incorporation in New England: A Statistical Study, 1800–1875," *Journal of Economic History*, VIII (May 1948), pp. 43–62.

[8] G. H. Evans, Jr., *Business Incorporations in the United States: 1800–1943.*

as an appropriate state for investigation. Before the people of New Jersey adopted a more felicitous nickname, their state had been called at various times "The State of Camden and Amboy," "The Home of the Trusts," and "A Traitor State." All these opprobrious designations had reference to the policy of the state with respect to its business corporations. Since by the early twentieth century New Jersey had become notorious for a "liberal" attitude toward business corporations and for the size and importance of many of the companies it had chartered, the background history of the development of public policy concerning the corporation in that state assumes a special significance.

The diversity of economic activity in nineteenth century New Jersey also recommended the state as a satisfactory choice for study. To present an undistorted picture of the development of the business corporation, it was desirable that the jurisdiction examined have a diversified economy of the kind enjoyed by New Jersey. Although small in total area, the state encompassed a considerable amount of productive agricultural land. It was also adequately, and in some respects richly, endowed with raw materials for manufacturing. There were, for example, iron and copper for the metal trades, clay for potteries, and sand for glass manufacturing. Sources of energy were available in the form of water power within the state and coal from near-by areas. Financial resources for industrial development as well as readily available markets for goods were afforded by the adjacent commercial and financial centers of New York City and Philadelphia. The transportation industry, too, was important in New Jersey, for the state stood astride the only direct north-south route along the Atlantic seaboard.

One of the most important nineteenth century developments in connection with business corporations in America was the widespread adoption of general incorporation statutes as substitutes for special or private acts of incorporation. New Jersey did not abandon the system of special charters suddenly. For three decades after general incorporation laws were available in New Jersey to those who wished to make use of them, most groups seeking charters applied for, and were favored with, special acts of incorporation. This long experience with a dual system of chartering makes New Jersey's history peculiarly significant to one who wishes to trace the development of the general incorporation law movement.

Finally, the relatively small size of New Jersey promised certain advantages in making the study. Since fewer charters were granted in New Jersey than in the larger states, it appeared that a more intensive study of the general development and a more detailed analysis of the charters could be made than would be feasible in connection with many other jurisdictions. This favorable feature was neutralized to a large extent, however, by the almost complete lack of uniformity in the terms of the special charters granted in New Jersey, by the paucity of official state documents, and by a scarcity of trustworthy secondary material bearing on the history of the state.

The period of years selected for investigation begins with 1791, the year in which New Jersey's first business corporation was chartered, and ends with 1875. Thus the study covers a period that witnessed the transformation of the American economy from a rudimentary form into the complex organization that emerged from the industrial revolution in America. The year 1875 was chosen as the terminal date because the constitutional amendments of that year brought to an end the system of chartering corporations by special act in New Jersey. Thenceforth all corporations had to be organized under general incorporation laws. The constitutional amendments forced a revolutionary change in New Jersey's corporation policy and hence mark the logical conclusion of one long chapter in the state's history.

The term "business corporation" has been used in the present study in a broad sense to include all profit-seeking enterprises chartered by the state. All stock-issuing corporations have been included in that category with the exception of a few friendly societies, academies, cemetery associations, and similar organizations where, in the judgment of the author, profit seeking was not the principal incentive. It has seemed desirable to include within the meaning of "business corporations" mutual savings institutions and mutual insurance companies that were incorporated by the legislature. These mutual institutions performed distinctly economic functions and operated in their appropriate spheres alongside stock companies chartered for the same purposes.

The study has been divided into two principal sections and a conclusion. Part I consists of a general and chronological survey of the development of public policy with respect to the business corporation in New Jersey through the year 1875. In the discussion, particular attention is directed to a consideration of public and official willingness to accept the device of the private corporation in the principal spheres of economic activity and to an examination of the various legislative procedures by which corporate privileges were granted to business enterprises. Throughout the section, emphasis has been placed on the political and economic factors that influenced the course of public policy.

Part II is designed to provide an analysis of the precise terms of the charters granted to business firms incorporated in New Jersey up to 1875. For this purpose a topical arrangement of the material has been adopted, and separate treatments are accorded such general subjects as the type and scope of business permitted to the companies chartered, their capital structure, the relationship between stockholders and directors, the liability of stockholders and directors for the business debts, state control of the corporations, and the relation of the corporations to the state revenues. The discussion under each of the topics is concerned with the provisions of special charters and charter amendments, with the provisions of the various general incorporation laws, and with other legislation affecting business corporations that bears on the subject under consideration.

Unfortunately it has been necessary to discuss many aspects of the development of public policy toward corporations in New Jersey without reference to what was occurring in other incorporating jurisdictions. Some attempt has been made, however, to provide comparisons when they appeared significant. Thus Part I contains an analysis of the clauses relating to business corporations that were found in the constitutions of the several states before 1875. A survey of such provisions does not by any means provide a complete picture of the policies pursued by these jurisdictions in the matter of chartering business corporations, but, in the absence of detailed studies for each state, it is useful as an indicator of the broad trends in the development of policy in the whole country. At numerous points in the study, comparisons between New Jersey statutes and the statutes of some other states have been made. To supplement the information about other states that is available in secondary works, a careful examination of the statute books of New York State was undertaken because New Jersey's legislature was frequently guided by the actions of this influential neighbor. Much intensive study must be devoted to the details of the treatment accorded business corporations in a number of American states, however, before a thorough and satisfactory comparative analysis will be possible.

The author wishes to take this opportunity to express his gratitude to Professor Stanley E. Howard of Princeton University for the interest he has shown in the development of this study and for the generous manner in which he has given of his time to read the manuscript at various stages in its preparation. The author is also grateful to the Committee on Research in Economic History of the Social Science Research Council for financial assistance during the time he was preparing the manuscript for publication.

J. W. C., Jr.

CONTENTS

PART III

CONCLUSION

APPENDIXES

TABLES

PART I

Development of Public Policy

CHAPTER I

Incorporation Procedure in New Jersey up to 1844

IN COMMON with most of the original constitutions of the independent American states, the first basic law of New Jersey contained no reference to the process of incorporation. The general interpretation in America was that in the absence of express designation of the incorporating authority, the power to incorporate was an implied and exclusive right of the legislature. This view was not shared by the first executive officer of New Jersey, with the result that the power of granting charters was established as the exclusive privilege of the legislature in that state only after a brief period of trial and error.[1] Governor Livingston of New Jersey made what appears to be the only attempt in independent America to take the incorporating power out of the hands of the legislators.[2] In 1778, that governor issued a charter to a Hopewell church and sealed the document with the great seal of the state. During discussion of a church charter application in 1779, a member of the assembly recalled the governor's action and questioned the necessity of an act of legislature for granting a charter. When the governor's charter was produced and read to the house, it was unanimously resolved:

> That the said Charter or Instrument of Writing is not warranted by Law, and therefore void . . .
>
> That the Power of granting Patents and Charters of Incorporation,

[1] The lack of agreement in New Jersey may have resulted from the fact that in the proprietary colonies of East and West Jersey and after 1702 in the royal colony of New Jersey the incorporating power was at various times exercised by the colonial assemblies and by the proprietary and royal governors. Cf. J. S. Davis, *Essays in the Earlier History of American Corporations*, I, 15–17, 66–69, and 85–86.

[2] Davis, II, 9; *Proceedings of the New Jersey Historical Society*, 3 ser. III, 117.

under the present Constitution, is vested solely in the Legislature of the State.[3]

The members of the council were less inclined to take such a firm stand in sweeping away gubernatorial power. They submitted a message to the assembly stating that the Hopewell congregation had presented a petition for a charter to the legislature in March 1778,

and it being the first Application of the Kind, under the present Government, and the Legislature, then sitting, not fully satisfied whether the Power of granting Charters was vested in the Legislative or Executive Authority, the said Petition being presented to the Governor, who being so advised by the Privy-Council, and having also the Opinion of the Attorney-General, did, in Pursuance of such Advice, grant and affix the Great Seal of the State to a Charter. . . . And the present Legislature having maturely considered the Constitution and Origin of the present Government, are rather of Opinion, that the Right and Power of granting Charters is vested in, and of Consequence must ever remain with, the Representatives of the People . . .[4]

The council's communication closed, however, with a plea not to consider a matter of "such Importance" so near the close of the session and at a time when the members were not all present. An attached resolution read:

That it be recommended to the next Legislature, to consider and determine the Subject-Matter above mentioned; and that the Petitions for Charters preferred to the present Council and Assembly, be deferred until such Determination is made.[5]

When the assembly took the message into consideration, the members refused to concur in the council's resolution. In presenting a series of arguments against the position of the council, the assemblymen denied that the Hopewell congregation had made an application to the legislature in 1778 and affirmed their

[3] *Votes and Proceedings of the General Assembly,* 3 sess., 3 sit. (1779), p. 182.
[4] *Ibid.,* pp. 192–93. [5] *Ibid.,* p. 193.

previous statement that there never was any doubt in the assembly that the chartering power was vested in the legislature. Their argument was that the Hopewell petition had been submitted to the legislature as early as October 1777, and leave to bring in a bill had been immediately granted.[6] Another objection made to the council's resolution afforded the assemblymen further opportunity to make a firm statement of opposition to non-legislative charters. The objection was that the resolution

> seems to imply Uncertainty and Doubt on that Subject, whereas this House is clearly of Opinion that the Right and Power of granting Charters is unquestionably vested in the Representatives of the People.[7]

This skirmish, taking place more than a decade before applications were made for business corporations, settled the question of the incorporating authority in New Jersey. Never again did a governor attempt to grant corporate privileges without the warrant of an act of legislature, and there is no evidence in the state documents of further differences of opinion in this matter between the two houses of the legislature.

Once established as the sole dispenser of corporate powers, the New Jersey legislature proceeded to exercise its prerogative by passing numerous special laws incorporating religious and educational groups. Applications for church charters became sufficiently numerous in a very few years to make an easier method of incorporation for religious organizations desirable. Early in 1786, the legislature enacted a general law enabling religious organizations, if composed of at least thirty family groups, to become incorporated upon filing a certificate with the clerk of the county in which their services were held.[8] The

[6] *Ibid.*, p. 199. It was admitted that the record of the action of 1777 had been "unaccountably omitted" from the printed journal, but it was claimed that it was in the original minutes. [The manuscript copy for 1777 is missing from the collection of the New Jersey State Library and could not be checked by the present writer.]

[7] *Loc. cit.*

[8] "An Act to incorporate certain Persons as Trustees in every religious Society or Congregation in this State, for transacting the temporal Concerns thereof." N. J. Laws, 10 sess., 2 sit. (1786), Ch. 129, p. 255.

general incorporation law was a relatively new and untried device in the America of 1786. It had been unknown in colonial America and apparently had been employed only in New York where such a law was passed in 1784 to provide for church incorporations.[9] Religious bodies were singled out for special treatment not merely because of the number of charter applications they occasioned; the device of a general law was seen as a means of implementing the policy of equal rights for all churches that was an essential feature of the new political philosophy.[10]

In 1794, New Jersey made similar provision for the incorporation of "Societies for the promotion of Learning," [11] and in 1799 extended the privileges of that act to library companies that had not already been incorporated by statute or letters patent.[12] A new general incorporation law for churches was also passed in 1799 to supersede the older one.[13]

Although New Jersey's first business corporation was created in 1791, it was many years later that general laws for the incorporation of profit-seeking groups were adopted in that state. Between 1791 and 1845, the strictly business corporations of New Jersey were created exclusively by special act of the legislature.[14] Several reasons can be given for the failure to extend the general-law system more speedily to incorporation for busi-

[9] Davis, I, 106, and II, 16.

[10] In this connection the preamble to the New Jersey general law for religious groups is interesting and enlightening: "Whereas Petitions are frequently presented to the Legislature from religious Societies or Congregations of different Denominations in this State, for Acts of Incorporation, for the better transacting the temporal Concerns of said Societies or Congregations, and many laws having been passed for that Purpose; and the Legislature being desirous of granting equal Privileges to every Denomination of Christians, and securing to them all their civil Rights . . . " *N. J. Laws,* 10 sess., 2 sit. (1786), Ch. 129, p. 255.

[11] *N. J. Laws,* 19 sess., 1 sit. (1794), Ch. 499, p. 950.

[12] *N. J. Laws,* 24 sess., 1 sit. (1799), Ch. 827, p. 644.

[13] *N. J. Laws,* 23 sess., 3 sit. (1799), Ch. 816, p. 572. The new law made provision for certain congregations whose religious tenets had prevented their incorporation under the previous law. It was more than a general incorporation law since it provided a blanket increase in property limitations applicable to all existing church charters.

[14] This statement is made with the qualification that some manufacturing corporations may have formed under the general incorporation law that stood on the statute books between 1816 and 1819, but evidence of the use of the law is totally lacking. Cf. *infra,* pp. 24–25.

ness purposes. It was not until the eighteen thirties that applications for business corporation charters became numerous enough to make special acts of incorporation a real burden to the New Jersey legislature, that representatives of any single type of business applied frequently enough to warrant a general law covering the group, or that ideas of equality of privilege such as impressed the legislators with respect to religious and educational endeavors were enlarged to include groups organized for profit-making ventures. Furthermore, during most of these years, the types of enterprises making most frequent application for corporate privileges were turnpikes and banks. Applications for turnpike charters directly concerned the public convenience and necessitated grants of authority to condemn private property or to occupy public highways, and those for banks had a necessary connection with the supply and quality of circulating media. These were considerations that would have made the lawmakers loath to permit incorporation without deliberation on the merits of each particular case. In the interest of chronology, the present discussion of the procedure involved in chartering business corporations in New Jersey before 1845 will first treat the process of incorporation by special act. An account of the movement for general incorporation laws for business concerns as it developed during the period will be presented at the end of the chapter.

The first step taken by a group seeking a special charter was the presentation of a petition to the legislature setting forth the public advantages to be expected from an act of incorporation.[15] Although the presentation of petitions is mentioned frequently in contemporary sources,[16] only a very few examples have been preserved.[17] Sometimes signatures were obtained not only from the groups immediately interested in the proposed projects but also from the general public in an effort to make the petitions as impressive as possible. On the occasion of a concerted effort

[15] The procedure outlined here for special charters applies also to special charter supplements.

[16] E.g., *Votes and Proceedings of the General Assembly,* 26 sess., 1 sit. (1801), p. 30; 28 sess., 2 sit. (1804), p. 119.

[17] Those available for examination are in the manuscript collection of the New Jersey State Library.

in 1812 to secure charters for a group of so-called "state banks," petition forms with printed headings were distributed widely over the state.[18]

It early became the practice of the New Jersey legislature to defer action on petitions until a succeeding sitting in order to allow opportunity for groups advocating and opposing the requested charters to present their arguments.[19] The condition on which leave to present bills for charters was generally given in early years was that notice of the intended application be advertised for a specified number of weeks in designated newspapers and in a number of "the most public places" in a specified region.[20] This method of bringing charter applications to the attention of the public was not, however, adopted as a uniform rule until 1833 when a law was enacted applying to all groups seeking special charters of incorporation and to companies desiring renewals of, or alterations in, their existing charters.[21] All applicants were required by the statute to publish notices of their intent in the papers of the counties where the corporations were to operate. The notices had to appear for six successive

[18] The collection of the New Jersey State Library contains a printed petition of January 13, 1812, from inhabitants of Elizabeth and other townships in behalf of the "state banks." This particular petition carried over 300 signatures. Another example of a petition for an act of incorporation that had been signed by several hundred persons can be found in *Votes and Proceedings of the General Assembly*, 39 sess., 1 sit. (1814), p. 126.

[19] In advocating publicity in connection with special charters, Governor John Jay of New York in a message of 1800 declared it would avoid the difficulty of "correcting the evils resulting to the public from unforeseen defects" and asked that charters be passed "only under such circumstances of previous publicity and deliberation as may be proper to guard against the effect of cursory and inaccurate views and impressions." New York State, *Messages from the Governors*, II, 450.

[20] E.g., *Votes and Proceedings of the General Assembly*, 28 sess., 1 sit. (1803), p. 79. The required advertisements appeared frequently in the newspapers. For an example see *The Federalist and New-Jersey State Gazette*, January 13, 1801. Sometimes the petitioners employed the required notice to reassure the public as to the inoffensiveness of their intentions. A group applying for a steam-boat company charter declared the desired law was to contain the "usual provisions in cases of the like nature, for guarding against extortions, negligence and such interferences as may prove detrimental to the public." *Trenton Federalist*, January 9, 1815.

[21] *N. J. Laws*, 57 sess., 2 sit. (1833), p. 99. New York had enacted a similar statute twenty years earlier. *N. Y. Laws*, 36 sess. (1813), Ch. 78, p. 79.

weeks before applications were presented. Notices concerning applications for new charters were to specify the objects and the amount of capital stock required, and those concerning alterations in charters were to state specifically the alteration desired.[22] Public notices of intention to apply for special acts may have had the desired effect in giving potential opposition an opportunity to be heard, for there is evidence that many petitions against proposed charters and charter supplements were presented to the legislature.[23]

Upon presentation of a charter application, the proposed bill, accompanied by petitions supporting and denouncing the project, was sent to committee. For many years, separate committees were appointed for the consideration of each application to the New Jersey legislature. As the number of charter applications increased, sporadic efforts were made to consider the applications as a group in order to standardize the terms of the proposed charters. Thus a committee was appointed in 1811 to consider all bank charter applications.[24] In 1824, a committee of the assembly was appointed to consider various applications for charters, and the council named a committee to meet with the assembly group to consider the bills and memorials for incorporating companies then before the legislature, "to be by them fairly and impartially investigated and decided upon agreeably to their merits respectively." [25] On other occasions, suggestions to commit all applications for business charters to standing committees were not acted upon.[26] It was not until the middle of the eighteen thirties that a standing committee on corporations was a regular feature of the organization of the

[22] The law was later altered to allow more time for public discussion by requiring that the six-week period end on or before the first day of the session during which the application would be made. *N. J. Laws*, 1849, p. 87.

[23] For example, in 1800 a bill to incorporate a navigation company was given to a committee "with a petition for and against it." *The Federalist and New-Jersey State Gazette*, November 11, 1800. Three petitions against the incorporation of a second water company in Trenton are preserved in the New Jersey State Library. Two were presented on November 1, 1810, and one in 1811.

[24] *Trenton Federalist*, January 21, 1811.

[25] *Votes and Proceedings of the General Assembly*, 49 sess., 1 sit. (1824), p. 115; *True American*, December 4, 1824.

[26] E.g., *Votes and Proceedings of the General Assembly*, 52 sess., 1 sit. (1827), p. 8.

assembly. This fact combined with the absence of general regulating statutes largely explains the lack of uniformity in the provisions of New Jersey charters of the period under consideration.

Once a bill for incorporation was reported to the legislature to be given the required three readings and opened for general discussion, the persons interested in the bill did not rely alone upon the support of formal petitions but usually attempted to give more personal attention to the welfare of their application. Lobbying appeared early and developed rapidly in connection with bills for special charters and became one of the most undesirable and most strenuously denounced features of the whole system of incorporation by special act. A letter written in 1809 by a man interested in securing a charter for a turnpike company shows that the value of outside agents in assuring passage of an incorporation law was recognized at an early date. In referring to opposition within the legislature, this applicant wrote to a friend: "There is I believe a majority in the House who would pass the Bill but there is wanted someone out of Doors to press the matter especially where the members from the County object." [27] There were frequent references in the press to the number of strangers evident in Trenton at the opening of the legislative sessions, with the comment that many came from New York and Philadelphia in search of profitable charters.[28]

Bribery of the legislators was freely charged in connection with the activities of lobbies, although usually the accusations were not supported by specific evidence. In fact, bribery was suspected by some in the case of the chartering of "The Society for establishing useful Manufactures," New Jersey's first busi-

[27] W. R. Fee, *The Transition from Aristocracy to Democracy in New Jersey: 1789–1829*, p. 147n.

[28] The *True American* of December 18, 1824, for example, declared that "the Wall street bees, attracted hither by the savor of New-Jersey honey, are buzzing about the State-House . . . Many very splendid offers have been made for our canals, and bank charters, by these gentlemen, who profess a great regard for the welfare of the state; but which some of our plain unlettered Jerseymen uncharitably interpret, to mean, a warm wish for the welfare of their own purses, and to make their fortunes out of the monopoly of our public favors if they can."

ness corporation.[29] Suspicions of bribery were strong enough by 1824 to occasion the appointment of a joint committee of the legislature to investigate the conduct of bank applicants and their agents. After hearing testimony, the committee reported that "it appears that an influence has been exerted and attempted, in favor of monied institutions, of which the people of New-Jersey, and we would fain believe the Legislature itself, has been heretofore entirely ignorant." [30] The report went on to exculpate the legislators by attributing the success of certain bank charter applications to offers of money and jobs made to people of influence who were in return to urge passage of the bills on their representatives in Trenton rather than to the corruption of a single member of the legislature. Stringent measures to punish bribery and corruption within the legislature were not taken until many years later.[31]

Another practice arising from the system of special charters, and one causing much concern, was the logrolling that occurred when numerous incorporation bills were before the legislature. No estimate of the prevalence of this practice can be hazarded because of the lack of positive evidence. Considering the sectional and special nature of the charters and the frequent charges of logrolling made, however, there is little doubt that special acts of incorporation became the state counterpart of federal tariff legislation in engendering logrolling tactics.

Bills for special acts of incorporation, having actively interested friends and sponsors, were often presented early in the sessions and were insistently pressed for rapid passage. Thus the argument was made that private legislation occupied so much of the time of the legislature that public legislation was neglected or at least relegated to second place. Although this objection to special charters was offered more frequently and with more cause after the middle of the nineteenth century, it was heard on earlier occasions. The argument was sometimes re-

[29] Davis, I, 449. A better-founded objection to the charter was that many legislators were subscribers to the project. *Ibid.*, I, 377, 449.

[30] *Journal of the Legislature Council*, 49 sess., 1 sit. (1824), p. 102. Cf. *True American*, August 27, 1825.

[31] Cf. *infra*, pp. 139–140, 163–164.

futed by those who claimed that private charters served public ends, especially when they were in the field of railroads or for new types of manufacturing concerns.[32]

Special incorporation acts as they were passed in New Jersey and elsewhere had numerous variations and do not form so simple and straightforward a category as is usually implied. The most familiar form of special charter is the legislative act bestowing upon a single group corporate privileges on specified terms for a particular object. In the early years in New Jersey, special acts for business corporations did not generally bestow the ordinary privileges of incorporation either immediately or in the future but left investiture of these powers with the governor who was authorized to issue his "letters patent." The governor's role was carefully restricted, however, since the special acts included a list of provisions regulating the formation and management of the corporations to be created. Six of the ten business charters passed before 1800 followed this prescription.[33] In 1800, the same formula was employed in chartering a navigation company and between 1809 and 1819 was used for eight Delaware River bridge companies.[34]

Apparently the formal investiture of corporate powers was originally left to the governor as an insurance that incorporation would not be effected until a designated number of shares had been subscribed, for all fifteen charters contained provisions making the governor's action contingent upon the securing of a specified subscription. Furthermore, eleven of these charters required that a minimum number of persons, ranging from twenty-five to fifty, should subscribe for the shares before the

[32] Cf. *Emporium and True American,* March 26, 1836.

[33] E.g., *N. J. Laws,* 17 sess., 1 sit. (1792), Ch. 406, p. 806; 19 sess., 2 sit. (1795), Ch. 544, p. 1041, Ch. 554, p. 1067; 22 sess., 2 sit. (1798), Ch. 708, p. 321.

[34] Davis' account of this type of incorporation act refers to its use for all "highway" companies of New Jersey up to 1800 and for most New Jersey companies of the same type until the second decade of the nineteenth century. Davis uses the term "highway" as a general one including bridges, and his statement is in error in two respects. Two eighteenth-century New Jersey bridge companies were incorporated directly by legislative act, and, in the early years of the nineteenth century, turnpike and other "highway" corporations greatly outnumbered the bridge companies for which this method of incorporation was used. *Op. cit.,* II, 20–21.

governor might act. Probably the reason for continuing this method of incorporation into the nineteenth century in the case of interstate bridge companies was the existence of an agreement made in 1783 requiring joint action by New Jersey and Pennsylvania in matters concerning the Delaware River. Thus the Delaware River bridge charters provided as a further restriction on the power of the governor to issue his letters patent that the legislature of Pennsylvania also approve the charters. The latter state was in this way assured that incorporation would not become effective until its consent was given.[35]

The majority of pre-1845 special charters bestowed corporate privileges upon a single group of persons by the legislative act itself, either at once or upon the fulfillment of conditions stated therein. When a condition was specified, it was most often the subscription of a certain capital,[36] but a number of charters granted corporate privileges only on the condition that another state pass similar acts. Thus eight interstate bridge charters granted corporate rights only after Pennsylvania had enacted equivalent charters,[37] and two ferry company charters were not to take effect as concerned the "concurrent jurisdictional right" of Pennsylvania until that state passed similar charters.[38]

Two minor variations of private acts bestowing corporate privileges appeared in New Jersey during these years. One type,

[35] E.g., *N. J. Laws,* 34 sess., 1 sit. (1809), Ch. 47, p. 164; 38 sess., 2 sit. (1814, private), p. 169. Apparently only New Jersey and Pennsylvania used this type of charter, a circumstance that suggests the interstate compact as a principal reason for its employment. Cf. Davis, II, 21. The failure of the Pennsylvania legislature to agree to one of the bridge charters led to the adoption of a joint resolution by the New Jersey legislature in the form of a message to the Pennsylvania lawmakers. The resolution called attention to the importance of free intercourse and suggested the concurrence of Pennsylvania "by granting a liberal authority to erect the said bridge on the site aforesaid, on such terms as are usual in such corporations, and such as will encourage individuals to make the investments necessary to complete the work . . ." *N. J. Laws,* 47 sess., 1 sit. (1822, private), p. 110.

[36] The details of such provisions are discussed below. Cf. pp. 242–243.

[37] E.g., *N. J. Laws,* 36 sess., 2 sit. (1812, private), p. 47; 55 sess., 2 sit. (1831), p. 106; 65 sess., 2 sit. (1841), p. 70. All these are, of course, distinct from those companies to be incorporated by the governor after Pennsylvania passed similar charters.

[38] *N. J. Laws,* 39 sess., 2 sit. (1815, private), p. 91; 41 sess., 2 sit. (1817, private), p. 45.

employed four times, involved reënactment of Pennsylvania bridge company charters by the legislature of New Jersey. In three cases the assents were given by publishing the Pennsylvania charters in full among the New Jersey session laws[39] and in the fourth by a mere statement that the Pennsylvania charter was "adopted, ratified and confirmed, by this state, as fully and as amply as if the same had been re-enacted at large, section by section. . . ." [40] The other variation appeared once and accomplished the incorporation of six separate and distinct banking companies by a single statute.[41]

An account of the forms of special charters would be incomplete without some mention of the practice of the legislature of passing supplementary acts modifying original charters. This became an integral part of the system of incorporation by special act. The charter of New Jersey's first business corporation was within a year of its passage supplemented by an act giving the directors power to enforce payment of subscriptions and rectifying a verbal error in the original charter.[42] The practice of enacting special supplements expanded to become of primary importance, and before 1845, 302 business charter supplements and special laws and joint resolutions pertaining to particular business corporations had passed the New Jersey legislature. The supplements covered a wide variety of subjects, ranging from mere correction of printers' errors to the revival or extension of charters or the bestowal of enlarged rights and privileges. Supplemental acts were sought as a means of providing for contingencies unforeseen at the time of the original incorporation or of securing some desired privilege that a former legislature had not seen fit to include in the charter. Charter supplements become of particular importance in a historical

[39] *N. J. Laws,* 19 sess., 2 sit. (1795), Ch. 554, p. 1067; 60 sess., 2 sit. (1836), p. 79; 66 sess., 2 sit. (1842), p. 119.

[40] *N. J. Laws,* 58 sess., 2 sit. (1834), p. 135.

[41] *N. J. Laws,* 36 sess., 2 sit. (1812, public), p. 3. On another occasion the legislature by a single law incorporated four fishing companies. Since these companies appear to have been intended merely to manage the fishing grounds in which the members operated as individual entrepreneurs, they have not been included in the statistics of business corporations. *Ibid.,* 63 sess., 2 sit. (1839), p. 75.

[42] *N. J. Laws,* 17 sess., 1 sit. (1792), Ch. 405, p. 804.

survey in the field of corporation finance, for, as will appear in Part II of this study, new departures in corporate financial practice or new attitudes on the part of legislators were generally reflected in the supplements before becoming apparent in original charter provisions.

It is worthy of comment that at no time during these early years did New Jersey have what can best be called "general regulating statutes" to guide the legislature in passing special acts of incorporation. General regulating statutes did not provide for incorporation by procedure but merely established the powers and restrictions applying to corporations created by the legislature. The increasing popularity of such statutes in other jurisdictions during this period can be explained by the facilitation in the creation of corporations and the uniformity in the restrictions and controls on corporations that resulted from their use.[43] If a state had general regulating statutes, the legislature granting corporate privileges had merely to make reference in the charter to the statute regulating that kind of company and add a few details such as the names of the corporators and the capital stock pertaining to the particular case. Special acts of incorporation under such a system were much simpler than the detailed charters of New Jersey. There was an obvious saving in the time a legislature would otherwise spend in debating each detail of every charter and a considerable decrease in printing expense. More important, however, was the improved quality of the resulting charters. The effort and

[43] Massachusetts seems to have made most general use of statutes of this type, enacting, for example, one regulating turnpike corporations in 1805, one for manufacturing companies in 1809 and another in 1830, one for insurance companies in 1818, and one for banks in 1829. Cf. C. C. Abbott, *The Rise of the Business Corporation*, pp. 43–44. Other examples are the turnpike act passed in 1807 by New York (*N. Y. Laws*, 30 sess. (1807), Ch. 38, p. 102) and the act of 1839 for manufacturing and mining companies chartered by Maryland (*Maryland Laws*, 1838–39, Ch. 267).

Oscar Handlin and Mary F. Handlin in writing of the first Massachusetts regulating law for manufacturing companies take the position that its passage by the legislature represented "a sweeping invitation to all who would to request charters. A general law laid down the conditions under which the state was ready, on petition, to organize manufacturing corporations." *Commonwealth, A Study of the Role of Government in the American Economy: Massachusetts, 1774–1861*, p. 136.

thought given to drawing up a general regulating statute was greater than could have been allowed for each particular charter application. Another desirable result was uniformity of charter provisions. This feature not only assured equal privileges to all corporations of a single type but also tended to simplify and accelerate legal actions involving interpretation of charter clauses. In the absence of general regulating statutes, the kind of provisions included in special charters varied widely. Even similar and partially standardized clauses differed from charter to charter so that each case was likely to involve special legal determination.

In spite of the advantages of general regulating statutes and their popularity elsewhere, the lawmakers of New Jersey continued throughout this period to include within each special charter a full catalogue of the provisions relating to each particular company.[44] Exactly how much pressure was brought upon the legislature during this time to pass general regulating statutes cannot be determined. It is clear that an act of this type to regulate turnpike companies was defeated in the assembly in 1814.[45] Twenty years later, the Democratic opponents of special privilege advocated general regulating statutes before they championed the cause of general incorporation laws. In 1835, a leading newspaper of their party printed in full the act then in force in Massachusetts as a regulator of the general powers and duties of manufacturing corporations.[46] A bill of this type was introduced in vain in the New Jersey legislature in 1836 under Democratic sponsorship, with the Democratic press supporting the measure.[47] The bill appealed to the Democrats, since by making special legislation "bend" to its provisions, the privileges of manufacturing corporations would

[44] New Jersey did have statutes governing various phases of corporation conduct. These differed from general regulating statutes, not being intended particularly to shorten or standardize charters but rather to supply details of proper action in case a charter was silent on particular points.

[45] *Votes and Proceedings of the General Assembly,* 38 sess., 2 sit. (1814), pp. 144–45.

[46] *Emporium and True American,* December 26, 1835. Although such laws were usually referred to in New Jersey as general incorporation laws, they did not provide for incorporation by procedure.

[47] *Ibid.,* April 9, 1836.

be regulated by general rules and the "doctrine of *equal rights*" restored.[48] Futile attempts were made in 1842 to secure passage of a bill that seems to have been a general regulating statute for manufacturing corporations.[49] All of the suggested laws relating to manufacturing companies contained stringent provisions in the matter of stockholder liability and probably failed of passage because of that feature. A newspaper correspondent writing in 1846 in support of a general regulating statute reviewed the struggles of earlier years in these words: "The difficulty in adopting such a law here, has arisen from the fact that while one political party, generally, sought to impose onerous and unreasonable provisions, the other on the contrary, seemed to consider all restraint as too stringent." [50]

Whatever the reasons for New Jersey's failure to adopt general regulating statutes during the pre-1845 years, the absence of such laws had considerable significance. When a group approached the legislature for a charter of incorporation, there was no general legislation to hamper them in pressing for any special privileges they desired. The road was open to secure a charter with as few or as many provisions and with as liberal terms as they had influence or tactical ability to obtain; there were no statutory obstacles to getting favors that would put the petitioning group at an advantage with respect to competitors or even with respect to the general public. In the absence of general regulating statutes, particular groups could obtain special assistance from a legislature that would have been unwilling to go so far as to change a general statute for their benefit. Finally, the New Jersey situation made it rather easy for petitioners and their legislative sponsors to include in special bills clauses or phrases conferring special privileges or to omit some generally used restrictive clause and have the fact go unnoticed as the bill progressed to final passage. These tactics had an increasing chance of success as the number of charter applications multiplied to the point where it became

[48] *Ibid.*, April 2, 1836.

[49] *Votes and Proceedings of the General Assembly*, 66 sess., 2 sit. (1842), pp. 363, 373, 442–43.

[50] *State Gazette*, January 30, 1846.

impossible for even the most conscientious legislator to give more than cursory inspection to every application acted upon during a session of a few weeks. The wide variety of privileges and restrictions appearing in business corporation charters granted by New Jersey bear testimony to the results of treating each charter as a separate and independent grant without the salutary influence of statutes of general applicability.[51]

Since the device of the general incorporation law was widely advocated in the United States after the middle of the eighteen forties as a cure-all for the many objectionable features attendant upon the system of incorporation by special act, it will be useful at this point to gather together the evidence concerning the use of and agitation for general laws in New Jersey before 1845. It has already been pointed out that even before any business corporations were chartered in New Jersey, a general law for church groups was in force and that before 1800 general laws existed for the benefit of several types of nonprofit organizations. An attempt has also been made to explain in a general way why such laws were not enacted for business corporations in those early years.[52]

There is considerable evidence of early interest in New Jersey in general incorporation laws as a means of stimulating the development of manufactures. During the period of the Embargo, a bill was reported from a committee of the assembly, which judging from the title, the only evidence available, was a proposal for a general incorporation law for manufacturing companies.[53] This "act to incorporate societies for the promotion of American Manufactures" was deferred to the next ses-

[51] The beneficial effect of standardization of clauses in special charters has often been stressed in discussions of the history of incorporation. It is true that in New Jersey many clauses came to be more or less standardized, but the use of stereotyped phraseology did little to correct the abuses suggested above. A standard clause could be altered slightly to change the effect in some important particular or, more important, omitted entirely in certain cases. Again it should be stressed that it was relatively easy to convince a legislature to make certain deviations from a norm in special cases when there was no general statute to set a pattern. Before 1845, the only New Jersey charters that showed almost no important variation were those of turnpike companies.

[52] Cf. *supra*, pp. 5–7.

[53] *Votes and Proceedings of the General Assembly*, 33 sess., 1 sit. (1808), p. 123.

sion and upon being reported at that time by a new committee was discussed and ordered dismissed.[54] A proposal for a general law in New Jersey followed closely on the heels of the enactment by New York in 1811 of the historically important general law for certain types of manufacturing concerns. A representative from the industrial county of Essex presented the following resolution to the New Jersey assembly early in 1812:

> *Resolved,* That a committee be appointed to enquire into the expediency of passing a law under the authority of which the citizens of this state may form companies for the further promotion of certain descriptions of manufactures.[55]

The committee appointed to consider the resolution evidently thought such a law expedient, for one day after their appointment they reported a bill entitled "An act relative to incorporations for manufacturing purposes." [56] An identity of titles suggests that the proposed bill was the same as the general law that had been enacted in New York in the preceding year, but the bill was rejected by the New Jersey solons and ordered dismissed.[57] In the following year, the assembly passed by a vote of twenty-five to fifteen "An act authorizing incorporations for manufacturing purposes," but the council was not in agreement with the measure and returned it.[58] The friends of a general manufacturing law did not, however, admit defeat, for in 1814 a member of the council presented a bill entitled "An act to incorporate manufacturing companies" which after two periods of discussion was postponed to the next sitting.[59] When the bill was brought as unfinished business before the next legislature, it was dismissed after the second reading.[60]

Unfortunately the specific arguments advanced during the debates on general manufacturing laws were not even indicated in the printed record, but probably the lack of support for the bills can be partly explained by the increasing prosperity of

[54] *Ibid.,* 34 sess., 1 sit. (1809), p. 180. [55] *Ibid.,* 36 sess., 2 sit. (1812), p. 122.
[56] *Ibid.,* pp. 165–66. [57] *Ibid.,* p. 182.
[58] *Ibid.,* 37 sess., 2 sit. (1813), p. 25; *Journal of the Legislative Council,* 37 sess., 2 sit. (1813), pp. 1312, 1316, 1334.
[59] *Ibid.,* 38 sess., 2 sit. (1814), pp. 1528, 1534, 1581.
[60] *Ibid.,* 39 sess., 1 sit. (1814), p. 1613.

New Jersey manufactures without the stimulus of fostering legislation as the second war with England progressed. Late in 1813, the governor was able to report to the legislature that amid war "our domestic and public manufactories have prospered beyond our most sanguine expectations." [61] A few months later, the legislature recognized the importance of securing accurate information on the extent and condition of manufacturing establishments in the state and ordered a report made.[62] The report, submitted just after the close of the war, was presumably pleasing to the lawmakers. The tabulation based on incomplete returns enumerated, for example, twenty cotton mills and fifty-six woolen goods factories.[63]

It was the welfare of these war-induced manufacturing establishments that received principal attention in the message of the governor to the legislature early in 1816.[64] After calling attention to the fact that the war had brought a new realization of the power and resources of the country by forcing capital formerly employed in commerce into pursuits that would otherwise have remained unattempted and had proved the practicability of supplying domestically many articles previously imported, the governor went on to make the following remarks on legislative policy:

> Our infant manufactures will undoubtedly claim your earnest attention. On this subject, New-Jersey is deeply interested. Much of our capital is already invested in manufacturing establishments; and many of those establishments must fail if left without protection, to struggle in a market inundated with goods of British manufacture . . . [The exigencies of war and the possible value to the nation of protected manufactures justified the adventurers] in calculating upon a liberal support, as well from the general government, as from the Legislatures of the several states . . .
>
> Although our manufactures must depend chiefly upon the wisdom

[61] *Votes and Proceedings of the General Assembly,* 38 sess., 1 sit. (1813), p. 69.
[62] *N. J. Laws,* 38 sess., 2 sit. (1814, public), p. 73.
[63] *Votes and Proceedings of the General Assembly,* 39 sess., 2 sit. (1815), p. 233.
[64] *Ibid.,* 40 sess., 2 sit. (1816), pp. 87–92.

of Congress for relief, yet I am confident they will receive from you such aid as the limited means of a state legislature can afford.[65]

The members of the assembly were sufficiently impressed to refer to a select committee the section of the governor's message "as relates to the expediency of extending Legislative encouragement to the manufacturing interest within this State." [66] While the committee was deliberating on the measures a state legislature might take to encourage manufactures, an Essex County assemblyman "presented a petition from a number of the inhabitants of Paterson, in the county of Essex, praying for a general law on the incorporating of Manufactories." [67] A committee appointed to consider the petition reported within a day a bill entitled "An act relative to incorporations for manufacturing purposes." [68] The bill progressed speedily to passage in the assembly[69] and just as rapidly in the council, although the latter house made some amendments and agreed to the bill only by the close vote of seven to six.[70] The amended bill was at once passed by the assembly with a more favorable vote than it had received when passed in its original form.[71]

[65] *Ibid.*, pp. 90–91. The industrialists were apparently already active in the federal capital, for a New Jersey newspaper reported accounts in out-of-state papers of two men "employed by the manufacturing interest of New-Jersey to look after their concerns at Washington." *Trenton Federalist,* January 1, 1816. New Jersey manufacturers also sent petitions to Congress asking encouragement of the textile and iron industries. *Annals of Congress,* XXIX, 105, 136, 931–32; XXXI, 446.

[66] *Votes and Proceedings of the General Assembly,* 40 sess., 2 sit. (1816), p. 107.

[67] *Ibid.*, p. 156. The origin of the petition is interesting. The count of manufactories made in 1814 and 1815 shows Essex County to have been the leading manufacturing district. Of the 20 cotton mills reported, 13 were in Essex, and 11,944 spindles were in use there as compared with 342 in Bergen County, the only other county in which the number of spindles was recorded. *Ibid.*, 39 sess., 2 sit. (1815), p. 233.

[68] *Ibid.*, 40th sess., 2 sit. (1816), p. 163.

[69] *Ibid.*, p. 192. The final vote was twenty-four to twelve, nearly all the opposition coming from nonindustrial counties.

[70] *Journal of the Legislative Council,* 40 sess., 2 sit. (1816), p. 1879. Here, too, the members from distinctly agricultural counties expressed their opposition to the proposed law.

[71] *Votes and Proceedings of the General Assembly,* 40 sess., 2 sit. (1816), pp. 217–18. The final vote was twenty-seven to nine.

Since no more was heard from the committee to consider methods of aiding New Jersey manufactures and since two of the three members of that committee were also on the committee of three that reported the general law, it is to be inferred that the former committee was of the opinion that a general incorporation law was the most effective measure a state legislature could adopt to foster the welfare of manufactures.[72] The New York general act of 1811 had perhaps been enacted for the same reason,[73] and the New Jersey legislators had reason to believe in the stimulating effect of a general manufacturing law when they considered the experience of New York. A note in the 1814 session laws of New York listing the companies that had organized under the general law during the preceding seven months was accompanied by the comment that "The capital stock of the manufacturing companies incorporated under the general act of March 22d, 1811, amounts to the enormous sum

[72] Previous proposals to relieve New Jersey textile manufacturers from taxation had been considered in the assembly but were never acted upon. Cf. *True American,* November 6, 1815, and *Trenton Federalist* of the same date.

[73] Probably New York's general incorporation law of 1811 was passed as a means of stimulating American industry to combat the effects of the Embargo and to prepare for the threatening war. Governor Tompkins of New York had in 1808 and 1810 exhorted his legislature to take measures to make the country independent of imported manufactured goods. New York State, *Messages from the Governors,* II, 622, 658. Furthermore the five-year limit put on the 1811 law suggests that it was considered to be a measure to meet a temporary situation. In 1816, when New York manufacturers were also faced with foreign competition, the same governor advocated legislative "patronage." *Ibid.,* II, 855. The legislature promptly extended the general law for one year and broadened its coverage. *N. Y. Laws,* 39 sess. (1816), Ch. 58, p. 58. A similar appeal by Governor DeWitt Clinton in 1818 stimulated the legislature to further action. New York State, *Messages from the Governors,* II, 899. They voted to revive the then expired 1811 law for a term of five years. *N. Y. Laws,* 41 sess. (1818), Ch. 67, p. 53. In 1821, the general law was continued indefinitely. *Ibid.,* 44 sess. (1821), Ch. 14, p. 9. The statutes of New York afford one other bit of evidence that general incorporation laws were viewed at this time as a means of stimulating a desired type of activity. In 1814, the legislature passed "An act to encourage Privateering Associations" under which groups operating private armed vessels might incorporate during the war and continue their corporate existence until one year after the war's end. *Ibid.,* 38 sess. (1814), Ch. 12, p. 11. It should be stated that in New York the measures taken to stimulate manufacturing did not end with the passage and continuance of the general law of 1811. Other measures to aid textile concerns granted permission to form fire companies, exemptions from jury and militia duty for certain operators, and exemption from taxation. *Ibid.,* 38 sess. (1815), Ch. 202, p. 204; 40 sess. (1817), Ch. 64, p. 54.

of 4,711,000 dollars." [74] A recent study shows that 110 companies had organized under the law between 1811 and 1815.[75] The New Jersey legislators were doubtless aware of the extent to which the New York act had been successful.

New Jersey's general law of 1816 [76] was nothing more than a duplicate of the New York law of 1811 with some slight changes. The law was limited to five years, and companies for the purpose of making woolen, cotton, or linen goods, glass, bar iron, anchors, mill irons, steel, nail rods, hoop iron, and ironmongery, sheet copper, sheet lead, shot, white or red lead [77] could file certificates of incorporation with the secretary of state. The terms of the charters that would be thus obtained will be discussed under appropriate headings in Part II of this study, but the differences between the acts of New York and New Jersey can best be mentioned here. In New Jersey ten was the minimum number of persons who might file a certificate, while in New York the number was five. Stockholder liability was slightly more severe under the New Jersey act. The New York law contained an ambiguous provision making stockholders at the time of dissolution of a company responsible for all debts then owing "to the extent of their respective shares of stock in the said company, and no further," but the New Jersey law added to this liability an additional amount equal to "the dividend and profits they may have received thereon." The New Jersey act also added a section requiring the president and directors of any company organized under the act to see that children employed by them, whether under parole agreement or indenture, were taught one hour a day in "reading, writing and arithmetic" and that they attended religious worship on the Sabbath.[78]

[74] *Ibid.*, 37 sess. (1814), Appendix, p. 289.

[75] W. C. Kessler, "A Statistical Study of the New York General Incorporation Act of 1811," *Journal of Political Economy*, XLVIII (December 1940), 879.

[76] *N. J. Laws*, 40 sess., 2 sit. (1816, public), p. 17.

[77] By an amendment of 1815, New York had added clay and earthenware goods to this list. *N. Y. Laws*, 38 sess. (1815), Ch. 47, p. 44. These products were not included in the New Jersey law.

[78] The matter of the education of children employed in factories had worried the legislature as the factory system spread in New Jersey. In 1814, the assembly had resolved: "That a committee be appointed to enquire into the propriety of

The passage of the general law of 1816 received surprisingly scant public attention; newspapers noting the event merely mentioned the act by name and did not even record the vote.[79] There was a similar lack of public interest three years later when the act was repealed.[80] Examination of a number of New Jersey newspapers published between 1816 and 1819 affords no indication of public opinion either for or against the principle of the general law, nor do the state archives or official state documents contain any reference to companies organized under the act.[81] The lack of evidence suggests that the law was not actually used, and this conclusion is strengthened by a consideration of the depressed condition of American manufacturing enterprises after the end of the War of 1812.[82] In October 1816, the New Jersey governor spoke to the legislature of the "new distress" into which the country had been plunged "by a ruinous importation of European goods." [83] Incorporations under the New York general law, previously so numerous, fell to as few as eighteen for the years 1816 to 1819.[84] Although no special charters for manufacturing companies were enacted in New Jersey during the life of the gen-

providing that the children employed in manufacturing establishments in this state be suitably educated, with leave to report by bill." *Votes and Proceedings of the General Assembly,* 39 sess., 1 sit. (1814), p. 12. In anticipation of some action, the special charters of three manufacturing companies passed in 1814 and 1816 provided that the employers were subject to any regulation that might be made subsequently for required education. *N. J. Laws,* 39 sess. 1 Sit. (1814, private), pp. 8, 13; 40 sess., 2 sit. (1816, private), p. 158.

[79] A typical mention is that in the *Trenton Federalist* of February 12, 1816.

[80] *N. J. Laws,* 43 sess., 2 sit. (1819, public), p. 25. The repeal bill originated in the assembly and was unanimously agreed to in both houses of the legislature. *Votes and Proceedings of the General Assembly,* 43 sess., 2 sit. (1819), p. 127; *Journal of the Legislative Council,* 43 sess., 2 sit. (1819), p. 65.

[81] The repealing act contained a proviso "that nothing herein contained shall in any ways [*sic*] affect any company heretofore incorporated, by virtue of the said act." The proviso may have been included either to protect companies known to have filed under the general law or because the legislators were uncertain as to whether any had filed.

[82] As early as January 2, 1815, the management of New Jersey's second manufacturing corporation, the Fairfield Manufacturing Company chartered in 1809, advertised in the *Trenton Federalist* that they desired to sell or rent the cotton section of the mill immediately and the wool section in the spring.

[83] *Votes and Proceedings of the General Assembly,* 41 sess., 1 sit. (1816), pp. 15–16.

[84] Kessler, "New York General Incorporation Act," p. 879. Only one company had filed in 1819.

eral law, there is no indication in the legislative journals that any applications were made.

The present writer has not, however, been able to discover why the legislators troubled to repeal an unused law two years before it would have expired by its own limitation. Perhaps by 1819 the financial losses to stockholders and creditors of the companies chartered during the War of 1812 had resulted in a popular reaction against manufacturing corporations. The New Jersey general manufacturing law of 1816, unheralded at its birth, apparently neglected during its life and buried quietly upon its demise, has been generally ignored or overlooked in later studies of American corporation history. It nevertheless has historical significance as one of the earliest general incorporation laws for business concerns in the United States.[85]

After this inauspicious beginning, the cause of business incorporation by procedure made no progress in New Jersey for over twenty-five years, but during the eighteen thirties discussions concerning general incorporation laws became frequent. It is important to note, however, that when the question was revived during the later period, the champions of general laws were no longer motivated by a desire to encourage industry by permitting an easy incorporation procedure but by Jacksonian doctrines that looked toward an end of "special privilege." In fact, the Democrats supported general laws in the late eighteen thirties only after a show of hostility toward all corporations for business purposes. When they found they could not abolish business corporations, they turned first to advocating general statutes regulating the terms of special charters and later to supporting general incorporation laws as the only practicable means to curb "monopolies."

Although no further general laws for the incorporation of business concerns were passed by New Jersey during the period treated in the present chapter, mention of several laws proposed during these years will provide a background for the general-law movement of the late eighteen forties. In 1837, an assemblyman from Hunterdon County, the principal stronghold of

[85] Its predecessors were a Massachusetts law for water companies (1799), the New York manufacturing act (1811), and the New York law for the incorporation of privateering associations (1814).

Democratic antagonism toward corporations, introduced a bill entitled "An act defining the general powers and duties of Manufacturing corporations in this state, and authorizing the Governor of the state, for the time being, to issue letters of incorporation creating the same." The bill had a brief and stormy history, being turned down, reconsidered, and finally postponed.[86] The year after the enactment of New York's general banking law of 1838, the council considered a similar law for New Jersey, but action on the proposed bill was postponed to the following legislature and apparently forgotten.[87] In 1842, while a general regulating law for manufacturing corporations was under consideration in the assembly, a member offered the following resolution:

> *Resolved,* That the committee on corporations be instructed to consider the expediency of enacting a general law for the formation and better regulation of incorporations for manufacturing purposes.[88]

The resolution was adopted in a slightly modified form and a select committee appointed, but there is no evidence that a report was formulated.

Further indication of the revived interest in general incorporation laws at the end of the period under discussion in this chapter is found in connection with beneficial or mutual aid societies, associations not considered for the purpose of this study to be business concerns. Between 1831 and 1841, sixteen such societies had received special charters in New Jersey.[89]

[86] *Votes and Proceedings of the General Assembly,* 61 sess., 2 sit. (1837), pp. 239, 300, 310, 322, 623–24.

[87] *Journal of the Legislative Council,* 63 sess., 2 sit. (1839), pp. 168, 219, 253. There is nothing to indicate whether the banks to be created by its terms were to be corporations. The one special bank charter passed during this session contained a clause anticipating the enactment of the general banking law. It read: "should there be a general banking law enacted [during] the present session of the legislature, then, and in that case, this charter shall be null and void, and of no effect." *N. J. Laws,* 63 sess., 2 sit. (1839), p. 131.

[88] *Votes and Proceedings of the General Assembly,* 66 sess., 2 sit. (1842), pp. 442–43. It is not entirely certain whether the intention here was to supplant the suggested regulatory law by a general incorporation law or to instruct the committee to study the advisability of passing the regulatory law.

[89] E.g., *N. J. Laws,* 55 sess., 2 sit. (1831), pp. 21, 103. This movement among working-class persons to provide for mutual assistance in the event of sickness,

The large number of applications for charters for beneficial societies before the legislature in 1842 was probably the principal reason for the unanimous adoption by the council of the following resolution:

Resolved, That the committee on Corporations be, and they are hereby instructed to report a general law for all associations, as humane or beneficiary Societies, to become Incorporated under the same instance of applying to the Legislature, for special acts, in each particular case.[90]

The recommended action was slightly delayed, however, and it was not until 1844 that a general incorporation law was enacted to provide for "Benevolent and Charitable Associations." [91]

The years up to and including 1844 thus form a period during which New Jersey business corporations were created by various types of special legislative acts. Except for one unsuccessful attempt after the War of 1812 to employ a general incorporation law to assist a manufacturing community threatened by depression, incorporation by procedure played no role in actual practice. As the period drew to a close, however, those who had once opposed corporations were wont to support a system of general incorporation laws to eliminate what they considered the worst evil of incorporation — the feature of special privilege. It was not until the second half of the decade of the eighteen forties that these men were instrumental in causing the adoption of general incorporation laws for business enterprises, but their ideas were formulated during the period under discussion here, and by 1844 the flood tide of agitation for general laws was rapidly approaching its peak.

---

accident, old age, or death is an interesting accompaniment to the industrial revolution in New Jersey. Concern lest such beneficial societies become machines for labor organization led to the inclusion in the charter of one a provision that the charter would be void and the property of the association would be forfeited to the state in the event that the group passed any "law or regulation respecting the rate of wages of any of the members, or the business which any of them may, or do follow, and shall be convicted thereof by due course of law . . ." *Ibid.*, 59 sess., 2 sit. (1835), p. 68.

[90] *Journal of the Legislative Council,* 66 sess., 2 sit. (1842), p. 152.

[91] *N. J. Laws,* 68 sess., 2 sit. (1844), p. 197.

CHAPTER II

The Position of the Business Corporation in New Jersey, 1791–1844

BETWEEN 1791, the year in which New Jersey's first business corporation was chartered, and 1844, the year in which New Jersey adopted its second constitution, the business corporation came to hold an important and secure place in the economic structure of the state. After 1844, the practice of granting corporate charters to enterprises operating for the personal profit of the owners was not seriously challenged in New Jersey, and the corporate form of business organization spread rapidly into many fields of economic activity. In the years previous to 1844, however, there was not complete unanimity of opinion as to what spheres of economic activity might appropriately be delegated to private corporations or even agreement as to the wisdom of creating business corporations of any type. The present chapter is concerned with tracing the attitudes of the public in general and the business community in particular toward corporations in these formative years in so far as published sources indicate these attitudes. The discussion is concerned primarily with New Jersey experience. When facts drawn from the records of other states seem useful as points of comparison or contrast, they are included. The procedure involved in the creation of business corporations during this period was discussed separately in the preceding chapter. Detailed analysis of the numerous restrictions and duties imposed upon business corporations as well as of the rights and privileges granted them is deferred to Part II; such matters are treated in the present chapter only as they are necessary to an understanding of public policy with respect to the business corporation between 1791 and 1844.

As in the majority of the North American colonies, there was no experience in New Jersey with business corporations during the pre-Revolutionary period.[1] It is interesting, however, to note that in 1765 the colonial assembly of New Jersey constituted a semipublic corporation by the title of The Trustees of the Road and Ferries from Newark to the Road leading from Bergen Point to Paulus-Hook.[2] The trustees formed a self-perpetuating board and were empowered to receive donations, collect tolls, and keep the road in good condition, their activities being subject to a county board of review. The preamble of the act of incorporation stated that the road desired by the inhabitants of the district "will be very expensive, and cannot well be effected unless assisted by the voluntary Contribution of others." Although the trustees did not constitute a private corporation, the example is important as a prelude to the subsequent employment of the device of the private corporation to accomplish the construction of transportation and communication facilities. In both cases corporations were created in order to finance public improvements without expenditure of public funds. Perhaps equally important was the constitution of special groups to carry out particular works at a time when the state government itself was not adequately organized to undertake such tasks.

There was little in the legislation passed in New Jersey during the first fifteen years after 1776 to indicate what the future policy of the state toward business corporations would be. The legislation concerned directly with economic activity was nearly all confined to the years of the Revolution. Such legislation as was passed during the war dealt with price-fixing and with the prevention of forestalling, regrating, and engrossing,[3] and with

[1] Davis, *Essays in the Earlier History of American Corporations*, II, Figure I, pp. 22–23.

[2] Samuel Allinson, ed., *Acts of the General Assembly of the Province of New-Jersey . . .* , Ch. 409, p. 276 (1765). Paulus (or Powle's) Hook subsequently became Jersey City.

[3] *N. J. Laws*, 2 sess., 1 sit. (1777), Ch. 8, p. 16; 4 sess., 1 sit. (1779), Ch. 11, p. 23, Ch. 12, p. 25. The price-fixing act of 1779 was soon discontinued as being too burdensome on New Jersey residents until such time as neighboring states should enact similar legislation for general price limitation. *Ibid.*, 4 sess., 2 sit. (1780), Ch. 24, p. 57. In 1781, all legislation restricting trade, except that with the enemy, was repealed. *Ibid.*, 5 sess., 2 sit. (1781), Ch. 28, p. 80.

state financial aid or exemption of workmen from militia duty in order to assure a continuing supply of the essential articles of salt, iron, powder, and paper.[4] This legislation, while interesting as war-emergency measures, gave no indication of what state policy toward business enterprise would be under normal conditions.

There is some evidence that during the period of the Confederation Jerseymen hoped to attract to their territory a larger share of commercial activity by appropriate legislative measures. Governor Livingston urged such a policy in 1783, and a year later a group of delegates from principal towns met at New Brunswick and petitioned the legislature to do something to induce merchants to establish themselves in New Jersey.[5] The legislature responded promptly and generously by passing "An act for establishing certain free Ports in the State of New-Jersey, and for the Encouragement of Commerce therein."[6] The ports of Perth Amboy, New Brunswick, and Burlington were declared free ports for the term of twenty-five years, and "all Foreigners, Mariners, Manufacturers or Mechanicks; and also all Subjects of the United States, or any of them" who removed to one of these cities and actually resided there one month pursuing "their professional Business, or any Kind of Commerce, shall be deemed and admitted Freemen and Citizens . . ." As a further inducement, merchant-citizens of the ports were offered a twenty-five-year exemption from taxes

[4] Maintenance of a supply of salt seems to have occasioned considerable concern. In 1776, the legislature agreed to make a loan of £500 to five individuals if in three months time they had erected a salt works capable of a certain output. In case of destruction of the works by the enemy, the state agreed to deduct part of the loss from the loan. *N. J. Laws,* 1 sess. (1776), Ch. 8, p. 8. A year later the legislature authorized a state owned and operated salt works. *Ibid.,* 1 sess. (1777), Ch. 15, p. 118. The authorization was rescinded when a large number of private works were being established. *Ibid.,* 2 sess., 2 sit. (1778), Ch. 17, p. 35. Most of the remaining legislation designed to encourage salt, paper, powder, and iron production exempted workmen in these industries from service in the state militia. E.g., *N. J. Laws,* 1 sess. (1777), Ch. 27, p. 47, Ch. 51, p. 114, Ch. 52, p. 115; 2 sess., 1 sit. (1777), Ch. 5, p. 12, Ch. 7, p. 16. All exemption laws pertaining to workmen in iron and salt works were repealed in 1779. *Ibid.,* 3 sess., 2 sit. (1779), Ch. 18, p. 49.

[5] H. M. Clokie, "New Jersey and the Confederation," Ch. 23 in I. S. Kull, *New Jersey: A History,* II, 541.

[6] *N. J. Laws,* 8 sess., 2 sit. (1784), Ch. 50, p. 105.

on "their Possessions as Merchants, and for their Stock and Vessels employed in Commerce . . ." Although the principal purpose of this legislation was to create ports in which foreign goods could be landed free of duties except such as might be levied by the Congress, there was even at this early date sufficient protectionist sentiment in the legislature to demand the following proviso leaving the door open for a possible change in policy: "That Nothing in this Act contained shall be construed or understood to debar the Legislature of this State . . . from laying an Impost or Duty upon any Goods, Wares or Merchandise, imported into the said free Cities or Ports, which may prove injurious to, and discourage the Manufactories in this State." When later in the same year, the state legislature granted its first municipal charters, it was made abundantly clear in the preambles that the towns becoming incorporated — New Brunswick, Perth Amboy, and Burlington — were favored with charters because of their present and potential importance as commercial centers.[7]

In turning to the early history of New Jersey's business corporations, it is desirable to distinguish certain of the more important and representative groups of companies. Only in this manner can an adequate discussion of the attitude of the public and of the legislators toward corporate enterprise in various fields of economic activity be presented and an indication of why enterprisers in various industries desired incorporation be given. The groups singled out for special examination are cor-

[7] *N. J. Laws,* 8 sess., 2 sit. (1784), Ch. 54, p. 110; 9 sess., 1 sit. (1784), Ch. 73, p. 143, Ch. 74, p. 150. The preamble of the Perth Amboy charter was the most explicit and stated in part that "the Improvement of Trade and Navigation in this State is of the utmost Importance to the Well-being of the same: And . . . the Prosperity of Trade requires the Collection of Merchants together in sufficient Numbers . . . and . . . it is necessary, in the present unprovided and disadvantageous Condition of this State, to bestow on Merchants peculiar Immunities and Privileges, in order to attract them to its Harbours, and to secure to them, for a sufficient and definite Duration, the entire Profits of their Commerce without burden, Abatement or Uncertainty, in order to excite in them a Spirit of useful Adventure, and to encourage them to encounter the Risks and Expences of a new Situation, and of important and beneficial Undertakings: and . . . commercial Cities require a peculiar Mode of Government for maintaining their internal Police; and commercial Transactions require more expeditious and summary Tribunals than others . . ."

porations for manufacturing and mining, those created for banking and insurance operations, and companies chartered to construct transportation and communication facilities.

MANUFACTURING AND MINING COMPANIES

New Jersey's first business corporation, "The Society for establishing useful Manufactures" — more conveniently referred to as "the S. U. M." — , was chartered by the legislature in 1791.[8] Since the company was conceived and financed principally by non-Jerseymen and was intended to be a "national" institution, it is important to note the considerations that led Alexander Hamilton, Tench Coxe, and others actively interested in the manufactory to approach the legislature of New Jersey for a charter. Subscriptions to the stock, payment of which was contingent upon success in securing a charter of incorporation, were secured in July and August of 1791, although even at this late date the promoters of the company had not decided definitely upon a location for the works. The prospectus, probably drafted by Hamilton, was first circulated privately to attract subscriptions and then published in various newspapers in September 1791. It contained the following passage relating to the selection of the state in which to establish the proposed works:

> There is scarcely a state which could be insensible to the advantage of being the scene of such an undertaking. But there are reasons which strongly recommend the State of New Jersey for the purpose. It is thickly populated—provisions are there abundant and cheap. The State having scarcely any external commerce and no waste lands to be peopled can feel the impulse of no *supposed* interest hostile to the advancement of manufactures. Its situation seems to insure a constant friendly disposition.[9]

A careful student of the history of the S. U. M. has concluded that New Jersey was selected as the home of the undertaking in the hope that the financial support of residents of

[8] *N. J. Laws,* 16 sess., 1 sit. (1791), Ch. 356, p. 730. (In the session laws, the charter is erroneously numbered Ch. 346.)

[9] A. H. Cole, ed., *Industrial and Commercial Correspondence of Alexander Hamilton,* p. 193.

both the rival cities of New York and Philadelphia would be forthcoming and because New Jersey boasted at the time of no rival manufacturing interests while manufacturing "societies" had already been formed in New York and Pennsylvania and had been given legislative support. The economies expected to result from operating in a nonurban community also seem to have received serious consideration.[10] There were, however, more concrete reasons to believe that the manufacturing project would receive favorable consideration by the people and government of New Jersey. A short time before, the members of the assembly had concerned themselves as to "most probable measures of encouraging the Manufactures of this State." One of the committees appointed to consider the subject reported a bill to incorporate a society similar to the Pennsylvania Society for the Encouragement of Manufactures and the Useful Arts that had been formed in 1787, and although the bill passed the assembly it was defeated in the council by a single vote.[11] Furthermore the prospectus of the S. U. M. was made public a few weeks before the New Jersey elections of October 1791. Since that document expressly favored New Jersey as the incorporating state, it was inevitable that the S. U. M. should become a New Jersey election issue.[12] The election results seem to have indicated approval of the scheme by the citizens of the state, for among the legislators chosen were several who were either then or soon afterwards subscribers to the stock.[13] The reception of the charter application in the New Jersey legislature was favorable. The requested bill became law only about three weeks after its introduction. The final vote in the assembly was thirty to four and in the council nine to four.[14]

[10] Davis, I, 375–377.

[11] *Ibid.*, I, 377. *Votes and Proceedings of the General Assembly,* 14 sess., 1 sit. (1789), pp. 67, 69–70; 15 sess., 1 sit. (1790), pp. 11, 23, 97. *Journal of the Legislative Council,* 15 sess., 1 sit. (1790), pp. 33–34.

[12] "ELIZABETH-TOWN, September 21. As our annual election is near at hand, it is hoped, says a correspondent, that the different counties will make judicious choice in their members, as business of a momentous nature, relative to the national manufactory, will be laid before them." *New York Journal,* September 24, 1791. Quoted in Davis, I, 377n.

[13] Davis, I, 377.

[14] *Votes and Proceedings of the General Assembly,* 16 sess., 1 sit. (1791), pp. 20, 54–59, 62–64, 70. *Journal of the Legislative Council,* 16 sess., 1 sit. (1791), pp. 6–7, 11, 17–18, 21.

There is no indication that the citizens of New Jersey regarded the act of chartering the society with anything but approbation.[15] Probably most of them were anxious to see legislative action in the form of a liberal charter if by that means industry could be attracted into a state that may have already begun to feel inferior to the neighboring states of New York and Pennsylvania, just as a few years earlier they had been desirous of fostering commercial activity in the state by legislative measures.

No other manufacturing company was chartered in New Jersey until 1809. The fact that nearly two decades elapsed between the charters of the S. U. M. and the Fairfield Manufacturing Company does not indicate hostility on the part of the legislature or people of New Jersey to corporate enterprise in the field of manufacturing. There is nothing in the official records of the New Jersey legislature to indicate that applications for manufacturing company charters were made during the intervening years.[16] For a variety of reasons, early manufacturing companies in the United States, both incorporated and unincorporated, failed to prosper in spite of rather than for lack of legislative encouragement.[17] Notwithstanding its generous special privileges and its influential and talented backers, the S. U. M. failed miserably in its manufacturing operations and discontinued them early in 1796 after a three-year trial. Manufacturing in New Jersey and elsewhere in the United States remained essentially a home industry until after the first decade of the nineteenth century. Since cotton manufacturing was the first American industry to adopt the features of the modern factory system, it is significant to note that a

[15] In writing of divided public opinion in regard to the S. U. M., Davis draws material from numerous American newspapers, but the unfavorable comment quoted by him was found in papers published outside of New Jersey. *Op. cit.*, I, 427–453.

[16] The situation was similar in other jurisdictions. After a thorough investigation of eighteenth century manufacturing companies of the United States, Davis wrote: "I have seen no evidence of refusal to grant charters which were seriously sought for this purpose." *Ibid.*, II, 283. Yet only eight manufacturing corporations were chartered in the United States through the year 1800. *Ibid.*, II, 269.

[17] *Ibid.*, II, 279–283.

study of that industry brought one author to the conclusion that the growth of the factory system in the United States must be dated from the years of the War of 1812 and not earlier.[18]

When the bill for the incorporation of the Fairfield Manufacturing Company, New Jersey's second manufacturing corporation, was introduced in the legislature in 1809, it met no opposition and speedily passed the assembly by a vote of thirty-five to one and was unanimously approved in the council.[19] The legislative history of the third manufacturing corporation, chartered somewhat over a year later, was similar. Introduced in the council, the charter received the unanimous approval of that house and passed the assembly by a vote of twenty-four to five.[20] There was also no apparent opposition to the numerous manufacturing company charters passed during the War of 1812.

In the years immediately following the war, Jerseymen seem to have become acutely conscious of the value to their state of manufacturing establishments. The governor recommended protection for American "infant manufactures" in a special message to the legislature in 1816,[21] and the general incorporation law for manufacturing concerns enacted in that year seems to have been designed especially to encourage such establishments.[22] New Jersey's concern for the welfare of the manufac-

[18] Clive Day, "The Early Development of the American Cotton Manufacture," *Quarterly Journal of Economics,* XXXIX (May 1925), 450–468. Day concluded that the commercial restriction of the Embargo period did not have the importance generally attributed to it in initiating industrial development. *Ibid.,* p. 463.

[19] *Votes and Proceedings of the General Assembly,* 34 sess., 1 sit. (1809), p. 191; *Journal of the Legislative Council,* 34 sess., 1 sit. (1809), p. 855. The corporation was to engage in textile manufacturing. *N. J. Laws,* 34 sess., 1 sit. (1809), Ch. 38, p. 137.

[20] *Journal of the Legislative Council,* 35 sess., 2 sit. (1811), p. 965; *Votes and Proceedings of the General Assembly,* 35 sess., 2 sit. (1811), pp. 411–12. The corporation was chartered for the "purpose of importing, printing, binding, publishing, and vending books at the city of Jersey; and also of establishing and conducting a paper manufactory, and type foundry, whenever they may deem the same beneficial to themselves and this state . . ." *N. J. Laws,* 35 sess., 2 sit. (1811), p. 349.

[21] *Votes and Proceedings of the General Assembly,* 40 sess., 2 sit. (1816), pp. 90–91.

[22] Cf. *supra,* pp. 18–23.

turing industry was manifested from that time on in frequent joint resolutions of the legislature supporting a system of protective tariffs.[23] The New Jersey lawmakers implemented their policy of favoring manufactures by chartering large numbers of manufacturing concerns during the decades of the eighteen twenties and thirties. During those years, manufacturing companies formed the most important single group of business corporations chartered in New Jersey both from the point of view of numbers and of aggregate capital stock authorized.[24]

Charters granted to manufacturing concerns frequently expressed legislative policy. Some made reference to the desirability of promoting American manufactures and of assisting domestic producers to compete with foreign-made goods.[25] Others made special mention of the benefit to New Jersey deriving from an increase in manufacturing capital.[26] A charter for a beet sugar refinery declared that the community would benefit if the necessary article of sugar could "by legislative aid" be produced from a vegetable that could be cultivated in the "middle states." [27] There are indications that early use was made of the incorporating power to attract industry into New Jersey from other states. It is difficult to determine in just what instances charters were granted to manufacturing companies as a means of encouraging the concerns to move into New

[23] For example, a resolution adopted in 1823 declared: "That manufactures form an important pillar of our national prosperity, and that their encouragement is an object, which deeply involves the present and future welfare of these United States." It recommended to the congressmen from New Jersey that "they use their exertions in promoting all measures calculated to cherish and advance the interest of manufacturers." *N. J. Laws*, 48 sess., 1 sit. (1823, private), p. 185. An 1828 resolution requesting further protection for manufactures concluded with the following statements: "The state of New-Jersey has the means of contributing large quantities of the raw materials of iron, wool, and flax, and has already made very great advances in the manufactures of these and other articles. The cultivation and improvement of these resources have become essential to the prosperity of this state." *N. J. Laws*, 52 sess., 2 sit. (1828), p. 216.

[24] Cf. *infra*, Table I, p. 206, Table V, p. 213.

[25] E.g., *N. J. Laws*, 34 sess., 1 sit. (1809), Ch. 38, p. 137; 49 sess., 1 sit. (1824), p. 64; 50 sess., 1 sit. (1825), p. 58.

[26] E.g., *N. J. Laws*, 49 sess., 1 sit. (1824), p. 8; 52 sess., 2 sit. (1828), p. 103; 59 sess., 2 sit. (1835), p. 111.

[27] *N. J. Laws*, 61 sess., 2 sit. (1837), p. 455.

Jersey, but two charters may be specially mentioned in this connection because of statements contained in their preambles. The Patent Cloth Manufacturing Company, incorporated by New Jersey in 1815, had been incorporated in New York the previous year.[28] In 1823, The Jersey Little Falls Manufacturing Company, then operating a carpet factory in New York City, was incorporated by New Jersey. The preamble of the charter declared that the managers contemplated moving the concern to New Jersey and that the legislature recognized the benefit to the state from the employment of the capital there.[29] A pamphlet published in South Carolina in 1845 called attention to the results of Pennsylvania's illiberal policy with respect to manufacturing corporations and declared that a large factory financed by Philadelphia capitalists had been recently established in New Jersey rather than in Pennsylvania because of the greater facility of incorporation afforded in the former state.[30]

It is clear that until the latter part of the eighteen thirties there was little opposition to charters for manufacturing purposes in New Jersey, and very few charters requested seem to have been refused.[31] On the contrary, the lawmakers seem to

[28] *N. J. Laws,* 39 sess., 2 sit. (1815, private), p. 172. No reason is assigned to indicate why a New Jersey charter was desired. It is not even certain that the intent was to move the company to New Jersey, for, in contrast to most charters of the period, nothing about the scene of manufacturing activity was specified.

[29] *N. J. Laws,* 48 sess., 1 sit. (1823, private), p. 124. A letter from "Livingston" in the *True American* of February 28, 1824, praised the charter as evidence of action rather than words to attract New York capital to New Jersey.

[30] "A very large manufacturing establishment has been recently put in operation at Gloucester-point in New-Jersey, three miles below Philadelphia. The owners are Philadelphians, who made choice of that location, because a more liberal charter could be obtained from that State than from Pennsylvania. What will be the result of this move? It will be the building up of a town in New-Jersey, and the investment of some millions of Pennsylvania capital, to give employment to the poor, and pay taxes to the former State." *An Enquiry into the Propriety of Granting Charters of Incorporation for Manufacturing and Other Purposes, in South Carolina:* By One of the People, p. 9.

[31] An accurate reckoning of the number of manufacturing charters actually refused could be made only after a minute examination of the records of the proceedings of both assembly and council. Even then, the investigator would learn nothing about the reasons for refusal — whether objection was made to corporate enterprise in a certain industry or whether the applications turned

have been eager to encourage the development of manufacturing by acts of incorporation. There appears to have been less opposition to manufacturing corporations in New Jersey than to two other major types of corporations, those for banking and transportation purposes, until 1835 when the whole policy of granting charters of incorporation to business units became a political issue and the anti-corporation group reserved a large share of its vituperation for manufacturing corporations.[32]

The early history of New Jersey mining corporations is in most respects similar to that of manufacturing companies.[33] The Soho Company, chartered in 1801 as New Jersey's first mining corporation,[34] was a typical case in that it had no difficulty in obtaining a charter. The final assembly vote on the question of its charter was thirty-three to three, and there were no opposing votes in the council.[35] Preambles to mining company charters frequently referred to the benefit to the welfare of the state that might be expected to result from the acts of incorporation. Many such charters were prefaced with the incontrovertible statement that "it will be for the public benefit, that the mines of this state should be worked." [36]

---

down had requested special favors in addition to the ordinary privileges of incorporation. For example, during the meeting of the legislature in the autumn of 1826, the assembly appears to have refused a few applications for manufacturing company charters, but no indication of the reasons for adverse action can be discovered. Cf. *Votes and Proceedings of the General Assembly,* 51 sess., 1 sit. (1826), *passim.*

[32] Cf. *infra,* pp. 75–80.

[33] Most mining company charters also authorized the manufacture of the metals extracted.

[34] *N. J. Laws,* 26 sess., 1 sit. (1801), Ch. 52, p. 116. This company, formed to operate the famous Schulyer's mines near Belleville, was probably the same group that had previously endeavored to obtain a charter and financial assistance from the federal government. Cf. Davis, II, 287, 287n.

[35] *Votes and Proceedings of the General Assembly,* 26 sess., 1 sit. (1801), pp. 120–21. *Journal of the Legislative Council,* 26 sess., 1 sit. (1801), p. 118. At one point in the proceedings of the assembly, the title of the corporation was expanded to the Soho Copper-Mine and Metal Company, perhaps as an additional assurance that the company would confine its activities to the contemplated objects. The company was thus designated when the bill went to the council, but that body restored the original and simpler title of the Soho Company.

[36] E.g., *N. J. Laws,* 49 sess., 1 sit. (1824), p. 19; 51 sess., 1 sit. (1826), p. 39. One company, chartered in 1837, was to operate Cuban mines, but the metals obtained were to be processed in New Jersey. *Ibid.,* 61 sess., 2 sit. (1837), p. 76.

It is important to look at the other side of the picture and consider, as far as the meager information available allows, the advantages to promoters and owners of early manufacturing and mining concerns of charters of incorporation. Then, as now, the principal advantage of incorporation seems to have been the limitation of individual liability for business debts that attached to corporate enterprise. This consideration must have been implicit in the statement in the 1791 prospectus designed to encourage subscriptions to the S. U. M. that "To effect the desired association an incorporation of the Adventurers must be contemplated as a mean necessary to their security. This can doubtless be obtained." [37] Early manufacturing company charters made no reference to limitation of liability as a reason for incorporation, but several charters for mining enterprises were explicit on this point. The preamble to the 1811 charter of a company organized to work the same mines that the earlier Soho Company had been interested in declared that the petitioners thought they could undertake mining operations if they were incorporated, "by means of which the private property of adventurers will be secure from loss . . ." [38] In 1824, still another company was chartered to work the same mines. The petitioners represented that they could finance the operations with the assistance of others who would associate with them if they succeeded in becoming incorporated "so as to secure the adventurers from other loss than the property they may choose to adventure . . ." [39] The same language was repeated in a mining company charter in 1835.[40]

The preambles of a few manufacturing and mining company charters justified the acts of incorporation on the ground that the enterprises required more capital than could otherwise be obtained. Although limitation of liability was not expressly mentioned as the attribute of incorporation that would make it possible to bring in outside investors, it can safely be assumed

[37] Cole, *ed.*, p. 193. Of course, the charter of the S. U. M. granted other valuable privileges such as the right to raise a certain sum of money through a lottery, the authority to build certain canals and to incorporate the district around the works as a town.

[38] *N. J. Laws*, 35 sess., 2 sit. (1811), p. 476.

[39] *N. J. Laws*, 49 sess., 1 sit. (1824), p. 19.

[40] *N. J. Laws*, 59 sess., 2 sit. (1835), p. 138.

that such an idea was implied. Thus the preamble of the charter of the first mining corporation, enacted in 1801, stated that the proprietors had spent large sums already and requested an act of incorporation because they did not have sufficient funds to complete the work.[41] An individual entrepreneur was granted a charter expressly to permit him to increase the size and scope of his textile manufactory.[42] A group associated for the purpose of exploring for and mining coal sought incorporation "to enable them more extensively to carry their intentions into effect . . ."[43] Another coal mining project was favored with a charter because the promoters represented that the undertaking entailed "expenses beyond the reach of individual enterprise . . ."[44] Because the proposed operations would be "attended with great expense and hazard," a group owning mining properties was incorporated by the legislature.[45] An iron works was granted a charter because the proprietor was alleged to have used his entire personal estate in construction, to have found his personal capital insufficient, and to consider corporate privileges and powers essential to his success.[46]

Final and more weighty testimony as to the importance of limited liability as a motive for seeking charters of incorporation during these early years can be found in the first edition of Angell and Ames' pioneer American treatise on private corporations that appeared in 1832. The authors, in contrasting private corporations with partnerships, wrote:

> It is frequently the principal object, in this and in other countries, in procuring an act of incorporation, to limit the risk of the partners to their shares in the stock of the association; and prudent men are always backward in taking stock when they become mere copartners as regards their personal liability for the company debts.[47]

[41] *N. J. Laws,* 26 sess., 1 sit. (1801), Ch. 52, p. 116.
[42] *N. J. Laws,* 49 sess., 1 sit. (1824), p. 8.
[43] *N. J. Laws,* 52 sess., 2 sit. (1828), p. 188.
[44] *N. J. Laws,* 56 sess., 2 sit. (1832), p. 184.
[45] *N. J. Laws,* 65 sess., 2 sit. (1841), p. 54.
[46] *N. J. Laws,* 66 sess., 2 sit. (1842), p. 105.
[47] Joseph K. Angell and Samuel Ames, *A Treatise on the Law of Private Corporations Aggregate* (1st ed., 1832), p. 23. The authors expressed the opinion that corporation charters benefited the public by stimulating investment in trade and public improvements. *Ibid.*, p. 24.

Davis arrived at a similar conclusion with respect to the importance of limited liability after investigating the history of eighteenth century business corporations of the United States.[48]

There were, however, other attributes pertaining to the corporate form of organization that appealed to businessmen as individual firms increased in size and complexity. These were the features of the corporation that made the problem of management and operation more simple than in the case of the unincorporated joint-stock company and included such advantages as the right of perpetual succession, the power to hold property and to bring suits in the corporate name, and the increased freedom with which ownership shares might be transferred. A further advantage enjoyed by incorporated proprietors, one deriving largely from the corporate attribute of limited liability, was the possibility of more safely delegating managerial functions to persons who were not owners. Such advantages were frequently set forth in manufacturing company charters as the reason for incorporation. An 1813 charter for an established textile factory stated that the proprietors, "in order that the business may be conducted with more facility, have prayed to be incorporated," [49] and eight manufacturing company charters passed between 1814 and 1816 contained similar expressions of purpose.[50] The charter of The New-Brunswick Society for encouraging domestic manufactures, passed in 1821, declared that the petitioners "finding a considerable difficulty in conducting the concerns of a company so numerous without the aid of a charter" sought incorporation in order to extend their operations and conduct business with "more facility." [51] In 1833, the proprietors of an "extensive and valuable" textile concern applied for a charter because "by

[48] Davis, II, 317–18. A different opinion concerning the importance of limited liability in the earliest American business corporations has been advanced by Oscar Handlin and Mary F. Handlin in "Origins of the American Business Corporation," *Journal of Economic History,* V (May 1945), pp. 8–17, and in *Commonwealth, A Study of the Role of Government in the American Economy: Massachusetts, 1774–1861,* pp. 155–162.

[49] *N. J. Laws,* 37 sess., 2 sit. (1813, private), p. 109.

[50] E.g., *N. J. Laws,* 39 sess., 1 sit. (1814, private), pp. 8, 13; 39 sess., 2 sit. (1815, private), p. 112, 115.

[51] *N. J. Laws,* 46 sess., 1 sit. (1821, private), p. 26.

reason of the great extent of said establishment, and the large capital required to carry on the same with advantage, it is inconvenient and difficult to be managed by one individual . . ." Since the legislators thought the argument sounded "reasonable," they granted a charter of incorporation.[52] It is interesting to note that in every case where ease of management was given as the excuse for incorporation, some degree of organization had already taken place. In each instance the language of the charter indicates that a factory had been actually established.[53]

TRANSPORTATION AND COMMUNICATION COMPANIES

When a bill to incorporate a company to improve the navigation of the Assunpink Creek was before the New Jersey legislature in 1796, James Ewing, mayor of Trenton, penned a long petition to the legislative council in protest against limiting the term of existence of the projected company to ninety-nine years. The petition is significant because in it Ewing discussed the methods by which works to facilitate transportation and communication could be carried forward. He wrote in part:

> Only three Methods present themselves by which works of public utility, attended by heavy expenses, can be effected.
>
> The first is, by Government undertaking the task at the public expense — here the Government having the Revenues of the State at command have more power than can be otherwise acquired — it is in this way without doubt, that all great improvements of general advantage to the Community ought to be effected, because where all are benefited all ought to be obliged to contribute; yet where the expense is certain and considerable and the Advantage or success problematical, Legislators will rarely think themselves justifiable in sporting with the property of their Constituents; therefore little is to be expected from this quarter. —

[52] *N. J. Laws,* 57 sess., 2 sit. (1833), p. 113.

[53] One further example, although it falls outside of the period under discussion, may be mentioned here because of the historical importance of the company involved. When Peter Cooper applied in 1847 for a charter of incorporation for his Trenton Iron Works, the express purpose was "to enable him to take in others to divide the cares and responsibilities of the enterprise." *Newark Daily Advertiser,* January 30, 1847; *Sentinel of Freedom,* February 2, 1847.

> The Second Method, is by men of large Fortune & Property, undertaking works of public Utility with a view to increase their Fortunes and advance the value of their property, but if we look through the State of New-Jersey we shall find few if any Men of property sufficient to induce us to expect any thing from them [.]
>
> The last Method then is the only one from which we are to hope for important public improvements, Viz. By Companies of Men joining together and risking a part of their property in order to form a joint Stock sufficient to defray the expense of the improvement contemplated; Under this Idea we see almost every State in the Union has encouraged the forming [of] such Companies, and especially for promoting an inland Navigation, by authorizing their improvements and ensuring to them and their Successors the emoluments arising from them should their undertakings prove successful — It was under an Idea that a like disposition prevailed in the Legislature of New Jersey that your Petitioners came forward on the present occasion. —[54]

At the time they were written, these reflections applied not only to navigation projects but equally to other types of improvements such as roads, canals, and bridges. Undertakings of this sort were deemed from the earliest days of American independence as fit subjects for governmental enterprise. The only serious discussion in eighteenth century New Jersey was concerned with the question of whether such projects should be carried out as governmental or private undertakings. There was little or no debate, once the decision was made to delegate a particular undertaking to private enterprise, as to whether or not the proprietors should enjoy the privileges of incorporation. The corporate form of organization was accepted as essential for private "highway" companies.

The eighteenth century history of New Jersey makes it quite clear that the legislators of that state were averse to "sporting" with public money to secure major transportation facilities. The legislature tried various means to encourage the improvement of navigation and the construction of bridges and roads by funds drawn from private sources, giving legislative aid in the form of granting legal status to "commissioners," guaran-

[54] Manuscript petition, dated March 15, 1796, in the collection of the New Jersey State Library.

teeing monopoly position, or authorizing the drawing of lotteries.[55]

National interest required the development of satisfactory transportation facilities across New Jersey, for the state stood athwart the only feasible land route between the principal cities of the Atlantic seaboard. The primary problem involved was the construction of bridges over three sizable New Jersey streams. Early attempts to execute the major bridges marked the transition in New Jersey from former schemes of lotteries and state commissioners to the method of corporate enterprise. Two principal eighteenth century bridge projects were undertaken in the first instance by private companies with legislative authorization. The companies were granted charters of incorporation only after the bridges were in place.[56] The decision to employ the device of the corporation to build future bridges may have been largely influenced by the experience of the state's first bridge company that was chartered in 1792 during the time the unincorporated companies were struggling to finish their works. The preamble of the bridge company charter declared that the work would be of "publick Utility," and that there were "ample Reasons for expecting that the same may be effected by individual Citizens, if proper Encouragement be given by the Legislature." [57] The incorporated company, although undertaking a less ambitious task than the unincorporated concerns, carried its work forward with such promptness that it could not have failed to excite public interest.[58] After 1800, all the principal bridges of the state were constructed and operated by incorporated companies.

The New Jersey legislature also attempted at an early date to accomplish the important task of improving inland navigation by chartering corporations for that purpose after previous measures to encourage private parties, without incorporation, to do the work had proved inadequate. The first navigation

[55] Cf. W. J. Lane, *From Indian Trail to Iron Horse*, pp. 70–71, 122–126, 143–145; J. A. Durrenberger, *Turnpikes*, pp. 43–44.

[56] Davis, II, 204–209.

[57] *N. J. Laws*, 17 sess., 1 sit. (1792), Ch. 406. p. 806. This was the second business corporation.

[58] Davis, II, 209–210.

company was chartered in 1795, and its act of incorporation employed the language of the above-mentioned bridge charter to the effect that there existed "ample reasons for expecting the same may be effected by individual citizens, if proper encouragement be given by the legislature." [59] The two other eighteenth century navigation companies' charters contained similar expressions of purpose.[60] Although the early navigation companies were not attended with the same success as the bridge companies, the private corporation appeared during the decade of the seventeen nineties as the accepted means of stimulating improvements in inland navigation.

New Jersey was more slow than its neighbors to delegate road building to private corporations. The other American states had chartered seventy-two turnpike companies before 1801, while New Jersey had created none.[61] The slowness with which the device of the corporation was applied to road building may have reflected some public hostility to private enterprise in a field that had been primarily the responsibility of governmental units.[62] An indication of the hesitancy with which road building was relinquished to private companies in New Jersey is found in a supplement of 1798 to a bridge company charter empowering the company to repair a section of road. Once the work was completed and before tolls were collected, the company was required to open books for voluntary public contributions for ninety days, at the end of which time the road was to become forever free if the subscriptions were adequate

[59] *N. J. Laws,* 19 sess., 2 sit. (1795), Ch. 544, p. 1041. This was the third business corporation.

[60] *N. J. Laws,* 20 sess., 2 sit. (1796), Ch. 586, p. 57; 21 sess., 2 sit. (1797), Ch. 627, p. 157. A later navigation charter was more explicit as to the advantage of an act of incorporation, declaring that the "expense of such an undertaking, would be too great for individual enterprise" and that the legislature was "desirous of affording all proper encouragement to enterprise and industry, especially when directed to internal navigation." *Ibid.,* 51 sess., 1 sit. (1826), p. 81.

[61] Davis, II, Table X, p. 216.

[62] There was considerable hostility to turnpikes in eighteenth century Pennsylvania, and in speaking of the paucity of toll roads in the southern states, Davis says: "Clearly the tradition of public building and control of land highways was much stronger than in the case of waterways, and business enterprise was not active enough to press into the field." *Ibid.,* II, 219–220, 226.

to pay the cost of the repair work.[63] After 1800, the people of New Jersey came to realize the value to their welfare of good and direct roads, and articles appeared in newspapers of the state to dispell the old prejudice against privately owned toll roads.[64] Failure of the earlier methods of improving roads by appointment of special commissioners, by drawing of lotteries and by direct governmental endeavor hastened the movement toward incorporated turnpike companies. An effective argument on behalf of turnpike companies was the existence of persons in New York City who were interested in developing their town as a market for the increasingly important products of the mines and farms of New Jersey and the upper Delaware valley. By creating turnpike corporations, New York capital could be introduced in large amount to build New Jersey's roads.[65]

New Jersey's first turnpike company was chartered in 1801.[66] By 1820, the legislature had created forty-five such corporations. Encouragement of corporate road building, however, was not at once accepted by all citizens as desirable public policy. During the first decade of the nineteenth century, some Democrats were loud in denouncing the turnpike movement as subversive of the liberties of the people, closing old roads and making the proprietors rich at the expense of the people's rights, and in general "a direct tendency to subvert our Republican Institutions." [67] There is no indication, however, that such hostility appreciably influenced the course of legislative action, and many turnpikes were chartered by Democratic legislatures. After 1810, most open hostility ceased,[68] and a Demo-

[63] *N. J. Laws,* 22 sess., 2 sit. (1798), Ch. 714, p. 342.

[64] Cf. Lane, pp. 145–46.

[65] *Ibid.,* p. 146. Durrenburger, pp. 70–71. Unlike most other states, New Jersey had little part in the rivalry for the western traffic.

[66] *N. J. Laws,* 25 sess., 2 sit. (1801), Ch. 38, p. 80.

[67] W. R. Fee, *Transition from Aristocracy to Democracy in New Jersey: 1789–1829,* pp. 144–147. Opposition to turnpikes is evidenced by protective provisions in charters imposing penalties for breaking down tollgates or milestones, for passing forcibly without payment of toll or for avoiding a tollgate by use of a "shun pike." E.g., *N. J. Laws,* 27 sess., 1 sit. (1802), Ch. 81, p. 172.

[68] On February 14, 1814, the *Trenton Federalist* noted that a Democrat who "some years ago" had objected to turnpikes on the ground they would "introduce an aristocracy" had actually become a stockholder in one.

cratic governor could, by 1816, speak in the following favorable terms of the accomplishments of turnpike companies:

> By enhancing the value of taxable property, they have increased the means of filling the state treasury, while they have taken nothing from it. No further legislative aid has been necessary, than to give a proper direction to the enterprize of our wealthy citizens.[69]

Up to 1820, the most important class of New Jersey charters, both in terms of numbers and of capital stock authorized, was that including highway projects such as bridge, navigation, and road companies.[70] In view of the relatively large capital required for the successful prosecution of such undertakings, charters of incorporation bestowing the privilege of limited liability upon the stockholders were indispensable if the requisite capital was to be obtained. There were other rights given in the charters, however, that were equally or more important than the ordinary corporate privileges. They included, for example, the right to take private land, materials, and ferries by condemnation proceedings, the right to locate works on existing public roads, and occasionally limited monopoly guarantees. The question of state financial assistance to companies constructing works of internal improvement arose early and was settled to the disadvantage of the companies. In only one case, the 1804 charter of the Newark Turnpike Company, did the legislature agree to subscribe to the stock.[71] In a few cases, when financial aid appeared necessary to success, the legislature

[69] *Votes and Proceedings of the General Assembly,* 40 sess., 2 sit. (1816), p. 90.

[70] A charter that has significance in the early history of railroading also dates from this period. In 1811, John Stevens, often called the father of American railroading, applied to the New Jersey legislature for a charter to construct a railroad across the state, but the conservative legislators rejected his proposal as being impracticable. Lane, p. 281. The assembly finally approved an act of incorporation for the railroad in 1814. *Votes and Proceedings of the General Assembly,* 38 sess., 2 sit. (1814), pp. 203–04. The council, however, postponed consideration of the bill. *Journal of the Legislative Council,* 38 sess., 2 sit. (1814), p. 1573. In 1815, the council passed the charter by a vote of seven to four, and the assembly gave it unanimous approval. *Journal of the Legislative Council,* 39 sess., 2 sit. (1815), p. 1686; *Votes and Proceedings of the General Assembly,* 39 sess., 2 sit. (1815), p. 193. This was the first railroad charter in America. *N. J. Laws,* 39 sess., 2 sit. (1815, private), p. 68.

[71] *N. J. Laws,* 29 sess., 1 sit. (1804), Ch. 151, p. 419.

merely authorized public lotteries in preference to appropriations from the public treasury.[72] By the end of the second decade of the nineteenth century, Jerseymen had established a definite policy of securing major transportation facilities by the device of the private corporation and without cost or financial obligation to the state.[73]

New Jersey's policy with respect to internal improvements faced its only serious challenge in the eighteen twenties. The controversy flared up in connection with the construction of two major canals — one to connect the Passaic River and the northern section of the Delaware River, the other to open navigation between the Raritan River and the lower Delaware.[74] Faced with the example of neighboring states that were constructing major waterways as state enterprises, Jerseymen debated whether their two obviously profitable routes should be turned over to private hands. Development of the southern and more important route, that from the Delaware to the Raritan, had been attempted as early as 1804 by an ill-fated company chartered to connect the two rivers by canalizing the intervening natural streams.[75] Interest in the project revived after the War of 1812, and in 1819, after Jerseymen's hopes of securing construction by the national government had faded, a committee of the assembly recommended that New Jersey follow the example of other states and construct internal improvements as state enterprises. The report, which was finally tabled, advocated the creation of a special fund for the purpose by earmarking certain state revenues such as the bank stock

[72] In one instance, a Delaware River bridge company was allowed to sell its Pennsylvania-authorized lottery tickets in New Jersey. *N. J. Laws,* 24 sess., 1 sit. (1799), Ch. 829, p. 646. The other cases involved two turnpike companies, one of which had been chartered by Pennsylvania. The "neat" sums realized from the lotteries were to be used to pay company debts, and the state treasury was to benefit by gifts of stock in the companies equivalent to the sums raised. *Ibid.,* 39 sess., 2 sit. (1815, private), p. 165; 40 sess., 2 sit. (1816, private), p. 155.

[73] It is important to note that the state did not forfeit irrevocably its right to own and operate transportation facilities. In many charters, the state reserved the right to purchase the works after a specified time. Cf. *infra,* pp. 385–388.

[74] Excellent accounts of the two canal projects can be found in Lane, pp. 221–277.

[75] *N. J. Laws,* 29 sess., 1 sit. (1804), Ch. 153, p. 433.

taxes.[76] In the following year, the assembly again turned the canal question over to a committee for consideration. The committee presented a bill to incorporate a private company to build the canal and reported against state construction in a document setting forth the prevailing New Jersey philosophy on internal improvements:

> 1st. That from the uncertainty which exists in respect to the cost of the canal and the future profits, if accomplished, and other reasons, it would not be advisable for this state to undertake the making of the said canal, nor to invest the public money in the stock of any company to be formed.
>
> They beg not to be understood as giving this opinion upon any evidence or data which should discourage a subscription to said undertaking by others, but upon the known policy of this state to avoid engagements of a pecuniary kind, tending to increase the public burthens, unless in case of necessity.
>
> 2d. That it appears to them, that the leading consideration should be, with this state, to hasten the commencement and completion of this great work, without too nice calculations upon the loss or gain to the stockholders — it being certain, if accomplished, the people of this state, will be abundantly remunerated now and in all future time for the liberality of the terms of incorporation.
>
> 3d. That to bring the enterprize immediately before the public, and engage capitalists in the undertaking, they have prepared a bill for incorporating a canal company, upon the most liberal principles, and at the same time containing all proper provisions for securing the attainments of its advantages.[77]

The views of the committee found a responsive audience, and the lawmakers speedily passed the charter for the New-Jersey

[76] "The obvious advantages arising from this source [*i.e.*, internal improvements] have been long foreseen and long admitted, but hitherto the exertions of individuals and the money of those individuals (most unequally afforded) have been the only means made use of to accomplish so desirable and beneficial an object . . . Private means are exhausted — the spirit of enterprise which dictated these measures, has subsided, and almost become extinct. It has died away, while the state has been a silent and (except in one or two instances) an unconcerned looker on." *Votes and Proceedings of the General Assembly,* 43 sess., 2 sit. (1819), pp. 141–143.

[77] *Votes and Proceedings of the General Assembly,* 44 sess., 2 sit. (1820), pp. 108–09.

Delaware and Raritan Canal Company.[78] Like its predecessor, however, this company failed to find financial support.

In 1822, when the Delaware and Raritan problem was still unresolved, the Delaware to Passaic project came to the forefront of public attention. Public interest in canals seems to have been thoroughly aroused by this date, and, influenced apparently by New York's success in prosecuting the Erie Canal, public sentiment for state construction became widespread in New Jersey. Newspapers such as the Trenton *True American,* the Morristown *Palladium of Liberty,* and the Newark *Sentinel of Freedom* campaigned heartily during 1822 for construction by the state,[79] and the legislature responded by appointing commissioners to investigate the matter.[80] The commissioners, reporting in 1823, declared the project would be a financial success and should be undertaken by the state.[81]

A joint committee appointed by the legislature in 1823 to make a statement of policy agreed on the probable profitableness of the undertaking. While they declared their unwillingness to decide on how the work should be financed, they did express the following opinion:

> The committee do not hesitate to say, that they believe it would comport with the present views of their constituents, and the interest of the state, to grant a liberal charter to a private company to make the contemplated canal.[82]

[78] *N. J. Laws,* 44 sess., 2 sit. (1820, public), p. 55.

[79] The principal arguments were that the revenue to be derived should go to the state and not "to enrich the monied men of our neighboring states, who would eventually, if not immediately, monopolize the stock, and thus render us forever tributary to them," that the example of New York proved a state could manage construction and operation as "discreetly and economically" as individuals, that the state could borrow the necessary funds to provide for the work "without the state advancing a dollar," and that the revenues would "finally shut up the books of the tax gatherer." Cf. *True American,* July 27, August 17 and 31, 1822.

[80] *N. J. Laws,* 47 sess., 1 sit. (1822, private), p. 79.

[81] DeWitt Clinton of New York and army engineers furnished by the War Department also examined the route and concurred in the commission's conclusions. Lane, pp. 225–26.

[82] *Votes and Proceedings of the General Assembly,* 48 sess., 1 sit. (1823), p. 87.

Although many newspapers continued to express a preference for state construction, those members of the legislature who feared that canal undertakings would imperil the financial position of the state won out, and in 1824 the Morris Canal and Banking Company was chartered to connect the Delaware and Passaic Rivers.[83]

While the Morris Canal plan was still being discussed, the failure of the second company chartered to build a waterway between the Delaware and Raritan Rivers caused renewed debate on the proper procedure to follow to secure construction of the latter work. A joint committee of the legislature reported in 1823 in favor of carrying the work forward as a state project, but at the same time the committee recommended further study of the anticipated costs and revenues.[84] A group appointed to make further investigation sent an interesting document to the next legislature. After weighing the arguments against entrusting the waterway to the "arbitrary control of individuals" and assessing the opportunity for profit that might result from state construction, the report recommended a plan that was to influence profoundly the future policy of New Jersey. It suggested construction by a private company under terms that would secure considerable profit to the state without pledging state financial aid in any form:

> The committee have . . . reflected, that although the prospect is flattering, yet the success of this project, like that of all new experiments, is in some measure problematical, requiring an immense expenditure, with but uncertain promise of a corresponding profit . . . Under these impressions, your committee are induced to recommend the *incorporation* of a private company, by a charter that will secure to the state, by subscriptions to the stock, or other means, a reasonable part and interest in the profits and direction of the said com-

[83] *N. J. Laws,* 49 sess., 1 sit. (1824), p. 158. Banking and trust powers were included in the charter "to induce capitalists and others to subscribe . . ."

[84] The committee were "of opinion that such a canal, if it could be effected at an expense not too great for the resources of the state, and without imposing a burdensome weight of taxation, ought to be carried into execution by the state itself." *Votes and Proceedings of the General Assembly,* 48 sess., 1 sit. (1823), p. 85.

pany, believing that in this way, most of the benefit expected, may be realized to the state, without assuming the great responsibilities which must be incurred by its undertaking the expense and future risk of the canal and its management, as a state property.[85]

These proposals were put into execution by the chartering of a third company to undertake the Delaware and Raritan project.[86] State participation in the venture was assured by reservation of one-fourth of the stock to be held at the option of the state for approximately three years, and a $100,000 bonus was to be paid the state "in part consideration" for the charter. The company sold its stock and paid the required bonus, but subsequent niggardliness on the part of Pennsylvania in the matter of the withdrawal of water from the Delaware discouraged the company from pursuing the project further.[87] It petitioned the legislature for a refund of the bonus, and the request was granted on condition that the charter and franchises be surrendered.[88]

Public demand for action to secure a waterway across New Jersey became insistent in 1827. By that date, the problem was also complicated somewhat by public interest in railroads.[89] Between 1827 and 1830, New Jersey's established policy with respect to transportation facilities met its greatest and final challenge. A committee of the assembly, reporting in 1827, advocated that the state build the canal between the Delaware and Raritan Rivers.[90] Many newspapers supported the proposal. One editor declared he could hear only one sentiment — that the state undertake the canal — ,[91] another favored state

[85] *Ibid.*, 49 sess., 1 sit. (1824), pp. 120, 122.

[86] *N. J. Laws,* 49 sess., 1 sit. (1824), p. 175.

[87] Lane, pp. 255–56.

[88] At first only $90,000 was returned. *N. J. Laws,* 51 sess., 1 sit. (1826), p. 87. Later the remainder of the bonus was refunded. *Ibid.*, 52 sess., 2 sit. (1828), p. 178.

[89] Stevens had given a demonstration of the practicability of railroads at Hoboken in 1825. Newspapers printed articles and letters to instruct the public on the relative merits of railroads and canals. E.g., *True American,* November 7 and 21, December 5, 1827.

[90] *Votes and Proceedings of the General Assembly,* 52 sess., 1 sit. (1827), p. 66–70.

[91] *True American,* November 28, 1827.

construction as promising the people ultimate relief from taxation.[92] A bill to provide for state construction of the canal actually passed the assembly in 1828, but it failed of passage in the council by a tie vote.[93]

In January 1829, an assembly committee submitted a report minimizing the financial risk involved in building the much needed canal and strongly advocated that the state undertake the work.[94] The report received wide notice in the press, and the canal became the leading topic of discussion in the state. Another bill providing for construction by the state itself passed the assembly in 1829, but consideration of this bill was indefinitely postponed in council.[95] A final bill for a state owned canal was introduced in the fall of 1829, but the measure was abandoned early in 1830 when applications for a canal charter and a railroad charter came before the legislature.[96] Rivalry between the canal and railroad groups, both of whom sought charters, had created a deadlock in the legislature for the two preceding years,[97] and the stalemate was broken only after a compromise was arrived at by the two groups.[98] On the same

[92] *Trenton Emporium,* November 24, 1827.

[93] *Votes and Proceedings of the General Assembly,* 52 sess., 2 sit. (1828), pp. 194–95; *Journal of the Legislative Council,* 52 sess., 2 sit. (1828), p. 105; *True American,* February 13, March 5, 1828.

[94] *Votes and Proceedings of the General Assembly,* 53 sess., 2 sit. (1829), pp. 126–152. "In fine, it would elevate the character of New Jersey; small in territory, and now subject to the constant encroachments of her more powerful sisters. It would place in her hands a means by which she might command their respect. Holding the right of way, which all of them would be compelled to use, it would give her a power and a consequence, which she could by no other means acquire."

[95] *Ibid.,* p. 227; *Journal of the Legislative Council,* 53 sess., 2 sit. (1829), p. 99; *Trenton Emporium,* February 21 and 28, 1829. The editor of the *Emporium* thought something would certainly be done the following year to secure to the state the revenue from canal tolls "which will prove to all future generations an exhaustless mine of wealth."

[96] *Emporium and True American,* January 23, 1830. The question of the state's building the canal had been made an issue in the election of 1829, and the outcome of the balloting showed that regions not to be directly benefited by the canal were opposed to being taxed in order that the state might undertake the work. Cf. Lane, pp. 257–58.

[97] Charters authorizing railroads across New Jersey had been defeated in 1828 and 1829. *True American,* February 13, March 12, 1828; *Trenton Emporium,* February 14, 1829.

[98] Lane, pp. 258–59.

day, February 4, 1830, charters were finally granted to The Delaware and Raritan Canal Company and The Camden and Amboy Rail Road and Transportation Company to open the major transportation arteries of New Jersey.[99]

The terms of these two important charters were drawn in accordance with the policy of securing construction of public works without risking state funds or credit yet allowing for state participation in the profits. Neither company was guaranteed state financial aid, although in each case one-fourth of the capital stock was to be held for a specified period at the option of the state.[100] On the contrary, transit duties based on the passengers and freight transported by the companies were to be paid to the state. The press endorsed the principle of transit duties, "the object of which is to secure a revenue to the Treasury without embarking in any expenditure of capital,"[101] and considered the charters the best solution to New Jersey's transportation problem because "a handsome revenue is secured from them without subjecting ourselves to any risk, and by the time the State is able to purchase them she can do so, at less probably than she could now construct them."[102]

Once the transportaton projects were entrusted to private corporations, it became clear that, rather than give the companies financial aid, the state could increase the public revenues by selling increased privileges to the companies. It was reported in the fall of 1830 that the Camden and Amboy offered the legislature a bonus in return for exclusive rights to railroad transportation between New York and Philadelphia, a suggestion that aroused much criticism from the newspapers of the state.[103] The papers, however, reversed their stand two months

[99] *N. J. Laws,* 54 sess., 2 sit. (1830), pp. 73, 83.

[100] It was later stated that the purpose of reserving the right of subscription for a period of time was to allow the state an opportunity to decide whether to subscribe after the chances of success of the projects were more certain. *Emporium and True American,* January 7, 1832.

[101] *Ibid.,* January 23, 1830.

[102] *Ibid.,* January 30, 1830.

[103] One editor declared it was only necessary to "*name* such a monstrous proposition, to secure the opposition of every citizen of the state. Can it be possible that a company of New-York and Philadelphia gentlemen are to be protected against competition from the people of New-Jersey, in engrossing the business

later when the legislature passed an act to make it lawful for the railroad company to present the state with 1000 full-paid shares of stock in return for a guarantee that no other railroad would be authorized to engage in transporting passengers and goods across New Jersey between New York and Philadelphia unless the stock gift was returned to the Camden and Amboy.[104] Newspaper editors made the flimsy excuse that no monopoly had been granted because a new road could be authorized at any time if the legislature surrendered the state's stock.[105] It was quite obvious, however, that the railroad had gone far in the direction of securing exclusive privileges.

The canal company had been, in the meantime, experiencing financial difficulties in getting started and, fearing "ruinous competition" from the railroad, agreed to a combination with that company. Happy to assure completion of both projects in this way, the legislature, in spite of some cries of "monopoly," passed an act of "union." [106] By the terms of the act, the two companies were allowed "to consolidate" their capital stock into a "joint stock" with equal rights to profits. Each company retained its separate organization, but direction and management of all affairs was to emanate from the directors sitting "in joint-meeting." When the union was effected, the railroad and canal corporations became known popularly as the "Joint Companies."

This rapprochement of the two corporations served not only to assure the execution of both railroad and canal projects; it also increased the effectiveness of the influence that they could bring to bear on the legislature. By 1832, the Joint Companies were able to secure passage of the infamous "monopoly bill" under the terms of which the companies presented the state with an additional 1000 full-paid shares on which dividends were to be paid "as if the state had subscribed for such stock

that has from time immemorial been the common property of our citizens and that the state can be brought into an alliance with them for such a purpose? We went to war once for 'free trade and sailors' rights,' and free trade and landsmen's rights are as precious." *Ibid.*, November 20, 1830.

[104] *N. J. Laws*, 55 sess., 2 sit. (1831), p. 74.

[105] E.g., *Emporium and True American*, February 19, 1831.

[106] *N. J. Laws*, 55 sess., 2 sit. (1831), p. 124.

and paid the several instalments thereon." [107] The interest of the state was protected by a requirement that the whole net profit, except for a maximum surplus for contingencies of $100,000, be paid out as dividends. It was further agreed that if the state revenues from both transit duties and dividends on the state stock did not equal $30,000 in any one year, the deficiency would be made up by the companies before any dividends were paid to ordinary stockholders "so as to secure to the state the aforesaid sum of thirty thousand dollars, at least in each and every year during said charter." In return for guaranteed revenue, the state gave the Camden and Amboy irrevocable monopoly privileges in the following passage:

> That it shall not be lawful, at any time during the said rail road charter, to construct any other rail road or rail roads in this state, without the consent of the said companies, which shall be intended or used for the transportation of passengers or merchandise between the cities of New York and Philadelphia, or to compete in business with the rail road authorized by the act to which this supplement is relative.[108]

Thus New Jersey was willing to surrender a large part of its freedom of action in return for revenue that promised to reduce state taxes to the vanishing point. At the time, there was little public opposition to this scheme that had been cleverly conceived by the Joint Companies. *The Emporium and True American* echoed the general sentiment by declaring a dislike "in the abstract" for the principle of absolute protection, at the same time excusing the legislators' act as necessary to make the public revenues secure and making the indisputable statement that "the Legislature have acted under powerful inducements." [109] The "powerful inducements" soon became still more

[107] *N. J. Laws,* 56 sess., 2 sit. (1832), p. 79.

[108] Lateral roads not intended for the "purpose of competition" were excluded from the prohibition. The Camden and Amboy, on its part, was to construct a branch line to serve New Brunswick.

[109] "The *right of way* across New-Jersey has always been considered a great state property — the inheritance of the people — and a source to which they were entitled to look for a state revenue as a relief from taxation, and a means of improving our condition as a people . . . The people pay nothing — become responsible for nothing — The state remains free from debt — a large present revenue is secured — " *Emporium and True American,* March 10, 1832.

powerful in convincing many Jerseymen that it was to the advantage of their state to protect and strengthen the monopoly. In 1833, Governor Seeley in addressing the legislature expressed the common sentiment that "we may with confidence look forward to no very distant period, when the revenue arising from the several great works of internal improvement in our state . . . will be amply sufficient to defray all the expenses of government, and enable the legislature to augment the school fund . . ."[110]

When, between 1833 and 1835, the monopoly met its first challenge, it became apparent that the actual and prospective revenues to be enjoyed by the state as the result of its virtual partnership with the Joint Companies fulfilled every expectation as effective insurance for legislative protection. The Philadelphia and Trenton Railroad purchased a controlling interest in the stock of the Trenton and New Brunswick Turnpike Company[111] in order to obtain a route across New Jersey and petitioned the New Jersey legislature for permission to lay tracks over the turnpike. The battle between the Joint Companies and the turnpike company, which was backed by the Philadelphia and Trenton Railroad, created turmoil in the legislature in 1834 and 1835. Advisory legal opinions were presented by both sides, the Joint Companies' council stressing the contractual nature of the monopoly grant. In the face of opinions on behalf of the turnpike company by such eminent jurists as Roger B. Taney, James Kent, and Daniel Webster,[112] the bill to authorize construction of a railroad by the turnpike company was defeated in the assembly in 1835.

The interesting fact about the decision to continue the monopoly was that neither the public nor the lawmakers were as much impressed by finely spun legal theories as they were by

[110] *Votes and Proceedings of the General Assembly,* 58 sess., 1 sit. (1833), p. 8.

[111] This company had been chartered in 1804. *N. J. Laws,* 29 sess., 1 sit. (1804), Ch. 137, p. 382.

[112] Although these men employed basically different reasoning, they all decided that a railroad could be constructed on the route of the turnpike. Taney took the stand that the "monopoly act" of 1832 was not binding on future legislatures. Kent and Webster emphasized the contractual nature of the turnpike charter and declared that the turnpike company was the injured party since subsequent legislation had diluted the value of its franchise. Cf. Lane, pp. 327–28.

the certain revenues derived by the state from the Joint Companies. The arguments presented in the press were concerned primarily with the question of state revenues. A published letter from "A Jerseyman" commended the legislature for having effectively, and without financial risk to the state, secured an income from the New York to Philadelphia traffic and lauded the "policy of using this advantage of position *for purposes of revenue.*" [113] Other writers stressing the loss of revenue if the "foreign monopoly" was allowed to build a competing railroad reminded the public that the existence of a competing road would also lessen the value of New Jersey's right to buy the Joint Companies' works at the end of the established period. They painted vivid pictures of the prosperity that could be expected if the state protected the monopoly until it could be taken over as a state enterprise.[114] The revenue issue was expressed with great frankness by the assembly committee appointed to report on the petition to allow railroad privileges to the turnpike company. The committee decided against the petition in order "to preserve inviolate, sacred, and unimpaired, the *faith,* the *integrity,* and the *revenues* of the state, by a strict adherence to that system of policy which has laid at the foundation of our Internal Improvements, *the principle of protection as a means of revenue.*" [115] Fear that a new legislature might be of a different opinion led influential newspapers to remind Jersey voters the following fall that if New Jersey did not alter its policy "this will be the richest State in the Union" and to issue warnings against electing legislators who favored diverting the revenues of the state into "the pockets of speculating stock-jobbers and foreign monopolists." [116]

The managers of the Joint Companies, fearing that a court

[113] *Emporium and True American,* November 29, 1834.

[114] "No mine of precious metal, or valuable jewels, could prove more inestimable. The proceeds would relieve us from all taxation . . . In a word, New-Jersey would be a land flowing with milk and honey." *Emporium and True American,* March 28, 1835. In order to present their case to the public, the anti-monopoly group found it desirable to establish a newspaper, the *Trenton Argus,* especially for the purpose. Lane, p. 328n.

[115] *Votes and Proceedings of the General Assembly,* 59 sess., 2 sit. (1835), p. 223.

[116] E.g., *Emporium and True American,* August 1, September 5, 1835.

decision might uphold the right of the turnpike company to lay rails without further legislation, bought a controlling interest in the Philadelphia and Trenton Railroad and averted any threat to their monopoly for the time being. After 1835, the Joint Companies ceased to rely solely on the power of their lobby and actively entered politics, exercising, mainly through the Democratic party, constantly increasing political control in the state government for the next thirty-five years. It was this deep-seated control that earned for New Jersey its nineteenth century name of "The State of Camden and Amboy." Political control was aided and abetted by the significant revenues paid by the companies into the state treasury. As early as 1836, the guaranteed sum was exceeded, and after 1838 the sums paid to the state continually increased. [117] It very soon became unnecessary in certain years for the state to resort to direct taxes,[118] and no direct state taxes were levied in any year between 1848 and the Civil War period. No circumstance could have been better calculated to engender public approbation of the monopoly policy. Thus through political control and financial tribute to the state, the monopoly group was able to weather a series of threats to its dominance. The vilification heaped on New Jersey by the press and public of other states, the efforts of other New Jersey railroad groups to break the monopoly, the ardent campaign of the Whig press of the state, and persistent and spirited opposition from such prominent New Jersey residents as the economist Henry C. Carey were unavailing. The monopoly companies remained secure in their position until their properties were leased to the Pennsylvania Railroad in 1871.[119]

The chartering of the Camden and Amboy in 1830 had inaugurated the railroad era in New Jersey. The legislature adopted the policy pursued with respect to other highway proj-

[117] P. M. Tuttle, "History of Railroad Taxation in New Jersey" (Harvard University doctoral thesis, typewritten manuscript in New Jersey State Library), p. 39.

[118] In 1837, for example. *Emporium and True American,* March 17, 1837.

[119] An excellent and detailed account of the influence wielded by the Joint Companies can be found in the chapter entitled "Monopoly and Politics" in Lane, pp. 323–370.

ects for the new mode of transportation. There was no audible agitation for state construction of railroads, and charters for private railroad companies were granted with liberality.[120] Furthermore, New Jersey did not, as did many other states, aid in financing the railroads,[121] and no action was taken in the several instances where subscription rights were reserved to the state. In order to encourage private investment in railroads, various inducements such as liberal tax treatment, amounting in many cases to virtual tax exemption, were included in the charters.[122] If railroad corporations found difficulty in raising funds necessary to complete their roads, the legislature came willingly to their aid by enacting supplements to make borrowing from private investors possible,[123] and in one instance a railroad was assisted by the award of banking powers.[124]

Thus New Jersey's policy with respect to transportation and communication facilities was well established before the eighteen forties. Construction of the facilities was accomplished in every important instance by private rather than governmental

[120] The continued existence of the Camden and Amboy monopoly, of course, distorted the railroad picture. The result of the legislature's assiduous protection of the monopoly was to make nearly every road in the central section of the state a mere subsidiary branch of the Camden and Amboy.

[121] The sole example of a state loan to a railroad company occurred in 1837 in connection with the New Jersey Railroad and Transportation Company. The legislature ordered the trustees of the school fund to loan the railroad $100,000 at six per cent. The loan was to be made "on good and sufficient security" and callable on twelve months' notice. In return, the expiring right of the state to subscribe for capital stock was extended in part for seven years. *N. J. Laws,* 61 sess., 2 sit. (1837), p. 71.

[122] Cf. *infra,* pp. 398–401.

[123] Cf. *infra,* pp. 282–286 and 291–293.

[124] *N. J. Laws,* 61 sess., 2 sit. (1837), p. 91. It is to be noted that in the case of railroads, as had been true of some earlier highway projects, the legislature did not renounce irrevocably the right to engage in the industry. Many railroad charters made provision for state purchase of the roads after a specified time had elapsed. Cf. *infra,* pp. 387–388. The same approach was recommended by Governor Throop of New York in 1832. In speaking of the prospects for railroads, the governor declared it might be a long time before all improvements worthy of government enterprise "can be undertaken upon the public means alone. Shall we then forbear to possess ourselves of these advantages, if they can be obtained without imposing public burthens?" He then recommended, however, that the legislature reserve "the right to take possession of them [railroads] as public property." New York State, *Messages from the Governor,* III, 375–76.

enterprise — private enterprise made effective by liberal grants of corporate charters. Nor did New Jersey follow the example of its neighbors and pledge the funds or the credit of the state to aid the corporations established.[125] The state was amply rewarded for its caution when the depression of 1837–1843 set in because it escaped the financial difficulties that plagued nearly every other state. It was in connection with charters for transportation companies that Jerseymen found overwhelming proof of the validity of a notion, conceived earlier in connection with bank charters, that a policy of granting liberal corporate privileges could be employed not only to foster the state's physical development but also to furnish plentiful funds for the financial support of the state government. The lesson was well learned and dictated the direction of New Jersey's corporation policy until the early twentieth century.

BANKING AND INSURANCE COMPANIES

New Jersey's initial banking legislation was "An act to promote and support the National Bank" passed in 1782.[126] This law did not grant a state charter to supplement the Bank of North America's questioned federal charter of 1781, but it did guarantee that no other bank would be established in New Jersey during the war with Great Britain.[127] No bank was, in fact, chartered by New Jersey until 1804 when the Newark Banking and Insurance Company was incorporated.[128] The preamble of the act of incorporation stated that the agricultural, manufacturing, and commercial interests of New Jersey would be advanced by the establishment of a "well regulated" bank and

[125] One author, in writing of New York's demonstration of the manner in which public credit could be employed to assist private corporations, declared "the way was open for other States to pursue the same course; and only New Jersey and the smaller New England States refused to enter upon it." G. S. Callender, "The Early Transportation and Banking Enterprises of the States in Relation to the Growth of Corporations," *Quarterly Journal of Economics,* XVII (November 1902), p. 153.

[126] *N. J. Laws,* 6 sess., 2 sit. (1782), Ch. 21, p. 67.

[127] The act imposed severe penalties for counterfeiting the notes of the Bank of North America and made the bank's notes legal tender at full face value for debts owing to the state. Six other states also passed legislation to assist the bank. Davis, II, 38.

[128] *N. J. Laws,* 28 sess., 2 sit. (1804), Ch. 109, p. 268.

that the capital raised for banking purposes would afford great public benefits.[129] There appears to have been little opposition to the creation of the bank,[130] and by 1808 three other banks had been chartered, one each at the towns of Powles Hook (later Jersey City), Trenton, and New Brunswick.[131]

In each of the four bank charters there was a clause reserving a certain amount of stock to the state if the legislature wished to subscribe. If the state exercised its option, it was to have the right of appointment of certain directors. The reservation to the state of the right to subscribe to bank stock was quite clearly not intended as an assistance to the banks in raising the necessary capital. It was realized that the banking franchise was a valuable one, and it was easy to find subscribers to bank stock. The right to subscribe was reserved by the state so that the state might participate in the large profits to be expected from the banking business.[132] The New Jersey government had either no funds or little inclination to become a large stockholder in banking enterprises,[133] for the legislature preferred to realize an immediate revenue from its subscription privileges and authorized the sale of its rights to subscribe to the stock of three of the banks.[134] In only one case, that of the Trenton Banking Company, did the lawmakers see fit to exercise their option and purchase bank stock.[135]

[129] After the bank was in operation, the *Trenton Federalist* of August 27, 1804, echoed these sentiments with the statement that the bank was "auspicious to the commercial, mechanical and manufacturing interests of the people of New-Jersey."

[130] The final assembly vote on the bill was thirty-two to six. *Votes and Proceedings of the General Assembly,* 28 sess., 2 sit. (1804), 128–29. It received unanimous approval in the council. *Journal of the Legislative Council,* 28 sess., 2 sit. (1804), pp. 299–300.

[131] Although the bank at Powles Hook was declared by its charter to be a branch of the bank at Newark and could not be established without the consent of a majority of the directors and stockholders of that bank, it was in effect a separate and distinct corporation. *N. J. Laws,* 29 sess., 1 sit. (1804), Ch. 135, p. 378. The "Branch" became widely known as the "Jersey Bank." For the charter of the Trenton Banking Company see *ibid.,* Ch. 154, p. 449; for that of the Bank at New-Brunswick see *ibid.,* 32 sess., 1 sit. (1807), Ch. 30, p. 80.

[132] Cf. Callender, pp. 159–162.

[133] This was in contrast to the situation in many states at this time. *Ibid.,* pp. 113–14.

[134] *N. J. Laws,* 29 sess., 1 sit. (1804), Ch. 165, p. 482; 32 sess., 1 sit. (1807), Ch. 26, p. 73; 34 sess., 1 sit. (1809), Ch. 54, p. 203.

[135] *N. J. Laws,* 35 sess., 1 sit. (1810), p. 249.

Beginning apparently in 1809, controversy over the question of increasing the number of banks beyond the four already chartered flared up in earnest, and opinion divided along party lines. The Democrats who were then in control of the legislature commenced agitation for a state-financed bank, the officers of which would be appointed by the legislature. The Federalist press issued a series of warnings against increasing the quantity of paper money and against a state-controlled bank as a scheme to create "fat offices" for party men.[136] At the same time, a bill to levy a special tax of one-half of one per cent on the capital stock of the existing incorporated banks was proposed in the legislature. The Federalists called the suggested tax a Democratic plan to raise revenue by taxing "*aristocrats* and *foreigners* [residents of New York City and Philadelphia]."[137] The bank tax law was finally passed in 1810.[138] The tax is significant as the first one in which the New Jersey lawmakers singled out a group of incorporated business units as subjects for special taxation. Its adoption reflected the early realization that the state was granting a valuable privilege in enacting bank charters and that the state treasury might benefit from such grants. The tax was applied consistently to all specially chartered banks thereafter created.

As the year 1811 approached and it became increasingly certain that the first Bank of the United States was to be discontinued, New Jersey's legislature was confronted with numerous applications for bank charters. In January 1811, the assembly appointed a special committee to examine the bank applications and to report on the course the legislature should pursue. The chairman of the committee was J. J. Wilson, a Democrat who had been the spokesman of his party on banking matters for several years.[139] Wilson reported for the committee that an increase in banking facilities was desirable but that

[136] E.g., *Trenton Federalist,* September 18, 1809. The Federalist opposition was probably based largely on loyalty to the first Bank of the United States, one of the party's principal measures. It may also have been to some degree the result of a desire to protect the large personal interests of Federalists in the existing state banks.

[137] *Trenton Federalist,* November 20, 1809.

[138] *N. J. Laws,* 35 sess., 1 sit. (1810), p. 244.

[139] *Trenton Federalist,* January 21, 1811. This paper considered Wilson "bank mad."

since the state's funds were all productively employed, it was inexpedient to create a state bank. The suggestion was made that five banks with a total capital of nearly one million dollars be chartered. The committee also recommended that "to guard against the evils which have in some instances already arisen from Banks . . . if the above capitals are authorized to be subscribed by *individuals,* an equal amount in each shall be created and reserved for the *state,* to be filled up as funds may be collected and the Legislature deem it expedient."[140] After suffering defeat in the council, the proposed bank bills were forgotten for the remainder of the session.[141]

The Democrats again formed a majority in the 1811–1812 legislature, and they seemed determined to create additional banks.[142] Early in 1812, backed by a large number of petitions that had been in an organized fashion circulated widely over the state,[143] they passed a bill creating six separate banks.[144] Although each of the banks included in its title the words "state-bank," the banks were not in a strict sense state institutions. One-half of the stock in each was reserved at the option of the state, the initial boards of directors were named in the

[140] *Votes and Proceedings of the General Assembly,* 35 sess., 2 sit. (1811), pp. 409–410.

[141] *Trenton Federalist,* February 18 and 25, 1811.

[142] *Ibid.,* December 9, 1811. [143] *Ibid.,* January 13, 1812.

[144] *N. J. Laws,* 36 sess., 2 sit. (1812, public), p. 3. This law has been sometimes erroneously referred to as a general bank law. E.g., J. J. Knox, *A History of Banking in the United States,* pp. 432–33.

It is interesting to note that not only New Jersey was plagued at this time by proposals for greatly enlarged banking systems. Governor Tompkins of New York addressed his legislature in 1812 speaking strongly against further chartering of business corporations in general and of banks in particular. *The Weekly Register,* I, No. 23, February 8, 1812. Evidences of bribery in connection with the numerous bank charters before the legislature influenced Tompkins to take the unprecedented step of proroguing the legislature for sixty days to permit the trial of persons offering bribes and to allow time for sounding public opinion on the question of banks. *Ibid.,* II, No. 32, April 4, 1812. New Jersey's other neighbor, Pennsylvania, was experiencing similar troubles that culminated in 1813 in Governor Snyder's unsuccessful veto of the "forty bank bill." *Ibid.,* IV, No. 82, March 27, 1813.

Between 1811 and 1816, the brief period intervening between the two United States banks, the number of state banking institutions in the whole country increased from 88 to 246. D. L. Kemmerer, article on "Banking" in *Dictionary of American History.*

law, and annually thereafter the legislature was to appoint one-half of the directors of each bank as well as the president of each who was to be "ex-officio a director." The plan was to keep the banks' management strictly under the control of the state, for the power of appointment was to be exercised by the legislature regardless of whether or not the state subscribed to its quotas of stock. The banks were immediately attacked by Federalists as "engines" to perpetuate the Democratic party in New Jersey.[145] The principal objections to the so-called state banks were made in a series of communications to the *Trenton Federalist* by a writer signing himself "Obadiah." They included criticism of party control evidenced by the fact that two supreme court justices and two members of the legislature had been appointed bank presidents, the charge that instead of increasing state revenues through capital stock taxes the new banks would merely lessen the value of the state's stock in the Trenton bank, and reflections on the fraud involved in designating the new institutions "state banks." [146]

The scheme of state control of the banking business was short lived. The Federalists were soon afforded an opportunity to change the bank plan, for in the 1812–1813 legislature they were for the first time in a number of years the majority party.[147] One of their early measures was a law designed to end any rapprochement between the judiciary and business corporations such as had been created by the appointment of supreme court justices to the presidencies of two of the state banks.[148] The Federalists next passed a law to authorize the governor to sell the subscription rights of the state in each of the six banks

[145] *Trenton Federalist,* February 3, 1812.

[146] *Ibid.,* February 17, March 2 and 16, 1812.

[147] The second war with England which the Federalists opposed, and not bank policy, had been the principal campaign issue.

[148] The law, entitled "An act to insure the faithful and impartial execution of office," declared that supreme court justices' salaries were to cease and their appointments terminate if they held "any office or appointment in any body corporate" in New Jersey. The announced reason for the measure was that "it is essential to the purity of the administration of justice within this state, and to the diligent and able execution of the same, that the justices of the supreme court of this state should not . . . become engaged as officers in corporate bodies and interests, to the great danger of the pervertion [*sic*] or neglect of justice." *N. J. Laws,* 37 sess., 2 sit. (1813, public), p. 3.

for not less than sums specified in the law.[149] In the event that no purchasers came forward within three months, anyone could pay into the state treasury one-half the minimum selling prices and thereby extinguish the rights of the state. Once the subscription rights of the state in a particular bank were sold or extinguished, certain of the terms of that bank's charter were changed. The principal charter alteration was that the president and all directors would be chosen thenceforth by the stockholders.[150] This skirmish ended all serious efforts to establish in New Jersey either state banks or banks in which the state government exercised managerial control.[151]

In 1814, the New Jersey assembly resolved

> That a committee be appointed to enquire if there is any law preventing individuals or associations of individuals without incorporation, from the discounting or issuing of paper money; and if no law exist, what laws should be enacted prohibiting the same.[152]

The committee appointed reported "An act to prohibit unincorporated banks" which was speedily and unanimously passed by both houses of the legislature.[153] The principal section of the law read as follows:

> That no association of citizens unincorporated or not incorporated for the express purpose of banking or establishing a banking-house or office of discount and deposit by the laws of this state or the United States, be permitted to establish directly or indirectly within this state any banking-house or office of discount and deposit, nor to discount any note, bond, bill or other obligation, as a banking insti-

[149] *Ibid.*, p. 19. The minimum selling prices for the rights totaled $30,000.

[150] When the governor refused to act, the legislators made provision for a commission to sell the rights. *Ibid.*, p. 42.

[151] The Federalist press rejoiced that the state's rights had been sold. It was declared that the bank law had afforded "good, snug, fat, easy offices" for Democrats and put their hands *"deep in the vaults besides!"* Wilson, the Democratic sponsor of the banks, was said to be certain that "the *state is undone and ruined forever!" Trenton Federalist,* March 15, April 5, 1813.

[152] *Votes and Proceedings of the General Assembly,* 39 sess., 1 sit. (1814), p. 20.

[153] *Ibid.*, 39 sess., 2 sit. (1815), p. 236; *Journal of the Legislative Council,* 39 sess., 2 sit. (1815), p. 1743.

tution, nor to continue the same after the first day of May next, if any such should have been heretofore established . . .[154]

Thus a little more than a decade after New Jersey's first commercial bank was chartered, the legislature set commercial banking apart as an activity reserved for those groups especially chartered for the purpose.[155] The writer has not been able to ascertain the extent to which banking had developed in New Jersey outside the jurisdiction of the incorporated banks,[156] but whatever the need for legislation to prohibit unincorporated banks, passage of the law greatly enhanced the value of bank charters. The legislature was so quick to take advantage of this fact that it appears as a distinct possibility that the lawmakers passed the law for that very purpose. Two bank charters passed while the legislature was preparing to prohibit unincorporated banks required payment of substantial bonuses to the state as "consideration" for the grants.[157] This was the first time the state had required outright bonuses in return for bank charters, and the policy was continued in connection with a number of bank charters passed during the decade following 1815.[158] The fact that incorporated banks had been set apart to pay a special capital stock tax may also have afforded a reason to prohibit banking by other groups. With no effective organization, the state had considerable trouble in collecting the bank tax even from the relatively few chartered institutions; it would have been futile at the time to have extended the tax

[154] *N. J. Laws,* 39 sess., 2 sit. (1815, public), p. 13.

[155] Similar measures had previously been taken in some other jurisdictions, ostensibly as a means of preventing the rapid increase of banks. In 1799, Massachusetts had forbidden its residents to join any unchartered association formed for banking purposes. *Laws of Massachusetts,* 1799, Ch. 2. New York passed "An act to restrain unincorporated Banking Associations" in 1804. *N. Y. Laws,* 27 sess. (1804), Ch. 117, p. 615. Maryland prohibited unincorporated banks in 1810. J. G. Blandi, *Maryland Business Corporations: 1783–1852,* p. 17. For the background of some of the early restrictions on unincorporated banks see Shaw Livermore, *The Early American Land Companies,* pp. 245–253.

[156] One bank charter approved while the legislature was considering the law to prohibit unincorporated banks stated that the banking association incorporated was already in existence. *N. J. Laws,* 39 sess., 2 sit. (1815, private), p. 21.

[157] *Ibid.,* pp. 21 and 32.

[158] E.g., *N. J. Laws,* 40 sess., 2 sit. (1816, private), p. 48; 42 sess., 2 sit. (1818, private), p. 49; 49 sess., 1 sit. (1824), pp. 35, 99, 105, 118, 140.

to a large number of unincorporated banks that could easily have eluded the levy.

The special value attaching to bank charters was used in yet another way. In order to assure the success of some project deemed advantageous to the state, banking privileges were occasionally awarded to corporations that were to prosecute the desired work. The Salem Steam-Mill and Banking Company was chartered in 1822 with banking powers contingent upon the establishment of a grist mill operating at least four pairs of stones.[159] A similar case of the same year was the Commercial Bank of New-Jersey that was required to employ a stated percentage of its capital in a fishing business at Perth Amboy.[160] The most important case historically was the Morris Canal and Banking Company of 1824.[161] The charter of this company stated that "for the encouragement of so great an undertaking, as the erection of said canal, and in some measure to induce capitalists and others to subscribe for the same, it shall be lawful for the said company, to increase the capital stock of said company, for the purpose of banking operations . . ." To stimulate construction of the canal, the amount of capital that could be devoted to banking operations was determined by the amount spent on the canal, and if a stated amount was not expended each year the company was required to cease banking operations. The same device was used in 1837 to aid the Belvidere Delaware Rail Road Company and the Bergen Port Company to construct their improvements, the banking capital allowed in each case being made contingent on the funds actually spent on the works undertaken.[162] The legislators were cautious, however, in granting banking powers as an aid to the accomplishment of some particular project.[163] In most cases

[159] *N. J. Laws,* 47 sess., 1 sit. (1822, private), p. 48. [160] *Ibid.,* p. 70.

[161] *N. J. Laws,* 49 sess., 1 sit. (1824), p. 158. In addition to ordinary commercial banking power, the canal company was authorized to act as a corporate fiduciary.

[162] *N. J. Laws,* 61 sess., 2 sit. (1837), pp. 91, 387.

[163] For example, the *True American* of November 5, 1825, reported two such applications in the assembly. One was for a company with banking powers to complete an unfinished Delaware River bridge, the other for a textile company that was declared to "crave a bank, as the best buttress of their establishment, and are willing to rest their hopes of success on a paper foundation." Neither of these bills was passed.

where ancillary banking powers were given, it soon became evident that the companies involved were interested principally in banking operations to the detriment of their supposedly primary objectives.[164] The combination banks failed most miserably in the panic of 1837, and the practice of linking banking and other operations was discontinued.

Until widespread feeling against every type of business corporation developed during the late eighteen thirties, banking companies formed the only group of corporations against which there was any effective and continuing hostility in New Jersey. Opposition to banks did not result from hostility to business corporations in general but from a distrust of expanding that particular type of business without the utmost caution. The arguments employed in New Jersey against increasing the number of banks were the same as those heard in all other states and were concerned primarily with the disturbing effect on the economy of expansion and contraction of bank currency and with the difficulty of protecting innocent holders of bank notes from loss. Influenced by such considerations, the legislators frequently refused to charter banks when they were requested to do so.[165] The refusals are significant, for the "sale" of banking privileges was a source of revenue to the state and bank charters were pressed with diligence by promoters attracted to that high-profit field. In contrast to legislative unwillingness to grant new bank charters, the wisdom of rechartering existing and

[164] By charter supplements passed in 1825, both the Commercial Bank of New-Jersey and the Salem Steam-Mill and Banking Company were released from their obligation to carry on the non-banking part of their businesses. *N. J. Laws*, 50 sess., 1 sit. (1825), pp. 6, 16. The banking privileges of the Morris Canal were "to prove fatal to the success of the company" when subsequent managements became exclusively interested in the financial aspects of the business and engaged in irregular and criminal schemes. Lane, pp. 228, 236–240.

[165] A letter from "Caution" printed in the *True American* of April 5, 1819, after the close of a legislative session in which several bank applications were defeated, expressed the prevailing sentiment on the question of chartering additional banks: "Tho' the Legislature have not done all the good in their power, they deserve credit for refraining from some of the evil which they were urged to. In refusing to establish any new banks, they did wisely. We have more now in the state than are of general utility — more than can long withstand the pressure of the times. Incalculable and innumerable evils are already experienced from the multitude of banks . . . Let us proceed no further in the delusive and destructive system; but await the result of the present difficulties."

solvent banks was not seriously questioned. Every bank chartered in New Jersey was limited in duration, but if one survived long enough to require rechartering, it was generally assumed to be well managed and deserving of continued existence.[166]

The policy of New Jersey with respect to insurance companies seems to have been from the beginning one of encouragement. The first New Jersey corporation to be granted insurance powers was the Newark Banking and Insurance Company, and the charter set forth relief from distress caused by fire as the primary object of the corporation.[167] The banking power was allegedly added because of a fear that the insurance business would not yield an adequate return on the capital employed.[168] The next three insurance companies incorporated were mutual companies, at least one of which seems to have had a previous history as an association.[169] The mutual plan seems to have been the more popular for insurance companies during the period under consideration in this chapter, for two-thirds of the insurance charters granted up to 1844 were for mutual companies.[170]

The first New Jersey stock company designed to undertake insurance functions exclusively was The Mechanics' Fire In-

[166] The importance attached to the quality of bank management is revealed in the report of an assembly committee to which the question of the advisability of rechartering five of the so-called state banks was referred. The committee, reporting favorably on extending the banks, stressed the fact that the institutions were in honest hands, a circumstance that "the committee consider an important fact, and is after all, the strongest guarantee the public can have. Much more depends on the character of the persons to whom a charter is granted, than upon the nature of the restrictions embodied in the charter itself. Honest men, need no restrictions, while experience has fully shown, that all the terms that may be imposed upon fraudulent men, furnish no protection to the public." *Votes and Proceedings of the General Assembly,* 53 sess., 2 sit. (1829), p. 158.

[167] *N. J. Laws,* 28 sess., 2 sit. (1804), Ch. 109, p. 268.

[168] Perhaps the insurance business was used as a screen in this instance, for the charter terms were almost exclusively concerned with the banking operations.

[169] *N. J. Laws,* 48 sess., 1 sit. (1823, private), p. 163. The preamble declared the association requested incorporation the better to carry out the "salutary objects of their institution."

[170] This is in contrast to the record of the years 1845 through 1875 when nearly two-thirds of the insurance companies chartered were stock corporations.

surance Company chartered in 1824.[171] The preamble of the charter is interesting because of its statement of the reasons for the establishment of the company. It declared that since residents of New Jersey often placed their fire insurances in New York City, "an Insurance Company in the town of Newark . . . would much tend to the convenience of the inhabitants aforesaid, and would confine at home a source of wealth which is now carried into another state." Three other stock companies chartered subsequently were launched with similar statements of purpose.[172] The first stock insurance company was subjected to a special annual tax on the capital stock as were four other similar companies chartered during the following ten years.[173]

The most interesting feature of the insurance business of these early years is that it occasioned, in 1826, the first New Jersey legislation dealing with out-of-state corporations. American insurance companies appear to have begun about 1816 to solicit business beyond the borders of the states of their incorporation, and there is strong evidence that for some years afterward they were the only group of corporations engaged significantly in interstate business.[174] The preamble of New Jersey's 1826 "Act relative to insurance companies" contained a clear statement of the problem:

> it is represented to the legislature, that associations or companies of individuals, not resident in this state, nor incorporated by its laws, do, nevertheless, by means of agents appointed by them, in this state, effect many insurances within the same, against losses by fire, and otherwise, thereby securing to themselves all the benefits, without being subject to any of the burthens of insurance companies regularly incorporated by law of this state.[175]

The law established regulations for New Jersey agents of companies not incorporated by New Jersey "(although such indi-

[171] *N. J. Laws,* 49 sess., 1 sit. (1824), p. 74.

[172] *N. J. Laws,* 51 sess., 1 sit. (1826), p. 70; 58 sess., 2 sit. (1834), p. 73; 59 sess., 2 sit. (1835), p. 102.

[173] E.g., *Laws of New Jersey,* 55 sess., 2 sit. (1831), p. 33. In each case the tax provisions did not become effective until three years after business had begun.

[174] Cf. Blandi, pp. 26, 89–90.

[175] *N. J. Laws,* 51 sess., 1 sit. (1826), p. 67.

viduals or associations may be incorporated by the laws of any other state or kingdom)." Agents were required to pay semi-annually for the use of the state a tax of 5 per cent of the gross premiums received by them.[176] There is a lack of definite evidence as to the intent of the legislators in enacting this measure. They may have wished to protect their domestic companies from competition, an action that would, incidentally, increase the revenues the state might expect from the capital stock tax levied on some of the domestic companies; or, if New Jersey companies were discriminated against by the laws of the other states, the Jerseymen may have been motivated by pique to institute retaliatory measures. On the other hand, the law may have been intended merely as a revenue measure, although the severity of the tax imposed makes this seem unlikely.[177]

It is impossible to state definitely whether any insurance business was conducted in New Jersey by unincorporated enterprises. Probably all such business was carried on by incorporated groups. The very nature of the insurance business makes a sizable capital and a continuing existence necessary features for companies engaged in it. It was apparently an easy matter to secure a charter for insurance purposes in New Jersey, for there is no evidence in the state documents of opposition to corporations of this type.

In concluding the discussion of the position of the business corporation in New Jersey before 1845, it is desirable to bring together the available evidence as to the public sentiment of the period toward the corporation. As concerns the years of the eighteenth century, the New Jersey literature affords almost no information. There is nothing, however, in the recorded experience of New Jersey that would refute the general conclusions reached by Joseph S. Davis who has attempted to determine the attitude of the public toward business corporations

[176] A bond of $1000 was required of each agent as security for payment of the tax, and penalties for noncompliance with the law were prescribed.

[177] The tax was halved in 1846. *N. J. Laws,* 1846, p. 4. The retaliatory nature of the levy was emphasised by an amendment of 1848 declaring that the tax would be imposed only on agents of companies chartered by states imposing a tax on the agents of New Jersey companies. *Ibid.,* 1848, p. 46.

in eighteenth century America. Davis gathered numerous quotations from contemporary sources, and examination of the assembled material makes it clear that the anti-corporation arguments of "aristocracy," "monopoly," and "special privilege," widely employed later during the period of Jacksonian Democracy, actually had their beginnings before 1800.[178] Although Davis found that the "*talk*" of the opponents of corporations sounded louder than the voices of the defenders, he drew the following conclusion from his investigation:

> Actions, however, proverbially speak louder than words. Despite the prevalence of such talk as has been quoted, the extent and intensity of the distrust and hostility is easily magnified. The unprecedented growth of corporations emphatically attests the weakness of the opposition. Not many charters were sought in vain, and these chiefly because of local objection to the particular project. And it is significant that expressions of fear and criticism were more common before 1792 than after, when more experience with actual corporations had accumulated. It is probably fair to say that the broader opposition rested on traditional antipathy to such corporations as the close corporations of the English boroughs, the restrictive gilds, and the monopolistic companies for foreign trade; and that the American business corporation turned out to be quite a different sort of creature.[179]

[178] Davis, II, 303–309.

One of the most thoroughgoing early statements in opposition to the corporate device was made by the Council of Revision of New York State. That body reported in 1785 against a bill incorporating a body of tradesmen and mechanics of New York City. Included among their objections to the act of incorporation were the following:

"Because all incorporations imply a privilege given to one order of citizens which others do not enjoy, and are so far destructive of that principle of equal liberty which should subsist in every community; and though respect for ancient rights may have induced the framers of the constitution to tolerate those that then existed, nothing but the most evident public utility can justify a farther extension of them . . .

"Because the reasons assigned in the preamble of this bill, may equally operate for the incorporation, not only of the mechanics but of every other order of men in every county, whereby the State, instead of being a community of free citizens pursuing the public interest, may become a community of corporations, influenced by partial views, and perhaps in a little time, (under the direction of artful men) composing an aristocracy destructive to the constitution and independency of the State." New York State, *Messages from the Governors,* II, 229–230.

[179] Davis, II, 309.

Except for some agitation against turnpike companies early in the nineteenth century, against banking companies after 1810, and against privately constructed canals in the eighteen twenties, the present writer has found no serious and widespread opposition to business corporations in New Jersey until the middle of the eighteen thirties. The legislature chartered numerous companies by nearly unanimous votes, and except for banks and projects against which there was considerable local objection there is no indication that even very generous charters were difficult to obtain.[180] The distrust of business corporations that did exist was reflected not in a refusal to incorporate business groups but in the increasing caution with which the charters were drawn up. The early decades of the nineteenth century witnessed the increasingly frequent inclusion in charters of such provisions as those specifying regressive voting arrangements in corporate elections, those limiting the duration of the grants, those reserving to the state the right to alter or repeal charters, and, in some instances, provisions whittling away a part of the limited liability with which corporate stockholders were invested.[181]

[180] One author concludes a survey of New Jersey's corporation policy during the early years with the following statement: "On the whole, the legislature inclined more to liberality than to niggardliness in investing corporations with power. Every possible encouragement was extended to aggregations of capital aiming at the development of state resources or industry, and many charters were granted for these purposes which provided for valuable privileges." H. W. Stoke, "Economic Influences upon the Corporation Laws of New Jersey," *Journal of Political Economy*, XXXVIII (October 1930), p. 553.

[181] The following quotation referring to American experience in general expresses a similar conclusion: "After the turn of the century [1800], corporation primacy was threatened by the growing tendency on the part of legislators to impose disabilities on the corporation, even while they continued to grant those particular legal advantages which set it apart from the association. That there was, in the generation 1795–1825, such a distinct legislative trend has been little realized by modern students of corporate development." Livermore, p. 258; see also pp. 258–271. Massachusetts affords a good example of this trend, especially in the matter of stockholder liability. Cf. E. M. Dodd, Jr., "The First Half Century of Statutory Regulation of Business Corporations in Massachusetts," *Harvard Legal Essays*, pp. 65–120. The exact extent to which disabilities were imposed on business corporations in New Jersey will appear in the analysis of charter provisions in Part II of this study. It is clear that a tendency to circumscribe the power granted to corporations existed in New Jersey for several decades after 1800, but it was not as significant there as Professor Livermore declares it was in many jurisdictions. It cannot be said to have "threatened" the corporation's "primacy" in New Jersey.

It is well known that during the Jacksonian era business corporations became a lively topic of public debate. Jackson vetoed the bill for the rechartering of the second Bank of the United States in 1832, and the bank was one of the leading issues in his successful fight for reëlection in the same year. The bank controversy touched off a sympathetic attack by Democrats on all business corporations. The attack first received attention in the New Jersey press in 1835 and constituted the only major threat to the practice of chartering companies for business purposes in the history of the state. It is interesting that the attack began before the depression years of 1837–1843 and that it arose during a time when the New Jersey legislature was enacting a constantly increasing number of charters for groups engaged in such industries as manufacturing and mining that were in direct competition with unincorporated enterprises. Unpleasant experience with insolvent corporations during the depression years undoubtedly prolonged the attack on corporations and was responsible for an increasing interest in enforcing some degree of individual liability on corporation stockholders.

Early in 1835, the Trenton *Emporium and True American*[182] called the attention of its readers to the anti-corporation sentiments of Democrats in neighboring states. The following quotation from a New York paper was offered as representative of the position of the Democrats of that state:

> All Bank charters, all laws conferring special privileges, with all acts of incorporations [*sic*], for purposes of private gain, are monopolies, inasmuch as they are calculated to enhance the power of wealth, produce inequalities among the people, and to subvert liberty.[183]

The Democrats of Dauphin County, Pennsylvania, were reported to have passed a resolution against acts of incorporation as "unequal, partial and unjust" exercises of government, threatening to destroy "the free constitution under which we

[182] In order to determine the exact nature of the anti-corporation arguments, the files of this paper have been carefully searched. The paper was representative of the influential Democratic press of New Jersey during this period.

[183] *Emporium and True American*, March 28, 1835.

live." [184] The editor of the *Emporium and True American* made clear his own position in the following statement:

> *We* say all incorporated companies are, more or less, Monopolies, and while the Legislature ought not to violate their rights, or stain the sacred faith of a whole people . . . yet the Legislature ought cautiously to refrain from increasing the irresponsible power of any existing corporations, or of chartering new ones . . . upon this great subject, we have all slept too long . . .[185]

The principal Democratic arguments against the creation of business corporations were presented by the *Emporium and True American* during the spring and summer of 1835 in a series of ten articles entitled "Monopolies." The initial article made it clear that the steadily increasing number of business charters enacted after 1820 and the ease with which charters were obtained were causing concern to many persons.[186] It was alleged that over one-half the annual cost of the legislative sessions could be attributed to the passing of charters, charter supplements, and general legislation governing corporation conduct.[187] This fact, the author contended, made the "original cost" of the "monopolies" very high. Nor was their subsequent cost to the people to be overlooked. Singling out for special attention four classes of corporations — banks, turnpikes,

[184] *Ibid.*, June 13, 1835.

[185] *Ibid.*, April 25, 1835. The editor thought that unless his advice was followed future generations of Jerseymen would be left the inheritance of Gibeon, "mere hewers of wood and drawers of water to jobbers, banks, and stock-brokers."

[186] *Ibid.*, May 9, 1835. The charge was made that charters were passed for persons "almost unknown to the body granting them corporate privileges. When any application was made for a charter, the only question asked, in nine cases out of ten, was, can it do any harm? And if none could point out the evil that was to flow from it, the charter became a law."

[187] *Loc. cit.* The regulatory laws were denounced as "so many statutory evidences of the danger of creating these institutions. They are laws to *protect the public* against this privileged order — these favored few." It was true that certain regulatory legislation had been enacted during the preceding two decades as corporations became more numerous. E.g., "An Act for the relief of creditors against corporations," *N. J. Laws,* 41 sess., 2 sit. (1817, public), p. 18; "An Act to prevent fraudulent elections by incorporated companies, and to facilitate proceedings against them," 50 sess., 1 sit. (1825), p. 81; "An Act to prevent frauds by Incorporated Companies," 53 sess., 2 sit. (1829), p. 58.

canals, and railroads — the writer calculated the cost to the people of the state for such corporations to have been about $8,000,000. This figure included losses to Jerseymen from bank stock investments and unredeemed bank currency[188] and tolls paid on turnpikes that were not in repair and that caused only inconvenience.[189] While the writer thought that most chartered companies had cost the people more than they had returned in the form of benefits, he did, however, have qualified praise for the "pecuniary reservations" made by the state in the case of the Camden and Amboy monopoly:

> As the character of Monopolies became better understood, the Legislature began to see the necessity of imposing upon them a share of the burdens of taxation . . . And, no doubt, if the State should now arrest the Monopoly policy, which has been fast carrying us away, while we shall derive from them a revenue, exceeding in proportion to our population, that of any other State in the Union, we shall still possess the vital Republican energy to keep in check the dangerous aristocratic tendencies of these bodies. To recede, we cannot; the constitution, laws and plighted faith, are an insurmountable barrier. To progress, is to rush headlong into a bondage worse than British.[190]

The author of the articles did not devote all of his attention to the measurable losses that business corporations had occasioned the people of New Jersey. He also stressed the more general arguments that had been voiced from time to time in the past and that were to be repeated many times during subsequent years. For example, he denounced business corporations on the grounds of the special privileges granted to them:

> To have the land scattered over with incorporated companies, is to have a class of privileged, if not titled, nobility — a nobility that will ever be reaching forward to higher emoluments, at the hazard of more deeply involving the rights of the public.[191]

Neither did he think corporations could be called "patriotic, benevolent, humane, or generous — and too frequently not

[188] *Emporium and True American,* May 16 and 23, 1835. Care was taken to deduct bank stock taxes collected by the state.

[189] *Ibid.,* June 6, 13 and 20, July 4, 1835.

[190] *Ibid.,* July 4, 1835. [191] *Ibid.,* July 18, 1835.

even *just*. To grasp all, and never voluntarily disgorge, are incident to their very nature." [192] A final political argument was that most corporations were of Federalist origin, sought by an "aristocracy" that wished to convert the government "into a mere money-making machine." [193]

Thus in 1835, political lines were drawn in the matter of the business corporation, and the Democratic governor of New Jersey, Peter D. Vroom, informed the legislature in his October message of that year that he opposed every kind of exclusive right:

> Hence corporations, of any description, should be sparingly created. If they are to compete with private and individual enterprise, they should be discountenanced. Powers and privileges are necessarily conferred by them, which individuals do not possess and cannot exercise. The contest between the two is an unequal contest, and the result is always in favor of the corporation.[194]

The Democratic attack on business corporations continued along essentially the same lines and with scarcely lessened intensity for the succeeding three or four years. The anti-corporation movement in New Jersey was, of course, no isolated phenomenon but part of a country-wide political development. The vociferous Locofoco or Equal Rights wing of the Democratic party was the principal instrument by which the attack was launched and sustained. During 1836 and 1837, the Locofocos broadcast their philosophy of hostility to all banks of issue, to special charters of incorporation, and to irrepealable corporate charters of any description.[195] This extreme position was reflected in the messages of various Democratic state governors during the late eighteen thirties and early forties as they warned their respective legislatures against a further increase

[192] *Loc. cit.* Since corporate managers are mere agents, "with the nobler feelings and sentiments of men, they have, in their capacity as agents, nothing to do."

[193] *Ibid.*, July 25 and August 8, 1835.

[194] *Votes and Proceedings of the General Assembly,* 60 sess., 1 sit. (1835), p. 20.

[195] Cf. F. Byrdsall, *The History of the Loco-Foco or Equal Rights Party . . . , passim.*

in the number of corporations. Manufacturing corporations designed to operate in fields already occupied by individual enterprises came in for their special denunciation, largely on the ground that the owners enjoyed a limitation of liability not granted to individuals or partners.[196] In some states the agitation against manufacturing corporations seems to have influenced legislative policy, as for example in South Carolina where a resident arguing in behalf of persons seeking charters for manufacturing companies in 1845 made the following observation: "Will South-Carolina refuse to grant charters of incorporation for manufacturing and other purposes, or will she not? She has heretofore acted with the utmost liberality in granting unrestricted charters, and not until 1837, did she seem to entertain apprehensions of harming the public weal by such acts." [197]

For several years, the Democratic press in New Jersey continued to publish expressions of opinion similar to those with which they had opened their attack in 1835. Their most harsh language was used against banks and manufacturing corporations, although a few kind words were reserved for corporations chartered to pioneer in new and risky fields of manufacturing.[198] At the same time, the political nature of the division of opinion over corporations became even more evident, and the

[196] For some examples see the 1836 message of Governor William L. Marcy of New York, New York State, *Messages from the Governors,* III, 554; Governor David R. Porter of Pennsylvania in 1840 and 1842, *Hazard's United States Commercial and Statistical Register,* II (January 15, 1840), p. 44, and VI (January 12, 1842), p. 22; Governor Henry Hubbard of New Hampshire in 1842, *ibid.,* VI (June 29, 1842), pp. 406–07.

[197] *An Enquiry into the Propriety of Granting Charters of Incorporation for Manufacturing and Other Purposes, in South Carolina*: By One of the People, p. 3.

[198] For example, the editor of the *Emporium and True American* commented in his issue of March 26, 1836, on the large number of manufacturing companies just chartered by the legislature: "So many of these bills as erected Companies, to go into any locality and business already occupied with individual capital and enterprise, (and some such there are,) we consider it impolitic to have granted. But those which were to occupy new and untried fields — silks, or fire arms, for instance — although in common parlance, private, are not without advantage to the public. Confined within their proper spheres, while they give employment to the industrious — create markets for produce — and foster enterprise by uniting its energies, they become the pioneers to future fields of wealth, which discovery and success will throw open to all."

Democratic papers openly accused the Whigs of being the "corporation party." Analyses of votes in the legislature were presented to prove that support for bank charters came principally from Whig members.[199] It was also alleged that most of the stock of New Jersey banks, referred to as "soulless incorporations," was held by Whigs and that these same people owned the Trenton manufacturing corporations.[200] Certain transportation corporations were accused during the hard-fought campaign of 1840 of carrying Whig candidates, as well as their log cabins and other campaign paraphernalia, free or at reduced rates while refusing to transport the United States mail or American soldiers at fair prices.[201]

Similar sentiments were heard in the legislative chambers. Petitions from agricultural counties were frequently presented asking that the legislature refuse to grant further charters of incorporation for any type of business.[202] Also Democratic members of the assembly spoke on various occasions against incorporated business units.[203]

[199] *Emporium and True American,* April 7 and 14, 1837; *True American* [Tri-weekly campaign series], September 27, 1838.

[200] *Emporium and True American,* July 14, 1837. [201] *Ibid.*, May 1, 1840.

[202] For example: "Your petitioners assert, that incorporated manufacturing companies . . . by a chartered monopoly of rights and privileges, become monopolizers of trade; the inevitable consequences of which are first to paralyze, and eventually to annihilate individual enterprise in the mechanic arts; compel mechanics in comfortable business, who have spent years in acquiring a knowledge of their profession . . . to abandon their vocation, and embark in a business, the elements of which they are entirely ignorant; or become operatives in the mammoth factories, of their incorporated competitors — blast the fair prospects of worthy, amiable and respected families, and finally turn all those streams of wealth, of which manufacturing is the fountain, into one broad channel, which thus is made to empty itself directly into the pockets of a privileged few . . .

"And that any incorporation, by throwing a mantle of protection around a few individuals, of which the great mass of the people are, and of necessity must be deprived, is incompatible with, and militates directly against the fundamental principles upon which the American Government is based . . .

"[Your] petitioners must earnestly entreat your honorable bodies, to refrain from granting any act or acts of incorporation, for any purpose or purposes, under any pretence whatever, during your present term." *Votes and Proceedings of the General Assembly,* 60 sess., 2 sit. (1836), pp. 204–209.

[203] For example: "It cannot be that public sentiment, upon the increase of these incorporated companies, whether in powers or numbers, is not well known . . . And yet this House has gone on adding power to power — company to com-

It is interesting that during the very years when anti-corporation sentiment was at its peak in New Jersey, the advisability of passing a statute authorizing limited partnerships was under discussion in the state.[204] Limited partnership bills were presented in the legislature between 1833 and 1836, and supporting petitions were presented from time to time, but they did not receive favorable response from the strongly Democratic legislatures of those years.[205] Many Democrats, especially those from farming districts, and some Democratic newspapers opposed limited partnerships as being too closely similar to corporations and lacking even the limitation of capital generally imposed on the latter bodies. The Essex County legislator who sponsored one of the bills endeavored to allay the fears of this group by declaring that the purpose of his bill was to end applications for charters of incorporation.[206] In a message of January 1837, the Democratic governor recommended passage of the bill in the belief that the limited partnership would provide most of the advantages of incorporation and at the same time be freely available to all who cared to adopt it.[207] Acting on the governor's recommendation, the legislature proceeded to pass the limited partnership act.[208] Those who expected that the

pany, until the natural rights of the people are well nigh monopolized in the hands of these bodies." *Emporium and True American,* March 2, 1838.

[204] The New York legislature had enacted a limited partnership statute in 1822, but there does not appear to have been any agitation for such a statute in New Jersey until the eighteen thirties.

[205] E.g., *Votes and Proceedings of the General Assembly,* 58 sess., 2 sit. (1834), p. 337; *ibid.,* 59 sess., 2 sit. (1835), pp. 244, 257.

[206] *Emporium and True American,* February 13 and March 19, 1836. The editor of this paper was opposed to the limited partnership as a "speculative" system.

[207] "As to corporations for manufacturing or other purposes, which may be considered of a private nature, as distinguished from those in which the public have a more direct and important interest, I am of opinion, that most, if not all, of the benefits to be derived from such corporations, may be obtained by adopting a general law upon the subject regulating limited partnerships. And I would recommend the adoption of such a system, not only because I consider its results will be beneficial, particularly to the commercial and manufacturing portions of our state, but because such a system being open to all alike, will do away with at least one odious feature of those corporations, and its adoption will tend to prevent incessant legislation upon the subject." *Votes and Proceedings of the General Assembly,* 61 sess., 2 sit. (1837), pp. 128–29.

[208] *N. J. Laws,* 61 sess., 2 sit. (1837), p. 121.

result of the law would be a reduction in pressure from the business community for charters of incorporation were to be disappointed. The special form of partnership organization was to be little used in New Jersey and was by no means considered by entrepreneurs to be a substitute for the corporation with its obvious advantages.[209]

Open opposition to the creation of business corporations lessened considerably in New Jersey after 1838. In the first place, the number of business corporations chartered fell rapidly after that year to a fraction of what it had been during the middle years of the eighteen thirties.[210] The great decline resulted from the business depression of 1837 to 1843 and not from a refusal on the part of the legislators to grant charters when they were requested. In fact, the political climate of the legislature was favorable to the development of business corporations during those years because the Whig party came into control of both houses in the fall of 1837 and retained a dominant position in the legislature for a number of years thereafter.

In the second place, there was an increasing realization on the part of those who demonstrated the most determined opposition to business corporations of the impossibility of stemming the tide of corporate development. In spite of outspoken hostility to business corporations on the part of New Jersey Democrats, the large number of charters granted between 1835 and 1837 were passed by Democratic legislatures. It had become quite evident that when the business community requested acts of incorporation they would be accommodated no matter which political party controlled the legislature. Thus those who expressed concern over the multiplication of business corporations recognized the development as inevitable and turned their energies from efforts to prevent the creation of corporations to the advocacy of schemes to rid the chartering system of what they considered its worst features. The principal proposals to reform

[209] For a detailed study of the New Jersey limited partnership statute and of its history see S. E. Howard, "The Limited Partnership in New Jersey," *Journal of Business,* VII (October 1934), pp. 296–317.

[210] To take the most extreme example, the number of charters dropped from a total of forty-five during the 1836–37 session to one during the session of 1842–43. Cf. *infra,* Table I, p. 206.

the system that were espoused between 1835 and 1844 have been detailed in the preceding chapter.[211]

In conclusion, it can be stated that the voices of the opponents of private business corporations, although they were raised at various times during the period under consideration in this chapter, had little actual influence in obstructing the passage of acts of incorporation in New Jersey. The statistics of incorporation reveal a direct relationship between the number of charters granted in various years and the state of business activity.[212] Regardless of the political composition of the legislatures, many charter applications were made and were favorably received during periods of business prosperity or optimism, and few applications were made during periods of business depression.

But if the opposition failed in preventing the multiplication of business corporations, it had a significance that deserves attention. Those who distrusted and resisted the business corporation played a major role in the controversies that held the center of attention in New Jersey for more than a decade after 1844. Specifically they intensified their demands for general legislation on the subject of business corporations and at the same time advocated that charters granted under general laws contain a variety of provisions designed to place corporations under more strict state control and to afford increased protection to the creditors of corporations. The results of their efforts in these directions will be treated in later chapters.

[211] Cf. *supra*, pp. 16–17 and 25–26. In brief, general regulating statutes were first proposed, and later attention was directed to general incorporation laws.

[212] Cf. *infra*, 205–210. A similar correspondence between the number of charters granted and the business cycle can be noted in the figures of incorporation for Maryland and Pennsylvania, two other states for which analyzed data are available. Cf. Appendix I, p. 445.

CHAPTER III

Constitutional Provisions Regulating the Corporation Policy of the States, 1776–1844; and the New Jersey Constitutional Revision of 1844

WHEN the New Jersey constitutional convention assembled in Trenton in May 1844 to revise the sixty-eight year old constitution of the state, it was acting in response to a demand long expressed by many Jerseymen for a more complete statement of the fundamental law. Agitation for constitutional change had been touched off at the end of the eighteenth century by William Griffith, a prominent New Jersey lawyer, who in 1799 published anonomously an "address" to the legislature and people to demonstrate the need for revision of the organic law.[1] Although Griffith's appeal had no immediate success in stimulating positive action on revision, it is of significance as an early exposition of all the main arguments for constitutional change that were to be continually used until 1844. The early date of the "address" is sufficient explanation of the fact that no attention was given to the lack of constitutional provisions or restraints concerning the granting of charters of incorporation. This subject was one that had not yet become of importance and had received only slight consideration anywhere in the United States. Griffith's treatise contained a discussion of corruption in the legislature, but the argument was confined to the subject of appointments to offices.

In 1827, a convention of citizens assembled in Trenton to discuss the problem of amending the constitution, and this group set forth their arguments in detail in petitioning the legis-

[1] William Griffith, *Eumenes*: *Being a collection of papers, written for the purpose of exhibiting some of the more prominent errors and omissions of the Constitution of New Jersey.*

lature for a constitutional convention.[2] In this case too, no specific reference was made to the problem of incorporation, but there was a general mention of the lack of any provision for internal improvements which the delegates considered important for the future progress of the state.[3] Criticism was made of the lobbies operating in the legislature, the "Intrigues, bargains, and improper arrangements" consummated there and the impediments to the public business, but again these evils were viewed as resulting merely from the wide power over appointments with which the legislature was vested.[4]

As late as 1841, a committee of the legislative council, appointed after a message of that year from the governor recommending one specific change in the constitution, thought the time not appropriate for revising the constitution. But in the event that a revision would be undertaken, they submitted their proposals as to the subjects that should receive close attention.[5] None of the recommendations, however, touched on the subject of corporate charters.

It had become evident to most by this time that some changes must be made in the basic law. For two years the legislature debated the proper procedure to follow, for the 1776 constitution made no provision for its own amendment. In February 1844, the legislature provided for a popular election of delegates to a constitutional convention and for the submission of the constitution they should propose to a popular vote.[6]

Although the need for constitutional provisions respecting corporations had not been set forth in the prominent proposals for revision of New Jersey's ancient charter, it was to be expected that the subject of corporations would arise in a convention assembled in the year 1844. It has been shown in the preceding chapter that all corporate bodies were under suspicion at that time. The United States Bank controversy had not

[2] *Memorial of the Convention of Delegates assembled at Trenton on the 22d of August 1827, on the subject of revising and amending the Constitution of New-Jersey.*

[3] *Ibid.*, p. 6. [4] *Ibid.*, pp. 5–6.

[5] *Report of the Committee of Council, on the Proposed Alteration of the Constitution of the State of New Jersey.*

[6] *N. J. Laws*, 68 sess., 2 sit. (1844), p. 111,

been forgotten, and antibank sentiment was turned against the state banks. The series of severe business depressions starting in 1837 and continuing into 1843 made many citizens distrustful of banks of circulation, of schemes for internal improvements, and of corporations generally since large sums had been lost through investment in the speculative securities of those organizations. The New Jersey legislature had each year chartered a considerable number of private corporations, but not without public criticism of the privileges and immunities that those groups enjoyed. By 1844, a number of other states had legislative enactments concerning restrictions to be imposed in corporate charters, and in some instances sentiment was so strong that the power of legislatures to grant charters had been restricted by constitutional provisions.

The first constitutional convention ever to meet in New Jersey assembled delegates from all parts of the state at a time when a rapidly expanding industrial community faced the opposition of a group who distrusted the corporate form of business organization. The convention was predestined to become the arena where friends and foes of corporations should champion their respective causes.

To understand the nature of the proposals concerning corporations put forth in the 1844 convention and to assess the importance of the constitutional provisions ultimately adopted, it will be helpful to survey the stipulations regarding corporation charters appearing in the constitutions of other states by this date. There were in all twenty-six states in the Union in 1844, and the subject of corporations received attention in the constitutions of exactly half of them.[7] In addition, Florida was awaiting admission under a constitution drawn up in 1838 which belongs properly to the pre-1844 group and has been included in the present discussion.[8]

In two of the states, the constitutional provisions were merely positive statements of the authority of the legislatures to charter corporations. The constitution of Vermont asserted the

[7] Two additional states had had constitutional provisions concerning corporations but had dropped them before this year.

[8] The actual admission of Florida occurred in March 1845.

right of the house of representatives to "grant charters of incorporation." This clause appeared in the constitution adopted in the district of Vermont in 1777 and was continued in the constitutions of 1786 and 1793.[9] Tennessee's organic law of 1834 gave the legislature express power to grant incorporation by special act in spite of a strict prohibition of special legislation on other matters.[10] No such constitutional provisions were necessary in New Jersey in 1844 since no one seriously questioned the right of the legislature to create corporate bodies.

The constitutions of Ohio and Florida imposed a positive duty on the legislatures to grant charters to certain nonprofit groups.[11] Ohio's constitution, ratified in 1802, declared that every group formed within the state for the support of educational institutions, having given themselves a name, were "entitled" to receive from the legislature "letters of incorporation" to enable them to hold real and personal estate.[12] The constitution of the Florida territory, dating from 1838, made it the duty of the legislature to pass a general law under which churches and religious or other societies might become incorporated, and the legislature was forbidden to pass special acts in these cases.[13] Provisions of this type would not be expected to engage the attention of the New Jersey convention, for the state legislature had long expressed a willingness to grant charters freely to nonprofit organizations and had very early passed general laws under which most societies of this type were free to incorporate.

[9] B. P. Poore, *The Federal and State Constitutions* (2d ed., 1878), II, 1861, 1870, 1878. The 1776 constitution of Pennsylvania which had formed the pattern for Vermont's constitution contained a similar clause (*ibid.*, II, 1543), but it was omitted in the 1790 constitution.

[10] *Ibid.*, II, 1687.

[11] The 1778 constitution of South Carolina had also guaranteed certain religious groups the right to be incorporated. Charters of the Church of England groups were to be continued, and any other group professing the "Christian Protestant" religion were for the purpose of worship "entitled to be incorporated and to enjoy equal privileges." The groups had first to qualify by including fifteen or more males at least twenty-one years of age, selecting a name by which to be known at law, and subscribing "in a book" to five articles of Christian faith as set forth in the constitution. *Ibid.*, II, 1626. These provisions were dropped from the constitutions of the state after 1790.

[12] *Ibid.*, II, 1463. [13] *Ibid.*, I, 327.

It is with constitutional restrictions that this discussion is most concerned, for it was over such provisions that heated battles were fought in the New Jersey convention. The earliest restrictive provisions appearing in the state constitutions limited the power of legislatures to charter banks. Five of the six states entering the Union between 1816 and 1821, influenced by a period of suspension of specie payments and bank failures during and after the War of 1812, had incorporated such provisions in their first constitutions. Indiana, entering in 1816, forbade all charters for private banks of issue. The legislature was permitted to establish one state bank with branches, provided at least $30,000 in specie was paid in by individuals.[14] In 1818, Illinois adopted a similar rule except that no private capital was required in the state bank.[15] Mississippi, when joining the Union in 1817, required at least one-fourth of the stock of any bank chartered to be reserved for the state to take at its option, and the state was to be allowed to appoint directors in proportion to the amount of stock for which it actually subscribed.[16] Alabama, in 1819, adopted the most detailed provisions regulating bank charters. The constitution seems to have prohibited new banks except for a state bank with branches. Existing charters could be renewed, but for this purpose, as well as to establish a branch of the state bank, a vote of two-thirds of each house of the legislature was necessary.[17] Other provisions restricted the legislature to the establishment of but one branch bank or renewal of one bank charter at each session, and the charters of the branches or the renewed charters were required to conform to certain provisions. The requirements were that two-fifths of the capital stock be reserved to the state and that the state have power in the direction of the banks in proportion to the stock it took, that business could not begin until one-half of the capital stock was paid in specie

[14] *Ibid.*, I, 509. The two banks chartered by the territorial legislature were allowed to continue.

[15] *Ibid.*, I, 447.

[16] *Ibid.*, II, 1063. These provisions were omitted in the constitution of 1832.

[17] *Ibid.*, I, 43. This appears to be the first state constitution to require more than a majority vote for granting corporate privileges.

and the amount so paid be at least $100,000, and that certain penalties for failure to discharge liabilities when due be provided.[18] The same section declared the state and other bank stockholders to be liable for the business debts "in proportion to their stock holden therein." [19] The provisions of the Missouri constitution of 1821 were more simple. The legislature was permitted to incorporate only one banking company, but this institution might have five branches. Only one branch could be established at a single session of the legislature, and the capital of the whole bank was never to exceed $5,000,000, one-half of which was reserved to the state.[20]

Eighteen years passed before any further provisions applying specifically to banking corporations were put into state constitutions. Influenced by the national experience during the money panic of 1837, the 1838 constitution of the Florida territory and a new constitution of Pennsylvania of the same year contained restrictions on bank charters. Florida required twenty incorporators for each bank, at least a majority of whom were to be residents of the state. Bank charters were to be limited to twenty years and could not be renewed.[21] At least $100,000 of a bank's capital was to be paid in specie, and the total liabilities could at no time exceed twice the capital paid in.[22] Upon forfeit of the charter or dissolution of the corporation, the stockholders were made individually and severally liable for debts in proportion to the stock owned by each.[23] The same article contained other detailed provisions with respect to banks, the most important of which was one prohibiting banks from paying annual dividends of over ten per cent of the capital stock paid in, additional earnings being set aside as a "safety fund." [24] No officer or director of a bank was eligible to be governor, state senator, or representative, and

[18] *Ibid.*, I, 43–44.
[19] *Ibid.*, I, 43. This is the first instance of a constitutional provision for stockholder liability. No other such provision appeared until 1838.
[20] *Ibid.*, II, 1113. [21] *Ibid.*, I, 327.
[22] *Ibid.*, I, 328. This is the first constitutional limit on corporate debt.
[23] *Loc. cit.*
[24] *Loc. cit.* This is the first constitutional restriction on dividend payments.

not until one year after holding such a position in any Florida bank.[25] In adopting a new constitution in 1838, Pennsylvania required that no corporation with banking privileges be incorporated unless a six-month public notice of the intended application had been made in a manner to be prescribed by law. No bank charter was to be granted for more than twenty years, and every such charter was required to reserve to the legislature the power to alter or revoke it whenever in the opinion of that body it was "injurious to the citizens of the commonwealth . . ."[26]

By 1844, six states had imposed constitutional restraints on legislative power to grant charters of incorporation of any type. The earliest of these provisions is to be found in the 1821 constitution of New York and required the assent of two-thirds of the members of both houses of the legislature to create, continue, alter, or renew any corporation charter.[27] The two-thirds rule was adopted by three additional jurisdictions before 1844: Delaware in 1831,[28] Michigan in 1837,[29] and Florida in 1838.[30] State constitutions imposed a few additional limitations on granting charters for any business enterprise. North Carolina by constitutional amendment in 1835 required a thirty-day notice,[31] Florida in 1838 a three-month newspaper notice,[32] Rhode Island in 1842 was more strict in requiring final action on any bill for incorporation to be delayed until another election of members of the general assembly should have taken place and public notice of the pendency of the bill have been given in the meantime.[33] Only three other provisions relating to corporations in general appeared during this period. In 1831, Delaware required that charters should not continue in force for more than twenty years without legislative reënactment

[25] *Ibid.*, I, 324. [26] *Ibid.*, II, 1559. [27] *Ibid.*, II, 1347.

[28] *Ibid.*, I, 292. In this case a simple majority could renew an existing corporation.

[29] *Ibid.*, I, 990. [30] *Ibid.*, I, 327.

[31] *Ibid.*, II, 1416. This regulation applied to all private laws.

[32] *Ibid.*, I, 327.

[33] *Ibid.*, II, 1608. Charters for certain nonprofit groups were exempt from this provision.

unless they be corporations for "public improvement" and that every charter reserve the power of revocation to the legislature.[34] Florida in 1838 required that no corporation be created unless it was composed of ten or more individuals, at least five of whom were Florida residents.[35]

An examination of state constitutions in force before 1844 brings the general attitude of many Americans of the period toward corporations into clear relief. When a people included in their constitution provisions restricting the exercise of legislative power in chartering corporations, they were endeavoring to correct what appeared to most of them to be serious evils about which there was widespread concern. Most such limitations dealt with bank charters, and these were in all cases put into the constitutions after severe financial crises. The provisions concerning banks were designed to limit the number of banks chartered, to bring those chartered more directly under the control of the state governments, to permit the governments through stock ownership to participate in the profits arising from this special privilege, and to protect bill holders and depositors by requiring a minimum capital paid in specie, by imposing a measure of liability on stockholders and by restricting dividend payments. The restrictions on granting other types of charters were less severe. It is interesting to note that in every case the special act was accepted as the procedure for dispensing charters for profit-making organizations. The aim of the constitutional provisions was to regulate the procedure by which special acts of incorporation were granted and to purify the system so that only generally acceptable charters would be approved. To accomplish this purpose, some states required the assent of more than a simple majority of the legislators for charter grants, some put their faith in enforcing publicity when applications for charters were to be made to the legislature, one even required that there be a general election between the time of application for a charter and the final grant of incorporation, and one limited the time for which charters could be

[34] *Ibid.*, I. 292. [35] *Ibid.*, I, 327.

granted without renewal and insisted that the charters reserve to the legislature the right of alteration or repeal.[36]

The year 1844 has a wider significance in the history of American corporation law than derives from the fact that it happened to be the year in which New Jersey adopted a new constitution. It is important to repeat that up to this time constitutional provisions dealing with corporations, except for some concerning nonprofit corporations that were required to be formed under general laws, were designed to correct abuses and weaknesses in the system of granting incorporation by special act without abandoning the system. Beginning in 1845, constitutional provisions respecting corporations were concerned to a large extent with eliminating the private act of incorporation. New Jersey's was the last constitution to be adopted before this new movement got under way.

In assigning to the proceedings and final decisions of the New Jersey convention of 1844 their proper importance in the whole development of the policy of the state toward corporations, it is also essential to regard the convention in correct historical perspective by referring to the feelings with which corporations were regarded at this time in other parts of the United States. The animosity toward corporations during this period is only partially revealed by the above outline of the constitutional provisions adopted in the years before 1844. It has been shown in the preceding chapter that at various times during the earlier part of the nineteenth century there had been sporadic attacks on incorporated business enterprises, particularly those with banking privileges, and that about 1835 attacks on all incorporated businesses began in earnest. One student of the corporation question as it was debated in constitutional conventions between 1835 and 1860 interprets the conflict as a phase of the economic growing pains of the country, describing the era as one when a "rapidly expanding nation, whose very growth brought with it new social and economic problems, was facing a new set of facts armed with legal and political theories

[36] Many states had statute laws dealing with special acts of incorporation, but these did not have the force of constitutional provisions and did not necessarily limit the actions of future legislators.

inherited from the past." [37] Experience with business failures in the years following the panic of 1837 intensified the opposition to incorporated businesses, and the early years of the eighteen forties were a critical time in the development of American business corporations in general and in the application of the principle of limited liability in particular. Owing to the depression of 1837–1843, the number of charters granted by the states had declined sharply in comparison with former years. The question of the moment was whether, when the demand for charters should revive with improved business conditions, the state legislatures should again be allowed to grant corporate privileges without rigid constitutional restraint.

The constitutional convention of New Jersey assembled on May 14, 1844.[38] After two weeks, the Committee on the Legislative Department, composed of four Democrats and three Whigs, reported the following two proposed sections on corporations:

[37] T. G. Gronert, "The Corporation in the State Constitutional Conventions of 1835–1860," *Proceedings of the Fifth Annual Convention of the Southwestern Political and Social Science Association,* 1924, p. 80. This study makes no reference to the New Jersey convention of 1844.

[38] According to I. S. Mulford in his *Civil and Political History of New Jersey,* published in 1848, on an extra-official recommendation of the legislature the districts, with one exception, elected equal members from each of the two political parties to the convention of 1844 (p. 495).

The "radical" Democrats had an effective representative and spokesman in the person of Moses Jacques. Jacques, over seventy years of age at the time of the convention, had retired to a New Jersey farm in 1837 after having been a prime mover in the establishment of the Locofoco or Equal Rights party in New York. He had drawn up the Declaration of Principles of the group in 1836 in which the party's hostility to banks of issue, to "monopolies by legislation," and to irrepealable charters had been enunciated. In an "address," also produced in 1836, he urged that the constitution of New York be amended "to prohibit future legislatures granting acts of incorporation to companies or individuals in any case whatever, as our only safeguard against temptation." The contemporary historian of the Locofoco wing of the Democratic party declared Jacques to be "the patriarchal leader of the Loco-Focos, for they never had in fact any other visible leader among them." Cf. F. Byrdsall, *The History of the Loco-Foco or Equal Rights Party . . . ,* pp. 39–43, 73, 115, 164; A. M. Schlesinger, Jr., *The Age of Jackson,* pp. 191, 199, 219, 261.

The delegates to the New Jersey constitutional convention divided as follows on the basis of occupation: twenty lawyers, fourteen farmers, seven physicians, seven merchants, and ten miscellaneous occupations. *Newark Daily Advertiser,* July 2, 1844.

XX. The assent of two-thirds of the members elected to each house shall be requisite to the passage of every law appropriating public money or property to local or private use, and also to the passage of every law granting prerogative rights or special privileges, or for creating, continuing, or renewing private corporations, other than those for religious, literary, or charitable purposes: and all such laws may be altered, modified, or repealed by the legislature, whenever, in their opinion, the public good may require it.

XXI. All charters for banks or money corporations shall be limited to the term of twenty years, but may be renewed.[39]

These recommendations were clearly influenced by a study of other state constitutions.[40] It has been shown that four states had adopted the two-thirds rule for all charters and one other for bank charters. One state required the reservation of the power to alter or repeal all charters, and another made this requirement in the case of bank charters. It had also been the general practice to make more harsh rules for corporations with banking privileges, and two constitutions had limited these corporations to twenty years, one forbidding any renewal.

Debate on the two suggested sections opened on June 10, and the proposal that the legislature have power to alter or repeal all charters was immediately attacked. It was understood, of course, that if such a provision was not inserted in the constitution, the legislature was powerless to amend or revoke any charter in which the power of amendment or repeal was not expressly reserved.[41] One of the delegates from Essex County, demanding removal of the clause from section XX, argued that the decision as to whether a charter should contain such reservation of power to the legislature should be left in each case to the lawmaking body. He did not wish to tie the hands of the legislature in the event that a charter without such

[39] *Journal of the Proceedings of the Convention to Form a Constitution for the Government of the State of New Jersey,* p. 54. This volume is cited hereafter as *Journal of the Proceedings.*

[40] Debates on the two sections indicate that many delegates had informed themselves about the details of constitutions adopted during the preceding twenty-five years. Some had also attempted to secure information as to the practical working of various provisions.

[41] For about twenty years, New Jersey legislatures had reserved this power in most charters. Cf. *infra,* pp. 380–382.

a clause might appear to be for the public good.[42] Another delegate spoke in support of this position, stating that although he realized it was "*the spirit of the age* — . . . which looks suspiciously at corporations," the two-thirds requirement was "sufficient security against hasty or party legislation . . ." He then employed the argument that appears to have had great weight in the convention. Maintaining that public works would never be undertaken if enterprisers thought that a mere majority of the legislature could confiscate their privileges, he declared: "Let us not in attempting to embody the *spirit of the present age,* prevent subsequent Legislatures, from embodying the spirit of future ages. Besides, Mr. Chairman, will not the effect of this clause, be to drive capital and enterprise from the State? Will capitalists first hazard their money in doubtful or dangerous undertakings, with the further danger of repeal always hanging over their undertakings?" [43] Another agreed that the early bridges would not have been built without guarantees of inviolability, and on the argument that the clause as it stood would "greatly embarrass investments of capital" in the state, the convention agreed that a two-thirds vote should be required to alter or repeal a charter.[44]

At this point, the delegate from Essex County again moved that the whole clause be struck out. He was supported by a colleague who argued that a charter should never be repealed except for being abused and that such cases should be dealt with as before in the courts. The chairman of the committee that had recommended section XX [45] came to the defense of the repeal clause with the following argument: "Something is necessary to guard and control these charters. And if this provision is stricken out, an effort will be made, and sustained, to introduce a provision for *personal liability,* in them." [46] A "radical" Democrat anticipated future debates by declaring that he would make such an effort anyway. The committee

[42] *Newark Daily Advertiser,* June 12, 1844. The Trenton correspondent of this newspaper reported the debates in considerable detail. The official published journal of the convention records merely the motions and votes.

[43] *Loc. cit.* [44] *Loc. cit.*

[45] Peter D. Vroom, a former Democratic governor of New Jersey.

[46] *Newark Daily Advertiser,* June 12, 1844.

chairman said stockholder liability was unnecessary if the repeal clause remained and that stockholders would not be injured by such a clause unless the legislature could not be trusted.

When debate on the clause opened again on the following day, the convention chairman, a former governor, declared in favor of its retention. The clause was not novel in constitutions, and he was certain the legislature would guard the public interest and repeal a charter only when necessary. Against him it was argued that confidence would be destroyed if charters that appeared to be inviolate could be repealed because of a provision of the state constitution. The committee chairman denied that situation would constitute a violation of contract as was implied, for if the repeal clause was fundamental law, all contracts would be made with reference to it. He admitted, however, that the principal object was to guard the public against "monied" corporations, but it appeared to him the clause would be "wholesome" if applied equally to all. He brushed aside the argument that corporations would be rendered unsafe, pointing out that the clause restricted repeal or alteration to cases where the public good required such action and that no legislature would tamper with a charter except in emergency. A similar provision, he declared, had caused no difficulty in Delaware. After a final appeal by the original opponent of the clause that it would limit the power of the legislature to grant sufficiently liberal charters to attract companies with capitals large enough to undertake major works and would put a damper on all enterprise in New Jersey, the repeal clause was defeated by a vote of twenty-four to nineteen.[47]

Later in the session, the question of a repeal clause came up in connection with bank charters. A Democrat who had formerly advocated such a clause applying to all charters stated that he had decided it was unnecessary to keep banks under the control of the legislature at all times if sufficient restrictions were imposed on their creation. In nine cases out of ten he considered a repeal might come too late to be any protection, but he declared that either a two-thirds vote for bank charters

[47] *Loc. cit.*

or the repeal clause would have to stay.[48] One delegate offered the irrelevant argument that a repeal clause was of no use since none had been included in bank charters until the eighteen twenties and that all the banks created in 1824 had failed except one where no power to alter or repeal had been reserved. A compromise amendment requiring a three-fifths vote to charter banks, a limit of twenty years on the charters, and a compulsory clause permitting the legislature by a three-fifths vote to alter or repeal the charters if they thought the public good required was offered to break the deadlock. This proposal was defeated by the close vote of twenty-six to twenty-four.[49] On the following day, several members of the convention declared that the compromise would pass if the repeal clause was removed entirely. This proved true, for when the clause was omitted, the bank section passed by a vote of thirty-seven to seventeen.[50]

Thus for the foes of irrevocable grants of special privileges the bitter fruit of several days of debate was that the New Jersey legislature should continue free to create corporations that might be free from legislative interference during their terms of life. This was contrary to the rule established in the great majority of constitutions ratified in the years immediately after 1844, but it continued to be the situation in New Jersey until the 1844 constitution was first amended in 1875.

Even before the repeal clause had been finally disposed of, proponents of a liberal incorporation policy turned their attention to the two-thirds vote required by section XX to effect or renew any charter. A Whig delegate from Essex County arose to declare that the section covered too much ground because corporations, aside from banks, had created no alarm in the public mind. He would not extend the provision to manufacturing companies and "tie down the Legislature from acting

[48] *Ibid.*, June 26, 1844.

[49] *Journal of the Proceedings*, p. 183. The vote was split on party lines, most Democrats favoring the amendment and most Whigs opposing it. Referring to this part of the debate, the reporter of the *Newark Daily Advertiser* declared on June 26, 1844: "The whole proceedings of the afternoon have been marked by considerable excitement and feeling — and the subject seems involved in great difficulty."

[50] *Newark Daily Advertiser*, June 26, 1844; *Journal of the Proceedings*, p. 186.

with the same liberality as heretofore." [51] Friends of the two-thirds rule came to its defense as a conservative measure that would tend to prevent hasty legislation. They contended that all corporations were productive of "mischief and injury"— people had lost money in them, and the companies influenced elections. The chairman of the convention also favored the rule as a means, already tested by the experience of other states, of ending the facility with which charters of incorporation were obtained. His principal objection to corporations was that they prevented individuals from carrying on business with their own capital, but he conceded that public improvements such as railroads and canals might be exempt from the provision since "they can only be made by corporations . . ." [52]

Acting on the latter suggestion, the convention proposed a new section that specifically exempted "works of public improvement" from the operation of the two-thirds rule. A motion was made to remove the exemption, but, on the plea that to do so would give existing transportation companies an entire monopoly, only nine votes were cast in favor of the motion.[53] An attempt to exempt renewals from the two-thirds rule was also rejected.[54] In an endeavor to resolve the whole dispute, it was moved that charters be granted by simple majorities in the legislature but require favorable action in two successive years.[55] Only four members were in favor of that plan.[56]

At this stage of the proceedings, the principal debates on the advisability of requiring more than a majority vote of the legislature for chartering corporations began. The chief justice

[51] *Newark Daily Advertiser,* June 12, 1844. He was supported by a member from Passaic, another industrial county, with the argument that he had worked for a whole session to get a bare majority to renew a charter. The delegate gave a hint of legislative logrolling by relating that he had first to secure "the aid of a gentleman who wanted a similar favor in another County."

[52] *Loc. cit.* [53] *Journal of the Proceedings,* pp. 158–59.

[54] *Ibid.,* pp. 159–160. It was successfully argued that once a locality profited from a bank or manufacturing company, it would be unwise to force a dissolution with unemployment as the probable consequence. *Newark Daily Advertiser,* June 24, 1844.

[55] Adoption of this proposal would have meant approval by two distinct legislatures, for annual election of the lawmaking body had already been established by the convention.

[56] *Journal of the Proceedings,* pp. 160–61.

of the state, a Whig, was opposed to the principle of allowing a majority to do everything except grant a charter and felt that "the principle owed its origin to a sort of political feeling or phrenzy [*sic*] against corporations" which, while they had not always prospered and had sometimes caused losses to workmen, had been "a great advantage to the community." [57] Another delegate was eloquent in his advocacy of easy incorporation as opposed to the "spirit of radicalism on the subject of corporations," declaring: "They have done more to increase the prosperity of our State than anything else. Let the Legislature grant all that may apply, if the object is to benefit the community; and if the public interest require them, they will be called into existence; if not, they can certainly do us no harm. But why this opposition to corporations? What have they done?" [58] He would not worry about business failures. Even though the stockholders lost, the works remained to benefit the state. In especially vindictive remarks he accused the proponents of a two-thirds rule of trying to prevent all charters by a "radical minority of one-third . . ." Since opponents of corporations declared them "dangerous to our liberties, injurious to our interests, and opposed to the theory of our government," they must feel that a corporation created by a two-thirds vote is just as dangerous. If they had ventured "to show their teeth at these little monsters" he felt they should "come manfully up to the work and strangle them at once . . ." [59]

The arguments in favor of a majority rule that had most direct application to New Jersey's peculiar situation were set forth in an extended address by another Whig delegate. This member, while he maintained that the two-thirds rule in any state violated the elementary principles of free government and in states where it existed was "an excrescence of arbitrary power and neither suited or adapted to the feelings or spirit of a free people," felt it particularly unsuited to New Jersey. His practical argument was that since New Jersey was between two large states and would not enjoy extensive commerce, since agriculture too was limited by a small and only partially pro-

[57] *Newark Daily Advertiser*, June 24, 1844.
[58] *Loc. cit.* [59] *Loc. cit.*

ductive area, the state should develop the local advantages with which it was favored by a commercial policy founded on equal protection and privilege to all. After appealing to a particular concern of Jerseymen — attracting capital to develop industry within the state, — he continued: "The soundness of the proposition is abundantly sustained by reference to the condition of those States where industry and enterprise have been fostered by legislative patronage. In what States of this Union do we find industry and productive labor in all its ramifications more abundantly rewarded than in Massachusetts?" The industrial supremacy of that state could be attributed to liberal legislation, and New Jersey could by similar means experience the same result. Trenton and Paterson would rival Lowell. He summed up his basic argument by declaring a preference for a "liberal yet judicious policy to one that is so stringent and prohibitory as to paralyze and unnerve the right arm of industry." [60]

In opposition to all these charges, the advocates of a two-thirds rule, led by the chairman of the Committee on the Legislative Department, denied they were caught in a political frenzy or departing from established principles. They held incorporation to be a special privilege "in derogation of the common right" not to be granted by a mere majority of the legislature. The weight of their argument was that to allow corporations with little responsibility for debts to be established to do the same kind of business that individuals carried on was an interference with the constitutional provision of equal rights.[61]

Various compromise suggestions were advanced. One was to require a two-thirds vote for bank charters but only a three-

[60] *Ibid.*, July 9, 1844. This speech made passing reference to an argument that had great influence in New Jersey later in the century — the possibility of raising revenue by taxing corporation stock, although here the point was confined to the existing tax on bank stock. Other delegates had called attention to the industrial records of states exercising liberality in granting charters. For example: "There is no more liberty, prosperity, virtue or happiness anywhere than in the New England States, and there is none of this jealousy of incorporations [*sic*] there." *Ibid.*, June 24, 1844.

[61] *Ibid.*, June 24, 1844. One farmer Democrat, however, frankly declared his determined opposition to all corporations.

fifths vote for other charters except those for public improvement companies and nonprofit organizations for which a majority would be sufficient.[62] After further and unsuccessful attempts to reinstate the unqualified two-thirds principle, the convention found agreement in restricting the requirement of a greater than majority vote to bank charters. Even in this case, those who would put difficulties in the path of petitioners for incorporation salvaged very little of that for which they had hoped. Only a three-fifths vote was specified for incorporating banking companies, clearly a compromise between the majority-vote and the two-thirds-vote camps.[63]

While this discussion was proceeding, the advisability of limiting bank charters to twenty years was debated. Section XXI as originally reported by the Committee on the Legislative Department had provided a twenty-year maximum duration for bank charters,[64] and this proposal met no organized opposition.[65] The convention delegates were unwilling, however, to extend the limitation to non-banking corporations and, without taking a formal vote, turned down a proposal to limit the charters of manufacturing companies to twenty years.[66]

In the heat of discussion over corporation policy, the provisions of section XX requiring a two-thirds vote for appropriating public money or property to local or private use or to grant special privileges were forgotten. When the convention's work was unified, practically nothing of section XX remained.

[62] *Journal of the Proceedings*, p. 161.

[63] Analysis of the recorded votes shows that the convention divided on party lines on the question of a lenient or strict corporation policy. The Democrats were in general in favor of making charter grants difficult to obtain; the Whigs favored easy incorporation. Since the two parties enjoyed nearly equal representation in the convention, the votes on this question of basic policy were close.

[64] Cf. *supra*, p. 94.

[65] An attempt to reduce the term to fifteen years was quickly defeated. *Journal of the Proceedings*, p. 182. Moses Jacques wished to prohibit the legislature from chartering any banks. He held that banking was "productive of great evil to all classes, not even excepting those engaged in it," and that if a state could not issue bills of credit it could not charter a corporation for that purpose. *Newark Daily Advertiser*, June 12, 1844.

[66] *Journal of the Proceedings*, p. 164. The suggestion had been put forth by Mr. Jacques.

What was left was combined with section XXI and became the following Article IV, Section 7, Paragraph 8 of the new constitution:

> The assent of three-fifths of the members elected to each house shall be requisite to the passage of every law for granting, continuing, altering, amending, or renewing charters for banks or money corporations, and all such charters shall be limited to a term not exceeding twenty years.[67]

It has already been indicated that the matter of the limited liability of stockholders and officers for corporation debts agitated the minds of many persons during the late eighteen thirties and early forties. Although no committee made formal recommendation to impose a measure of liability and no liability section was incorporated in the constitution, it is not surprising that the question was debated on the floor of the convention. While the convention was sitting as committee of the whole to discuss the powers of the legislature, a Democratic delegate moved to add to the section on bank charters the requirement that "in all cases, the President, Directors and Stockholders shall be personally liable for the debts of such corporation." [68] The Democratic chairman of the Committee on the Legislative Department favored the proposal and wished to see its application extended. He voiced the sentiment of the group favoring stockholder liability for debts by stating: "If there is any danger to be feared in a republican Government, it is the danger of associated wealth, with special privileges, and without personal liability. It is the aristocracy of wealth we have to fear . . ." He considered a provision for unlimited liability to be a necessary protection and did "not see why the provision

[67] Poore, II, 1318. The compromise rule of a three-fifths vote does not appear in any other state constitution during the whole period covered by this study. Whenever corporation charters could be granted by special act, the required vote was either a simple majority or two-thirds.

In connection with procedure for granting special charters of incorporation, it should be mentioned that the 1844 constitution gave a veto power to New Jersey governors for the first time. The veto could be overridden by a simple majority in each house.

[68] *Newark Daily Advertiser,* June 12, 1844. The suggestion was made by Moses Jacques who had previously announced his opposition to all banks.

should not extend to manufacturing establishments . . ." The speaker observed that when people were willing to risk their private capital in business, there appeared "some overgrown capitalists from the East, and they get an act of incorporation. They enjoy privileges which men of moderate means cannot obtain. And why should they enjoy these without being personally responsible?" He regretted that whenever reforms were proposed the argument was advanced that capital would be driven out of the state and denied that this situation had resulted when some degree of liability was imposed on directors. The result, he believed, had been to attract responsible men as directors rather than the reverse.[69]

The opposition employed the usual argument that enforced liability would deter any prudent man from taking shares of stock and that banking capital would be driven from New Jersey.[70] After the chief justice spoke at length to illustrate how such liability would put irresponsible men in control of banks and cause disastrous failures, the proposed amendment was rejected.[71]

Ten days later, an unsuccessful attempt was made to add the following more temperate clause to the section on banks: "the president and directors shall be individually liable for the debts of their respective companies, to the amount of their estates, and the stockholders to double the amount of stock held by them, respectively." [72] The failure of this endeavor brought to an end efforts to impose liability on directors or stockholders of corporations. Little support had been found for the principle — never more than eight votes and those from representatives of distinctly rural communities. Up to this time, however, only two states had imposed stockholder liability by constitutional provision, and in both cases only banking corporations were affected. Immediately after 1844, the movement gained momentum, and many states specified a degree of stockholder liability

[69] *Newark Daily Advertiser,* June 12, 1844. Other Democratic delegates expressed their agreement.

[70] *Loc. cit.* [71] *Ibid.,* June 13, 1844.

[72] *Journal of the Proceedings,* p. 164. Only eight delegates supported the proposed amendment.

in their constitutions. In most cases the provisions applied to banks only but in a few to all business corporations.

There remain to be discussed a few miscellaneous actions of New Jersey's 1844 convention that have a bearing on the policy of the state with respect to business corporations. Article IV, Section 7, Paragraph 9 of the new constitution read:

> Individuals or private corporations shall not be authorized to take private property for public use without just compensation first made to the owners.[73]

Prohibitions against governmental taking of private property for public use without compensation were standard in the bills of rights of state constitutions, and the New Jersey constitution of 1844 included such a prohibition. The paragraph quoted above was inserted as additional security that the legislature would not attempt to charter a turnpike, canal, railroad, or other company with power to make use of private land before actually providing payment for it.

Article IV, Section 6, Paragraph 3 of the 1844 constitution provided that:

> The credit of the State shall not be directly or indirectly loaned in any case.[74]

This prohibition was accepted without debate, for the delegates desired that New Jersey should avoid in the future, as it had in the past, the problems created in other states by overgenerous state financial aid to corporations established to execute internal improvements. Influenced by the events of 1837, Florida had in 1838 forbidden the pledge of public credit "in aid of any corporation whatsoever," [75] and in 1842 Rhode Island had denied the legislature the right to pledge the "faith" of the state without the express consent of the voters.[76] After 1844, numerous other states hastened to include more or less similar clauses in their fundamental law.

[73] Poore, II, 1318. [74] *Ibid.*, II, 1317. [75] *Ibid.*, I, 328.
[76] *Ibid.*, II, 1607.

One of the original proposals of the Committee on the Legislative Department [77] became with no opposition and only slight amendment Article IV, Section 6, Paragraph 4 of the constitution. The paragraph as amended was in part as follows:

> The legislature shall not, in any manner, create any debt or debts . . . which shall . . . at any time exceed one hundred thousand dollars . . . unless the same shall be authorized by a law for some single object or work, to be distinctly specified therein, which law shall provide the ways and means, exclusive of loans, to pay the interest of each debt or liability as it falls due, and also to pay and discharge the principal of such debt or liability within thirty-five years from the time of the contracting thereof . . . and no such law shall take effect until it shall, at a general election, have been submitted to the people, and have received the sanction of a majority of all the votes cast for and against it at such election . . .[78]

The effect of this provision on the future policy of New Jersey with respect to its corporations was to reduce the likelihood that the state would exercise the right reserved in many charters to buy various transportation facilities at the end of specified periods. It was later charged that the officials of the Joint Companies had been instrumental in securing acceptance of this section in order to render nugatory the charter provisions giving the state the right after a certain date to buy the Camden and Amboy Railroad and the Delaware and Raritan Canal.[79] The argument offered in support of this accusation was that the words "single object or work" made an effectual check on any attempt of the state to buy the companies' property that consisted of two separate works. Even if the provision did have this effect, the convention had been warned of it. One delegate expressed to the assembled group his belief that unless the section was amended the state would be powerless to buy the works of the Joint Companies.[80]

[77] *Journal of the Proceedings*, pp. 53–54.

[78] Poore, II, 1317–18. Debts created for the purposes of war, to repel invasion, or to suppress insurrection were expressly excluded.

[79] Cf. W. J. Lane, *From Indian Trail to Iron Horse*, pp. 337–38.

[80] *Newark Daily Advertiser*, June 13, 1844. Dr. Lane appears to be in error in stating that the interest of the Joint Companies in the new constitution was

Whether or not the state was thus prevented from purchasing those valuable properties, the significance of the clause went far beyond such a consideration. The more obvious intent of the delegates was to prevent the creation of a large state debt on any pretext, whether for buying existing private works, for embarking on a program of new state-constructed works, or for other purposes without the express consent of the citizens in each particular case. The probable purpose of the words "some single object or work, to be distinctly specified" was to prevent the legislature from proposing a blanket program of purchasing or building works of internal improvement or from including in the law to be voted upon several proposals in the hope that the popularity of one might secure consent for the others.[81] That the principal object of the section was to prevent the creation of state debt by unrestrained legislative action rather than to prevent state participation in internal improvement schemes becomes still more clear when it is considered that the legislature was free to purchase or build works of this nature if that could be done without creating a debt in excess of the established maximum. Or if a particular scheme necessitated additional borrowing, it could be undertaken if a plan providing "ways and means" to discharge the debt within thirty-five years was approved by the voters.[82]

Constitutional limitations on debt were popular in this period

---

not clear until considerably later and incorrect in his comment: "It is curious that this provision of the constitution was accepted without comment or debate in the convention." Lane, p. 338.

[81] In his annual message of 1845, Governor Wright of New York called attention to a proposed constitutional amendment originated by the legislature of that state early in 1844. The provisions of the amendment were nearly identical with the New Jersey section under discussion here. The governor expressly stated that the provision requiring specification in each law of a single work or object was necessary to enable a freeman at the polls to form and express his decision. He declared this language to be necessary in order that each work should stand on its own strength. New York State, *Messages from the Governors,* IV, 104–05.

[82] The section as originally proposed had specified a period of twenty years for discharging the debt. Various suggestions were made in the convention to change the time to ten years, to twenty-five years and to an indefinite period. The thirty-five year term was accepted as a compromise. *Journal of the Proceedings,* pp. 152–154.

when many states had been brought to the verge of bankruptcy by lavish borrowing programs. The 1842 constitution of Rhode Island forbade creation of a debt of over $50,000 without consent of the people,[83] and an 1843 amendment to Michigan's constitution provided that if a debt was created the law authorizing it should be submitted to the voters at a general election.[84] In its 1845 constitution, Louisiana included a section on state debt very much like New Jersey's.[85] In 1846, Iowa introduced a similar clause in its constitution,[86] and New York did likewise in the same year.[87] These examples were subsequently followed by other states. In view of the general popularity of this type of provision, it seems that New Jersey's stand on government borrowing was more a part of the widespread reaction of the period against extravagant excursions into debt than a veiled plot on the part of the officers of the Joint Companies. That these men and the proprietors of other transportation companies may have rejoiced to see obstacles put in the way of future attempts by the legislature to purchase their properties should be regarded as incidental.[88]

The convention debates on the subject of business corporations have been examined in detail because of their importance in making clear the attitudes of leading citizens from all parts

[83] Poore, II, 1607.

[84] *Ibid.*, I, 993. The amendment required that the law submitted to the voters "embrace no more than one such object, which shall be simply and specifically stated . . ."

[85] *Ibid.*, I, 721. [86] *Ibid.*, I, 545.

[87] *Ibid.*, II, 1362–1363. Louisiana, Iowa, and New York employed the phrase "for some single object or work" in referring to the law to be approved by voters. Iowa and New York set higher maxima to which debts might rise before appealing to the people than the limit set in New Jersey. Iowa required provision for discharging the debt within twenty years; New York within eighteen.

[88] It was concern for the interest of the people of the state in the right to take over certain transportation facilities that prompted one convention delegate to suggest adoption of the following section: "In view of the rights reserved by the state, in several charters of incorporation heretofore granted for internal improvements . . . it shall be the duty of the legislature to take such action as will give to the people of the state timely information of the extent and value of these rights, so as to enable them to act wisely in reference thereto, and to the exclusive grants contained in said charters." *Journal of the Proceedings*, p. 232. The section was rejected, for there was by this date little interest in New Jersey in state operation of transportation facilities that had been anticipated at the time the charters were enacted.

of New Jersey at a time when the business corporation was everywhere on trial. The positive actions of the convention on the problem of corporations are significant principally because they were so limited. This outcome is not surprising for as already indicated the question of New Jersey's corporation policy had played no part in the agitation for a new constitution. When other state constitutional conventions produced definite reform provisions concerning corporation policy, the corporation question held an important place in the reasons for calling the conventions.[89] The 1776 constitution of New Jersey had so many glaring defects that had disturbed the minds of Jerseymen for a half century that the corporation problem was relegated to a secondary position.

Nevertheless the matter of corporation policy had arisen once the convention met and had occupied the attention of the delegates for several days. The final decision of the convention was to leave the legislature almost free from constitutional restraints in granting charters of incorporation. The lawmaking body was to be at liberty to grant charters of incorporation, irrevocable charters if they so desired, in most cases by the vote of a simple majority and in the case of banks by a three-fifths vote.[90] Only a single restriction on the terms of charters had been adopted — bank charters were to be limited to twenty years. With respect to such restrictions, New Jersey's constitutional policy was

[89] For example, in New York in 1846. S. Croswell and R. Sutton, *Debates and Proceedings in the New-York State Convention, for the Revision of the Constitution,* p. 172. Also in Illinois in 1847. Gronert, p. 89.

[90] Perhaps in rejecting the plan of requiring a two-thirds vote for all charters the delegates showed more foresight than many persons thought at the time. Only one other state, Texas, was to adopt this principle in the future, the rule being included in the constitution of that state in 1845. Poore, II, 1778. New York abandoned the two-thirds rule in 1846 in favor of general laws. Experience indicated that the principle had not reduced the number of charters granted. James Kent, *Commentaries on American Law* (7th ed.), II, 297–98. Some felt it merely "led to greater scandals in the legislature, since more money was required to secure the necessary two-thirds vote." J. H. Dougherty, *Constitutional History of the State of New York,* p. 167. It had even been stated in the New Jersey convention that New York had adopted the rule in 1821 against the warnings of the "best" men. *Newark Daily Advertiser,* June 26, 1844. Michigan dropped the two-thirds vote policy to substitute a general law system in 1850. Florida took a similar step in 1868 and Delaware in 1897. The 1868 constitution of Texas omitted all mention of the subject of corporations.

more liberal than that of the majority of states adopting new constitutions or amending old constitutions during the middle years of the nineteenth century.

It is of significance that the group desiring this generous policy argued principally that the future economic prosperity of the state demanded an unfettered legislature — one free to seize future opportunities as they unfolded, encouraging industrial and transportation development by liberal charter terms when such action seemed desirable. In the light of later New Jersey policy, it is interesting that this point was particularized by stressing the disadvantages suffered by the state because of its small area and its geographical position and by insisting that its future importance depended upon the liberality of laws designed to encourage enterprise in the state. It was this type of appeal that vanquished those who would restrict business corporations and carried the day in New Jersey in 1844.

Perhaps the most remarkable feature of the debates was the absence of any open suggestion to solve the corporation problem by requiring that incorporation be granted only under general laws. Although the intensity of the debates was the result of a fundamental conflict between those who favored easy incorporation and those who feared the result of a further growth of corporations, mandatory adoption of general incorporation laws would have offered ground for compromise. General laws might have appealed to the proponents of corporations since all who would conform to the laws could become incorporated. Of course, if this group were interested in leaving the door open so that special privileges could be secured by a relative few, any provision requiring general laws would have been unwelcome. On the other hand, those who opposed the chartering of business corporations might have compromised on general laws as devices for eliminating the exclusiveness of corporate privileges which was the principal objection expressed by them against incorporation by special legislative act. If these latter men, however, were really interested, as was charged in the convention, in destroying all business corporations, they would not have subscribed to general laws.

The principle of incorporation by formal procedure under

general laws was well understood by 1844. New Jersey for years had had such laws on the statute books for incorporating certain nonprofit organizations, and the legislature only a few weeks before the convention had passed a similar law to provide for the incorporation of benevolent societies. New Jersey had also had between 1816 and 1819 a general law for the incorporation of certain types of manufacturing companies. No state, however, had yet based its constitutional policy on the notion that the solution to the problem of granting charters of incorporation lay in prohibiting all special acts, but beginning in 1845 that notion was to be quite generally accepted in state constitutional conventions. Possibly the New Jersey delegates, if they considered the idea at all, shared the opinion expressed in later conventions in some other states that it was impossible to design general laws to provide for all types of business.

Because New Jersey did not adopt a requirement for general incorporation laws in 1844, the unfortunate results of special charter legislation were to continue for a longer time in that state than in a majority of others. The result of this fault in the new constitution was that New Jersey embarked in 1844 on a thirty-one-year period of conflict and struggle over the question of special acts of incorporation as against general laws providing for incorporation by procedure. The dispute was not to be resolved until the constitution was amended in 1875 to forbid special laws.

CHAPTER IV

Incorporation by Special Act and under General Laws in New Jersey, 1845–1875

DURING the years from 1845 to 1875, controversy in New Jersey over legislative policy with respect to the business corporation was somewhat more restricted in scope than it had been in earlier years. No longer was there an active question as to the expediency of chartering private companies to build certain works that the state itself might undertake. The line between state and private enterprise was by this time well established in New Jersey — drawn, as has been shown, practically to exclude the former. Neither was there any effective opposition to corporations as such.[1] In the period of business expansion following the depression of 1837 to 1843, the corporate form of organization came to be recognized as an indispensible engine of business finance. The whole discussion during the thirty-one-year period revolved around the question of whether corporations should be created by special act or by procedure under general incorporation laws and around the accompanying problem of what rights and restrictions to include in the charters granted. It is important to remember that during the whole period the legislators had complete constitutional freedom to incorporate any type of concern by special act or, on the other hand, to provide for incorporation by procedure in any or all cases. The dichotomy of opinion that resulted from this situa-

[1] There is some evidence of ineffectual opposition to incorporated business organizations in certain fields. In 1862, for example, the Editorial Association of New Jersey petitioned the legislature that "the incorporation by the Legislature of Joint Stock Companies for the purpose of publishing newspapers, is contrary to good policy, would destroy the independence of the Press, and place it entirely within the control of a few wealthy individuals, to the detriment of the personal enterprise by which practical printers with limited means, are enabled to establish newspapers in various parts of this State, in fair competition with each other." *Votes and Proceedings of the General Assembly,* 1862, pp. 321–22.

tion makes New Jersey a particularly interesting case study in investigating the origin and checkered history of the movement toward general incorporation laws. The dual system of incorporation that was adopted caused continued warfare between those favoring a system of special acts of incorporation and those advocating general laws. The records of legislative debates and evidences of contemporary public opinion that have been preserved for present-day study are disappointingly sketchy, but enough material remains to put together a fairly complete account of the long controversy.

Analysis of the background and operation of the nineteen general laws for business corporations enacted in New Jersey between 1845 and 1875[2] necessitates dividing the whole period into two parts: first, the years through 1857 and, secondly, those from that date through 1875. Thirteen general laws were passed between 1845 and 1857 and six between 1858 and 1875.[3] Since the two groups of laws had different backgrounds and formed two distinct movements, they can best be discussed separately.[4]

1845–1857

The first legislature under New Jersey's new constitution found itself confronted with numerous applications for special charters when it convened in January of 1845. The Democratic members had by this date abandoned their unsuccessful campaign to defeat all incorporation for ordinary business purposes and had turned their attention instead to a program to end mo-

[2] Not included in this count are the revised statutes of 1875 that were passed after the regular legislative session of that year.

[3] The complete titles, citations, and dates of enactment of all New Jersey general incorporation laws for both business and nonbusiness organizations passed up to 1875 are given in Appendix II, pp. 447–448.

[4] W. C. Kessler in "Incorporation in New England: A Statistical Study, 1800–1875," *Journal of Economic History,* VIII, May 1948, remarked a similar grouping of general laws in the New England states, noting that general laws in all except Connecticut clustered around two periods—"1851–1855, in which the movement was launched by the Massachusetts Manufacturing Act of the former year, and the decade after the Civil War." (p. 44). Speaking of the general-law charters recorded in New England from 1863 to 1875, Professor Kessler says: "These charters constituted the second wave of the movement toward general incorporation, the first having occurred in the 1850's . . ." (p. 59).

nopolies of "privilege" by the enactment either of general regulating laws or of general incorporation laws. Thus, early in the session, Jonathan Pickel, a Hunterdon County Democrat,[5] announced his intention of introducing in the assembly a bill entitled "An act to authorize associations for manufacturing and other purposes." [6] The scanty account of the bill's history does not make clear whether the "associations" to be formed would be corporations, but the bill did contain a clause of the type favored by Mr. Pickel making "share-holders" unlimitedly liable for business debts in case the joint property of the association was insufficient to discharge them.[7] The assembly promptly rejected the liability clause and committed the bill to the committee on corporations,[8] which group later reported that "in consequence of the near approach of the close of the session, they deem it not advisable to report a bill on that subject," thus effectively killing the proposal.[9]

While Mr. Pickel's bill was still under consideration, the special charter of the New Jersey Manufacturing Company

[5] The name of Jonathan Pickel will appear frequently in this chapter, as well as in the later discussion of stockholder liability, not because Pickel was the only member of the assembly during the eighteen forties and fifties who was anxious to bring reform into the existing incorporation procedure but because he was the most persistent and articulate single member of the reform group. Of all the members of the New Jersey legislature during the eighty-five years covered by this study, Pickel alone emerges from the terse and formal official accounts of legislative sessions as a definite personality and an individual marked by unusual singleness of purpose. This man, a farmer by occupation, bore the brunt of the ridicule heaped on the reformers in the assembly by the public press. During the weeks he was in the constitutional convention and during the years he fought in the assembly for individual liability for corporate stockholders, limitation of corporate debts, and a system of general incorporation laws, the Trenton correspondents of the Whig *Newark Daily Advertiser* headed their reports dealing with Pickel's activities with such titles as "Pickelania" and "Pickel scriptum." The papers opposed to Pickel, rather than argue the merits of the questions raised by him, preferred to descend to ridiculing the misspellings in the bills and amendments suggested by him and his apparently untutored mode of pronunciation.

[6] *Votes and Proceedings of the General Assembly,* 1845, pp. 211, 414.

[7] *Ibid.,* p. 548.

[8] *Ibid.,* pp. 548–49. The bill had originally been reported by the committee on the judiciary. *Ibid.,* pp. 418, 437.

[9] *Ibid.,* p. 637. Pickel made an attempt to have the committee report rejected, but he failed and the committee was discharged from further consideration of the bill. *Ibid.,* pp. 746–47.

came up for discussion. Pickel expressed the views of members of his party by opposing the charter as being against the "natural rights" of citizens, an exercise of "exclusive privilege," and "legislation for the few at the expense of the many," but the bill was approved by a large majority.[10] Unable to secure the total defeat of special manufacturing company charters in anticipation of the suggested general law, Pickel tried to amend the charter of the Morris and Hanover Manufacturing Company under consideration a few days later by imposing "personal responsibility" on the stockholders,[11] but the charter was passed without the liability clause.[12]

The 1846 legislature was likewise besieged with applications for charters, and at the opening of the session the governor, a member of the Whig party, warned the legislators of the danger of neglecting public business in order to act on private bills. The governor did not, however, suggest general laws to expedite incorporation procedure but merely exhorted the members to dispose of public business early in the session.[13] Private acts nevertheless received early attention, but at the same time a series of proposals for reforming incorporation procedure was introduced. The proposals were of two kinds — some for general regulating laws and some for general incorporation laws. An Essex County assemblyman introduced a general regulating act for manufacturing corporations based on the statute then in force in Massachusetts.[14] The arguments advanced in support of the bill were the same as those used previously when similar bills had been suggested: namely, reduction of legisla-

[10] *Newark Daily Advertiser,* March 6, 1845. Pursuing its campaign of ridicule, this paper reported words from Pickel's remarks mispronounced as *"nateral"* and *"ligislation."*

[11] *Ibid.,* March 12, 1845. The paper claimed nearly every word of the amendment was misspelled and reported a motion in the assembly to have 500 copies printed and distributed to the "Common schools." *Ibid.,* March 15 and April 3, 1845.

[12] *N. J. Laws,* 1845, p. 211.

[13] *Votes and Proceedings of the General Assembly,* 1846, p. 15. The governor's advice went unheeded, and after forty days had passed a resolution was offered in the assembly that no more private bills be considered until a certain date since the session had been devoted almost exclusively to such legislation. The resolution was not adopted. *Ibid.,* p. 506.

[14] *Ibid.,* pp. 142–43, 155.

tive expenditures, simplification of judicial processes, and advantage to the public of properly regulated corporations in contrast to the evils resulting from a "loose and ill-devised mass of legislation, and the loose management flowing therefrom.[15] It is clear that there was still some apprehensiveness of incorporation by procedure, for a correspondent of a Whig newspaper stressed the fact that if this bill were passed the creation of corporations would continue under the control of the legislature. He declared that the "creation of companies by their own act, by filing certificates or in any other way, may answer; but I can forsee difficulty, if there be looseness in arranging preliminaries by *blank-filling* scriveners." [16] The bill was never acted upon by the assembly, partly perhaps because of the stringent liability imposed on stockholders and directors before the whole capital should be paid in and because the committee on corporations had under consideration at this time another general regulating act entitled "An act concerning corporations" that applied to all corporations and contained no unpopular liability clause. Only the latter bill was reported by the committee.

The "act concerning corporations" had been introduced in the assembly with the explanation that it did not interfere with any bill then under consideration since it "merely by a general law, invested every corporation, with certain powers which the legislature was in the habit of giving to all of them and about which there was no difference of opinion. The object of this bill was to save the necessity of granting these powers expressly in every special act." [17] The sponsor later assured the legislature that the bill did not interfere with existing corporations and was merely to save time in writing future charters.[18] The measure passed the house with no opposing votes,[19] within two days passed the senate without opposition,[20] and was approved by the governor on February 14, 1846.[21]

The first section of this act enumerated the powers that every

[15] *State Gazette,* January 30, 1846. [16] *Loc. cit.*
[17] *Ibid.,* February 2, 1846.
[18] *Newark Daily Advertiser,* February 12, 1846.
[19] *Votes and Proceedings of the General Assembly,* 1846, pp. 354–55.
[20] *Journal of the Senate,* 1846, p. 330.
[21] *N. J. Laws,* 1846, p. 16.

corporation, "as such," should enjoy. They were perpetual succession unless limited in the charter to a specified number of years or in the case of banks to the time limited by the state constitution; the right to sue and be sued, complain and defend in any court of law or equity; the right to use a common seal and alter it at pleasure; the right to hold, purchase, and convey real and personal estate required by the business but not exceeding the amount limited in the charter; the right to appoint subordinate officers and agents; and finally the right to make bylaws not inconsistent with the constitution or laws of the United States or of the state of New Jersey. The second section declared the powers of the first section to vest in each corporation thereafter created even though they might not be specified in the charter or in the act under which it should be incorporated. The act further forbade corporations to engage in any kind of banking activity unless expressly chartered for that purpose or to exercise any corporate powers except those necessary to the exercise of the powers expressly granted. Stockholders who had not paid up their shares were made liable in case the capital proved insufficient to satisfy creditors' claims, but only to a sum necessary to "complete the amount of such share" or such proportion of that sum necessary to satisfy the debts of the company. A section regulating dividend payments was included, permitting dividends only from "surplus profits" and forbidding divisions of the capital among the shareholders without consent of the legislature under penalty of making assenting directors liable for the amounts divided. Another section provided: "That the charter of every corporation which shall hereafter be granted by the legislature, shall be subject to alteration, suspension, and repeal, in the discretion of the legislature." [22]

Although the "act concerning corporations" had been advo-

[22] It is interesting to compare this law with the *Revised Statutes of New York* (1827), Chapter 18, Title 3. The close similarity of language and arrangement suggests that the New York statute, or a similar one of another state, was used as a model by the author of the New Jersey law. The New York law contained rules not in the New Jersey statute dealing with dissolution and one especially important provision declaring any charter void if the corporation did not organize and commence business within one year from the date of incorporation.

cated as a time-saving device, it did not fulfill the claim made for it. Many special charters enacted after the new law was in force did not, it is true, enumerate the ordinary corporate powers but merely made reference to this general regulating act.[23] Yet the charters were thereby shortened only to an imperceptible degree, for enumeration of ordinary corporate rights had previously been accomplished in two or three lines. Since such rights pertained to all corporations by virtue of the common law as it had been developed by the courts, many charters had not even included the list of corporate powers. In short, New Jersey had not enacted a truly effective general regulating act. The only really significant feature of the act was the section declaring all future charters subject to alteration or repeal, and that section seems to have passed without comment.

The real significance of the year 1846 in the history of incorporation for business purposes in New Jersey derives from the fact that in that year the first of a series of general incorporation laws for business concerns was enacted. It is to the background of that law that principal attention will be directed. George F. Fort, a Democrat from Monmouth County, introduced into the senate in January 1846 a bill entitled "An act to authorize associations for manufacturing purposes." [24] Mr. Fort had been a member of the assembly in 1845, and it is important to note that he had been a member of the Pickel reform group and had invariably given his vote in support of Pickel's efforts. The bill offered by Fort in 1846 was given to the senate committee on corporations, and that group reported what seems to have been a somewhat similar substitute bill entitled "An act to authorize the establishment and prescribe the duties of manufacturing companies." [25] The bill took only four days to pass through the senate and was given a unanimous vote.[26]

[23] E.g., *N. J. Laws,* 1846, pp. 83, 100, 151.

[24] *Journal of the Senate,* 1846, pp. 170, 220. It will be noted that the title of this bill was nearly the same as that of the one introduced in the assembly by Pickel in 1845.

[25] *Ibid.,* p. 236. On motion of Fort, both original and substitute bills were ordered printed (*ibid.,* p. 237), but the substitute was agreed to by the senate without opposition from Fort (*ibid.,* pp. 301–02).

[26] *Ibid.,* p. 338. No significant debate is recorded, but Fort attempted to increase the liability of directors consenting to illegal dividends. *Ibid.,* pp. 309–10.

The senate bill, coming to the assembly, was referred to the committee on corporations and reported to the assembly for debate.[27] The principal opposition to the bill came from those members who declared a section making stockholders unlimitedly liable for debts until the capital stock was paid up to be too severe. Attempts to strike out the section and to make directors rather than stockholders liable were defeated.[28] Another section requiring annual publication of figures on capital stock paid in and existing debts, with unlimited liability of stockholders the penalty for neglect, came in for special denunciation. Some members wished to strike out the provision on the ground that manufacturing companies would be driven out of the state, that no prudent man would invest under such conditions, and that it made stockholders suffer for indiscretions of directors.[29] Others thought it a "wholesome section." [30] Several nearly successful attempts were made to postpone consideration of the whole bill,[31] but passage was finally achieved by a vote of thirty-one to twenty-three.[32] The senate concurred in minor assembly amendments,[33] and the bill became law on February 25, 1846.[34]

The New Jersey manufacturing law of 1846 takes a place as one of the earliest general incorporation acts of wide coverage in the United States. Its predecessors were the New York act of 1811,[35] the New Jersey law of 1816, a Connecticut law of

[27] *Votes and Proceedings of the General Assembly,* 1846, pp. 383–84, 395. By the time this bill was presented to the assembly, that body had already approved a bill entitled "An act authorizing joint stock companies." *Ibid.,* pp. 316–17. Unfortunately there is nothing in the record to indicate whether this was a general incorporation law of broad coverage or a law dealing with unincorporated joint stock companies, but it did not come up for consideration in the senate until after the general incorporation law for manufacturing companies had been finally approved, and on motion of Senator Fort consideration of it was postponed. *Journal of the Senate,* 1846, p. 450.

[28] *State Gazette,* February 18, 1846.

[29] *Votes and Proceedings of the General Assembly,* 1846, p. 395; *Newark Daily Advertiser,* February 18, 1846; *State Gazette,* February 18, 1846.

[30] *Newark Daily Advertiser,* February 18, 1846.

[31] *Votes and Proceedings of the General Assembly,* 1846, pp. 399 and 429–431.

[32] *Ibid.,* pp. 431–32.

[33] *Journal of the Senate,* 1846, p. 430.

[34] *N. J. Laws,* 1846, p. 64.

[35] To the list of the kinds of manufacturing companies permitted to organize under the New York law given above in the text and footnote on page 23,

1837,[36] and one enacted in 1837 in Michigan which while authorizing the formation of several types of manufacturing corporations withheld from the stockholders the privilege of limited liability.[37] Other early general incorporation laws were very restricted in scope, having been designed to encourage the development of some particular type of enterprise.[38]

Realization that the terms of the 1846 general incorporation law were too strict led the New Jersey assembly in 1849 to instruct its committee on corporations to "perfect" the law, and that group reported a new and somewhat less severe measure.[39] The *Newark Daily Advertiser* announced the bill as being "more broad" than the existing law and declared that its sponsors hoped it would "reach every application for private incorporations." [40] As debate on the bill proceeded, it became evident that the Democratic reformers, while not wishing to relax the liability provisions of the general law, were anxious to extend its coverage. "In this the people-guarding Mr. Pickel again figured conspicuously, seeking to extend its provisions to every imaginable case." [41] He was defeated in an attempt to extend

the New York legislature had added companies for making pins, beer, ale, and porter, and for smelting lead (*N. Y. Laws,* 39 sess. [1816], Ch. 58, p. 58), companies for manufacturing leather in certain counties (*ibid.,* 40 sess. [1817], Ch. 223, p. 265), and companies to make coarse salt (*ibid.,* 44 sess. [1821], Ch. 231, p. 234).

[36] *Public Statute Laws of the State of Connecticut,* May Session, 1837, Ch. 63, p. 49. This law was the most general in its application of all. It provided for the incorporation of companies for "manufacturing or mechanical or mining or quarrying or any other lawful business."

[37] *Acts of the Legislature of the State of Michigan,* 1837, No. 121, p. 284. The law permitted the formation of corporations for manufacturing woolen, cotton, or linen goods, paper, beet sugar, glass, leather, and iron, or for sawing lumber or flouring grain.

[38] For example: the 1799 Massachusetts law for aqueduct companies and the 1814 New York law for privateering ventures (cf. *supra,* pp. 22n, 25n); a Pennsylvania law of 1832 "to promote the culture of silk" (*Laws of the General Assembly of the State of Pennsylvania,* 1831–1832, No. 180, p. 470) which was amended in 1836 (*ibid.,* 1835–1836, No. 67, p. 211) and replaced in 1840 by a somewhat broader law "to promote the culture and manufacture of Silk . . ." (*ibid.,* 1840, No. 252, p. 672); and another Pennsylvania law of 1836 "to encourage the manufacture of Iron with Coke or Mineral Coal . . ." (*ibid.,* 1835–1836, No. 194, p. 799).

[39] *Votes and Proceedings of the General Assembly,* 1849, p. 562.

[40] *Newark Daily Advertiser,* February 7, 1849.

[41] *Ibid.,* February 21, 1849.

the law to mercantile establishments, but he succeeded in reducing the minimum capital necessary for companies organizing under the law.[42] The new manufacturing act passed the assembly by a vote of thirty-seven to twelve.[43] After some attempts to postpone it for a year in the senate, it was amended and repassed by the assembly with only one dissenting vote.[44]

Jonathan Pickel seems to have been the chief instigator of a general law for banks, the only other law of real importance of the thirteen general acts comprising the first group. In 1848, he opposed the charter of the Newark City Bank and gave notice of his intention to introduce a general banking law on the ground that special bank charters gave monopoly power to certain individuals and that he wished less favoritism in banking and better security for bank notes.[45] Pickel introduced his bank law in 1849 and was appointed a member of the special committee to which it was referred.[46] When he reported a bill to the assembly on behalf of a minority of the committee, he was ruled out of order until after the majority had reported,[47] and further consideration of a general banking law was postponed until the following year upon the adverse report of the majority of the special committee.[48] Passage of the bank act was finally

[42] *Loc. cit.*

[43] *Votes and Proceedings of the General Assembly,* 1849, p. 868.

[44] *Journal of the Senate,* 1849, pp. 834, 911–12; *Votes and Proceedings of the General Assembly,* 1849, pp. 1083–84, 1092–93. Pickel was the only dissenter on the final assembly vote. He may have been displeased either because the coverage of the act was not sufficiently broad or because the liability provisions had been slightly relaxed.

[45] *Newark Daily Advertiser,* February 17 and 24, 1848. Pickel revealed the influence of New York's experience on his thinking when he stated that he had sent for a copy of a bill then in the New York legislature revising the general bank law of that state. Free banking had been similarly sponsored in other states by Democrats who sought to destroy "monopoly" in banking and open the field to all. As expressed by Bray Hammond in "Free Banks and Corporations: The New York Free Banking Act of 1838," *Journal of Political Economy,* XLIV (April 1936), p. 184, "Free banking is a direct heritage from Jacksonian democracy."

[46] *Votes and Proceedings of the General Assembly,* 1849, pp. 565–66.

[47] *Ibid.,* pp. 612–13.

[48] *Ibid.,* p. 957. The majority objected to the great increase of banks in New York State, declaring that the "rapid increase of banking capital is at all times to be deprecated as an evil." They opposed putting banking within reach of every "sharper" and favored special bank charters containing provision for

achieved in 1850 after senate amendments making banks organized under it corporations rather than "associations" and subject to the provisions of the "act concerning corporations." [49]

The foregoing discussion of the debates over general incorporation laws has been confined to the most important of the laws. It will be useful to outline at this point the extent of the general legislation enacted in New Jersey during this early general incorporation law movement. The 1846 manufacturing law was followed in 1847 by a law providing for the incorporation of mutual savings institutions.[50] In the following year, the operation of the manufacturing law of 1846 was extended to mining companies.[51] The legislature of 1849 was responsible for passing an act for the formation of mutual loan and building associations[52] and the new manufacturing law to supersede that of 1846. Not only corporations for manufacturing and mining could organize under the 1849 manufacturing act but also those formed for "mechanical, agricultural, or chemical business, within this state, and also for purposes of inland navigation . . ." [53] In 1850, the general banking act was passed,[54] and corporations under the 1846 manufacturing law were given the option of coming under the 1849 law.[55] Three general laws were approved in 1852 providing for the incorporation of homestead and building companies,[56] plank road companies,[57] and

note redemption. A few objections to details of the bill also were made, the most important of these being directed against real estate bonds and mortgages as security for currency on the ground of their illiquid nature. For the majority report see *ibid.*, pp. 640–643.

[49] *Newark Daily Advertiser,* February 8, 20, 22, and 23, 1850. Hunt's *Merchants' Magazine and Commercial Review,* XXII (April 1850), pp. 422–23, declared, without giving reasons, that this was the "most remarkable" of the various state bank laws.

[50] *N. J. Laws,* 1847, p. 172.

[51] *N. J. Laws,* 1848, p. 9.

[52] *N. J. Laws,* 1849, p. 227.

[53] *Ibid.*, p. 300.

[54] *N. J. Laws,* 1850, p. 140. It should be stressed that the banks formed under this law were definitely declared to be bodies "corporate and politic" in contrast to the terms of the New York banking act of 1838 which was not explicit as to the exact nature of the banking associations formed under its authority.

[55] *Ibid.*, p. 280.

[56] *N. J. Laws,* 1852, Ch. 41, p. 83.

[57] *Ibid.*, Ch. 51, p. 95. Companies under this law were required to secure consent and apparently voluntary appropriation of land from three-fourths in interest of the landholders through whose property the roads were to run. If a

marine, fire, health, and life insurance companies.[58] During the same year, the manufacturing act was extended to include persons associated for the "transportation of goods, merchandise, or passengers, upon land or water, to build wharves and docks, and to reclaim and improve submerged lands." [59] An act providing for the incorporation of telegraph companies passed the 1853 legislature,[60] and the same body extended the operation of the manufacturing law to persons associating "to erect buildings and provide steam or other power, for the purpose of letting or renting such buildings and power to other persons, to carry on any kind of manufacturing business authorized by said act." [61] Incorporation of companies to navigate lakes, oceans, and inland waters was provided by a law of 1854.[62] An act to incorporate vessel building associations was enacted the following year[63] as well as a law to incorporate associations for the purchase and development of agricultural land by persons of "limited means." [64] In 1857, a general law, limited in its operation to three counties, provided for the incorporation of groups desiring to construct factory buildings to sell or rent.[65] With this act the first movement toward a system of general incorporation acts ended.

Mention should be made of the significant absence of a general railroad law from the group of general laws passed during this period. There was a proposed general railroad law in the assembly in 1849, but consideration of it was postponed.[66] In 1850, a general railroad law was introduced and passed in the assembly.[67] A similar situation followed in 1851,[68] and a final

---

road was to occupy a public highway, the highway first had to be vacated by the established legal procedure. When the bill was under discussion in the legislature, the *Newark Daily Advertiser* of February 5, 1852, referred to its "nullifying restrictions."

[58] *N. J. Laws*, 1852, Ch. 74, p. 159. [59] *Ibid.*, Ch. 44, p. 87.

[60] *N. J. Laws*, 1853, Ch. 122, p. 304. [61] *Ibid.*, Ch. 184, p. 427.

[62] *N. J. Laws*, 1854, Ch. 201, p. 470. [63] *N. J. Laws*, 1855, Ch. 245, p. 706.

[64] *Ibid.*, Ch. 256, p. 754. [65] *N. J. Laws*, 1857, Ch. 130, p. 373.

[66] *Newark Daily Advertiser*, February 17, 1849; *Sentinel of Freedom*, February 20, 1849; *Votes and Proceedings of the General Assembly*, 1849, p. 1002.

[67] *Votes and Proceedings of the General Assembly*, 1850, pp. 88, 459–461, 463, 503, 516–17.

[68] *Ibid.*, 1851, pp. 393, 777, 793–94, 798–99, 951–52.

attempt to find agreement between the assembly and senate failed in 1852.[69]

The favorite argument of most legislators against throwing the railroad industry open to all who cared to compete was the alleged impropriety of releasing to private companies and to the courts the decision to take land for railroads instead of leaving that decision to be made by the legislature in each individual case.[70] During the 1852 debate on a general railroad bill, the senate attempted to resolve this difficulty by amending the bill to require legislative consent before a corporation formed under the general law could take land for a right of way. The result would have been a modified form of general incorporation law leaving with the legislature the decision as to whether a proposed road was necessary and desirable enough to warrant taking a right of way.[71]

The underlying reason for the lack of agreement on the terms of a general railroad law was probably the opposition of the Joint Companies. During this period the Joint Companies were in virtual control of the Democratic machine, and they were opposed to all efforts to enact a general railroad law for fear of losing their monopoly position. The numerous petitions presented to the legislature in behalf of a railroad law came from "anti-monopoly" groups organized in opposition to the Joint

[69] "This is probably the end of the general R.R. law paroxysms. Two Legislatures have rejected it, and most allow that it is impossible to make it practicable. There has been a great deal of time and breath wasted this session in hypocritical homage to general laws, while all the *votes* have been given for special charters . . ." *Newark Daily Advertiser,* March 24, 1852.

[70] *Ibid.,* February 2, 1850. In the same issue of the *Advertiser* it was made clear that the fear of losing the revenue contributed by the transportation monopoly was an important element in the unwillingness of the New Jersey lawmakers to adopt a general railroad law: "Another doubt arose upon the question of transit duties — whether a road might not be constructed under it which would produce a forfeit on the part of the State of the transit duties we now receive from the Camden & Amboy Co."

[71] *Ibid.,* March 19, 1852. The assembly disagreed with the senate proposal and returned the bill. *Ibid.,* March 26, 1852.

The notion of requiring railroad corporations forming under a general law to obtain permission of the legislature to condemn land was not new. The plan had been followed in the first general railroad law of New York in 1848. *N. Y. Laws,* 1848, Ch. 140, p. 221. That state, however, had abandoned the principle in the 1850 general law for railroads. *Ibid.,* 1850, Ch. 140, p. 211.

Companies,[72] and while a Democratic governor spoke in 1851 in favor of such a law, he hedged his statement with the qualification that the law contain "such restrictions and limitations as will properly protect private property and the [financial?] interests of the state." [73] In a leading editorial surveying the legislation of 1851, the *Newark Daily Advertiser* blamed the failure of a general railroad bill on the Democratic "reformers." The editor declared that the Democratic legislators had spoken "most vehemently" in favor of such a law during the fall elections but had failed to do that for which they were expressly sent to Trenton.[74] The political influence of the Joint Companies was instrumental in forestalling passage of a general railroad law until the eighteen seventies.

A significant fact about the first movement for the enactment of general incorporation laws in New Jersey was that it found its principal support in the Democratic party. This was the party that for a decade before 1844 had made a political issue of corporations as "monopolies" — objecting to these institutions on the ground that all groups of citizens were not able to enjoy equal privileges under a system of incorporation by special act. The objections voiced had aimed at two forms of inequality: the disparity in privileges granted by special charters and the advantage that any corporation enjoyed relative to unincorporated concerns, particularly in the matter of liability for business debts. The leading Democratic arguments in support of general laws followed these lines although occasional references were made to the heavy burden of special laws on the legislature. The Democrats, however, while supporting a general incorporation system, continued to express apprehension that the limited liability feature of the corporation might work to the disadvantage of business creditors. Thus the early general laws sponsored by the Democrats contained provisions to make reasonably certain that adequate capital would be paid in and maintained to afford creditor protection.

[72] Cf. W. J. Lane, *From Indian Trail to Iron Horse,* p. 347. The economist Henry C. Carey was active in this movement.

[73] *Votes and Proceedings of the General Assembly,* 1851, p. 32.

[74] *Newark Daily Advertiser,* March 27, 1851.

Although the Whigs enjoyed a slight majority in the legislature in the late eighteen forties when the first general acts were passed, it is evident from the Whig press that the party was not overly enthusiastic about incorporation by procedure. The Whig *State Gazette* had favored a proposed general regulating statute for manufacturing companies in 1846 on the ground that it was desirable to leave the creation of corporations in the hands of the legislature.[75] Similar opposition to uncontrolled multiplication of business corporations was expressed by the same paper in commenting upon the large number of applications announced to come before the legislature in 1849. The editor thought charters should be granted only with caution and admonished the legislators that it was "one of their imperative and most sacred obligations" to weigh each case on its merits.[76] The *Newark Daily Advertiser,* another organ of the Whig party and one representing the views of a large section of the commercial community, gave only qualified support to a substitute for incorporation by special act. In commenting upon the large number of charter applications facing the 1849 legislature, the editor reflected: "It is, perhaps, wise and unavoidable that the whole municipal machinery of society should be required to put in motion a water-wheel, or drain a meadow, but it would seem to superficial observation that some less onerous, and equally safe mode of attaining such ends might be found among the resources of human wisdom." [77] Apparently the editor did not have much faith in the general incorporation laws then in force.

It was not, however, until the Democrats attempted to abandon the system of special chartering and force incorporation under the rather illiberal general laws that the Whig press became definitely hostile. At the time of the passage of the 1846 manufacturing law, doubtful members of the legislature had been assured that enactment of the general law would not prohibit special charters, and the general notion of the object of the general law was that it merely afforded an alternative system of incorporation for those who wished to "save the time

[75] *State Gazette,* January 30, 1846. [76] *Ibid.,* January 6, 1849.
[77] *Newark Daily Advertiser,* January 2, 1849.

and trouble of applications for special acts . . ." [78] Legislators opposing the 1846 law on the ground that its terms were too strict to permit any "healthy" company to rise under it had been reassured by other members of the assembly in words that foreshadowed troubles to come. Citing the dual system in New York, one member declared that he did not suppose the bill would prevent the legislature from incorporating other companies by special act at its discretion, and another said anyone who thought the law was "fire" did not have to play with it.[79] In accord with this position, six special acts for manufacturing companies were passed in the two years after the first general law was in operation. [80]

Very soon it became evident that the Democratic plan for general laws was not merely to make such laws available for those who did not wish to take the trouble to secure special charters. The Democrats intended to go further and force all incorporation under general statutes. A foretaste of the Democratic campaign of blocking special charters when a general act was applicable was given in 1848. In that year, Jonathan Pickel unsuccessfully opposed a mining company charter in the following words:

> I am not, as has been said, opposed to all corporations; I am anxious to give every facility to make researches for the metals of our state, but this perpetually increasing these corporations will be the very way to defeat this object. There has been enough of fancy stocks in New York and Philadelphia: they are more intended to put coppers into speculators' pockets, than to get them out of the earth. If they wish to work in good faith, we have already a general law on the subject which is liberal enough, and sufficient for any honest purposes.[81]

In the 1849 legislature, a test case was made of the charter of the Paterson Manufacturing Company. After Pickel had attempted to put individual liability for stockholders into the

[78] *Sentinel of Freedom,* February 24, 1846.

[79] *Newark Daily Advertiser,* February 20, 1846.

[80] E.g., *N. J. Laws,* 1847, p. 61; 1848, p. 215.

[81] *Newark Daily Advertiser,* February 10, 1848.

bill, "a demonstration of a desire to get the general manufacturing law into general use was made . . ." A member of the assembly moved to strike out the enacting clause of the charter not only to "drive this, and all other manufacturing companies, who want charters, to organize under the general law, which was enacted especially for the benefit of such persons," but also to save time for the applicants and the legislature. The purpose of this move, as stated in the assembly, was to give an early answer to the question "whether we shall spend time with private applications for Manufacturing Companies, when we have a general law for this purpose, or whether we shall not refer them back to this general law . . ." [82] The answer was the defeat of all special manufacturing charters in 1849 and the passage of a revised general manufacturing law.

Early in 1850, a resolution was adopted by the assembly declaring the legislators' intention not to act on special charters if the applications could be brought under an existing general law,[83] but in spite of this expression of sentiment one manufacturing company charter went through to final passage.[84] During the session, applications for bank charters and extensions were postponed until the general bank law then under discussion could be passed.[85] No new banks were created that year by special act, but one special charter of a banking institution was renewed near the end of the session.[86]

The whole controversy increased in intensity in 1851 when the Democrats enjoyed a majority in the legislature, and Daniel Haines, the retiring Democratic governor, sent a message to the legislature in which he expressed a preference for general laws:

> That laws and privileges should as far as possible be equal and alike to all, cannot with truth be denied. Partial laws and special privileges are not usually consistent with justice or sound policy, and

[82] *Ibid.*, January 18, 1849. The newspaper's correspondent reported that the legislators were determined to fix the general law if it was defective.

[83] *Ibid.*, January 9, 1850. [84] *N. J. Laws*, 1850, p. 258.

[85] *Newark Daily Advertiser*, January 11 and 24, 1850.

[86] *N. J. Laws*, 1850, p. 291.

should be enacted or conferred only in cases of manifest expediency or urgent necessity.[87]

Governor Fort's inaugural address of a few days later indicated unqualified opposition to special charters on the part of this Democrat who had voted with Pickel in the constitutional convention and in the assembly and who as a senator in 1846 had sponsored a general manufacturing bill:

> All applications for special privileges and monopolies should be discarded. General Laws, judiciously framed, embracing subjects of the same class, should be enacted, so as to enable all citizens under proper restrictions and guaranties, to avail themselves of the benefits they may confer.[88]

Fort stood ready to implement his views in so far as he was able. In spite of the strongly Democratic complexion of the 1851 legislature, charters were passed early and by wide majorities for a manufacturing concern and a mining company.[89] The governor immediately vetoed the special charters.[90] The veto message, being one of the best single statements of the position of New Jersey Democrats on incorporation procedure and coming from a leading advocate of general laws, deserves the following lengthy quotation:

> I would call the attention of the Legislature to the fact of the existence of a general Law . . . under which persons desirous of embarking in enterprizes of this character may become incorporated without resorting to the law-making power for a special act. The law referred to [the manufacturing law of 1849], is in lieu of one of a similar kind [the manufacturing act of 1846] . . . which had been considered impracticable, on account of the restrictive nature of

87 *Votes and Proceedings of the General Assembly*, 1851, p. 31.

88 *Ibid.*, p. 127. The governor also spoke in favor of "personal liability of stockholders in banks and other chartered companies." *Ibid.*, pp. 127–28.

89 One of these charters had been delayed slightly in the assembly because some members wanted to test the chance of "squeezing it in under the general law" although advocates of the special charter declared the general law "inadequate" in this case. *Newark Daily Advertiser*, January 31, 1851.

90 This was the first occasion on which a governor had used the recently acquired veto power to negative corporate charters.

some of its features, with the view of relieving the objections urged against the original, the present law was enacted . . .

It will be perceived . . . that the bills returned are of a character capable of being comprehended within the provisions of an existing general law.

The advantages of general over special laws are so apparent, that it seems only necessary to call your attention to a few prominent points.

General laws save the time of the Legislature otherwise unnecessarily consumed, at the expense of the State treasury and the true interests of the people.

They obviate the necessity of special applications, and thereby prevent the operation of private influences in legislation, to the delay of public business and the detriment of the public good.

They are considered and enacted in view of their equal benefit to the whole people, and to every section of the State, affording an unrestrained opportunity of incorporating salutary provisions, protective of popular rights and interests.

They are equal in their operation, and enable all citizens "to avail themselves of the benefits they may confer." Associations organized under them are more immediately under legislative control, and consequent responsibility to the state.

They avoid an infringement of those great principles of equal rights, liable to be violated by special charters, and which are usually sought, for the purpose of obtaining privileges and grants in their tendency directly subversive of those rights.

My chief object is to present for your consideration the necessity of applying remedies to such evils in legislation as exist, entertaining a firm conviction that they must increase in extent, frequency and degree, unless we revert at once to fundamental principles.

In addition to these objections, permit me to remark that it would appear to be judicious to enact general laws, embracing subjects of the same class, in a great variety of cases, founded upon the sound principles which pervade the general manufacturing and mining act.

Special Laws, will be deemed necessary while we have no general act to meet the case, but in regard to every application coming within the plain design of any public statute, we should not hesitate to require a strict conformity to its provisions, otherwise our laws will become nugatory. Supplemental statutes may be provided to remedy defects, should any exist, and to render the law feasible in its operation.

It will gratify me to co-operate with the legislature in effecting such wholesome reforms as are needed and undoubtedly demanded by an enlightened public sentiment.[91]

After hearing the governor's objections to the two charters, the legislators passed both bills over the veto, but with somewhat less favorable votes than were originally given them.[92] Later in the session, two additional manufacturing company charters were enacted.[93]

Governor Fort addressed the legislature at the opening of the next session in a message containing reflections on the matter of special charters similar to those he voiced in 1851 and a threat to veto any further special charters for manufacturing companies.[94] In an effort to accomplish his aims, Fort proceeded during the year to veto two mining company charters.[95]

[91] *Votes and Proceedings of the General Assembly,* 1851, pp. 680–81. The single veto message applied to both charters.

[92] *Ibid.,* pp. 722–23; *Journal of the Senate,* 1851, pp. 589–592. For the charters see *N. J. Laws,* 1851, pp. 45, 89. During debate on the veto message, one speaker contradicted the governor's statement that the general law covered the cases and declared that until the general law was improved special acts would be necessary. On the same day, another said he could show all general laws to be unconstitutional on the ground that the legislature could not deputize others to exercise its authority in such a way. *Newark Daily Advertiser,* February 28, 1851.

[93] *N. J. Laws,* 1851, pp. 214, 338.

[94] "For many years past our statute book has been encumbered with a variety of special acts of incorporation. That the major part of these chartered associations could have organized under the provisions of judicious general laws, embracing subjects of the same class, I do [not] entertain a doubt. The evil has long existed, is increasing, and ought to be diminished. To you as conservators of the public weal, the people look for relief, and I trust will not be disappointed . . .

"Of the acts passed at the last session of the legislature, full one-third were of a character to have been embraced within the scope of general laws . . .

"Special charters will be demanded, while we have no general act to meet the case. All applications coming within the purview of a general statute, should be discarded; otherwise, our laws will become uncertain and nugatory.

"For a more extended view of the advantage of general over special acts, permit me to refer you to my message [of last year] . . . returning two charters of incorporation for manufacturing companies. The principles which governed my action in those cases have been adopted on mature reflection, and will be adhered to, should bills of the like character be presented for my approval." *Appendix to the House Journal,* 1852, pp. 16–17.

[95] *Votes and Proceedings of the General Assembly,* 1852, pp. 501–02, 685–86. The governor said many more corporations would form under the 1849 gen-

He then turned his attention to two bills extending the lives of specially chartered banks and submitted vigorous vetoes.[96] In these messages the governor advocated the "propriety and policy of requiring all existing banks to comply with said general law [for banking corporations] . . . I think we should hesitate to grant the application, and defer action thereon until time is afforded to mature a law obliging every special bank within a limited period, or at the expiration of their charters, to comply with the salutary provisions of said general law."

For his message of 1853, Governor Fort tabulated the figures on the number of special charters and supplements passed during the preceding nine years "to indicate the importance of perfecting our system of general laws, and of adhering to the principle of granting no charters where a general act will meet the case." [97] Nevertheless, five manufacturing and mining charters were passed during the session of 1853. No new banks, however, were chartered nor were any existing ones renewed. On the other hand, a suggestion of the governor to make all special banks come under the general bank law after a suitable time for adjustment[98] was not acted upon, although a bill designed to carry out the governor's idea was introduced.[99]

Fort relinquished the governorship in 1854 and at that time made a final plea for more extensive use of general laws. In reviewing the achievements of his administration, he put emphasis on the general laws passed in the preceding three years.[100] The incoming Governor Rodman M. Price, also a Democrat, recommended general laws in the following words:

---

eral law if the legislature would cease treating it as a "nullity." He asserted that if he did not take the safe course of observing existing statutes, the whole fabric of general laws would break down.

[96] *Ibid.*, pp. 832–834; *Journal of the Senate*, 1852, pp. 725–727.

[97] *Appendix to the House Journal*, 1853, Message of the Governor, pp. 13, 14.

[98] *Ibid.*, p. 10.

[99] *Newark Daily Advertiser*, January 19, 1853. This paper's correspondent analyzed opinion in the legislature on the matter of banks by identifying three groups: those who were doubtful of the general law and preferred special banks, those who, like the governor, had "all confidence in the general law" and would grant no special privileges, and the "moderate Democracy" who were interested in certain existing banks and would extend their charters with the idea of making them general banks later on. *Ibid.*, February 4, 1853.

[100] *Appendix to the House Journal*, 1854, Message of the Governor, pp. 6–8, 25.

Special enactments are to be avoided, and ought only to be granted when general laws will not apply. The people have declared in favor of general laws, and are opposed to special legislation, as it often confers a privilege or monopoly which is against the spirit of our institutions . . . The principles of equal, exact and general laws, no privileged classes, no monopolies, should be the basis of legislation, and will prove alike honorable and advantageous to the state. "The blessings of good government must fall alike upon the rich and the poor." [101]

The session had not even commenced when it was clear that the whole battle over general laws would revolve about one issue: what policy to adopt with respect to the banks. The large number of applications for bank charters and renewals announced to come before the legislature caused the press to comment that even friends of the general bank law would be "sorely tried," that Price was ready to veto any special bank bill, and that the only course open to "Democracy" was to compromise and renew all charters for a brief time until the general law might be tried.[102] It was reported that the lobbies were filling with friends of bank applications and that with more than one-half the members directly interested "a more splendid opportunity for a completely organized system of logrolling, was never presented to the Legislature." [103]

The assembly committee on corporations promptly discountenanced all special banks in a strongly worded report on the question of extending the life of one of these institutions.[104] The committee thought the old specially chartered banks should be thankful they had been allowed as long as they had to issue as much money as self-interest dictated; to grant new favors of the same kind would be to create "a hereditary moneyed aristocracy." They reviewed the principles of note issue under the special and general laws and concluded that the two systems could not run parallel but that "one system must displace the other." Because of the inequality and insecurity resulting from

[101] *Journal of the Senate*, 1854, p. 59.
[102] E.g., *Newark Daily Advertiser*, January 10, 1854.
[103] *Ibid.*, January 12, 1854.
[104] *Votes and Proceedings of the General Assembly*, 1854, pp. 75–79.

special bank charters, the committee was "of the opinion that neither should the bill for the re-charter of the Sussex Bank be passed, or that of the re-charter of any other bank." [105]

The finance committee of the senate also reported at some length on the question of banks created by special acts *versus* banks organized under general laws.[106] Their report, while reviewing the evils of special banks, reopened the whole matter of general incorporation laws and made it quite evident that the Democrats were, officially at least, against all corporations unless they were formed under general laws providing a certain measure of protection to creditors. One section of the report read:

> Your committee . . . look upon all special acts of incorporation as of doubtful expediency, except in a few instances where the same may be necessary to promote the development of state resources, or the encouragement of some new branch of manufacturing industry . . . [Special charters are particularly undesirable in the field of banking] . . . The banks who are now asking an extension of their charters will organize under the free banking laws, (their declarations to the contrary, notwithstanding,) and will add the force of their influence, example, and usefulness to perpetuate the system of security banking.
>
> Your committee do not deem it out of place to remind the Senate that the now dominant party in this legislature [the Democratic party] has given pledges to the people that general, instead of special laws, should be enacted, as shown by the resolution of the state convention of 1850.
>
> "*Resolved,* That general laws should be substituted for special legislation — and that, where chartered privileges are necessary, they should be freely *open to all who will give the guarantees proper* TO SECURE THE PUBLIC AGAINST FRAUD AND ABUSE."
>
> Under this pledge political power has passed into the hands of that party. From various reasons the legislature have but partially redeemed that pledge, except, perhaps, upon the subject of banking.

[105] The *Newark Daily Advertiser* (January 18, 1854) thought the report placed the Democratic party in a "peculiar position" and indicated that there was strong objection to it in private party circles. The paper stated that although it was adopted by "nearly a full vote of the party" it would not influence later action on particular bills.

[106] *Journal of the Senate,* 1854, pp. 72–81.

The enactment of the "act authorizing the business of banking" has been a partial performance, on the part of the legislature, to redeem the pledge under which they have been elected. And now it remains to be determined, whether in this one instance of banking, we shall maintain that pledge by sustaining the general banking law. It is time that the masses of the people should understand whether the well considered and solemnly enunciated principles of the now dominant party in favor of general laws, are anything beyond idle pretensions and delusions to entrap the popular vote.[107]

The report was accepted by the senate, and a newspaper correspondent declared the bank question settled for the session: "The free banking law has been sustained as the policy of the State. — Whether it becomes the permanent policy or not, depends upon the success of the probable future attempts of the incorporated bank interests, to combine and carry the Legislature." [108] Shortly after the acceptance of the senate report, the assembly adopted a resolution offered by a member of its committee on corporations that it was "[in]expedient and improper to either extend the charter[s] of the Banks who are

[107] *Ibid.*, pp. 73, 75–76. Other parts of the report reveal the distrust with which the Democrats continued to view business corporations:

"Your committee are fully of the opinion that, by and through the aggregation of capital by means of legislative grants, the same difference in the conditions of men is being hastened in this country that has been the bane of European civilization, where the open and acknowledged principle of legislation has been property, in contra-distinction to humanity — the dollar instead of the man. We had hoped that the exploded doctrine of taking care of the rich by legislative means and expedients, that the rich might take care of the poor, had no longer advocates in this State.

"Through a multitude of corporations now in existence . . . the paths of life are becoming narrower and steeper and more rugged to our working city and manufacturing population . . . Gigantic corporations and capitalists have now the almost entire possession and control of the mechanical and manufacturing branches of industry in this country, insomuch that it has now become necessary for the individual to have the aid of these artificial moneyed powers, in order that he may emerge from the hopeless condition of being chained three hundred and thirteen days in the year to the piston of the steam engine . . .

"Your committee submit that in republican governments the appliances of legislation should not be used to create and widen that abyss which exists between poverty and wealth; it is likely always to be sufficiently wide without the aids of special legislation to widen it." *Ibid.*, pp. 74–75.

[108] *Newark Daily Advertiser*, January 26, 1854.

now applying to the Legislature for such extension or to grant new acts of incorporation for special Banks." [109]

Several attempts were made during the session to resolve the bank controversy by introducing general regulating statutes for specially chartered banks that imposed personal responsibility for payment of the circulating notes on directors and stockholders. The corporation committee of the assembly reported against one such bill as an impairment of the "vested rights" of stockholders in existing banks.[110] A nearly similar bill was defeated in the senate.[111]

The legislature adjourned without having taken favorable action on any special bank charter or bank charter renewal. Since many special charters were on the verge of expiration, it was evident that the Democratic determination to adhere only to general laws in the matter of banks would soon undergo its acid test.[112]

In spite of their performance with respect to specially chartered banks, the legislators of 1854 demonstrated signs of increasing unwillingness to force other types of corporations to form under general laws. Early in the session, the assembly refused to adopt a resolution declaring it the intention of that house not to pass any further private acts of incorporation.[113] The great number of applications for special charters for manufacturing and mining companies presented to the legislature, however, revived the question of a revision of the manufacturing law of 1849. A resolution was passed that "a committee be appointed to confer with the Attorney General, to review the said act and supplements and make their report on the same, concerning the amendments and alterations necessary thereto,

[109] *Votes and Proceedings of the General Assembly,* 1854, p. 173.

[110] *Ibid.,* pp. 1037–1040. It was claimed that the proposed bill had sought to alter some irrepealable charters of pre-1846 institutions. *Newark Daily Advertiser,* February 18, 1854.

[111] *Newark Daily Advertiser,* February 18 and March 14, 1854. The paper claimed that the senate bill applied only to post-1846 banks.

[112] At least two charters, those of banks at Mount Holly and Princeton, were to expire before the next session. The *Trenton Gazette* claimed to know that the stockholders of the Princeton institution would organize under the general law. *Newark Daily Advertiser,* April 5, 1854.

[113] *Votes and Proceedings of the General Assembly,* 1854, p. 174.

for Manufacturing Companies &c., to organize under the same." [114] The resolution was adopted, and a committee was appointed, but no report was made. The result was that twelve manufacturing and mining companies were given special charters in 1854.

The legislative session of 1855 witnessed the final serious contest over general and special incorporation laws to be fought during the first reform movement. With some special bank charters already expired and others nearing expiration, it was inevitable that the principal issue would be joined on the battleground of the banks. Governor Price opened the session with a message exhorting the legislators to resist the pressure for special bank charters:

> There should be no specialty in banking; the system in the State should be uniform and general, governed by one law. Nothing is so obnoxious to the sense of the people as exclusive special banking privileges, or so opposed to the general Democratic Republican principle of equal and general laws. The essence of law consists in its being equal and general; special legislation should never be resorted to, when it can possibly be avoided . . .
>
> The danger of special laws is greatest when they relate to moneyed institutions: the disastrous influence of banking interests in other States is well known. It is believed that special bank charters have been obtained by corruption or yielding to personal solicitations, and the danger and suspicion of being controlled by such motives should be avoided.[115]

The *Newark Daily Advertiser* prophesied that the coming struggle over bank charters would be resolved in favor of spe-

[114] *Ibid.*, p. 205.

[115] *Appendix to the House Journal*, 1855, pp. 9 and 12. At the close of his message, Price made a plea for greater use of general regulating statutes for special charters of all types: "In the construction of bills granting charters of incorporations [*sic*], a simple reference to the provisions of the general statutes concerning corporations which are intended to be enacted, might be advantageously substituted for the present practice of repeating such provisions in each bill, thereby diminishing the expense of printing and engrossing, and avoiding the risk of unguardedly granting improper corporate privileges." *Ibid.*, p. 24. As it always had in New Jersey, this suggestion fell on deaf ears. The passage is important, however, in indicating a decreasing interest in general incorporation laws for most types of companies.

cial charters in spite of the governor and other friends of the general law.[116]

Early in the session, the finance committee of the senate reported favorably on the view of the governor as representative of the political pledges of the Democrats since 1850 and offered the following resolution:

> *Resolved,* That in the opinion of the Senate it is inexpedient and unjust to extend the charters of specially incorporated Banks, or to grant new acts of incorporation for Banks, so long as the General Banking Law remains unrepealed.[117]

The resolution, however, was finally turned down.[118] A similar expression of sentiment by an assembly Democrat was not even voted on.[119] One member of the assembly thought it was impossible to learn the sentiment of the public from a study of petitions presented for and against specially chartered banks and wished to submit the question at a special election, but his suggestion received the support of only about one-third of the assemblymen.[120]

Applications for bank charters and extensions occupied the attention of the legislators during most of the session. After various proposals were introduced to regulate the liability of directors and stockholders for the circulating notes of specially chartered banks, a compromise was reached subjecting directors to unlimited and stockholders to double liability for bank notes. Having settled on an acceptable formula, the legislature proceeded to pass twelve bank charters and to extend eight specially chartered banks.[121] In every case, the banks were subjected to the new liability provisions. The new provi-

[116] *Newark Daily Advertiser,* January 16, 1855. The paper declared that there were still some who adhered to the idea of the general law:

> "For Faith, deluded Faith once wedded fast
> "To some dear object, hugs it to the last."

[117] *Journal of the Senate,* 1855, p. 89. [118] *Ibid.,* pp. 102–108.

[119] *Votes and Proceedings of the General Assembly,* 1855, p. 311.

[120] *Ibid.,* pp. 470–71.

[121] At least four of the new charters were for banks that had gone into operation under the general law: namely, The Newark City Bank, The Hunterdon County Bank, The Princeton Bank, and The Bank of New Jersey.

sions were said to have satisfied everyone except those who supported the general law "upon principle,"[122] but it was soon apparent that the governor was numbered among the latter group.

Governor Price promptly sent a message to the legislature announcing that he had vetoed the first charter passed.[123] He expressed his opposition to any specially chartered banks unless the general law was repealed, and he suggested that the bank question be made the campaign issue in the fall elections. The veto message emphasized the governor's opposition to special bank applications because of the accompanying pressure from special interests:

> . . . I have sympathized with the members of both Houses in the natural embarrassment caused them by the great pertinacity with which these numerous bills have been pressed, by personal friends, through private interests. I have witnessed the combination of those interested in bank applications, from one end of the state to the other, to the number of near thirty charters, pending at one time, in one solid phalanx, in your legislative halls. Was there ever a legislature so besieged, by so numerous and powerful a lobby? . . . Are we legislating for the good of the people, or for corporations alone? . . . [The legislators] who can resist this mighty torrent which a large, influential, wealthy and talented lobby has been pressing upon them, will deserve and receive the thanks and favors of a grateful constituency.[124]

The bill was nevertheless speedily repassed by a vote of forty to twelve in the assembly and thirteen to six in the senate.[125] The governor submitted four more vetoes of bank charters,[126] but they were in every case overridden by votes closely approximating those defeating the first veto.[127]

[122] *Newark Daily Advertiser,* March 22, 1855.

[123] *Votes and Proceedings of the General Assembly,* 1855, pp. 1053–1058.

[124] *Ibid.,* pp. 1055–1058 *passim.*

[125] *Ibid.,* p. 1058; *Journal of the Senate,* 1855, pp. 1157–58.

[126] *Votes and Proceedings of the General Assembly,* 1855, pp. 1108–1112.

[127] *Ibid.,* pp. 1121–1124; *Journal of the Senate,* 1855, pp. 1231–1233. The *Newark Daily Advertiser* (March 24, 1855) was correct in its guess that if the governor vetoed the first bill the legislature would override the veto. The cor-

Price was more successful in his opposition to special charters for insurance companies. He vetoed two such charters on the ground that insurance companies should organize under the general insurance act of 1852 so long as that act remained on the books.[128] Both vetoes were sustained, thereby maintaining a three-year record of no special insurance charters.

The general-law movement had received during this session, however, a staggering blow from which it did not recover. For five years the legislature had resisted all pressure to charter new special banks and during that time had extended the charters of only three existing banks;[129] now that policy was irrevocably abandoned. It is true that several manufacturing and mining company charters had been enacted in the preceding few years, but so long as the general law was adhered to in the important and widely discussed field of banking, the movement for general laws had been kept alive.

During the 1855 session, the issue of bribery in connection with special charters had come once more to the forefront. Rumors of payments offered a legislator for favorable votes on bank charters caused the legislature to appoint a special investigating committee. Both majority and minority reports issued from the committee, but the results of the investigation seemed to be inconclusive.[130] Such suspected attempts at bribery might have afforded good reason to adhere to the policy of permitting only general banks, but the legislators saw fit rather to pass legislation aimed at ending bribery while they continued to act on special charters. A law passed near the close of the session declared that both parties to legislative bribery were to be judged guilty of high misdemeanor and to be "forever disqualified to hold any office of honor, trust, or profit under this state." The law also recognized the problem of logrolling. It declared

respondent thought that the "general banking law, so far as any legitimate respect for it is concerned, is a dead letter, and its friends will be no more numerous hereafter than those of a bankrupt Schuyler."

[128] *Votes and Proceedings of the General Assembly,* 1855, pp. 270–71 and 446–47.

[129] *N. J. Laws,* 1850, p. 291; 1851, pp. 275, 281.

[130] *Reports of Majority and Minority of Committee, appointed to investigate into the Charge of attempting to bribe one of the members of the House of Assembly, to vote for the Re-Charter of Certain Banks* (Trenton, 1855).

a legislator guilty of high misdemeanor if he agreed with another member to vote or abstain from voting on any measure before the legislature in return for a similar favor in connection with some other proceeding before the legislature.[131] Thus by 1855 it was evident that the New Jersey lawmakers were again thinking in terms of purifying the procedure of special chartering rather than of ending the practice altogether.

In 1856, the advocates of general laws were again active in the legislature, but their lack of accomplishment made it clear that the general-law movement of the eighteen forties and fifties was a failure. Price submitted a message in which he voiced rather milder objections than before to special acts of incorporation.[132] A Democrat from Morris County introduced a resolution that a special committee of the assembly be appointed to investigate and report on the expediency of refusing to pass any acts of incorporation for any of the objects that could be accomplished under the existing general laws.[133] In spite of the fact that there was a Democratic majority in the assembly, it was voted to lay the report on the table.[134] The *Newark Daily Advertiser* interpreted this action as final evidence of the failure of the Democrats to implement their professions in behalf of general laws.[135] Concerning banking, the assembly committee on banks reported without avail against special bank charters on two occasions,[136] and the assembly also soundly defeated a resolution against specially chartered banks.[137] The record of senate actions during the session shows a similar disposition on the part of that house to go contrary to the official Democratic stand on specially chartered banks. A report of the committee

[131] *N. J. Laws*, 1855, Ch. 230, p. 654.

[132] *Votes and Proceedings of the General Assembly*, 1856, pp. 32–33.

[133] *Ibid.*, p. 340. [134] *Ibid.*, pp. 349–50.

[135] ". . . Democracy as now exemplified is the veriest sham, counterfeit, swindle and humbug out of State Prison . . . Thus gradually are the impositions of the spurious Democracy renounced — the end of deceiving the people having been served." *Newark Daily Advertiser*, February 15, 1856.

[136] *Votes and Proceedings of the General Assembly*, 1856, pp. 230–233, 967. The committee recommended "strict adherence to general over special laws, to abstain from that veering vacillating policy which has too much of late characterized and contra-distinguished New Jersey from her sister states . . ." *Ibid.*, p. 232.

[137] *Ibid.*, pp. 619–620, 628–630.

on corporations against a bank charter was not accepted,[138] and the same committee's resolution to refuse all applications for special banks was also turned down.[139] The result was that one more bank was chartered during the session, and although final action on some other bank bills was postponed, there was no successful move to force new banks to come under the general law.

On the eve of his retirement in January 1857, Governor Price reiterated his objection to special bank charters.[140] However, the inaugural address delivered one week later by Governor Newell, New Jersey's first Republican governor,[141] heralded a new era of special bank acts:

> Legislative enactments ought to have in view the greatest good of the entire community, and to this end a system of general legislation would seem to be desirable; but experience has proved that this theory cannot be made uniformly available. Prominent among other exceptions is the General Banking Law, passed a few years since, under which numerous banks were established; but notwithstanding the frequent efforts of its friends to improve the law so as to make it of practical utility, many of these institutions have either ceased to exist, or have relieved their disabilities by obtaining special charters. It is quite apparent, therefore, that if any banks be hereafter required, they will be established by separate acts of incorporation . . . The greatest circumspection should be exercised by the Legislature, in granting charters for monied corporations, and in all cases the interests of the billholder ought to be most carefully protected.[142]

Although the Democrats had a strong majority in the legislature in 1857, the *Newark Daily Advertiser* prophesied that the system of general laws, "one of the theoretical tenets of Democracy," would be heard of no more, that the legislature would subside "into the old routine of discriminating between worthy and unworthy applications, or leaving their fate to be decided simply by the strength of their support," and that the

[138] *Journal of the Senate,* 1856, pp. 356–57, 446, 775.
[139] *Ibid.,* pp. 608, 615.
[140] *Appendix to the House Journal,* 1857, p. 16.
[141] Newell had begun his political career as a Whig.
[142] *Journal of the Senate,* 1857, pp. 47–48.

settled policy of the state should be to charter banks by special act, "the general law having gone the way of all flesh, and being a mere empty slough on the statute books." [143] This forecast was substantiated as the session proceeded. The senate committee on corporations reported against two special bank charters in a document covering the entire history of New Jersey banking and declaring strongly in favor of the general-bank law.[144] The report was looked upon as merely *"pro forma,"* [145] and it was rejected by the senate.[146] When a few days later another special bank charter bill was introduced in the senate, it was referred to a specially appointed committee on banks. This committee submitted a favorable report on the bill, stating that for most sections of New Jersey a "system of special charters is preferable" to adherence to the general law and is the only system that could accommodate the people. The committee explained that the people should have the "liberty of choosing for themselves between the two systems" and that if they wanted special charters, "common sense, in opposition to theory, dictates the granting thereof . . ." [147] In the assembly the situation was similar, for it was the minority of a committee appointed to consider a special bank application that filed the only report against private bank acts.[148]

The extent of the failure of the first general-law movement can be illustrated by a comparison of the number of business corporations organized under general and special laws from 1847 to 1857.[149] If the figures of Tables II and III are com-

[143] *Newark Daily Advertiser,* January 12, 1857.

[144] *Journal of the Senate,* 1857, pp. 70–74.

[145] *Newark Daily Advertiser,* January 28, 1857.

[146] *Journal of the Senate,* 1857, p. 154; *Newark Daily Advertiser,* February 6 and 7, 1857.

[147] *Journal of the Senate,* 1857, pp. 147, 170–172.

[148] *Votes and Proceedings of the General Assembly,* 1857, pp. 264–271. This minority group expressed the well-worn case against special charters. For example: "The strongest position to be taken against special charters, is on the broad basis of EQUALITY *of rights and privileges* to every citizen of the State; on which principle also repose with perfect security the liberties of the people." *Ibid.,* p. 266.

[149] Since the first of the general laws was passed near the close of the session of 1846, that year is excluded from consideration.

pared, it is found that during those years 414 business corporations were chartered by special act and only 129 were organized under general laws.[150] Merely to cite these total figures, however, would give an incomplete and misleading impression of the actual situation by failing to take into account the fact that during all or part of the period there were no general laws to provide for certain types of corporations chartered by special act and would obscure the fact that for a few years the general laws enjoyed a measure of success. An adequate picture of the experience of the period is obtained only by examining the separate histories of certain of the more significant general laws.

The general manufacturing laws not only came first in time but were more frequently employed than other general laws. Between 1847 and 1857, sixty-four manufacturing and mining companies filed certificates under the laws of 1846 and 1849, while sixty-eight were created by special act.[151] Comparison of Tables II and III shows that legislative opposition to special charters in the late forties and early fifties resulted in more corporations of this type filing under general laws than were created by special act. After 1855, however, the lawmakers' resumption of the practice of granting special bank charters had repercussions in the fields of manufacturing and mining. Only six manufacturing and mining corporations filed under the general law in 1856 and 1857, while in the same two years seventeen were specially chartered.[152] Also the legislature's action of 1855 in converting several general into special banks was the signal for offering similar favors to manufacturing companies, with the result that three companies

[150] Table II is found on page 207, Table III on page 208.

[151] If four manufacturing companies that filed certificates in 1846 after the close of the legislative session are included, the number under general laws is increased to sixty-eight. There were in addition three transportation companies, a gaslight company, a quarrying concern, and two agricultural groups whose certificates of incorporation were filed under the manufacturing law between 1847 and 1857.

[152] In addition to the manufacturing and mining companies organized under the general law, one gaslight concern filed in 1856 under the 1849 manufacturing law. The following year, however, the company was granted a charter by special act. *N. J. Laws,* 1857, Ch. 110, p. 309.

already organized under the general manufacturing law were given special charters in 1856.[153]

Although the legislators seem to have had some initial success in forcing manufacturing concerns to organize under general laws, it is impossible to determine how many of the companies so formed had any actual operating experience. In 1851, opponents of the general law intimated that no company had gone, or could go, into actual operation under its provisions.[154] Although those desiring wider employment of the general law for manufacturing concerns frequently declared their willingness to modify the act in any necessary particular, nothing of the sort was done during this period except the replacement of the 1846 manufacturing act by the slightly less stringent law of 1849.

The only other general law of the first group to receive wide attention was the general banking act of 1850. In one sense this act was marked by more success than the others, for from 1850 through 1854, in spite of strong pressure on the legislature, no special bank charters were granted and only three specially chartered banks were extended. But in another respect the bank law was the worst failure of all, for the forces favoring special legislation brought about its early defeat. Governor Haines informed the legislature in January 1851 that the general banking law was so stringent that no group had been organized under it, and he advocated its amendment.[155] The law's provisions were relaxed, and in 1852 Governor Fort, a principal proponent of the bank law, was able to report that sixteen general-law banks had been organized up to the end of 1851.[156] But the seeds of failure of the banking act were already sown. Governor Fort pointed out that the law had been seized on by speculators. He declared that many general-law banks, while ostensibly located in New Jersey, were actually operated by "brokers" in other states and that the banking houses were sometimes intentionally put in places difficult of access. The governor, anxious to

[153] *N. J. Laws,* 1856, Ch. 52, p. 102, Ch. 122, p. 239, Ch. 166, p. 367. Two of these had filed their certificates in 1855 and one in 1854.

[154] *Newark Daily Advertiser,* January 31, 1851.

[155] *Votes and Proceedings of the General Assembly,* 1851, p. 32.

[156] *Appendix to the House Journal,* 1852, p. 23.

see the general law corrected, suggested a board of bank commissioners who would approve the location of new general-law banks and see that they were organized with reference to the needs of the community.[157]

The legislature proceeded to amend the law by requiring all general-law banks to have *bona fide* banking houses and to provide attendants during regular banking hours.[158] It is significant that the same amendment also required the banks to assume names different from those of any other New Jersey banks, to state their location on their notes in "large legible letters," and to have agents in specified cities for the redemption of notes. A board of bank commissioners with power of investigation of both general and special banks was created, but the governor's proposal to have the commissioners approve the location of any new general-law banks was not put into the law. In 1853, the bank commissioners reported twenty-one banks under the general law, but of these only four were reported as having gone into "full and *bona fide* operation," seven were declared to be about to wind up, and most of the rest were said to have no *bona fide* banking houses.[159] The commissioners felt that the confidence of the legislature had been abused and suggested changes in the law.[160] In support of their position the commissioners cited the case of Cape May County. Five of the general-law banks were announced as located in this least accessible and most sparcely populated section of the state, four of the five being centered at Cape May Court House, a village of less than 200 inhabitants. The situation was little changed when the commissioners submitted their next annual report, and they repeated their suggestions for reform.[161] It has already been shown that in 1855, rather than amend the general bank law with a view to making it more workable, the legislature preferred to grant special charters to new banks and to some banks already organized under the general law and also to extend the charters of existing special banks. In 1856, the report

[157] *Ibid.*, pp. 13–15. [158] *N. J. Laws*, 1852, Ch. 193, p. 478.

[159] *Appendix to the House Journal*, 1853, Report of the Bank Commissioners, pp. 4–6.

[160] *Ibid.*, pp. 6–12.

[161] *Ibid.*, 1854, Report of the Bank Commissioners, pp. 6–8.

of the state treasurer included statements for only six general-law banks.[162]

The 1852 general law for insurance companies was an even greater failure. As was indicated earlier, a few special insurance company charters were successfully vetoed after the act was on the statute books, and no special charters for insurance purposes were granted in 1853, 1854, or 1855. Only three companies, however, had filed certificates of incorporation under the general law by the end of 1856, and one of these received a special charter in 1857.[163] The legislators' lack of fidelity to the general law is indicated by the fact that beginning in 1856 special charters for insurance companies became more numerous than they had been previous to the enactment of the general law.

As concerns the other general laws of the first group, nine telegraph companies, six land development associations, and one steamboat company filed certificates under general incorporation laws during these years. There is no evidence, however, that any companies were organized under the acts for mutual savings institutions, plank road companies, or vessel building associations.

It might seem that by the decade of the eighteen fifties, advocates of chartering business corporations by special act of legislature could have few arguments to advance in support of their position. A study of editorials and news reports in the *Newark Daily Advertiser,* one of the more articulate representatives of the Whig press, shows a paucity of well-founded argument. The paper's campaign against the Democrats who advocated wider use of the general laws was largely one of ridicule. Agitation against general laws did not gain its full momentum until 1851 when the Democrats had gained a strong majority in the legislature and began to carry out their campaign promises of the autumn of 1850 by obstructing special charters with a view to forcing persons desiring incorporation to file under

[162] *Ibid.,* 1856, Report of the State Treasurer.
[163] *N. J. Laws,* 1857, Ch. 18, p. 36.

the general laws. A few quotations will indicate the principal type of attack made against the general-law system. When the 1851 legislature was considering a bill to prevent swine from running at large, the *Advertiser* suggested that the Democrats would probably pass a "*General Swine Law*, the principal provisions of which will be to allow every hog to root wherever it pleases, by contributing a reversion of pork to the School Fund . . ." [164] When in the same year Governor Fort vetoed a special charter, the newspaper declared his action to be "in accordance with the chimera of general laws, which, like Peter's sheet, are to reach all the four corners of heaven, and take in fish, flesh, and fowl, and everything else beside." [165] Later it was declared that the "general law making has become a little nauseating. As the possession of their large harems is said to make the Turks great misogynists, this wild and indiscriminate passion after general laws most probably will result . . . at least in a return to *the good old sober patient special law making*." [166] When Governor Fort threatened in 1852 to veto all special bills of incorporation, the *Advertiser* declared: "If this be so, a 'higher law' is at once established, which is that although the constitution does not forbid special charters, the Governor will whenever he thinks that they should come under the scope of a general law." [167] As signs of the disintegration of the general-law system appeared, the editor in reviewing the session of 1853 remarked that the Democrats had done nothing about general laws "which caused so much rapid ranting about Equality this, and Generality that, and other catchwords three years ago, but the special acts are intensely special." [168]

The whole attack, however, was not composed of vague statements in disparagement of general laws. The strongest argument against the existing general laws was furnished by the Democrats themselves: namely, that the laws were ignored by Democratic legislatures that passed special charters. The *Advertiser* frequently pointed out that although the Democrats

[164] *Newark Daily Advertiser*, February 26, 1851.

[165] *Ibid.*, February 28, 1851.

[166] *Ibid.*, March 8, 1851. Italics supplied.

[167] *Ibid.*, January 15, 1852.

[168] *Ibid.*, March 16, 1853.

had "resolved and re-resolved" to substitute general for special charters, those most loud in favor of general laws were most forward in pressing certain special charters.[169] When special charter bills were held up by talk of general laws, it was pointed out that the "ardor could not of course hold out even if it had been real — which it was not, as it originated in mere check and counter-check among a few members — for too many have private bills which they wished to have passed." [170] Lack of Democratic opposition to special charters for plank road companies immediately after the general plank road law had been enacted caused the *Advertiser* to draw the inference that the Democrats had "no practical trust in the general law system, and that the one already passed is inadequate." [171] The many instances of the Democrats' disregard for their own general laws in the face of pressure for private acts were powerful ammunition when used by opponents of the existing system of general laws. When the Democrats virtually abandoned the general banking act in 1855, the whole program of general laws was on the way to temporary eclipse.

A thorough discussion of the reasons for the failure of general incorporation laws to displace special acts of incorporation before the constitutional amendments of 1875 forced a change is deferred to the close of the following chapter after the experience of the whole period from 1845 to 1875 has been recounted.[172] The considerations given there apply with equal force to the first general-law movement and to the later period. There were, however, a few factors working against the success of the general-law system that apply particularly to the years under discussion in the present chapter. These considerations can best be rehearsed here.

First of all, the force of the New Jersey movement for general laws between 1845 and 1857 was greatly weakened when the issue became a matter of party politics. The Democrats who championed the cause of general incorporation laws had been widely known as antagonists of the business corporation,

[169] E.g., *ibid.*, January 24, 1852. [170] *Ibid.*, February 4, 1852.
[171] *Ibid.*, March 11, 1852. [172] Cf. *infra*, pp. 169–182.

members of the party having in the late eighteen thirties declared their opposition to incorporation for business purposes. When the party undertook at the end of the forties and in the early fifties to force all business corporations to organize under general laws, their intent was not to provide a simple and generous incorporating procedure. Rather it was the purpose of party members to make it impossible for one corporate group to receive more favorable charter terms than any other group and to whittle away one of the principal advantages of the corporation as compared with the proprietorship and general partnership, the privilege of limited stockholder liability. Although attempts made by some Democrats to include unlimited liability for debts in the general laws were unsuccessful, the most discussed laws, those for manufacturing and mining companies and that for banking corporations, contained provisions aimed at creditor protection that were onerous to the business community. Stringent personal liability of stockholders and directors in the event that the announced capital was not paid in or in case certain required statements were not filed, requirements for publicity concerning corporate financial affairs, limitations on corporate debts, and similar restrictive provisions were distinctly irksome to businessmen and could be avoided in special acts of incorporation. Had the Democrats been willing to liberalize the general laws to gain the support of businessmen, the fate of the early laws might have been very different.

Another factor tending to defeat the general-law system once the movement became associated with party politics was the domination of the Democratic party by the Camden and Amboy monopoly group. Since this domination was so nearly absolute in the years under discussion here, no general railroad law was possible at the time. The party was in the anomalous position of supporting measures aimed at ending "monopoly" and special privilege and at the same time advocating the continuance of the only true monopoly in the state. This open inconsistency could not fail to weaken public respect for Democratic efforts to establish a general incorporation procedure in non-railroad industries and to lose for the party the potential support of many true friends of the principle of equal privileges.[173]

If there is any one circumstance more responsible than another for the failure of the first general-law movement, it is the fact that the battle came to be fought out on the matter of banks chartered by special act *versus* banks organized under the general law. There is some likelihood that if the bank question had not become the principal issue, the outcome of the struggle would have been more satisfactory to the general-law group. The nature of the banking business under the two systems was entirely different. Specially chartered banks had the very desirable privilege of note issue restricted only by very liberal upper limits. Even such limits as there were on note issue seem to have been impossible to enforce at the time. Banks with charters obtained by filing under the general law were required to deposit with state authorities securities to furnish full backing for every dollar of notes issued. The vast disparity in profit opportunities under the two systems is evident. The very profitableness of the specially chartered banks made it inevitable that applicants for special bank charters would bring all possible financial and personal influence to bear on the lawmakers. The legislators also had to acknowledge an unhappy experience with the speculator-controlled general-law banks set up immediately after the general banking law was enacted. The resulting pressure for special bank charters was more than the legislators could resist.

In 1854, the year before the legislature succumbed to the temptation to revert to a system of special bank charters, a committee of the assembly in reporting on an application for rechar-

[173] The press was not backward in pointing out the contradictory position in which the Democrats stood. For instance, an editorial in the *Newark Daily Advertiser* of January 18, 1854, commenting on the inaugural address of Governor Price in which the governor supported the principle of general laws as opposed to "special legislation" and "monopoly" observed: "The commentary on this is not given by him of course; and so we will state it. It began in the creation by the Governor's party of the only monopoly of the State; but that is a fat one, and no mistake — we mean the *Camden & Amboy Companies,* which has introduced a *privileged class* into New Jersey, outraged equality, and continues a standing and flagrant example of special legislation."

tering a bank had foreseen "that the re-charter of this or any other of the banks . . . is in effect equivalent to a repeal of the free banking law . . ." [174] This view was thoroughly vindicated after 1855 when the legislature resumed the practice of chartering banks by special act. The legislators' decision to disregard the banking law also affected the fate of other general laws. If the solons were of a mind to grant the very special bank charters, they could not be expected to refuse special charters for much less controversial purposes. The almost complete collapse of the whole general-law movement after 1855 was, under the circumstances, inevitable.

[174] *Votes and Proceedings of the General Assembly*, 1854, p. 76.

CHAPTER V

Incorporation by Special Act and under General Laws in New Jersey, 1845–1875 (Continued)

1858–1875

THE GENERAL incorporation laws of New Jersey went into partial eclipse from 1858 through 1864. It is interesting that the new era of special charters was ushered in by the passage in 1858 of "An act to increase the revenues of the state of New Jersey" levying assessments on special charters and charter supplements for business concerns.[1] The fees established by the act were to be paid before the charters or supplements were to be published or have the force of law. The tax was justified by some as a means of discouraging many applications, especially those not "legitimate," from coming before the legislature at all and thus save time and money for the government.[2] Passage of the new revenue law, however, seems rather to indicate a willingness on the part of the legislature to pass special acts and an expectation that a large number of special charters and supplements would be enacted. It soon became apparent that the lawmakers were not much interested in saving time and publishing expense. In 1859, the revenue law was altered to permit publication of all special acts of incorporation and charter supplements even though the assessments were unpaid.[3]

Between 1858 and 1864, an occasional "spasmodic exhibition of fealty to the exploded system of general laws" was reported, "scapegoats" were claimed to be made of a few applicants for special charters, and in 1860 the senate corporation committee

[1] *N. J. Laws,* 1858, Ch. 95, p. 220.

[2] *Newark Daily Advertiser,* February 19 and 20, 1858.

[3] *N. J. Laws,* 1859, Ch. 167, p. 490. Any act, however, was to become inoperative if the fees were not paid by July 1 of the year in which it was passed.

reported against all special charters on the ground that "many private acts which have been obtained during the past few years are still in the hands of individuals, and have never been brought into use, but are merely held for speculative purposes." [4] But except for the extension of the manufacturing law in 1860 to associations "for the purpose of making, purchasing and selling manufactured articles, and also of acquiring and disposing of rights to make and use the same" [5] no further progress was made in the direction of a system of general incorporation laws until 1865.

Between 1865 and 1875, a series of new general incorporation laws and several amendments extending the scope of existing general laws were enacted in New Jersey. The second group of general laws was ushered in by an act for the incorporation of real estate development concerns in 1865.[6] More important was an act of the same year to permit incorporation under the general manufacturing law of "all persons exceeding four, who shall associate themselves together for the purpose of carrying on any lawful business whatever." [7] Another law for land improvement companies was enacted in 1867.[8] Other general laws were one for companies to dig and cut peat, stone, and other articles passed in 1869,[9] the general railroad law of 1873,[10] the gas company law of 1874,[11] and an 1875 law for companies to erect buildings in New Jersey.[12] During those same years, the general manufacturing act was modified to permit the establishment of dairy product concerns with less paid-in capital than was required by other types of companies[13] and to permit the formation of coöperative organizations to trade in general merchandise with the privilege of having branch stores.[14]

In April 1875, the corporation laws of New Jersey were revised. One section of the revision, "An act concerning corpora-

[4] *Newark Daily Advertiser,* February 3, 1858, March 9, 1859, January 25, 1860; *Journal of the Senate,* 1860, pp. 61–62.

[5] *N. J. Laws,* 1860, Ch. 117, p. 267.

[6] *N. J. Laws,* 1865, Ch. 379, p. 707.

[7] *Ibid.,* Ch. 491, p. 913.

[8] *N. J. Laws,* 1867, Ch. 378, p. 855.

[9] *N. J. Laws,* 1869, Ch. 374, p. 1001.

[10] *N. J. Laws,* 1873, Ch. 413, p. 88.

[11] *N. J. Laws,* 1874, Ch. 509, p. 124.

[12] *N. J. Laws,* 1875, Ch. 379, p. 85.

[13] *N. J. Laws,* 1874, Ch. 314, p. 59; 1875, Ch. 173, p. 35.

[14] *N. J. Laws,* 1875, Ch. 16, p. 12.

tions," [15] has been said by one author to have "embodied many provisions long sought by business and gained in individual instances by particular companies through special enactment" and to be "commonly viewed as the first modern 'liberal' incorporating statute." [16] Since the revision was approved after the regular legislative session of 1875, it does not fall within the period under study in this essay. No detailed analysis of it will, therefore, be attempted here, but it should be stated that a thorough investigation of earlier legislation reveals that nearly all the provisions of the revised statute stood scattered over the session law volumes at the time of the revision and were merely codified in 1875.[17]

Beginning in the middle of the eighteen sixties, the number of special charters passed annually was generally double and triple the number passed during any of the preceding years, and other forms of special legislation showed a corresponding increase. It was this circumstance that forced the attention of the public and the legislature to the necessity of alleviating the tremendous burden of private bills. One suggestion made to solve the problem of the large volume of legislation was to secure the earlier introduction of bills and thereby reduce the evils of the end-of-the-session rush.[18] It was obvious, however, that nothing short of an end to special legislation was an adequate solution. The debate over general incorporation laws was revived and soon held the center of attention. Thus the keynote of the second movement toward a system of general incorporation laws was the necessity of bringing to an end the rapidly increasing burden of special legislation. The argument of equality

[15] *Revised Statutes of the State of New Jersey* (1875), p. 3.

[16] C. C. Abbott, article entitled "Corporations," in *Dictionary of American History*. See the same author's *The Rise of the Business Corporation*, p. 47.

[17] The principal new provisions were those reducing the minimum capital stock required for ordinary business corporations and permitting stock to be given in payment for property.

The manufacturing law of 1849 was expressly repealed. *Revised Statutes of the State of New Jersey* (1875), p. 37. Six of the other general incorporation acts previously in force were reprinted in the revision. Pp. 38–131 *passim*.

[18] For instance, the president of the senate made this proposal, stating that "in not a few cases [I] have, in my short experience here, been called upon to face laws which I have assisted to pass, of which I was heartily ashamed." *Journal of the Senate*, 1868, p. 11.

of privileges was still heard in support of general laws, but it seems to have become a distinctly secondary appeal. In this respect the period differs from that of 1845 through 1857, and the campaign for general incorporation laws was spared from becoming once again a matter of party politics.

In 1867, the assembly appointed a special committee to inquire into the possibility of amending the general manufacturing law so as to make most special charter applications unnecessary, but no report was made.[19] In a message of 1869, accompanying a signed bill incorporating a manufacturing company, Governor Theodore F. Randolph pointed out certain tax exemptions granted the company and suggested that

> Much of the confusion and inequality as to taxes upon the property of private corporations would be avoided if the Legislature should see fit to refuse to create a private corporation by special charter in every case where the legitimate purposes of the proposed corporation can be attained by organizing the corporation under the general law . . . [of 1849, amended in 1865] so as to embrace within it all persons exceeding four, who shall associate themselves together for the purpose of carrying on any lawful business whatever.[20]

The same governor devoted a long section of his 1870 message to a plea for early passage of a set of general incorporation laws to reduce the special legislation that was passed annually in such quantity that neither the legislators nor the governor were able to give it careful consideration.[21] The legislature responded by appointing a joint committee that promptly engaged Cortlandt Parker, a Newark lawyer, to draft the necessary general laws.[22] At the end of the session, the committee made a report. The report did not propose to end the abuses mentioned by the governor by abandoning the granting of spe-

[19] *Votes and Proceedings of the General Assembly,* 1867, p. 441–42.
[20] *Ibid.,* 1869, pp. 566–67.
[21] *Legislative Documents,* 1870, pp. 13–14.
[22] *Newark Daily Advertiser,* January 19, 1870. The paper stated: "It is possible that certain laws general in their provisions, may be passed, but they will need to be carefully framed in order to escape opposition at the hands of some of the more cautious members."

cial charters altogether. Rather, it envisaged a dual system of incorporation both by procedure and by special acts. The latter, however, were to be guarded by general regulating statutes.[23] Probably owing to the lack of time, the proposals were not acted upon during the session.

In 1871, Randolph again set apart much of his annual message for an appeal to the lawmakers to perfect a system of general laws. The following sections of his message indicate the nature of the arguments he employed:

There is but one efficient remedy for such an evil [the vast amount of special legislation], and that lies in the prompt adoption by your bodies of a system of general laws — simple in form, convenient and inexpensive in their operation, affording no reasonable pretext for special legislation. Where such legislation is had, it should be made to compensate the state fully for the costs and trouble incurred. It is difficult to conceive why any man, or body of men, should receive special grants or favors from the Legislature, that are not equally free to all other men, or bodies of men. If in earlier days the protective policy that special legislation represents, was necessary to foster enterprise, no such reasoning holds good now.

Capital can only properly demand that it shall not be legislated against; for the rest, like individual labor, it must take its chances.

An evil long felt, and now becoming almost unendurable, is the lobby system, mainly the offspring of special legislation. The system fathers a class of shrewd men, who, zealous of success, resort to

[23] The report introduced the suggested code with the explanation that it secured reform by "general laws, which shall apply to every Corporation hereafter to be created by act of the Legislature; and in such a manner as that all their provisions shall attach at once to every Corporation chartered; saving thus endless repetition of similar provisions conferring or regulating corporate powers," and also by "acts providing means by which without application to the Legislature, Corporations for any lawful purpose, can be organized, regulated, and, if need be, wound up." *Votes and Proceedings of the General Assembly,* 1870, p. 1074. In a letter from Parker that accompanied the report, the author of the code explained that "in addition to this [a plan for general regulating statutes], it has seemed to me that the power of being incorporated without a particular act of the legislature might safely be extended; and that it was well to suggest a system for such incorporation, which would comprehend, as far as possible, everything. This method of legislation has long existed in Great Britain, and has been adopted by some of our sister States. Nowhere, however, has the scheme been so carefully elaborated as in England; and after looking at the acts of other States, I have taken those of the English Parliament, as, for the most part, my model." *Ibid.,* 1870, p. 1076.

means first questioned, next accepted, and thus becoming blunted to quick perception of right and wrong, these men, in turn, attempt to pervert the minds of others, and they the law makers. With special legislation, as an occasional act, this whole system would naturally die.

A code of general laws has been prepared by direction of your predecessors; and though your honorable bodies may not concur in all the suggestions therein contained, you will not fail to find abundant material from which to adopt one desirable in character, and beneficial in results.[24]

The *Newark Daily Advertiser* was at this time willing to advocate adoption of general statutes to deal with those who had looked upon the state as a "mere machine for the furtherance of individual ends and the promotion of private gain" but doubted the efficacy of any cure for special legislation unless the constitution was amended to outlaw private acts.[25] Although all of the bills prepared the previous year by Parker were introduced during the 1871 session, none of them was acted upon. Perhaps the principal reason for the neglect of the suggested laws was that the attention of the legislature was so completely absorbed for several years by the struggles over the general law for railroads that finally passed in 1873.

In his message of 1872, Governor Randolph spoke again in favor of a system of general laws.[26] Again the legislature did nothing to implement the governor's words.

[24] *Legislative Documents,* 1871, pp. 18–19.

[25] *Newark Daily Advertiser,* January 17, 1871.

[26] "The evils of special legislation have become so manifest, that the oft-repeated arguments in favor of general laws, scarce need rehearsal.

"Our statute books are filled with laws, that are substantially, mere repetitions of each other — convenience and economy, therefore, dictate their operation under the general system.

"To the legislative branch of the government, a vast saving of time would be secured by its adoption. To the judicial department, the economy of labor would be a manifest advantage. To the public, the certainty of just and equal privileges, which such laws establish, would go far toward insuring the accretion of capital within our own borders, the healthful and steady development of industrial enterprises, and security against the wrongs, which special privileges, by legislation, are calculated to engender.

"There is no railway enterprise, which capital may desire to develop, that cannot now be left to the protecting care of a law universal in its application. There can scarcely be a manufacturing or other industrial interest that will not obtain, under such enactment, all necessary protection." *Legislative Documents,* 1872, p. 11.

Governor Joel Parker, in 1873, advocated a change in the constitution to prohibit private acts of all kinds, expressing his belief that if general laws were made "comprehensive and liberal" all corporations could organize under them.[27] Recognizing the reluctance of the legislature to forfeit the right to grant special charters, Parker offered several alternative suggestions for amending the constitution in case general laws were not acceptable. He proposed a constitutional requirement that a list and summary of all legislation to be offered during a legislative session be made by the secretary of state for public information and for the benefit of legislators and that certain specific privileges such as exemption from the operation of general tax laws and permission for nonuniform rates by railroad and turnpike companies be absolutely forbidden.[28] The legislature showed no disposition to reduce the volume of special legislation passed during the session, but the members did respond to prevailing public opinion as it had been expressed through the governor and appointed a constitutional commission to propose changes in the basic law.

The constitutional commission reported the following year and included among its principal proposals one to interdict all special and private legislation. Governor Parker referred to this suggestion in 1875 in his last annual message in the following words:

> Among the most important of the proposed amendments is the one which forbids special legislation, and provides for general laws on the various subjects therein specified. Should this be adopted, the general railroad law, which was passed with such unanimity two years ago, will be secured, and hereafter there can be no monopoly of routes of travel in any part of the State . . . Neither can corporate powers be granted except by general legislation, and the Legislature would hereafter be relieved from the mass of business which now engrosses attention, the sessions would be shortened and the expenses of government diminished.[29]

[27] *Ibid.*, 1873, Message of the Governor, pp. 30–31. Parker pointed out that the public laws passed in 1872 were contained in about 100 pages of the published session laws, while the private and special acts occupied over 1250 pages of the same volume.

[28] *Ibid.*, pp. 31–32 [29] *Ibid.*, 1875, Annual Message of Governor Parker, p. 20.

In his inaugural address of the same year, Governor Joseph Bedle took an equally strong position in favor of the adoption of the commission's report:

Another evil is special legislation. This we have been slow to correct. In England the tendency has been against it for years. Attention has been called to it by several of the governors since the new constitution, and yet the statute books year after year show an increase of special favors. In these a vast amount of public time and expense is wasted, and thereby the sessions of the Legislature prolonged. Besides, such a policy does not give sufficient encouragement to capital and concentrated labor. Corporate privileges in many matters of legitimate trade and enterprise should be open alike to all, and readily obtainable on compliance with general laws whenever the demands of business require it. The Free Railroad Act of 1873 is eminently just and wise, and is a most important advance towards a thorough system of general laws. Competition should be encouraged, and reasonable corporate facilities readily acquired.

Exclusive or perpetual privileges should be most scrupulously avoided, for it is incompatible with the dignity and interest of a free people to create odious monopolies, or hamper its sovereign power.[30]

The legislature agreed in 1875 to submit to the people the proposed amendment requiring general laws on a number of specified subjects including the chartering of corporations.[31] At the same session, however, private acts of incorporation were quite generously passed. Bedle, in an effort to bring manufacturing companies under the existing general law, vetoed the first special manufacturing company charter sent to him for approval. In his veto message he expressed his objections to special charters of this type:

Its provisions are not peculiar, nor objectionable, in themselves, but it belongs to a class of special legislation by which corporate privileges in an ordinary business are conferred, and which privileges in my judgment should be obtained only through general laws. We have now an act under which a corporation may be organized for the

[30] *Ibid.*, 1875, Inaugural Address of Governor Bedle, p. 13.

[31] The vote was unanimous in the assembly. *Votes and Proceedings of the General Assembly*, 1875, p. 362. In the senate, three votes were cast against the proposed action. *Journal of the Senate*, 1875, p. 74.

purpose of carrying on any lawful business whatever, except banking. If some of its clauses may be regarded as too exacting, a change could readily be made, so as to make it conform to the usual scope of such bills as this. In common business matters corporate powers should be procured with discrimination and under general laws.[32]

In messages setting forth the same views, Bedle vetoed four more manufacturing company charters.[33] Although the governor's veto action was unanimously sustained in each case, the legislators persisted in passing other special charters. The considerable number of special charters passed later in the session went unnoticed or unchallenged by the governor. In the summer of 1875, however, the people of New Jersey approved the constitutional amendment prohibiting special acts of incorporation and the long struggle between the two systems of incorporation came to an end.

Altogether the period 1858 to 1875 was the heyday of special chartering in New Jersey. This situation arose in spite of the availability of general incorporation laws and in spite of the fact that the final decade of the period was marked by a revived public and legislative interest in the potentialities of incorporation by procedure. The renewed interest had, it is true, resulted in the passage of six general incorporation laws between 1865 and 1875, but except for the railroad and gaslight company acts, passed at the end of the period, these laws were of limited scope and minor importance.

The most significant fact about these years is that the legislature did not manifest the slightest disposition to cease chartering by special act. That special charters were the order of the day can be readily seen from a brief summary of the experience between 1858 and 1875, inclusive. The special charters for those years totaled 1455 while only 361 corporations filed certificates under general laws. A breakdown of these figures reveals that 398 manufacturing and mining company charters were granted by special act and only 156 by virtue of the gen-

[32] *Votes and Proceedings of the General Assembly,* 1875, p. 256.

[33] *Ibid.,* 1875, pp. 442, 938; *Journal of the Senate,* 1875, pp. 670–71. The governor also refused to sign two special charters for lodges. *Votes and Proceedings of the General Assembly,* 1875, pp. 267, 458.

eral law of 1849. Taking the years individually, special charters for manufacturing and mining purposes greatly outnumbered the companies filing under the general law except in 1858 when they were equal and in 1875 when the constitutional amendments prohibited further special charters. The general banking act was used from time to time, but banks receiving special charters outnumbered those filing under the general law. Furthermore, general-law banks appear to have operated for only brief periods. The report of the state treasurer in 1862 recorded only eight general-law banks in operation while forty-three were doing business under special charters,[34] and the 1867 report of the state comptroller indicated that all the general-law banks were being wound up.[35] Only two insurance companies filed certificates under the general insurance act as compared with the 128 that were granted special charters. Ninety-nine land development companies filed certificates under general laws with 145 receiving special charters, and many of the general-law companies were small homestead associations of minor importance and coöperative in nature. The railroad act of 1873 was successful in that no special charters for steam railroads were granted in 1874 or 1875.[36] The remaining general laws were very little used.

Thus special charter legislation came in for attack. It has already been pointed out that the principal complaint made against private acts during the eighteen sixties and seventies was the manner in which they crowded the sessions of the legislature. An examination of the statute books leaves no doubt that this particular charge was justified. Between 1858 and 1875, the legislature of New Jersey approved 1191 amending acts and joint resolutions dealing with particular corporations in addition to the 1455 special charters passed during those same years. The greater part of the legislation dealing with specially chartered corporations came in the years immediately following the Civil War, and the burden of it increased as the

[34] *Legislative Documents,* 1862, Annual Statements of the Several Banks in the State of New Jersey, p. 3.

[35] *Ibid.,* 1867, p. 160.

[36] The only special railroad charters passed during those years were three for horse roads.

years went on.[37] For example, the legislature of 1868 alone passed 143 charters and 102 charter amendments. Remembering that legislation relating to corporations was only one form of special legislation, it is not surprising that a movement for reform was inaugurated. When laws were enacted in such volume during a two or three month legislative session, they could not but be lightly considered. More serious than incompletely weighed special legislation, however, was the poorly conceived and ill-considered public legislation that necessarily resulted when the time and attention of the lawmakers was so largely monopolized by a flood of private bills.

The expense to the state of private acts also became an increasingly important problem. Since special charters and supplements were not only passed but also published before it was known whether the required assessments would be paid, the state went entirely uncompensated for a part of the special legislation dealing with corporations. In 1867, the comptroller of the treasury reported on the considerable outlay of money occasioned by the increased private legislation and declared in favor of general incorporation laws as a means to reduce the expenses of government.[38] Again in 1873, the comptroller related the problem of increasing state expenditures directly to the swelling stream of private legislation.[39]

[37] Indicative of the trend was the determination of the senate in 1870 to have two standing committees in addition to the regular committee on corporations. One of these was to consider bills concerning railroad, canal, and turnpike corporations, the other those dealing with banks and insurance companies. *Journal of the Senate,* 1870, p. 17.

[38] "If the state 'is governed too much,' as the world is said to be, then this is one of the appliances by which the thing is done, the unnecessary multiplication of the laws. Why should any insurance company, or manufacturing company, or banking company ask of the legislature a special charter, when there are general laws under which they might organize? Simply because the special charter is the cheaper and more expeditious, and perhaps the safer expedient.

"If they make this choice they should pay for it. It is submitted, that at present rates, these fees do not reimburse the state for the expenses which are annually paid out of the public fund in this regard, and that the legislature cannot go amiss, if they enact a law raising the rates of assessment from thirty to fifty per cent." *Legislative Documents,* 1867, p. 133.

[39] "The annual expense of the Legislature is a greater tax upon the treasury than it should be. Theoretically, the annual session is held for the purpose of legislating for the people; but a very large proportion of the business done at each session is the consideration of bills of a private nature, which are to prove

Still other objections made to special legislation during the period were the lobbying, the logrolling, and the bribery that were alleged to accompany it. The charge of bribery in the legislature caused, of course, the most serious concern. The fear that corporations sometimes paid legislators for special favors was strong enough to cause the enactment of new legislation against bribery. It will be recalled that after 1855 corporation directors and officers and legislators involved in bribery were deemed guilty of high misdemeanor.[40] Apparently it was felt that the law was not sufficiently strict and that punishment should be meted out to the corporation itself in cases of proven bribery. In 1871, when a bill to accomplish this was under consideration, Governor Randolph was sufficiently impressed with the need for such a law to send a special message to the legislature urging its adoption. The governor declared that the "greatest danger to executive or legislative independence lies in the rapidly growing power of Corporations." Referring to the "notorious" fact that most legislation was guided by the powerful influence of corporations, he warned: "Whatever means, then, the state has left to protect itself from the danger of such a condition of affairs, cannot be too promptly or effectually used." [41] The bill which was made law related both to corporations influencing citizens in their voting and to those bribing members of the legislature. It provided that if any officers or agents of a corporation used the corporate money or property or any other money or property for the purpose of bribery, the corporation's charter would be forfeited, providing such use of the money was allowed by the corporation or the money repaid by the corporation. Furthermore, any company officer consenting to such an appropriation of money would be guilty of misdemeanor and on conviction be deprived of the

a source of profit to individuals or corporations, who should therefore bear a greater proportion of the expense than is now imposed upon them. An increased assessment upon private acts would have the effect either to increase the revenue from this source, or diminish the number of such acts, and thus lighten the expenses of the Legislative session." *Legislative Documents*, 1873, Annual Report of the Comptroller of the Treasury, p. 18.

[40] Cf. *supra*, pp. 139–140. In 1869, in an apparent attempt to aid in the detection of instances of bribery, either party was allowed to escape the penalty upon giving evidence. *N. J. Laws*, 1869, Ch. 518, p. 1237.

[41] *Votes and Proceedings of the General Assembly*, 1871, pp. 1166–1169.

right of suffrage.[42] Just before the state elections of 1872, Governor Parker issued a proclamation as a reminder of the stringent laws against bribery by corporations.[43]

The matter of special and unequal privileges resulting from special chartering also came in for critical attention, but to a less degree than it had in the eighteen forties and early fifties. Special tax exemptions seem to have been the principal evil to which objection was raised during the later years. Although several suggestions were made for reforming the procedure followed in enacting special charters to avoid unwise grants of special privilege, nothing substantial was accomplished. Reverting to the old idea of purifying the special charter system by requiring publicity in connection with special grants, a bill was introduced without success that would have forced every applicant for a charter not only to advertise his intention to apply but also to publish the complete act desired.[44] Some sporadic attempts were made to standardize the terms of special charters, as in 1869 when a special committee of the assembly was appointed "to examine and perfect all Insurance Bills that are now in or may hereafter come in this House during this session, and so amend them as to place them on an equal footing . . ." [45] Occasionally the legislature chartered a company with the same, or partly the same, privileges as an existing corporation of a similar type by merely making reference to that corporation's charter. In this way the terms of a land improvement company charter of 1866 were made to apply to two other land companies.[46] Particular sections of special charters were a few times made to conform to general-law rules, as

[42] *N. J. Laws*, 1871, Ch. 399, p. 70. This law also contained a clause exempting from the penalty the party to an attempt at bribery first complaining in writing to a magistrate.

[43] *N. J. Laws*, 1873, pp. 841–42. The governor enjoined all officers of the law to use vigilance in enforcing the bribery statutes and "good" citizens to aid in enforcement, promising executive assistance to protect the purity of the elective franchise.

[44] *Newark Daily Advertiser*, March 14, 1867. The paper thought the proposal "cruel" since many could not afford such a long advertisement. "It is the indefeasible right of every pea-nut stand in New Jersey to have a charter, with the broad seal stamped upon it."

[45] *Votes and Proceedings of the General Assembly*, 1869, p. 581.

[46] *N. J. Laws*, 1867, Ch. 462, p. 984; 1868, Ch. 543, p. 1171.

in two cases where specially chartered corporations were given power to increase their capital stock if they proceeded according to the rules of the 1849 manufacturing law.[47] None of these measures was, however, employed frequently enough to have significant results. New Jersey consistently failed to enact any comprehensive general regulating acts, and the result was a great disparity among the specially chartered corporations as to their rights and privileges.

In spite of the justifiable criticism of the system of special chartering, no significant attempt was made in the legislature to solve the problem by rendering the existing general laws more palatable to the business community. The manufacturing law of 1849 was amended in 1865 to permit companies formed under it to do a part of their business out of the state provided a majority of the persons "associated" were citizens of New Jersey.[48] The same general law was improved in 1870 by the addition of rules for procedure in cases of voluntary dissolution of corporations organized under it.[49] In 1872, land and water transportation companies under the act were allowed to mortgage their land and issue bonds.[50] One onerous requirement of the law demanding annual publication of statements of the capital stock paid in, the assets deemed "good," and the debts was repealed, but not until 1875 in anticipation of the law revision of that year.[51] Aside from these and some other very minor changes,[52] the 1849 law remained as unattractive as ever to prospective incorporators.[53] Nor was the much discussed

[47] *N. J. Laws,* 1868, Ch. 296, p. 678, Ch. 486, p. 1094.

[48] *N. J. Laws,* 1865, Ch. 201, p. 354. The proviso may have destroyed most of the usefulness of the amendment, for the capital for many New Jersey concerns was supplied largely by New York and Philadelphia investors.

[49] *N. J. Laws,* 1870, Ch. 29, p. 8.

[50] *N. J. Laws,* 1872, Ch. 531, p. 77.

[51] *N. J. Laws,* 1875, Ch. 101, p. 24.

[52] The law was relaxed to allow dairy companies to begin business with a smaller capital stock than that required for other companies. *N. J. Laws,* 1874, Ch. 314, p. 59; 1875, Ch. 173, p. 35.

[53] In 1870, there was a bill before the assembly for a new general incorporation law to replace the 1849 law and confer on general-law corporations "more liberal powers than are now enjoyed." Among the proposed new powers were the right to mortgage the corporate property and borrow by bond any money

general banking law modified in the years after 1858 except for unimportant amendments enlarging the list of securities that could be deposited as backing for the circulating notes.[54] None of the other general laws was amended.

Thus during the eighteen sixties and early seventies, while the subject of general incorporation laws received wide attention in New Jersey, the state's general laws became virtually dead letters so far as their actual employment was concerned. Their status was even worse than the statistics recording the number of companies organized under them indicate. It has already been stated that only 361 corporations were organized under general laws between 1858 and 1875, inclusive. It is probable that many companies included in that figure were not organized as general-law corporations because the corporators preferred to organize in this fashion for the permanent conduct of their business. Nor were many organized under the general laws because they had been refused special charters and had no alternative. It is quite clear that the general laws became for many a mere temporary convenience. If a group wished to form a corporation, they, of course, could obtain a special charter only when the legislature was in session and only if they decided to apply a sufficient time in advance of the session to give the required public notice. Since a wait of many months might be entailed before the next meeting of the legislature, it is probable that the best plan in many cases was to effect a temporary corporate organization under a general law. It is also probable that in the tremendous volume of legislation in any particular year some charter bills may have been neglected. Rather than lose a full year's time until the application or bill could be

required if three-fourths of the stockholders consented, the right to issue preferred stock under certain restrictions and to purchase necessary real and personal property and "issue stock to the amount of the value thereof in payment therefor . . ." *Newark Daily Advertiser,* February 17, 1870. This bill never became law.

[54] E.g., *N. J. Laws,* 1863, Ch. 249, p. 467; 1864, Ch. 59, p. 102, Ch. 236, p. 357. The tax laws, however, were changed in 1859 to reduce the annual tax on general-law banks to one-quarter of one per cent of the paid-in capital while specially chartered banks continued to pay one-half of one per cent. This change was made in recognition of the greater profit opportunities of specially chartered banks. *Ibid.,* 1859, Ch. 185, p. 535.

reintroduced as unfinished business, the applicants could proceed under a general law and apply later for conversion into a specially chartered company. Also if a charter was refused in one year, the applicants expecting a more favorable reception during the succeeding session could in the meantime make use of the general laws. Or again, the general laws may have been used by some as a testing ground. There was doubtless uncertainty in many cases as to the success a projected corporation would have in securing support from the investing public; rather than sacrifice unnecessarily the time and money to obtain a special charter, promoters may have sometimes preferred to test the public reception accorded their project by the simple and cheap procedure of filing under a general law. If the enterprise promised success, a special charter could subsequently be obtained.

There is much evidence in the New Jersey statute books to indicate that some such considerations as these motivated many persons who organized corporations under general laws. The preambles of twenty-six special acts of incorporation passed after 1857 stated that the new charters were for corporations then existing under general laws. Six of these were bank charters,[55] ten were mining or manufacturing company charters,[56] and the remaining ten were charters for a variety of businesses. If six examples of conversion from general-law to specially chartered corporations occurring in 1867 are examined, it is found that the organization under general laws had been merely a temporary expedient in each instance.[57] All of the companies had filed certificates in the year 1866 on dates after the close of the legislative session of that year. In other words, organization was begun under the general laws with the intention of securing a special act at the earliest opportunity. The other special acts converting companies from a general-law status indicate similar temporary sojourns under the general laws. It

[55] E.g., *N. J. Laws,* 1859, Ch. 13, p. 23, Ch. 73, p. 183; 1862, Ch. 51, p. 70, Ch. 61, p. 103.

[56] E.g., *N. J. Laws,* 1866, Ch. 32, p. 67; 1872, Ch. 280, p. 633.

[57] *N. J. Laws,* 1867, Ch. 46, p. 75, Ch. 86, p. 139, Ch. 115, p. 202, Ch. 170, p. 344, Ch. 234, p. 488, Ch. 465, p. 987. These included three manufacturing concerns, two marl companies, and one ice company.

is also of significance that inspection of the filing dates of companies organized under general laws between 1858 and 1875 shows the great majority to have fallen in the long intervals between legislative sessions. It is thus clear that after 1857 the New Jersey general incorporation laws, except possibly those for the formation of certain small land associations, fell into a desuetude that was quite complete as far as providing an incorporating procedure for the permanent organization of business firms was concerned.[58]

It is interesting and important to search for the reasons that led persons forming business corporations to manifest such a decided preference for special charters. The preambles of the acts designed to convert companies organized under general laws into specially chartered corporations give but a slight clue. Some made vague references to the desirability of having the "advantages of an act of incorporation." [59] Others merely expressed a request for a special charter the better to carry out the objects of the corporation.[60] In a few preambles more frankness was apparent. A manufacturing company wishing to carry on a part of its business in other states and in foreign countries thought the New Jersey general law was causing "unnecessary inconvenience and expense." [61] A company organized in October 1867 under the 1849 manufacturing law to operate a railroad or other transportation agency and a telegraph line across Nicaragua applied for a special charter the following year on the indisputable ground that the general law "is not of sufficient scope, nor admits of sufficient freedom of corporate

[58] It is probable that some special charters other than the twenty-six referred to above were designed to benefit corporations initially organized under general laws. If the acts did not contain preambles to that effect, such cases would be difficult or impossible to detect. Perhaps, too, a number of other groups organizing under general laws with the intention of obtaining special charters later, failed to raise the desired capital or for some other reason disbanded before they had a chance to apply to the legislature. When all factors are considered, it seems unlikely that many corporations filing under general laws after 1857 had long-continued existences as general-law corporations.

[59] *N. J. Laws,* 1866, Ch. 32, p. 67, Ch. 141, p. 305.

[60] *N. J. Laws,* 1867, Ch. 86, p. 139, Ch. 170, p. 344; 1870, Ch. 15, p. 116.

[61] *N. J. Laws,* 1867, Ch. 234, p. 488.

action" for the purpose.[62] A general-law manufacturing company was given a special charter accompanied by the statement that it was desirable that the company's powers and privileges be enlarged.[63]

In drawing together the reasons why business groups in New Jersey preferred special charters to the simpler and less expensive procedure of filing under general statutes, the more favorable terms that could be obtained through the former device stand out as the most impelling consideration. The analysis of the terms of New Jersey business charters contained in Part II of this study should make this point quite evident. To anticipate, a few important privileges sought in special charters can be enumerated here. More liberal borrowing privileges than the general laws allowed was one. By securing a special charter a company might escape the over-all debt limits established in a number of the important general laws as well as secure certain positive borrowing rights such as power to mortgage property and issue bonds that most general laws did not expressly permit. Another was the expectation of less strict rules on director and stockholder liability than were imposed by the important general laws. Still others were the right to issue stock in exchange for property other than money and special exemptions from taxation. The publicity requirements of the manufacturing act of 1849 were very unpopular and could be avoided by securing special acts of incorporation. These and other privileges were awarded with equanimity by the legislators in one special case after another, but the same men were distinctly timid about opening the door wide enough to allow similar favors to all who cared to enroll under general laws. The result was a complete failure to keep the general laws abreast of new fashions in corporation finance and to make the general laws increasingly less desirable to businessmen as the years went on.

A minor consideration predisposing business groups in favor of special charters may have been apprehension of future hostile

[62] *N. J. Laws,* 1868, Ch. 362, p. 816.
[63] *N. J. Laws,* 1874, Ch. 220, p. 1071.

legislatures. It may have been thought that alterations of general laws to restrict the rights and privileges of all corporations under them would be more likely than legislation aimed at restricting the rights of any one specially chartered company.

The prestige attaching to a charter given by special act of the legislature was important to business promoters. This was a factor worthy of consideration even in cases where the powers obtainable under general laws would have been sufficient for the objects of the corporation. Governor Dix of New York stated the case clearly in his message of 1874 to the legislature of that state. In pleading for observation of constitutional restrictions on special legislation, he declared that

> it is well known that charters are frequently sought and obtained by individuals desirous of being associated for private purposes, not because there is any difficulty in effecting their object under existing laws, but because a special act of the legislature is regarded as attaching to such associations a higher public estimation, even when conferring no additional privileges or powers.[64]

Although the writer found no reference in New Jersey literature to the prestige value of special charters, there is no reason to believe these observations were not equally applicable to the situation there. If promoters could, by obtaining special charters, make their enterprises seem especially important or appear to have the badge of legislative approval, their chances of success in appealing to the investing public and to prospective customers might be enhanced.

For a variety of reasons, therefore, the attitude of the business community was not calculated to discourage special chartering in New Jersey. On the whole, businessmen appeared to prefer the system of incorporation by special act, not only in New Jersey but, as has been observed by some recent writers, in other states as well.[65] Granting an ordinary charter for busi-

[64] State of New York, *Messages from the Governors,* VI, 640.

[65] A. M. Schlesinger, Jr., in *The Age of Jackson,* pp. 334–339, comments on the Democratic background of early general incorporation laws and on the opposition with which they were met by the business community. In writing of Pennsylvania's general incorporation legislation of 1849 and 1853, Louis

ness purposes had become a matter of mere legislative courtesy, so there was little danger that at least the ordinary privileges of incorporation could not be obtained by private act. At the same time, this system inherently possessed the advantage to charter applicants that they might get more generous terms from the legislature than rival groups already in the field had obtained. Conversely, the possibility was always open to existing corporate groups to prevent potential competitors from entering the field on as favorable terms as they themselves enjoyed. In speaking of the struggle of the railroad monopoly against the proposed special charter for a competing company, a New Jersey newspaper declared editorially: "We believe it is the habit of all corporations to resist the charter of competitors. They do not willingly divide their business . . ." [66] Since the observation was no doubt true, influential firms standing securely behind their own special charters had reason to oppose truly "liberal" general incorporation laws.

It thus became evident that a group of legislators constantly courting the favor of their constituents and coöperating willingly in order that the private bills of all members received favorable attention would do nothing to withhold the flood of private charters in the face of the great clamor for them unless such action was specifically required of them by the constitution. If the New Jersey observers were aware of the experiences of other states, it is not surprising that they became convinced in the early eighteen seventies that nothing short of a constitutional amendment absolutely prohibiting all special charters would cure the pernicious disease from which their legislature suffered.

In New England, for example, where the state constitutions did not prohibit special acts of incorporation, special charters had continued to be passed in large numbers all through the middle of the nineteenth century in spite of the availability of

---

Hartz observes: "There is ample evidence to indicate that industrial capitalists themselves preferred a policy of special legislative charter grants . . . At the same time capitalists and promoters sought repeatedly to extract from the legislature special charters with more lenient provisions." *Economic Policy and Democratic Thought: Pennsylvania, 1776–1860,* pp. 40–41.

[66] *Newark Daily Advertiser,* April 8, 1872.

a number of general incorporation laws. Between 1844 and 1862, 2551 special charters were granted while only 982 corporations were organized under general laws. In the years from 1863 to 1875, the number of general-law corporations increased greatly, totaling 2205 as compared with 2390 special charters, yet nearly all of the general-law corporations of those years can be attributed to Connecticut and Massachusetts with Connecticut the only state showing more general- than special-law companies.[67]

The experience of New Jersey's neighboring state of New York is an even better case in point. The 1846 constitution of that state had prohibited special charters for commercial banks, but in regard to other types of corporations the constitution left a small loophole for special charters by prohibiting special acts of incorporation except in cases where, in the judgment of the legislature, the objects of the corporation could not be obtained under general laws.[68] As a result of this ban on special charters the New York legislature between 1847 and 1875 passed thirty general incorporation laws for various types of business organizations, but it became evident soon after 1847 that the "judgment" of the legislature could be easily warped to the opinion that incorporation by general law was impossible in a great many cases. The legislature took nearly thirty years to provide general laws for certain important groups of corporations. Savings banks, for example, continued to be created by special laws for many years, the first general savings bank law passing the New York legislature in 1875,[69] and that was after the constitution had been amended in 1874 to require that all savings bank charters be made uniform.[70] Even more remarkable was the fact that the New York legislators continued to pass special acts of incorporation for types of corporations already provided for by general laws. Governor Hamilton Fish sent to the New York senate in 1850 three veto messages that

[67] W. C. Kessler, "Incorporation in New England: A Statistical Study, 1800–1875," *Journal of Economic History*, VIII (May 1948), p. 46.

[68] B. P. Poore, *The Federal and State Constitutions* (2nd ed., 1878), II, 1363.

[69] *N. Y. Laws*, 1875, Ch. 371, p. 404. [70] Poore, II, 1377.

were occasioned by the legislature's action in extending the existence of a specially chartered bridge company and in incorporating another bridge company and a dock company by special act.[71] In each case the governor pointed out the existence of general laws under which the companies might file. During the following twenty-five years, the legislature continued to pass special charters even when general laws were available to cover the cases. Some of the governors made free use of the veto power in attempting to stem the tide. By 1872, however, the pressure for private acts of incorporation was still so strong that the governor declared in his annual message: "There should be more specific constitutional restraints upon legislative power to grant special charters for private corporations . . ." [72] If the New York legislature, with constitutional authority in that state leaning strongly against special charters, was not able to resist the temptation to incorporate by private act, there was no reason to expect that the New Jersey lawmakers, entirely unrestrained by their constitution, would of their own free will insist on a system of general-law incorporation.

There were, in fact, two factors peculiar to New Jersey that help to explain why that state was destined to be more tardy than a number of others in abandoning incorporation by special act. The first of these considerations had an effect the extent of which cannot be calculated. It was the existence of the railroad monopoly in the state. Mainly through control of the Democratic party, the monopoly group was able to defeat a series of attempts to secure a general railroad law which would have threatened its entrenched position as sole carrier of the New York–Philadelphia traffic. Since the railroad situation was the most flagrant example of special privilege in the state, a general railroad law would necessarily have to be the keystone

[71] State of New York, *Messages from the Governors,* IV, 513–516, 521–524, 525–26. The vetoes were sustained in all three cases. In the same year, the governor sent to the assembly vetoes of special charters for two benevolent societies and one academy that he thought should file under existing general laws.

[72] *Ibid.,* VI, 402.

of any comprehensive plan of reform. After the lease of the Camden and Amboy and its associated companies to the Pennsylvania Railroad in 1871, public sentiment in New Jersey turned strongly against perpetuation of a transportation monopoly in the hands of a "foreign" corporation. In order to defeat a special charter for a competing company, the Pennsylvania group compromised by supporting a general railroad law the terms to which seemed to offer less of a threat to their welfare.[73] Passage of the general railroad law in 1873 brought to an end the last organized opposition to a program looking toward complete abandonment of the system of special chartering.[74]

The second factor calculated to prolong the use of special acts of incorporation by New Jersey concerned the state's location between the great financial and commercial centers of New York and Philadelphia. There are indications that from very early years it had been the conscious policy of New Jersey legislators to attract capital into their relatively poor state by grants of special favor. In individual incorporation acts passed for the benefit of out-of-state petitioners, New Jersey was willing to give terms more attractive to businessmen than any that would have been approved in general laws in the middle years of the nineteenth century. Since the New York constitution of 1846 made it difficult for promoters to obtain special acts of incorporation in that state, New Jersey maintained a competitive advantage in the field of chartering by retaining its system of special acts of incorporation. As early as 1847, the

[73] Accounts of the political skirmishes and pressure politics connected with New Jersey's general railroad law have been given by W. E. Sackett, *Modern Battles of Trenton*, pp. 19–65 *passim;* Lincoln Steffins, "New Jersey: A Traitor State," *McClure's Magazine*, XXIV (April 1905), pp. 651–655; and H. W. Stoke, "Economic Influences Upon the Corporation Laws of New Jersey," *Journal of Political Economy*, XXXVIII (October 1930), pp. 562–566.

[74] The *Newark Daily Advertiser* of January 13, 1874, could state in an editorial on the opening of the next legislature: "The accusation made against us of monopoly has been refuted by a general law [for railroads] more generous and free than that of any other State. The same policy might well be extended to other forms of corporate enterprise, so that special acts shall be the exception rather than the rule."

opportunity thus offered to outbid New York in the matter of business charters had been recognized. In debating a special insurance company charter in that year, several New Jersey assemblymen remarked on the number of "improvements" financed by New York capitalists, declaring that these men had a feeling of "uncertainty" under their new constitution and that it was a matter of New Jersey's self-interest to induce capitalists in from other places.[75] When during the same session of the legislature a bill for the relief of the New Jersey Iron Company was introduced, an assemblyman stated that the "members of the Company were not Jerseymen, but it was our policy to offer every facility to persons out of our state to come and work our mines for our benefit,"[76] and a few days later discussion of a manufacturing company charter sought by out-of-state persons elicited the remark in the assembly that it was "our true policy to encourage such institutions."[77] In 1864, the assembly was debating another manufacturing company charter desired by capitalists resident outside of New Jersey. Objection was made to the charter on the ground that it did not contain the safeguards of the general manufacturing law. Defenders of the bill quickly pointed out the large amount of New York and Pennsylvania capital that had been "attracted" to New Jersey "by liberal charters," and they thought "it was scarcely good policy to discourage such investments."[78] Any number of similar expressions could be cited, but excerpts from two messages of Governor Randolph are sufficient additional evidence to indicate the attitude of Jerseymen on this subject. Randolph in 1869 reminded the legislators:

> The community that invites labor and capital within its borders by liberal legislation, adds to its own stability and enriches its citizens . . .

[75] *Newark Daily Advertiser,* February 3, 1847.

[76] *Ibid.,* January 29, 1847.

[77] *Ibid.,* February 11, 1847. It was maintained that the company had been attracted to East Newark because of "the low rate of taxes, its being conspicuous, and on the road to Philadelphia and New York; land was held at reasonable prices there, and it was upon a navigable stream."

[78] *Ibid.,* February 3, 1864.

I feel assured you will fully appreciate the propriety of continuing that policy which has heretofore induced manufacturing enterprise and capital to seek our protection.[79]

The same governor in 1870 advocated higher taxes on New Jersey corporations, but at the same time he made it clear that if new rates were established they should be lower than those imposed in neighboring states because:

We possess peculiar advantages in every respect for corporate enterprise, and it is the right, as it is the duty of the State, to avail itself reasonably of its advantages.[80]

The corporation policy of New Jersey did not, of course, go unnoticed in other states. Although almost none of its recommendations were adopted, the 1867 constitutional convention of New York is interesting to the student of corporations because the subject of incorporated business was thoroughly aired in the sessions. During discussions of the undesirable economic, social, and political effects of large corporations, New Jersey was frequently referred to as nothing more than a "tool and machine" of corporations, railroad corporations in particular. One speaker, however, defended New Jersey's policy as having achieved results for the state:

And, first and foremost, that much abused and often referred to State of New Jersey has been brought here to view; and we have been shown that State ridden and deprived of social and religious liberty by corporations of her own creation. New Jersey is used to this kind of treatment; often in derision has she been called the State of Camden and Amboy, and yet her people — her good, solid citizens — care little, very little, for this. One of the smallest States of the Union, with not more than two-thirds of her area susceptible of being devoted to agriculture, she has placed herself, by the aid of her location and corporations, as a power in the Union. Strip her of what her corporations have made her, the wealth and position she has obtained through them, and where would New Jersey be today? [81]

[79] *Legislative Documents*, 1869, pp. 185–86.

[80] *Ibid.*, 1870, p. 13.

[81] E. F. Underhill, reporter, *Proceedings and Debates of the Constitutional Convention of the State of New York, Held in 1867 and 1868*, II, 1075.

In 1873, the governor of New York expressed concern over the liberal policies of New Jersey and Pennsylvania, primarily their tax policies, aimed at attracting labor and capital into those states. Commenting particularly on the rapid growth of New Jersey's population, the governor declared:

> The natural advantages of New York, especially for commerce, far exceed those of other States; but they are not great enough to enable us to contend successfully with the rivalry of neighbors, quite as enterprising as ourselves, unless labor and capital are encouraged by laws as liberal as theirs.[82]

It is impossible to make any accurate statement as to the number of enterprises attracted to New Jersey by the gift of more generous charters than could be obtained elsewhere, but there is abundant evidence that the number was not small. The corporators named in many special charters were obviously New York and Philadelphia operators, and many examples can be shown where special authority was given to hold stockholders and directors meetings in New York and Philadelphia — an indication that the capital was supplied from those centers.[83] In two charters it was clearly stated that the companies had been originally incorporated under the laws of New York State, and they were apparently transferring at least part of their activity to New Jersey.[84] During the eighteen sixties, simple special laws enabling certain "foreign" corporations to hold land and establish works in New Jersey became numerous, but in some cases the New Jersey legislators went further and included in the authorizations simple charters under which the out-of-state companies might organize as New Jersey corporations if they desired.[85]

The policy of encouraging industry to enter New Jersey by

[82] State of New York, *Messages from the Governors,* VI, 530.

[83] E.g., *N. J. Laws,* 1866, Ch. 243, p. 576; 1873, Ch. 455, p. 1360.

[84] *N. J. Laws,* 1860, Ch. 93, p. 226; 1863, Ch. 134, p. 252.

[85] E.g., *N. J. Laws,* 1865, Ch. 363, p. 689; 1866, Ch. 121, p. 277. The 1866 offer of a New Jersey charter was apparently accepted, for an amendment to it was later passed authorizing an increased capital stock. *Ibid.,* 1872, Ch. 184, p. 439.

granting liberal special charters caused little adverse comment from citizens of the state. When the policy went further, however, and embraced special charters for out-of-state promoters whose projects were not to be put into operation in New Jersey, a considerable clamor was heard. An early example was the criticism arising when in the early eighteen sixties a group of New York men applied to New Jersey for a charter for The Central American Transit Company. The sponsor of the bill in the assembly remarked that the men wished to obtain their charter in New Jersey because "they feel more confidence in the legislation and legal decisions of this State, and because we had more than once granted charters to companies out of the State." In the senate, however, it was declared that the true reason for applying in New Jersey was that a New York charter would have cost the promoters $50,000.[86] Although the company was to be chartered in New Jersey, it was under no obligation to transact any business there except, as expressed by a supporter of the bill, "the guarantee of one of the corporators — a gentleman whose word no one can doubt, that he would use all his influence to fix the place of business in Jersey City." [87] While the debate on the bill was in progress, the *Newark Daily Advertiser* ran a leading editorial entitled "Legislating for other States." Brief excerpts from the long discourse will illustrate the editor's attitude toward the formation of such companies by New Jersey:

> It is certainly derogatory to the character of our legislators to have an impression exist abroad that it requires but little management, in connection with a judicious hospitality, to secure the passage of bills through our Legislature. That such an impression does exist is apparent from the attempt made by citizens and residents of other States, from time to time, to secure the passage of acts of incorporation, and other measures for private emolument, which their own States either utterly refuse to grant, or do so only after proper examination and criticism. Nor have such attempts been always unsuccessful . . . Other incorporations [besides a series of ephemeral banks] . . . —

[86] *Newark Daily Advertiser,* February 27, March 6, 1862.
[87] *Ibid.,* February 27, 1862.

some of them, perhaps, very respectable, valid and useful in their tendency — with no relations whatever to New Jersey, transacting no business within her limits, having no stockholders, no officers, not even an office in the State, and consequently having no right to be identified with it in any way, have at different times been created by our pliant legislators . . .

Is it to be supposed that such men as constitute the majority of our legislators, were considered better qualified to estimate the important bearings of such a magnificent scheme [as one for giving financial aid to railroads that sought incorporation here several years ago], than the legislators of New York, Pennsylvania, or Massachusetts? Or, was it not rather owing to a belief that they could be more easily cajoled in giving a legal existence to the incorporation than personages in like positions elsewhere? . . .

[At present there is in the legislature a charter for The Central American Transit Company.] The dignity and interests of the State should certainly call for such an identification with it, as to the management of the Company and the transaction of its business, as would unquestionably give the corporation a New Jersey character. Let its chief office be in New Jersey; let its vessels, if it is to have any, sail from our own ports; *let its property be taxed* as our own State institutions and corporations, and let its directors be residents among us.[88]

Not until the governor himself objected to the lack of identification of the company with New Jersey, was the bill modified to require the principal depot of the company to be located in Jersey City and elections of directors to be held in the same place.[89]

A series of case studies would be required to determine the extent to which New Jersey legislators accommodated out-of-state promoters of businesses located outside New Jersey, but a number of examples can be detected from a study of the charters themselves. It is probable, for instance, that some of the large number of mining and oil companies given liberal

[88] *Ibid.*, February 25, 1862.

[89] *N. J. Laws*, 1862, Ch. 187, p. 328. The revised bill received stronger support in the legislature than its predecessor had. *Newark Daily Advertiser*, March 28 and 29, 1862.

charters by New Jersey during and after 1865 with power to hold real estate in any state or territory were instigated by New York and Philadelphia interests.[90] In other cases it is entirely clear that New Jersey was used as a mere accommodation. The corporators of the Lower California Company, chartered in 1867, were such well-known New York financiers as August Belmont, Leonard Jerome, and William Fargo.[91] The company, with authorized stock of $15,000,000, was established as a mining company and as an agency to transport immigrants westward, its only identification with New Jersey being the obligation to maintain one "office" in the state. The Hispano-American Telegraph Company, holding a franchise from the government of Peru, had been organized under a New York general law. On the ground that the New York law was not of sufficient scope and did not admit enough freedom of corporate action for the objects intended, New Jersey obliged with a special charter in 1868.[92]

The desire to accommodate non-New Jersey projects was probably not so important a factor in continuing a system of special chartering as was the wish to offer favorable terms to projects that might be attracted into the state.[93] The state government did not benefit directly by way of increased revenues on account of such out-of-state enterprises except for the minor item of assessments on the special acts themselves. The possibility of increasing state revenues by new taxes on all corporations chartered by the state, however, figured in the thoughts

[90] The stipulation made in the case of the Ruby Gold and Silver Mining Company of Colorado that land could be held anywhere except in New Jersey and Pennsylvania raises the question of whether the New Jersey legislators were not wary of the effects of the creatures of their own creation. *N. J. Laws,* 1867, Ch. 360, p. 820.

[91] *Ibid.,* Ch. 471, p. 992.

[92] *N. J. Laws,* 1868, Ch. 562, p. 1203.

[93] On at least one occasion, however, a charter for a company only slightly identified with New Jersey contained a clause intended to stimulate New Jersey business. This was the case of the New Jersey Navigation Company with provision for special treatment in the matter of local tax assessments if the proceeds from increases in stocks and bonds were used to purchase iron ships built in New Jersey by residents of or by corporations chartered by the state. *N. J. Laws,* 1873, Ch. 425, p. 1341.

of the legislators after the Civil War. An abortive attempt in 1869 to institute a tax on the net income from all sources of corporations chartered by or doing business in New Jersey was in part a result of the new line of thought.[94] In a defense of the corporation income tax in 1870, the governor had the following to say about corporations with no connection with New Jersey other than their creation by the state legislature:

> A large number of corporations, seeking to avail themselves of our liberal grant, or desiring the confessed protection of our Courts, or purposing, perhaps, the evasion of imposts elsewhere, have their capital, labor and interests entirely beyond our limits. Surely they might justly be reminded of the power that created and protects them, without trespass upon their rights.[95]

Doubts as to the constitutionality of the income tax law and difficulties of administration were responsible for the repeal of the law in 1872,[96] and hopes of large financial benefits to the state from corporations chartered in New Jersey for out-of-state operation failed temporarily to materialize.

When consideration is given to the facts that the influential business community did not lend support to the general incorporation law movement in New Jersey, that special charters were so desirable to business organizations that great pressure for them was brought to bear on the legislature, and that New Jersey was confronted with two peculiar situations tending to defeat a system of general laws — political control by the railroad monopoly and location between two active commercial and financial centers —, the fate of the general law movement in the state between 1845 and 1875 is not surprising. Little could be done to eliminate special chartering of business corporations until public opinion in the state became sufficiently antagonistic to the system to force a constitutional change with

[94] *N. J. Laws*, 1869, Ch. 380, p. 1014.

[95] *Legislative Documents*, 1870, p. 13.

[96] *N. J. Laws*, 1872, Ch. 490, p. 65. The small amount of money that had been collected was returned.

a view to prohibiting special charters of incorporation altogether. This condition was fulfilled in the early eighteen seventies, and the result was that when the state constitution was amended in 1875 a clause was inserted in the basic law requiring incorporation to be effected only by general laws. The exact terms of this and of the other 1875 amendments concerning state policy with respect to the business corporation are discussed in the following chapter.

CHAPTER VI

Constitutional Provisions Regulating the Corporation Policy of the States, 1845–1875; and the New Jersey Constitutional Amendments of 1875

THE two preceding chapters have been primarily concerned with a description of New Jersey's experience with a dual system of chartering business corporations. It was this experience that led directly to public demand for the constitutional amendments of 1875. A complete understanding of the significance of the alterations in New Jersey's basic law requires more, however, than a knowledge of the internal affairs of that state. To a considerable degree, the constitutional changes approved by Jerseymen in 1875 were influenced by the trend of constitutional developments in other states after 1844, the year in which New Jersey's second constitution had been adopted. Not only must the influence of the actions of other states on public opinion in New Jersey be understood, but a full appraisal of the particular attitude of Jerseymen on the subject of business corporations must take into consideration constitutional provisions popular in many other jurisdictions that made, for one reason or another, no appeal in New Jersey.

Thus a considerable part of the present chapter will be devoted to an examination of the constitutional provisions adopted by other states between 1845 and 1875 insofar as the provisions reflected public policy with respect to business corporations. The remainder of the chapter will be concerned with the actual constitutional changes made in New Jersey in 1875 and with an appraisal of their significance and subsequent effect.

During and after the decade of the eighteen forties, there was a distinct tendency in various states to restrict the power of state legislators to treat the problem of incorporation for business purposes in any manner they might see fit. Owing principally to a great increase in the number of business corporations and the use of the corporate form of organization by an ever-increasing variety of business enterprises, constitutional restraints on the freedom of legislatures to incorporate business units became much more numerous in the years after 1844 than they had been previously.[1] Not only were the limitations more numerous, but they applied to a wider range of corporate enterprises.[2]

In discussing the constitutional provisions of the years from 1845 to 1875, it is convenient to divide the provisions affecting business corporations into three classes: first, regulations concerning the procedure by which incorporation was to be achieved; second, clauses governing the terms of the charters granted; and finally, restrictions on governmental aid to and interest in business corporations.

Although the principal feature of post-1844 constitutional provisions on the matter of the incorporating procedure was the trend toward the prohibition of special acts of incorporation, there were clauses put into a few state constitutions with a view to retaining at least a partial system of special chartering but making the system less objectionable in its operation. The first constitution of West Virginia, adopted during the Civil War, required that public notice be given in a manner to be prescribed by law of every intended application for an internal improvement or banking company charter, the only two types of special charters the constitution allowed.[3] The 1850 constitution of Michigan required notices of intended applications for charter amendments to be given previous publicity in a manner to be prescribed by the legislature, although the same constitution forbade the enactment of new special charters.[4]

The requirement of a two-thirds vote of the legislature for

[1] It must, of course, be remembered that the number of states was continually increasing. Eleven states joined the Union between 1844 and 1875, raising the total number at the later date to thirty-seven.

[2] For a discussion of the pre-1844 constitutional provisions see *supra*, pp. 86–92.

[3] B. P. Poore, *The Federal and State Constitutions* (2nd ed., 1878), II, 1990–91.

[4] *Ibid.*, I, 1009.

granting special charters, having been tried before 1844 in several states as a means of reforming the special chartering system, was virtually abandoned as the general-law movement progressed.[5] After 1844, Texas alone adopted a provision requiring a two-thirds vote for all special charters, including it in its first constitution adopted in 1845,[6] but omitting it when drawing up a new constitution in 1868. After 1844, the two-thirds rule was adopted in Georgia and Michigan as a special safeguard in the matter of bank charters. Georgia's constitutions of 1865 and 1868 required a two-thirds majority for all new bank charters or bank charter extensions.[7] Michigan, in 1862, amended its constitutional prohibition of special charters to allow the legislature to create a single bank with branches, but the charter was to be approved by a two-thirds vote in each house of the legislature.[8] In 1848, Illinois and Wisconsin took an even more cautious stand with respect to acts authorizing banks by requiring approval of such acts by the citizens at a general election.[9]

Since the constitutional provisions described above comprise the whole list of those adopted between 1845 and 1875 to improve the special chartering process, it becomes clear that constitutional conventions of the period under discussion in this chapter had turned their attention from measures calculated to regulate special chartering to proposals for the partial or complete abandonment of the system. Most of the constitutional clauses of the period that relate to incorporation procedure reflect this change in attitude.[10] The new movement

[5] Cf. *supra*, p. 108n. [6] Poore, II, 1778. [7] *Ibid.*, I, 406, 417.
[8] *Ibid.*, I, 1017. [9] *Ibid.*, I, 465; II, 2040.

[10] The notion of prohibiting special charters in favor of general laws by writing such a provision into the state constitution seems to have appeared rather suddenly upon the American political scene in the middle of the eighteen forties. A close approximation of the idea of prohibiting special charters can be found in a resolution offered by Henry Wheaton during the 1821 convention in New York. In this instance, however, the speaker probably had in mind compulsory adoption not of general incorporation but of general regulating laws: "*Resolved,* That the constitution ought to be so amended, as to provide, that it shall be the duty of the legislature to make uniform laws on the subject of private corporations, and that no religious, civil, or eleemosynary corporation, (except for the government of cities and towns,) shall hereafter be established, unless according to the general rules and regulations prescribed from

found its first concrete expression only one year after New Jersey revised its basic law in the 1845 constitution of Louisiana. That constitution prohibited all special acts of incorporation for business organizations and made it the duty of the legislature to provide general laws.[11] Once inaugurated, the movement to prohibit special acts of incorporation spread rapidly to other states. By 1875, eighteen states had followed the example of Louisiana and had made all special acts of incorporation unconstitutional.[12]

The constitutional convention of New York that completed its labors in 1846 also manifested a desire to eliminate the evils

---

time to time in such laws: *Provided,* that nothing herein contained shall be construed to impair the obligations of the charters already granted to the several corporations in this state." N. H. Carter, W. L. Stone and M. T. C. Gould, *Reports of the Proceedings and Debates of the Convention of 1821, Assembled for the Purpose of Amending the Constitution of the State of New York,* p. 294.

[11] Poore, I, 721. The complete article read: "Corporations shall not be created in this State by special laws, except for political or municipal purposes but the legislature shall provide, by general laws, for the organization of all other corporations, except corporations with banking or discounting privileges, the creation of which is prohibited." The corporation clause received but little discussion in the Louisiana convention, but it was made clear that a principal objection to the special charter was the time spent by the legislature in enacting this type of legislation. Cf. T. G. Gronert, "The Corporation in the State Constitutional Conventions of 1835–1860," *Proceedings of the Fifth Annual Convention of the Southwestern Political and Social Science Association,* p. 84.

[12] The complete list of states with the dates of their original adoption of absolute constitutional prohibitions of special acts of incorporation and with page references to Poore is as follows: Louisiana, 1845, I, 721; Iowa, 1846, I, 546; California, 1850, I, 199; Michigan, 1850, I, 1008; Ohio, 1851, II, 1477; Indiana, 1851, I, 524; Minnesota, 1858, II, 1039; Oregon, 1859, II, 1503; Kansas, 1861, I, 640; Nevada, 1864, II, 1258; Missouri, 1865, II, 1152; Nebraska, 1867, II, 1211; Alabama, 1867, I, 74; Arkansas, 1868, I, 140; Illinois, 1870, I, 488; Tennessee, 1870, II, 1708; Wisconsin, 1871, II, 2050; West Virginia, 1872, II, 2012; Pennsylvania, 1873, II, 1574.

The principle of prohibiting special acts had a stormy history in Louisiana, for it was abandoned when a new constitution was adopted in 1852, reinstated in 1864 (*ibid.,* I, 751), and omitted from the constitution of 1868. In Indiana, the legislature was allowed the privilege of chartering by special act one bank with branches. Pennsylvania, endeavoring to secure impartial operation of the general laws, added a prohibition against indirectly passing special laws by partially repealing a general law. It is interesting to note that in 1875 Alabama retreated from its position and allowed special acts for manufacturing and mining companies, for certain internal improvement companies, and in other cases where the legislature thought such laws were necessary. *Ibid.,* I, 94–95.

that flowed from a system of special chartering. This group, however, apparently in doubt that all possible objects of corporations could be covered by general laws, drew up a qualified form of constitutional provision. Commercial banks were to be created only under general laws; all other business corporations were to be created under general laws except "in cases where, in the judgment of the legislature, the objects of the corporation cannot be attained under general laws." Between 1846 and 1875, four additional states incorporated similarly qualified prohibitions into their constitutions.[13] Experience with such provisions proved that the "judgment" of the legislatures permitted the passage of a large number of special charters.[14] Two of the states that had tried the qualified prohibition had, by 1875, adopted absolute prohibitions of special charters.[15]

Three cases remain to be mentioned to complete the list of measures taken by the states in endeavoring by constitutional provisions to reduce the volume of special charters. Before West Virginia prohibited all special acts of incorporation in 1872, it had a constitutional provision dating from its first constitution prohibiting special charters for all companies "not having in view the issuing of bills to circulate as money or the construction of some work of internal improvement . . ."[16] Florida, where special acts for certain nonprofit corporations had been prohibited since the first constitution of the state,[17] did not extend the prohibition to acts of incorporation for business enterprises. When a new constitution was adopted in 1868, however, it was declared that the legislature "shall provide by general law for incorporating such municipal, educational,

[13] The states with the dates of original adoption of qualified constitutional prohibitions of special acts and with page references to Poore, are as follows: New York, 1846, II, 1363; Illinois, 1848, I, 465; Wisconsin, 1848, II, 2039; Maryland, 1851, I, 848; North Carolina, 1868, II, 1431.

[14] For the experience of New York cf. *supra,* pp. 172–173. Apparently there was difficulty in Maryland in forcing corporations to form under general laws. The constitution of 1867 made special charters void if enacted in cases where a general law was available and also directed the governor to appoint a commission to draw up additional general laws, to revise the existing general laws, and to submit their suggestions to the legislature for action. Poore, I, 900.

[15] Illinois in 1870, and Wisconsin in 1871. Cf. *supra,* p. 186n.

[16] Poore, II, 1990. [17] Cf. *supra,* p. 87.

agricultural, mechanical, mining and other useful companies or associations as may be deemed necessary," but it does not appear that special acts for profit-seeking enterprises were actually prohibited.[18] An amendment of 1873 to the Texas constitution made special legislation unconstitutional "in any case where a general law can be made applicable," but the amendment made no express mention of acts of incorporation.[19]

The trend away from special acts of incorporation thus resulted in the adoption of some type of constitutional mandate for the passage of general incorporation laws by twenty-four states before 1875. Of the states that in this period gave serious consideration to the adoption of constitutional provisions on the subject of general incorporation laws, Massachusetts was the only one ultimately to reject the idea.[20] The movement toward general laws is not, however, to be interpreted as marking the end of distrust and apprehension regarding corporate enterprises. The general-law movement in all states seems to have grown out of the widespread distrust of the monopolistic character of corporations arising soon after 1830 and out of a desire to make it impossible for certain groups to gain privileged positions denied to others.

An outline of other constitutional provisions concerning cor-

[18] Poore, I, 350.

[19] *Ibid.*, II, 1823. It was not until 1876 that special acts of incorporation were expressly prohibited by the Texas constitution. *Ibid.*, II, 1847.

[20] In 1853, a constitutional convention dominated by "radical" Democrats presented the citizens of the commonwealth with eight propositions to vote upon, among which was one prohibiting special charters "when the object of the incorporation is attainable by general laws." Convention debates show that supporters of the latter proposition desired to institute equality of opportunity, save the time of the legislature, and defeat the attempts of corporations under the existing general law to change to a special-law status to "dodge the wholesome provisions" of the general law. *Official Report of the Debates and Proceedings in the State Convention, Assembled May 4th, 1853, to Revise and Amend the Constitution of the Commonwealth of Massachusetts,* III, 50–75. All the propositions offered were defeated in the election. *Ibid.*, III, 756–768. T. G. Gronert, pp. 95–96, has remarked that an analysis of the vote demonstrates that support for the corporation proposition came largely from the rural areas while the financial and industrial sections, especially Boston, opposed it. It should be noted, however, that other and diverse propositions were turned down by a similarly distributed vote.

poration policy will make it clear that during the same period when special charters were being abandoned in favor of general incorporation laws a wide variety of constitutional clauses regulating the terms of charters granted by either special or general laws were adopted. Constitutional limitations on the power of legislatures to include in corporation charters any terms they saw fit are worth investigation as an illustration of the attempts made to circumscribe the powers and privileges of corporations at the same time that the general-law movement was progressing.[21]

A few state constitutions adopted between 1845 and 1875 actually withheld from legislators the power to create corporations for particular purposes. As in the pre-1845 period, it was the banking business that was generally discountenanced. In 1845, the constitutions adopted by Texas[22] and Louisiana[23] forbade the creation of corporations with banking privileges, and Arkansas amended its constitution in 1846 to prohibit banks.[24] The 1848 constitution of Wisconsin left it to the citizens to decide at a general election whether or not the legislature should be allowed to create banks.[25] Five states restricted freedom of legislative action by requiring the provisions of any bank law to have the approval of the voters before taking

[21] Although it is necessary in this study to confine the analysis of increasing restrictions on American business corporations in the period 1845 to 1875 to those dictated by constitutional provisions, a survey of the terms of general incorporation laws actually adopted by state legislatures during those years would demonstrate more conclusively that the period was marked by a desire not only to achieve equality of privilege as between corporations themselves but also as between incorporated and unincorporated enterprises. The numerous general laws examined by the writer contained provisions more onerous to promoters than those ordinarily included in special charters. This was clearly the situation in New Jersey. No complete study of the restrictions and safeguards included in the general incorporation laws adopted by the various states in the middle years of the nineteenth century is available, but a broad sample of these can be found in Justice Brandeis' dissenting opinion in the case of *Liggett* v. *Lee* (288 U.S., 517).

[22] Poore, II, 1778. The prohibition was dropped in 1868.

[23] *Ibid.*, I, 721. The rule was abandoned in 1852, reinstated in 1864 (*ibid.*, I, 751), and dropped again in 1868.

[24] *Ibid.*, I, 119. The clause was omitted in the constitution of 1864.

[25] *Ibid.*, II, 2040.

effect.[26] The constitution with which California entered the Union in 1850 did not allow banks with the right to issue paper money.[27] The constitutions of four other states subsequently prohibited the creation of banks with the privilege of note issue.[28] A unique clause appeared in the constitutions framed in Georgia in 1865 and 1868 withholding from the lawmakers the power to incorporate certain types of non-banking enterprises. The legislature was enjoined from granting charters of incorporation to private companies except for banking, insurance, railroad, canal, plank road, navigation, mining, express, lumbering, manufacturing, and telegraph purposes.[29]

Inasmuch as the matter of the limited liability of corporation stockholders held the center of attention during these years in discussions about desirable public policy with respect to business corporations, it is not surprising that many state constitutions included clauses designed to regulate stockholder liability. The only two constitutional provisions concerning stockholder liability adopted before 1844 had referred merely to the holders of bank stock,[30] and it was banking corporations that were affected by the majority of provisions adopted after 1844. Liability of bank stockholders and officers was unlimited under Michigan's 1850 constitution.[31] The provision was softened in 1860 by an amendment declaring those persons liable only "equally and ratably to the extent of their respective shares of stock . . ."[32] In 1857, Minnesota's constitution made bank stockholders liable "in an amount equal to double the amount of stock owned by them . . ."[33] Before 1875, seven states had

[26] Iowa in 1846, *ibid.*, I, 546; Wisconsin in 1848, *ibid.*, II, 2040; Michigan in 1850, *ibid.*, I, 1008; Ohio in 1851, *ibid.*, II, 1478; and Kansas in 1861, *ibid.*, I, 641.

[27] *Ibid.*, I, 199.

[28] Oregon in 1859, *ibid.*, II, 1503; Nevada in 1864, *ibid.*, II, 1258; Missouri in 1865, *ibid.*, II, 1152; and Mississippi in 1868, *ibid.*, II, 1093. It should also be noted that before 1875 ten states had adopted constitutional provisions requiring special security for any notes issued by state chartered banks. This generally took the form of securities deposited with state authorities. *E.g.*, Iowa in 1846, *ibid.*, I, 546; Michigan in 1850, *ibid.*, I, 1009.

[29] *Ibid.*, I, 406, 417.

[30] Cf. *supra*, p. 89.

[31] Poore, I, 1008–09.

[32] *Ibid.*, I, 1016.

[33] *Ibid.*, II, 1039. The individual liability was to continue for one year after a sale or transfer of the stock.

adopted constitutional provisions making bank stockholders, as a special class, subject to double liability for corporate debts.[34]

Although bank stockholders were the principal group to be affected by constitutional provisions for individual liability, some states saw fit to include in their constitutions a variety of clauses governing as well the liability of stockholders in non-banking corporations. California went further than any other state in the matter of stockholder liability by providing in its first constitution that "Each stockholder of a corporation or joint-stock association shall be individually and personally liable for his proportion of all its debts and liabilities." [35] Three state constitutions declared that "in all cases, each stockholder shall be liable, over and above the stock by him or her owned, and any amount unpaid thereon, to a further sum at least equal in amount to such stock." [36] Another made stockholders individually liable "to an additional amount equal to the stock owned by each stockholder . . ." [37] Two others stated that "Each stockholder in any corporation shall be liable to the amount of the stock held or owned by him." [38] Michigan's 1850 constitution awarded special security to one class of creditors by providing that "stockholders of all corporations and joint-stock associations shall be individually liable for all labor performed for such corporation or association." [39]

Concern with protecting the creditors of corporations was

[34] The states with dates of original adoption of double liability clauses and page references to Poore are as follows: Iowa, 1846, I, 546; New York, 1846, II, 1363–64; Illinois, 1848, I, 465; Indiana, 1851, I, 523; Maryland, 1851, I, 848; South Carolina, 1868, II, 1662; West Virginia, 1872, II, 2012.

[35] Poore, I, 199.

[36] Ohio in 1851, *ibid.*, II, 1477; Missouri in 1865, *ibid.*, II, 1152; and Arkansas in 1868, *ibid.*, I, 140. The above quotation is from the Ohio constitution; the language of the others varied only slightly. The Missouri provision was amended in 1870 to read that "in no case shall any stockholder be individually liable in any amount over or above the amount of the stock owned . . ." *Ibid.*, II, 1164. The 1874 constitution of Arkansas did not contain any liability clause.

[37] Kansas in 1861, *ibid.*, I, 640. Railroad corporations were exempt from the operation of the liability clause.

[38] Minnesota in 1857, *ibid.*, II, 1039; Alabama in 1867, *ibid.*, I, 74. The 1875 constitution of Alabama forbade individual liability for more than the unpaid stock. Poore, I, 95.

[39] *Ibid.*, I, 1009.

also responsible for constitutional provisions respecting overstatement of the corporate capital. In 1868, South Carolina's constitution provided that all general incorporation laws and special acts of incorporation must contain provisions for the prevention and punishment of fraudulent misrepresentations of the capital, property, and resources of corporations.[40] The 1870 constitution of Illinois enjoined railroad corporations from issuing stocks or bonds except for money, labor, or property actually received and applied to the purposes for which they were chartered, and it declared void all stock dividends and other "fictitious" increases of capital or indebtedness.[41] Pennsylvania adopted a somewhat similar rule in 1873 but extended its application to all corporations.[42] Arkansas followed the example of Pennsylvania in 1874.[43]

A large number of states attempted to restrain their legislatures from creating corporations over which the state government would have no future control. The 1845 constitution of Louisiana enjoined the legislature from creating corporations to endure more than twenty-five years and from granting any monopoly or exclusive privilege for longer than twenty years.[44] Michigan, in 1850, forbade the creation of corporations with a term of life of over thirty years except in the case of corporations for railroad, plank road, or canal purposes.[45] In 1851, Indiana joined New Jersey in prohibiting the granting of bank charters for a term of over twenty years.[46] The most popular means of retaining control over corporations, however, was by constitutional provision that all corporation charters be subject to amendment or repeal by the legislature. Although such provisions had seldom appeared before 1844,[47] nineteen states adopted them during the thirty-year period after 1844.[48]

There remain to be considered briefly a few other types of

[40] *Ibid.*, II, 1662. [41] *Ibid.*, I, 489.

[42] *Ibid.*, II, 1588. No mention was made of stock dividends in this case.

[43] *Ibid.*, I, 172. This particular type of clause seems to have been popular at the time, for in 1875 three other states included it in their constitutions, although in one of those cases its application was restricted to railroad corporations.

[44] *Ibid.*, I, 721. This prohibition was dropped in the constitution of 1852.

[45] *Ibid.*, I, 1009. [46] *Ibid.*, I, 523. [47] Cf. *supra*, pp. 90–91.

[48] The states, the dates of adoption of constitutional requirements that all corporation charters be subject to amendment or repeal by the legislatures, and

constitutional restrictions on the authority of the various legislatures to grant rights and privileges to business corporations. One of the most prized privileges sought by business corporations was special treatment in the matter of taxation. Iowa seems to have inaugurated the movement to end this particular abuse by constitutional prohibition. That state included in its 1846 constitution a clause requiring the property of corporations to be "subject to taxation, the same as that of individuals." [49] By the beginning of 1875, nine other states had somewhat similar provisions to outlaw special tax treatment for business corporations.[50]

Because of previous liberality in granting certain corporations the right to take land by condemnation proceedings, eleven states, following New Jersey's example of 1844, adopted constitutional provisions before 1875 requiring compensation to the owners to be paid or secured before property was taken.[51] Michigan and Pennsylvania imposed constitutional

page references to Poore are as follows: Texas, 1845, II, 1778; Iowa, 1846, I, 547; New York, 1846, II, 1363; Wisconsin, 1848, II, 2039; California, 1850, I, 199; Michigan, 1850, I, 1008–09; Maryland, 1851, I, 848; Ohio, 1851, II, 1477; Pennsylvania, 1857, II, 1569; Oregon, 1859, II, 1503; Kansas, 1861, I, 640; West Virginia, 1863, II, 1990; Nevada, 1864, II, 1258; Missouri, 1865, II, 1152; Alabama, 1867, I, 74; Arkansas, 1868, I, 140; North Carolina, 1868, II, 1431; South Carolina, 1868, II, 1662; Tennessee, 1870, II, 1708. Texas and Iowa required two-thirds votes for the alteration or repeal of charters, the former state stipulating that in cases of revocation or repeal "compensation for the franchise" be made. Michigan required a two-thirds vote for altering special acts in existence before the adoption of the 1850 constitution. Repeals and alterations in Pennsylvania were somewhat restricted by the requirement that they be done in such a manner that no "injustice" be done to the corporators. In Oregon the power was not to be used "so as to impair or destroy any vested corporate rights," and a similar restriction was adopted by Tennessee. The repeal power in West Virginia does not appear to have applied to banks or internal improvement corporations, the only two classes that could be incorporated by special act, nor does it seem to have applied to special charters in South Carolina.

[49] Poore, I, 546.

[50] Of these, the constitutional provision of Pennsylvania in 1873 is most interesting in the light of New Jersey experience. It stipulated that the power to tax corporations or corporate property was not to be surrendered by any contract or grant to which the state was a party. *Ibid.*, II, 1585.

[51] The majority provided expressly for the right of appeal to a jury in cases of disagreement over the valuation. Minnesota added the requirement that if a corporation was accorded the right to take land for public purposes, the corporation was obliged to carry the goods of all "on equal and reasonable terms." *Ibid.*, II, 1039.

limitations on the power of corporations to hold real estate. Michigan, in 1850, made it unconstitutional for any corporation to hold real estate acquired after that date for a period of more than ten years except property actually occupied by the corporation in the exercise of its franchises,[52] and Pennsylvania, in 1873, prohibited any corporation from holding real estate beyond that necessary for its legitimate business.[53]

In the early eighteen seventies, state constitutions reflected a general interest in securing representation on the boards of directors of corporations for minority stockholders. The constitution adopted by Illinois in 1870 required that in all elections for corporate directors each stockholder be allowed one vote, in person or by proxy, for each share owned for as many persons as there were directors to be elected. Or if the stockholder desired, he might cumulate his votes and give one candidate as many votes as the number of directors to be elected multiplied by the number of his shares, or distribute the votes among as many candidates as he wished. Elections of directors were not to be conducted in any other manner.[54] West Virginia adopted the same rule in 1872.[55] A less stringent provision was included in the 1873 constitution of Pennsylvania to permit all corporate stockholders to cast the whole number of votes to which they were entitled for one candidate or to distribute them.[56]

Discussion of the principal constitutional restrictions on the terms of corporation charters should not be concluded without referring to provisions adopted in the early eighteen seventies for the regulation of railroad charters. Shortly before 1875, six states adopted detailed constitutional provisions pertaining to railroad corporations. Some provisions were concerned with rate regulation, some with prohibiting consolidation of competing lines, and others with a wide variety of railroad manage-

[52] *Ibid.*, I, 1009. [53] *Ibid.*, II, 1588. [54] *Ibid.*, I, 488.

[55] *Ibid.*, II, 2012. Interest in cumulative voting continued, and in 1875 Missouri and Nebraska made constitutional stipulations similar to those of Illinois and West Virginia.

[56] *Ibid.*, II, 1588.

ment and operating practices.[57] Thus in the eighteen seventies railroad corporations replaced banking companies as the special target of constitutional restraints.

It is worthy of note that up to 1875 six of the thirty-seven states then in the Union had not seen fit to place any constitutional limitations on their legislatures as to the manner in which business corporation charters were to be granted or as to the terms to be allowed in the charters. Five of these states were in the New England group: namely, Massachusetts, Connecticut, New Hampshire, Vermont, and Maine; the sixth was Kentucky.

The third and final group of constitutional provisions concerning corporations is comprised of those clauses relating to the financial relationship between state governments and business corporations. Provisions of this type became popular as a direct result of the nearly disastrous experience after the panic of 1837 of many states that had undertaken to give financial assistance to internal improvement companies. Three types of provisions were adopted: those regulating the right of the state to hold corporation stock, those governing grants or pledges of state credit in aid of corporations, and, less directly, rules on the matter of state indebtedness.

Between 1845 and 1874, inclusive, clauses forbidding state ownership of stock in any corporation were written into the constitutions of sixteen states.[58] Two states adopted prohibi-

[57] For examples of detailed provisions pertaining to railroad corporations see the 1870 constitution of Illinois (*ibid.*, I, 488–89) and the 1873 constitution of Pennsylvania (*ibid.*, II, 1589–90).

[58] The states, the dates of adoption of constitutional prohibitions against state stockholding, and page references to Poore, are as follows: Louisiana, 1845, I, 721; Texas, 1845, II, 1778; Iowa, 1846, I, 546; Michigan, 1850, I, 1008; Indiana, 1851, I, 523–24; Ohio, 1851, II, 1473; Pennsylvania, 1857, II, 1569; Oregon, 1859, II, 1503; Nevada, 1864, II, 1258; Missouri, 1865, II, 1155; Mississippi, 1868, II, 1093; Georgia, 1868, I, 418; Tennessee, 1870, II, 1701; Virginia, 1870, II, 1970; West Virginia, 1872, II, 2011; Arkansas, 1874, I, 172.

The rule was relaxed in Louisiana in 1852 to permit the state to subscribe up to one-fifth of the capital of companies for internal improvements. *Ibid.*, I, 735. The constitution adopted in Louisiana in 1868 made no reference to state stockholding. The Texas provision was also dropped in that state's 1868 constitution. In Missouri an exception was made if the stock was taken to secure loans pre-

tions on state stockholding that applied only to bank stock.[59]

In the same period, constitutional limitations on the power of legislatures to pledge or loan the credit of the states to corporations became popular. Provisions of this type had previously been adopted by New Jersey and two other states,[60] but it was not until the full effects of the business depression after 1837 were felt that other states took similar steps. Between 1845 and 1874, inclusive, twenty states put provisions into their constitutions forbidding the practice of extending loans of state credit in aid of private corporations.[61]

Since constitutional limits on state debt had a connection with the ability of state legislators to exercise reserved rights to purchase certain works of internal improvement or to build competing state-owned and -operated projects as well as with their power to give financial aid to private corporations, those limitations deserve brief mention here. It has been shown that before 1845 three states, including New Jersey, had adopted constitutional clauses to limit state debt.[62] During the following twenty years, six states followed this example and adopted

---

viously made to certain railroads. The Tennessee provision prohibited the state from becoming the owner in whole or part of any bank or from becoming a stockholder with others in any corporation.

In five cases the prohibition of stockholding was extended to include the political subdivisions of the states. New York, in 1874, also prohibited its subdivisions from owning stock in any corporation. *Ibid.*, II, 1378.

[59] Kansas in 1861, *ibid.*, I, 641; West Virginia in 1863, *ibid.*, II, 1988. The West Virginia prohibition was extended to include all corporations in 1872. See preceding footnote.

[60] Cf. *supra*, p. 104.

[61] The states, the dates of adoption of constitutional prohibitions against the loan of state credit, and page references to Poore, are as follows: Louisiana, 1845, I, 721; Iowa, 1846, I, 545; New York, 1846, II, 1362; Illinois, 1848, I, 453; Maine, 1848, I, 804; Wisconsin, 1848, II, 2037; Kentucky, 1850, I, 672; Virginia, 1850, II, 1929; Indiana, 1851, I, 523–24; Maryland, 1851, I, 846; Ohio, 1851, II, 1473; Pennsylvania, 1857, II, 1569; Minnesota, 1858, II, 1038; West Virginia, 1863, II, 1988; Nevada, 1864, II, 1258; Missouri, 1865, II, 1155; Alabama, 1867, I, 75; Georgia, 1868, I, 418; Mississippi, 1868, II, 1092–93; Tennessee, 1870, II, 1701. Some exceptions were made in the case of internal improvement companies by Alabama and Georgia. In Ohio and Pennsylvania political subdivisions of the state were also refused the right to loan their credit to corporations. In 1874, New York extended the prohibition to political subdivisions. *Ibid.*, II, 1378.

[62] Cf. *supra*, pp. 105–107.

regulatory clauses that were quite similar to New Jersey's. They were Louisiana in 1845;[63] Iowa in 1846;[64] and New York in the same year;[65] Wisconsin in 1848;[66] Maryland in 1851;[67] and Nevada in 1864.[68]

The foregoing summary of the three major types of constitutional provisions respecting business corporations adopted by various states between 1845 and 1874 is indicative of contemporary public policy in the matter of these institutions. It becomes evident that after the middle of the eighteen forties there was a distinct tendency to curb the power of legislators to use their own discretion in granting corporate charters. The principal change was in the direction of refusing legislators the right to grant special charters. Nearly as important were the constitutional requirements that the legislators retain a measure of control over the corporations they chartered. Numerous states forbade the chartering of certain types of corporations, and many prescribed a measure of liability for corporate stockholders. Finally, the people attempted to deny their representatives authority to extend the financial aid of the states to corporations.

New Jersey itself had had a small part in the new movement. It had been, in 1844, in the vanguard of states requiring compensation to be made to owners before land could be taken for public purposes, of those forbidding state credit to be loaned to corporations, and of those curtailing legislative power to create state debt. But the most important constitutional changes made in other states had long been neglected in New Jersey. It was with the above-outlined provisions of other state constitutions before them as object lessons that in 1873 the New Jersey constitutional commission began its work of suggesting amendments to be submitted to the people.

Most important among the reasons for amending New Jersey's constitution was the constantly increasing evil of special legislation. As was to be expected, the principal attention of

[63] Poore, I, 721. [64] *Ibid.*, I, 545. [65] *Ibid.*, II, 1362–63.

[66] *Ibid.*, II, 2037.

[67] *Ibid.*, I, 845–46. This state also adopted certain prohibitions making state-sponsored public works unconstitutional.

[68] *Ibid.*, II, 1259.

the commission was directed toward a means of ending that undesirable situation. The commissioners suggested the method, already adopted in many states, of prohibiting special laws altogether in a wide variety of cases. The amendments written by them included a new Paragraph 11 in Article IV, Section 7, removing all authority from the legislature to enact special laws in ten specific instances. Included among the ten were the following two that had direct bearing on business corporations:

> Granting to any corporation, association, or individual any exclusive privilege, immunity, or franchise whatever.
>
> Granting to any corporation, association, or individual the right to lay down railroad-tracks.[69]

The same new paragraph contained the following important clause:

> The legislature shall pass no special act conferring corporate powers, but they shall pass general laws under which corporations may be organized and corporate powers of every nature obtained, subject, nevertheless, to repeal or alteration at the will of the legislature.[70]

The provision that all charters of incorporation were to be subject to repeal or alteration by the legislature meant a definite end to grants of irrepealable charters. Efforts to include a similar provision in the constitution had failed in the convention in 1844,[71] but the 1846 "act concerning corporations" had in

[69] *Ibid.*, II, 1326.

[70] *Loc. cit.* There seems to have been some doubt in New Jersey as to the desirability of sweeping away all legislative power to create corporations by special act. Governor Bedle, referring to this paragraph in his message of 1876, had the following to say: "One marked feature of this paragraph is, that it cuts off all right to grant exclusive corporate privileges, and prevents the Legislature from conferring, by special law, any corporate powers. This is a very sweeping change. Exclusive privileges should never be granted . . . but the wisdom of an entire restriction, except by general laws, is not free from doubt, and can only be determined by its practical results. In common with the large majority in favor of this amendment, I am satisfied that it was best to adopt it and try it, for gross abuses need radical remedies." *Legislative Documents,* 1876, Message of the Governor, p. 7.

[71] Cf. *supra,* pp. 93–97.

fact made all charters subsequently enacted liable to repeal or alteration.

A new Paragraph 12 in Article IV, Section 7, restricted the power of the legislature to grant certain favors in the realm of taxation. The paragraph read:

> Property shall be assessed for taxes under general laws, and by uniform rules, according to its true value.[72]

It is significant that no other restrictions were imposed on the legislature regarding the terms of the corporate charters to be granted under the new general-law system. In fact, the only restriction previously imposed by the 1844 constitution, that limiting bank charters to a term of twenty years, was expressly repealed.[73]

The 1844 constitution's restrictions on governmental assistance to private corporations were broadened and strengthened by amendments suggested by the 1873 commission. Article I, Paragraph 19, added to the 1844 prohibition of loans of state credit to corporations an even more stringent curb on the ability of the political subdivisions of the state to become financially interested in private business ventures. The paragraph read:

> No county, city, borough, town, township, or village shall hereafter give any money or property, or loan its money or credit, to or in aid of any individual, association, or corporation, or become security for or be directly or indirectly the owner of any stock or bonds of any association or corporation.[74]

Paragraph 20 of the same article forbade grants of money or property by the state or by municipal corporations:

> No donation of land or appropriation of money shall be made by the State or any municipal corporation to or for the use of any society, association, or corporation whatever.[75]

[72] Poore, II, 1326. [73] *Loc. cit.*

[74] *Ibid.*, II, 1325. In view of the interest of the state in the stock of certain transportation companies, New Jersey did not follow other states and prohibit state stockholding.

[75] *Loc. cit.*

All of the amendments suggested by the constitutional commission were approved without change by the legislature and by the voters and became effective in 1875. With its constitution thus modified, New Jersey entered a new era in its dealings with business corporations. Special acts of incorporation were no longer possible.[76] On the other hand, the legislature of New Jersey was at an advantage as compared with the legislatures of many states, for it was permitted an almost free hand in deciding on the terms of charters to be granted under general laws. Almost at once it became evident that the lawmakers would move in the direction of extending and enlarging the corporate privileges that could be obtained by filing under general laws. The governor, in fact, called their attention to the necessity of such action in his message delivered at the opening of the 1876 session:

> Inasmuch as private corporations can hereafter be organized only under general acts, such acts now in force will have to be thoroughly examined and adapted to the wants of the public, and, wherein they fail to furnish all necessary corporate privileges, other general laws should be passed.[77]

The salient features of the policy pursued by New Jersey in succeeding years in granting ever more "liberal" terms to corporations organizing under its general laws are well known. That policy was formulated both to attract industry into the state and to increase the public revenues. The history of the years before 1875 offers considerable evidence to explain why New Jersey was a leading participant in the late nineteenth century phenomenon of competitive lowering of standards in the matter of charters for business corporations.

In the first place, there had long existed in New Jersey a sentiment that the geographical situation of the state made it desirable to permit the lawmakers to grant corporate charters on the terms deemed necessary to encourage capital investments

[76] Some existing corporations, however, received special amending acts after 1875. E.g., *N. J. Laws,* 1876, Ch. 114, p. 539, and Ch. 164, p. 540.

[77] *Legislative Documents,* 1876, Message of the Governor, p. 9.

to be made in the state. It was that notion that was responsible for the defeat of all attempts to put restrictive clauses into the 1844 constitution and that probably was responsible for the omission from the 1875 amendments of types of constitutional restrictions previously adopted by many other states. Furthermore, New Jersey lawmakers were fully experienced in listening to the entreaties of out-of-state groups for generous charter terms, and they knew the value of such favors to the petitioners. If valuable favors could no longer be granted in the form of special charters, the only way to respond to continued requests for more favorable charters than could be obtained elsewhere was by amendments designed to make the general laws more attractive.

It is also significant that almost from the beginning of business corporation history in their state, Jerseymen had foreseen the possibility of providing for the state's financial needs through the sale of corporate privileges. In this New Jersey may not have differed greatly from other jurisdictions, but it was unique in having for a time actually arrived at the happy situation in which the revenues derived from the corporations chartered by the state paid all the cost of the state government. As the state budget grew and the revenues derived from the railroad monopoly diminished, it was almost inevitable that New Jersey should turn once again to an old plan — that of making its corporations the source of supply for the public purse. In looking back, it appears that the stage was finally and fully set in 1875 for the drama that was soon to make New Jersey nationally famous as the bountiful provider of generous charters of incorporation under "liberal" general laws.

PART II

Analysis of the Charters

CHAPTER VII

Nature and Scope of Business

BETWEEN 1791 and 1875, the state of New Jersey incorporated 2318 business enterprises by special acts of the legislature, and 494 companies filed certificates of incorporation under the various general laws. It is the primary purpose of this chapter to present data that will illustrate the nature and scope of the business activities contemplated by these corporations and that will indicate the relative numbers of companies that were chartered to engage in various fields of enterprise. The chapter also includes a discussion of the most significant special privileges awarded to business corporations to assist them in carrying out their undertakings and something about the most important types of restrictions put upon them.

Figures showing the number of business corporations chartered by special acts between 1791 and 1875, inclusive, are presented by legislative sessions and by types of business in Tables I and II.[1] Table III gives similar data for companies that filed certificates of incorporation under the general laws between 1846 and 1875, inclusive. It should be noted in connection with Tables I and II that the total number of corporations chartered by special act fluctuated greatly from year to year. The fluctuations follow very closely the pattern of changes in the general level of business activity in the United States, significant increases in the number of special charters

[1] A certain amount of arbitrary treatment was necessary in classifying the corporations. For example, companies whose original charters authorized them to engage in both banking and other activities were classified as banks on the assumption that banking would be their most important function. The only instance in which that assumption might be seriously challenged is the case of the Morris Canal and Banking Company. In other cases where corporations were empowered to engage in two or more types of activity, the writer has classified the companies according to what appeared to him to be their principal function.

TABLE I

Business Corporations Chartered by Special Acts in New Jersey, 1791–1844

Legislative Sessions	1791–92	1792–93	1793–94	1794–95	1795–96	1796–97	1797–98	1798–99	1799–1800	1800–01	1801–02	1802–03	1803–04	1804–05	1805–06	1806–07	1807–08	1808–09
General																		
Manufacturing	1																	
Mining											1							
Land Development														1				
Quarry																		
Fishing																		
Market																		
Dairy																		
Peat																		
Hall																		
Financial																		
Bank													1	2			1	
Insurance (Mutual)																		
Insurance (Stock)																		
Savings Inst. (Mutual)																		
Local Utility																		
Water									1	1	1		1	1			1	
Water Power																		
Gas																		
Transportation and Communication																		
Turnpike										1		1	1	2	9		2	5
Railroad																		
Bridge		1		1		1	1	1				1						
Steamboat																		
Canal and Waterway				1	1	1				1		1		2				
Ferry																		
Transportation																		
Totals[a]	1	1		2	1	2	1	1	1	3	2	3	3	8	9		4	5

Legislative Sessions	1809–10	1810–11	1811–12	1812–13	1813–14	1814–15	1815–16	1816–17	1817–18	1818–19	1819–20	1820–21	1821–22	1822–23	1823–24	1824–25	1825–26	1826–27
General																		
Manufacturing	1	1		1	2	6	1						1		1	3	3	1
Mining		1														1	1	1
Land Development											1							
Quarry																		
Fishing																	1	1
Market																		
Dairy																		
Peat																		
Hall																		
Financial																		
Bank			6			2	1		2					2	1	6		
Insurance (Mutual)			1	1											1			
Insurance (Stock)																1		1
Savings Inst. (Mutual)																		
Local Utility																		
Water	1	2															1	
Water Power							1											
Gas																	1	
Transportation and Communication																		
Turnpike	1	6		3	3	3	5	1		2							2	
Railroad						1												
Bridge	2	1	3		1		1			1								
Steamboat						1											1	
Canal and Waterway							1				1			2	1	1		1
Ferry						2		1	1						1	1		
Transportation																		
Totals[a]	5	11	10	5	6	15	10	2	3	3	2		1	4	5	13	10	5

Legislative Sessions	1827–28	1828–29	1829–30	1830–31	1831–32	1832–33	1833–34	1834–35	1835–36	1836–37	1837–38	1838–39	1839–40	1840–41	1841–42	1842–43	1843–44	Totals
General																		
Manufacturing	7	4	2	1	3	5	3	5	18	21	2	6	4	1	3	1	2	110
Mining	5		1		2		2	1	1	2	1	1		1				22
Land Development										2	3						1	8
Quarry										1								1
Fishing																		2
Market			1															1
Dairy						1												1
Peat						1												1
Hall								1										1
Financial																		
Bank	2		2	1	2		4		1	5		1						42
Insurance (Mutual)						1	1				4	1	1	3	2		4	20
Insurance (Stock)	1			1	1		1	1		2					1			10
Savings Inst. (Mutual)	1											1					1	3
Local Utility																		
Water	1		1	1		1		1				1						16
Water Power				1									1					3
Gas											1							2
Transportation and Communication																		
Turnpike	1					1				1		1						51
Railroad			1	4	3	1	1	1	11	9				1			2	35
Bridge				2	1		1	1	3			1		1	2			27
Steamboat	3	1	1		1		1		1	1	1	1	1				1	15
Canal and Waterway	1		1			1	1		1	1								20
Ferry	1								1			1		1				10
Transportation				1			1											2
Totals[a]	23	5	10	12	13	12	16	11	37	45	12	15	7	8	8	1	11	403

Source: *Laws of New Jersey.*
[a] The totals arranged by calendar years rather than by legislative sessions can be found in Appendix I.

TABLE II

BUSINESS CORPORATIONS CHARTERED BY SPECIAL ACTS IN NEW JERSEY, 1845–1875

Legislative Sessions	1845	1846	1847	1848	1849	1850	1851	1852	1853	1854	1855	1856	1857	1858	1859	1860	1861	1862	1863	1864	1865	1866	1867	1868	1869	1870	1871	1872	1873	1874	1875	TOTALS
GENERAL																																
Manufacturing	9	12	5	1		1	3	1	3	5	5	7	8	5	7	11	4	5	9	11	16	22	23	28	34	24	17	35	31	24	8	374
Mining		4	3	9	1		1		2	7	4	1	1	1	1	1	3	1	1	1	17	8	14	9	5	4	8	1	6	3		117
Land Development	1	2		1			2	2	2	4	8	1		1	1	1	1			2	3	18	18	12	16	18	9	19	17	6	3	168
Quarry											2					1							2				3	3	2	3		16
Hall			1	1	2		1	1	1	1	1	2		2		1	1					4	1	2	7	5	2	3	2	6	2	49
Hotel						1	1	1	2	2		1	1	3		1	1			8	1	5	3	6	3		1	1	4	2		48
Market											1	1										2		3	1	1	4	1	2	1		17
Ice											1											1	4	3	1	2	2		3			17
Coöperative																	1			1			2	4	1	1	1	1	1			13
Marl																						1	2	2	1		1					7
Miscellaneous						1																	4	2	1	6		2	2	2	3	23
FINANCIAL																																
Bank				1	1						12	1	1		4	4	1	3								2	6	3		2		41
Insurance (Mutual)	4	3	1	1	4		1	1				2	2	3	3	3			3		1	1	2	4	3	5	5	3		2	2	59
Insurance (Stock)			2	1	2		1	2					4	2	4	1	1				2	5	5	14	4	11	13	6	7	10	3	100
Savings Inst. (Mutual)			1	1		1	2			1	1		3				1		1	1	1		5	5	7	10	14	1	6	4	3	69
Savings Inst. (Stock)																									1			2	2	1		6
Miscellaneous					1																		2	4	1	2	5	6	9	2	4	36
LOCAL UTILITY																																
Water	2			1	2			2	1	2	3		2		3	1		1		2	2		3	2	1	3	3	6	1	2	1	46
Water Power									1										1				1	1	1	1			1			7
Gas	1		1	1	3		1	1	7	3	2	1	7		1	5	3	3	3	5	2	2	1	4	2	5	2	2	3	4	2	77
TRANSPORTATION AND COMMUNICATION																																
Turnpike			1	1	7	2	11	15	6	9	10	7	8	8	7	3	2	4	4	4	7	17	9	6	5	8	2		3	3	2	171
Plank Road					1	4	3	4	4	4		2														1						23
Railroad (Steam)		2	2	6	3	6	4	2	8	6	4	3	3	1	4	1	8	1	4	6	4	16	18	12	13	10	6	11	7			171
Railroad (Horse)										1					9	8	4		2	3	2	5	6	6	6	2	7	5	7	1	2	76
Bridge				1	1				1	1				2	2	2				1				2	2			1				16
Steamboat	4	1	2	2			1	6		3	3	2	1			1	1			2	1	2	3	1	2	1	1		1	2		43
Canal and Waterway			1									1				2						2	1	1	2	1	1			2		14
Ferry				1	4	2	4	2	1			3	1	1	1		1			2	1			4	3	3	3		2	1	1	41
Transportation				1	1	1					3	3	1					1		2	3	6	6	5	1	2	2	5	2	1	2	48
Telegraph	1					1	2		1		2				1		1							1	1		2			2	2	17
Miscellaneous											1																2	1	1			5
TOTALS	22	24	20	30	33	20	38	40	40	49	63	38	43	29	48	47	34	19	28	51	63	117	135	143	125	128	122	118	122	86	40	1915

Source: *Laws of New Jersey.*

TABLE III

Business Corporations Created under the New Jersey General Incorporation Laws, 1846–1875

Date of Filing	1846	1847	1848	1849	1850	1851	1852	1853	1854	1855	1856	1857	1858	1859	1860	1861	1862	1863	1864	1865	1866	1867	1868	1869	1870	1871	1872	1873	1874	1875	Totals
General																															
Manufacturing	4	2	5	1	7	2	7	9	10	12	3	3	6	2	1	1		4	8	7	10	9	9	7	12	10	6	11	10	25	203
Mining		3													3						2	4		1			2	2	2	2	21
Land Development (Stock)									1					1							5	8	4	4	4	10	9	10	6	8	70
Land Development (Mutual)								3	2										3	1	2	4	2	5	1	1	7	2	2		35
Quarry												1	1													1				1	4
Hall																												1	1	1	3
Hotel																														3	3
Market																									1					1	2
Ice													1							1	1						1				4
Marl													1					1			1										3
Miscellaneous							1	1																		2	1		5		10
Financial																															
Bank						16	4	4	3	2	3	7	7	1			8		1			1			1	2	1				61
Insurance (Stock)									1	1	1			1	1																5
Local Utility																															
Water																								1						1	2
Gas											1		2					2	2					1							8
Transportation and Communication																															
Railroad																												11	8	6	25
Steamboat							1																								1
Ferry																1															1
Transportation								2	1				2				2				2	1				1	1				12
Telegraph								3	5	1			1		1		1		1							1			1	1	16
Miscellaneous															1						1	1					1		1		5
Totals	4	5	5	1	7	18	13	22	23	16	8	11	21	5	7	2	11	7	15	9	24	28	15	19	19	28	29	37	36	49	494

Source: *Corporations of New Jersey: List of Certificates Filed in the Department of State from 1846 to 1891, inclusive.* Compiled by the Secretary of State.

appearing, for example, in 1814 and 1815, between 1835 and 1837, between 1851 and 1855, and from the Civil War to 1873, with noticeable decreases in periods of reduced business activity such as occurred between 1816 and 1821, in the years following the panic of 1837, in 1858, and in 1874 and 1875. The totals of the maximum authorized capital stock of the corporations chartered by special act during each legislative session beginning with 1800 are given in Table IV, and the amounts show a similar correspondence with cyclical fluctuations in business. It is not surprising, of course, that the number of special charters should vary with the business cycle, but it is significant that the principal determinant of the number of companies chartered was the tempo of business activity rather than any discernible legislative policy.[2]

It should be emphasized that the statistics presented in Tables I and II record merely the number of corporations receiving charters. It is certain that in a large number of instances no actual organization took place or, organization having been accomplished, no actual business operations were commenced. To discover exactly how many charters were never fully implemented would necessitate hundreds of case studies, but a few bits of evidence can be given here to show that the number was of considerable magnitude. Nearly one-half of the turnpike companies chartered in New Jersey during the first three decades of the nineteenth century failed to construct roads.[3] The first three canal companies chartered to connect the Delaware and Raritan rivers did not accomplish the task.[4] In 1873, the governor announced the names of companies chartered by special act between 1860 and 1873 whose charters were void because the required fees had never been paid. His list included, for example, twenty-two railroads, nineteen turnpike companies, seventeen insurance companies, and eighty-one companies in the industrial group.[5]

[2] The number of special charters granted each year up to 1844 in New Jersey, Maryland, and Pennsylvania varied according to much the same pattern. Cf. Appendix I, p. 445.

[3] W. J. Lane, *From Indian Trail to Iron Horse,* p. 151.

[4] Cf. *supra,* pp. 48–50, 51–52.

[5] Published in *N. J. Laws,* 1874, pp. 756–791. The legislature enacted a law under which these charters might be revived. *Ibid.,* Ch. 368, p. 67.

TABLE IV

CAPITAL STOCK AUTHORIZED BY SPECIAL ACTS OF INCORPORATION IN NEW JERSEY, 1800–1875[a]

Year	Capital Stock[b]	Year	Capital Stock[b]
1800	$ 490,000	1838	$ 2,585,000
1801	500,000+	1839	850,000
1802	145,000	1840	1,090,000
1803	600,000+	1841	1,370,000
1804	2,825,000+	1842	150,000
1805	1,215,000	1843	3,330,000
1806	...		
1807	280,000+	1845	3,460,000
1808	132,500	1846	6,560,000
1809	220,000+	1847	5,020,000
1810	1,298,000+	1848	3,990,000
1811	2,420,000	1849	3,124,000
1812	140,000	1850	3,760,000
1813	472,500	1851	5,620,000+
1814	2,153,000	1852	4,635,500
1815	677,500	1853	9,101,000
1816	56,000	1854	17,103,000
1817	420,000	1855	13,097,000+
1818	630,000+	1856	7,911,000
1819	1,100,000	1857	4,882,000
1820	...	1858	2,773,000
1821	50,000	1859	12,028,000
1822	230,000+	1860	8,945,000
1823	1,170,000	1861	6,911,200+
1824	5,256,250	1862	7,115,000
1825	995,000	1863	4,335,000+
1826	980,000+	1864	17,034,000
1827	3,430,000	1865	30,723,000+
1828	750,000	1866	42,924,000
1829	2,845,000	1867	82,947,000+
1830	2,879,000	1868	71,085,000+
1831	5,280,000	1869	48,581,500
1832	1,107,000	1870	44,892,000
1833	3,180,000	1871	50,729,000+
1834	1,750,000	1872	53,034,000+
1835	8,370,000	1873	40,150,000+
1836	16,455,000	1874	40,790,000+
1837	6,925,000	1875	7,760,000+

[a] Before 1845, the dates indicate the years in which the legislative sessions began; between 1845 and 1875, the dates indicate the years in which the legislative sessions were held. Figures are not given for the years before 1800 because of the impossibility of assigning definite dollar figures to the capital stock of many early corporations. The plus signs indicate that there were corporations the amount of whose authorized capital stock could not be determined.

[b] The totals represent the maximum capital stock authorized by special charters. The amounts of capital actually raised and employed would, undoubtedly, be much smaller. On the other hand, the figures do not include additions to the authorized capital that were granted to numerous corporations by acts supplementary to their original charters.

Although Tables I and II are sufficient in themselves to indicate the number of corporations that were chartered from time to time to engage in particular fields of economic activity, a few general observations are in order. During the seventeen nineties, corporations were created almost exclusively for the construction or improvement of transportation facilities. Corporations of this type continued to be dominant in numbers during the first two decades of the nineteenth century, although banks, manufacturing corporations, and water companies appeared on the scene in significant numbers. The transportation group yielded first place to other types of companies during the eighteen twenties and continued to lose relative to the others during the eighteen thirties. It should be noted that manufacturing and mining companies, so greatly outnumbered before 1820, account for 32.8 per cent of all corporations chartered in New Jersey through the year 1844.[6]

The relative importance of the different types of corporations can be assessed more accurately perhaps by comparing the total amounts of capital stock that were authorized by special charters for corporations engaged in each type of activity. Tables V and VI have been prepared for this purpose. Here again the figures are self-explanatory, but a few of the interesting points they reveal when compared with the date in Tables I and II can be mentioned. Tables V and VI demonstrate clearly the increasing importance of companies chartered to carry on manufacturing, mining, and other ordinary business activity after the middle of the decade of the eighteen twenties. Such companies accounted for 58.7 per cent of the total capital stock authorized by special charters during the last five years of the eighteen twenties and for 61.5 per cent in the last half of the eighteen thirties. The figures based on the amount of authorized capital serve to decrease the significance of certain types of corporations that seem important when only the number of charters is considered. For instance, between 1850 and 1854, inclusive, forty-three turnpike companies were chartered by special

[6] In Maryland they accounted for 27.9 per cent, but in Pennsylvania only 7.1 per cent of the companies chartered during the same period were manufacturing or mining concerns. Cf. Appendix I, p. 446.

act and only twenty-three manufacturing and mining companies. Yet the latter accounted for 25.0 per cent of the total authorized stock during those years while the turnpike companies, because of their small average size, accounted for but 3.9 per cent. Many similar comparisons can be made from the tables.[7]

The descriptive titles used in Tables I, II, V, and VI are sufficient in most cases to indicate the nature of the business in which various corporations were authorized to engage. In the cases of corporations listed as manufacturing, mining, insurance, and banking companies, however, some further explanation of the exact nature and scope of their business is desirable.

Corporations were chartered by special act in New Jersey for a wide variety of manufacturing operations. Considering first the group of 110 manufacturing companies chartered before 1845, one is surprised at the latitude over one-third of the companies were permitted in their operations. Five, including the S. U. M., were allowed to make any products that were not prohibited by law.[8] In two 1814 charters the products that were to be manufactured were not specified.[9] Ten other companies were

[7] The great disparity in the average amounts of authorized capital stock for certain types of companies can be seen from the following figures based on the special charters passed between 1800 and 1875:

Type of Business	*Average Authorized Capital Stock*
Manufacturing	$273,000
Mining	675,600
Land development	410,000
Hotel	169,200
Bank	278,200
Water	87,000
Gas	133,000
Turnpike	59,400
Plank road	78,300
Railroad	622,800
Horse railroad	174,300

These figures must, of course, be used with caution because great differences exist between individual corporations of the same type. For example, the authorized capital of the manufacturing group ranged between the extreme limits of $5,000 in an 1857 charter and $6,000,000 in an 1874 charter, and only 26 of the 222 turnpike companies had an authorized capital larger than the average amount given in the tabulation.

[8] E.g., *N. J. Laws,* 16 sess., 1 sit. (1791), Ch. 356, p. 730; 55 sess., 2 sit. (1831), p. 139.

[9] *N. J. Laws,* 38 sess., 2 sit. (1814, private), pp. 148, 240.

TABLE V

AUTHORIZED CAPITAL STOCK OF NEW JERSEY BUSINESS CORPORATIONS, 1800–1844

(Expressed as percentages of the total capital stock authorized in each period)

Legislative Sessions[a]	1800 to 1804	1805 to 1809	1810 to 1814	1815 to 1819	1820 to 1824	1825 to 1829	1830 to 1834	1835 to 1839	1840 to 1843
GENERAL									
Manufacturing....	..	2.7	33.3	3.5	18.3	35.6	22.9	26.6	35.3
Mining...........	11.0	..	3.9	..	3.7	22.2	6.6	3.1	8.4
Land development	..	..	..	10.4	..	..	..	31.3	..
Quarry...........	..	..	..	..	..	..	..	.5	..
Fishing...........	..	..	..	..	.3	.7	..	..	..
Market..........	..	..	..	..	..	.2	..	..	..
Dairy............	..	..	..	..	..	..	1.1	..	..
Peat.............	..	..	..	..	..	..	.7	..	..
Hall.............	..	..	..	..	..	..	.5	..	..
Totals	11.0	2.7	37.2	13.9	22.3	58.7	31.8	61.5	43.7
FINANCIAL									
Bank............	66.3	10.8	42.2	17.3	41.8	4.4	13.7	8.1	..
Insurance........	..	..	..	..	3.0	4.4	5.3	.6	1.7
Totals	66.3	10.8	42.2	17.3	44.8	8.8	19.0	8.7	1.7
LOCAL UTILITY									
Water............	2.0	..	.1	..	..	.7	.3	.1	..
Water power......	..	..	..	3.5	..	..	1.4	.8	..
Gas..............	..	..	..	..	..	.8	..	.8	..
Totals	2.0	..	.1	3.5	..	1.5	1.7	1.7	..
TRANSPORTATION AND COMMUNICATION									
Turnpike.........	16.9	80.0	6.8	9.0	..	.8	.1	.3	..
Railroad.........	..	..	7.7	..	..	11.1	42.9	21.9	50.5
Bridge...........	.5	6.5	2.9	22.0	..	..	.7	.3	1.9
Steamboat........	..	..	.8	..	..	6.0	.9	3.8	.5
Canal and waterway	3.3	..	..	28.4	32.1	12.5	.8	.3	..
Ferry............	..	..	2.3	5.9	.8	.6	..	1.5	1.7
Transportation....	..	..	..	..	..	..	2.1	..	..
Totals	20.7	86.5	20.5	65.3	32.9	31.0	47.5	28.1	54.6
	100.0	100.0	100.0	100.0	100.0	100.0	100.0	100.0	100.0

Source: *Laws of New Jersey.*

[a] The dates indicate the years in the October of which the legislative sessions commenced. Thus each group includes five sessions except the last which covers only four.

TABLE VI

AUTHORIZED CAPITAL STOCK OF NEW JERSEY BUSINESS CORPORATIONS CHARTERED BY SPECIAL ACT, 1845–1875

(*Expressed as percentages of the total capital stock authorized in each period*)

Legislative Sessions	1845 to 1849	1850 to 1854	1855 to 1859	1860 to 1864	1865 to 1869	1870 to 1875
GENERAL						
Manufacturing	36.5	5.4	17.0	18.7	14.8	18.7
Mining	19.3	19.6	7.4	9.8	20.0	5.7
Land development	1.4	3.5	8.3	8.8	7.5	12.6
Quarry	..	..	.9	.7	.1	1.7
Hall	.6	..	.6	.1	.3	.4
Hotel	..	2.4	.8	3.5	1.2	.9
Market	..	.1	.4	..	1.5	1.1
Ice	..	..	.1	..	.4	.5
Coöperative	..	..	..	.1	.1	.1
Marl	..	..	..	..	.6	..
Miscellaneous	..	.2	..	.1	.5	2.6
Totals	57.8	31.2	35.5	41.8	47.0	44.3
FINANCIAL						
Bank	.9	..	9.0	3.6	..	1.3
Insurance	3.4	1.1	5.0	.9	4.2	7.2
Savings institution	..	..	..	..	.1	.3
Miscellaneous	.7	..	..	..	4.6	4.1
Totals	5.0	1.1	14.0	4.5	8.9	12.9
LOCAL UTILITY						
Water	1.0	.7	1.7	1.1	.5	.6
Water power	..	.1	..	.2	.7	1.5
Gas	2.0	2.0	2.2	3.2	.9	1.7
Totals	3.0	2.8	3.9	4.5	2.1	3.8
TRANSPORTATION AND COMMUNICATION						
Turnpike	2.1	3.9	2.2	.8	.3	2.5
Plank road	.3	4.1	.2	..	..	..
Railroad (steam)	20.9	48.5	18.4	19.9	16.4	10.2
Railroad (horse)	..	.2	4.2	4.0	1.4	2.4
Bridge	.2	.1	.1	.2	6.5	..
Steamboat	5.9	2.7	3.5	10.5	6.0	3.8
Canal and waterway	.1	..	5.0	.5	4.2	6.8
Ferry	3.6	3.8	2.2	.9	.4	2.1
Transportation	.7	.2	2.9	12.4	4.8	2.7
Telegraph	.4	1.4	5.0	..	2.0	.4
Miscellaneous	..	..	2.9	..	..	8.1
Totals	34.2	64.9	46.6	49.2	42.0	39.0
	100.0	100.0	100.0	100.0	100.0	100.0

Source: *Laws of New Jersey.*

empowered to produce certain enumerated products "and other articles." [10] The charters of 24 companies each authorized the manufacture of a number of different and often unrelated products.[11] The operations of the remaining companies were confined in each instance to fairly well defined spheres of manufacturing. Companies chartered to engage solely in the textile industry numbered 44 and formed by far the largest single group.[12] The metal and machine trades were represented by 10 charters,[13] glass manufacturing by 4,[14] and the pottery industry by 3.[15] The other companies chartered to manufacture a particular type of product form a miscellaneous group whose products included books and type, flour, beet sugar, paper, artificial fertilizer, cement, and ship bread, biscuits, and crackers.

Although 18 of the 374 manufacturing companies chartered by special act during and after 1845 were largely unrestricted as to the products they might manufacture[16] and 30-odd were allowed some choice as to the type of manufacturing in which they would engage, the operations of all the others can be classified fairly accurately. The numbers of companies in the more important categories were as follows:

Metal and machine	106
Textile	60
Pottery, brick, etc.	32
Chemical	18
Printing and publishing	16
Glass	10
Paper	9
Rubber	9
Food preserving	7

[10] E.g., *N. J. Laws,* 51 sess., 1 sit. (1826), p. 53; 52 sess., 2 sit. (1828), pp. 107, 168, 209.

[11] For example: Silk, wool, cotton, iron, machinery, hardware, steel, and glass; printing, bleaching, and dyeing textiles; raising silkworms. *N. J. Laws,* 56 sess., 2 sit. (1832), p. 49. Grain products (except liquor), cotton, wool, flax, hemp, silk, iron, copper, and machinery; printing, bleaching, and dyeing cotton fabrics. *Ibid.,* 61 sess., 2 sit. (1837), p. 265.

[12] E.g., *N. J. Laws,* 34 sess., 1 sit. (1809), Ch. 38, p. 137; 52 sess., 2 sit. (1828), pp. 103, 123, 149.

[13] E.g., *N. J. Laws,* 60 sess., 2 sit. (1836), pp. 128, 259.

[14] E.g , *N. J. Laws,* 49 sess., 1 sit. (1824), p. 49.

[15] E.g., *N. J. Laws,* 50 sess., 1 sit. (1825), p. 115.

[16] E.g., *N. J. Laws,* 1847, p. 109; 1872, Ch. 220, p. 554.

It is interesting to note that about ten of the manufacturing companies chartered during the eighteen sixties and seventies were expressly authorized to hold patents which they could use themselves or license others to use under a rent or royalty arrangement.[17] Apparently the manufacturing operations of nearly all the companies were to be carried on in New Jersey, but in a few instances the charters stated that manufacturing could be carried on either in or out of New Jersey,[18] and one company was chartered in 1870 to manufacture tanning materials in Virginia "or elsewhere." [19]

If a company wished to manufacture products other than those permitted by the terms of its charter, it could always ask the legislature to amend the charter. Between 1828 and 1875, fifteen manufacturing companies were granted charter amendments that increased considerably the scope of their authority.[20]

The corporations included in the mining group seem to have been chartered to engage primarily in extractive industry, but almost without exception they were also empowered to perform refining and manufacturing operations on the ores and minerals they obtained from their lands. All the earliest companies and many chartered at various times around the middle of the nineteenth century were to operate copper, iron, and zinc mines in New Jersey. Five companies chartered about 1830 were interested in exploring for and mining coal.[21] The most significant thing about the mining group is that a large number of companies were chartered by the New Jersey legislature to operate out of the state. As early as 1837, a company was incorporated to operate mines in Cuba, although its manufacturing processes were to be carried on in New Jersey.[22] Beginning in 1865, the New Jersey legislature did a wholesale business in chartering mining companies with authority to operate outside the state. Nearly forty such companies were incorporated between 1865 and 1875. Most of them were specifically authorized to carry on

[17] E.g., *N. J. Laws,* 1860, Ch. 56, p. 130; 1874, Ch. 48, p. 893.

[18] E.g., *N. J. Laws,* 1863, Ch. 134, p. 252; 1873, Ch. 86, p. 971.

[19] *N. J. Laws,* 1870, Ch. 304, p. 673.

[20] E.g., *N. J. Laws,* 52 sess., 2 sit. (1828), p. 156; 1864, Ch. 213, p. 326.

[21] E.g., *N. J. Laws,* 52 sess., 2 sit. (1828), pp. 93, 114.

[22] *N. J. Laws,* 61 sess., 2 sit. (1837), p. 76.

their operations in western territories such as Colorado, Montana, and Nevada, and usually the choice of geographical location was left wide open by allowing them to operate in any other state or territory or merely "elsewhere." [23] The companies chartered to operate in the west were created for the purpose of extracting gold, silver, and petroleum. One that was permitted to operate in Kentucky and "elsewhere" was authorized to mine coal.[24] Anticipating the fact that the laws of some jurisdictions in which these companies might wish to operate would not allow them to hold, convey, or lease the necessary real or personal estate, the charters frequently permitted the corporations to "hold . . . lease and convey any . . . beneficial estate or interest, as cestui que trust or otherwise, on any property which may be purchased . . . for the use or benefit of said company . . ." [25]

Approximately 70 per cent of the insurance companies created by special act in New Jersey were chartered to insure against fire or marine risks.[26] It was not until the eighteen thirties that any other type of insurance company was chartered in the state. In 1834, one of the fire insurance companies was granted an amendment to its charter empowering it to take marine risks and "to make insurances upon the lives of persons, and valuable beasts, and grant annuities." [27] On the very next day, a new company was chartered to write fire, marine, and life insurance and to grant annuities.[28] Twenty-five companies were chartered during the succeeding years to insure lives and another seven to write both life and other forms of insurance. Three other companies had their charters amended to permit them to do a life insurance business. Toward the end of the

[23] E.g., *N. J. Laws,* 1865, Ch. 309, p. 579; 1867, Ch. 222, p. 469. Between 1860 and 1870, most of the New England states also chartered a number of mining and petroleum companies that intended to carry on their business in the west. Cf. W. C. Kessler, "Incorporation in New England: A Statistical Study, 1800–1875," *Journal of Economic History,* VIII (May 1948), p. 60.

[24] *N. J. Laws,* 1866, Ch. 424, p. 962.

[25] E.g., *N. J. Laws,* 1867, Ch. 163, p. 326.

[26] Seventy-nine companies were to carry on the business of fire insurance exclusively; fifty-two could take either fire or marine risks; two were to insure against marine losses only.

[27] *N. J. Laws,* 58 sess., 2 sit. (1834), p. 73.

[28] *Loc. cit.*

period of special chartering, a few companies were incorporated for a variety of purposes such as insuring live stock or issuing health or accident insurance.

The banking companies listed in Tables I and II were all empowered to do a general commercial banking business. They could make loans of credit either in the form of circulating bank notes or demand deposits.[29] Although the banks were required to honor their obligations by the payment of specie on demand, their demand deposits outstanding and their notes in circulation needed in actual practice to be covered by only a fractional reserve.[30] It was considered necessary from the time of the earliest bank charters to limit the amount by which banks could increase their liabilities lest the companies be tempted by the promise of greater profits to increase the amount of credit they extended until they were unable to meet their obligation to pay specie on demand. The first four bank charters limited the total debts of the banks to twice the amount of the "capital in specie on hand."[31] The debt provision written into most bank charters passed between 1812 and 1850, however, was less exacting and merely limited the total debt to twice the capital stock paid in.[32] Two 1818 charters dealt more strictly with the problem of the bank notes by adding clauses that limited the note circulation to twice the amount of specie or notes of specie-paying banks actually in the vaults at the time the notes were issued.[33]

[29] There was one bank chartered in 1871 that apparently did not have the privilege of issuing bank notes, but by that date the federal tax on state bank notes had destroyed the value of the privilege. *N. J. Laws,* 1871, Ch. 232, p. 573.

[30] In this respect the specially chartered banks were at a great advantage as compared with banks that received their charters by virtue of the general banking law of 1850. The latter banks were required to deposit with state officials a dollar-for-dollar reserve of securities against the bank notes they issued. *N. J. Laws,* 1850, p. 140.

[31] Actual deposits of cash for "safe keeping" were not to be counted as part of the debt. E.g., *N. J. Laws,* 32 sess., 1 sit. (1807), Ch. 30, p. 80.

[32] Here, too, actual deposits of money were not to be counted as debt. E.g., *N. J. Laws,* 49 sess., 1 sit. (1824), pp. 35, 99, 105.

[33] In addition, the notes outstanding were not to exceed twice the amount of cash on hand for a period longer than ninety days. *N. J. Laws,* 42 sess., 2 sit. (1818, private), pp. 49, 75. The following year, one of the banks was relieved of the special limitation on the amount of its note issue. *Ibid.,* 43 sess., 2 sit. (1819, private), p. 16.

The Morris Canal and Banking Company of 1824 and the Princeton Bank of 1834 were unhampered by any restrictions on either their total debts or their note issues.[34] After 1850, legislative policy on the matter of limiting bank credit underwent a major revision. The older form of provision limiting total debts to twice the paid-in capital appeared in only four special bank charters passed after that date, but in every new bank charter and in most supplementary acts extending the lives of existing banks the lawmakers limited the note issue to twice the amount of capital paid in.[35]

Some New Jersey corporations were empowered to act as trustees. Since the companies that could engage in a trust business cannot be identified in the tables presented earlier in the chapter, a word should be said about them here. The Morris Canal and Banking Company chartered in 1824 was the first corporate fiduciary in New Jersey. In fact, it appears to be one of the earliest American corporations to be given authority to act as trustee, following by only a few years the very first cases in Massachusetts and New York.[36] The Morris Canal and Banking Company's trust powers were very broad and were probably granted as an inducement to New York and Philadelphia capitalists to purchase stock in the canal enterprise. Its charter gave the company the right to "receive and take by deed or devise any effects and property, both real and personal, which may be left or conveyed to said company, in trust . . . and to execute any and all such trust or trusts in their corporate capacity and name, in the same manner and to the same extent as any private trustee, or trustees, might or could lawfully do, and no further . . ."[37] When in 1836 the company was seeking an amendment to its charter, the question of the propriety of the trust power was raised in the legislature. The company

[34] *N. J. Laws,* 49 sess., 1 sit. (1824), p. 158; 58 sess., 2 sit. (1834), p. 150. In 1836, the charter of the Morris Canal and Banking Company was amended to limit the amount of notes outstanding at any one time to $2,000,000. *Ibid.,* 60 sess., 2 sit. (1836), p. 262.

[35] E.g., *N. J. Laws,* 1855, Ch. 190, p. 519, Ch. 220, p. 621.

[36] J. G. Smith, *The Development of Trust Companies in the United States,* pp. 248–250.

[37] *N. J. Laws,* 49 sess., 1 sit. (1824), p. 158.

maintained that the trust power was one of the most valuable privileges conferred by the charter and was important in attracting out-of-state capital into New Jersey.[38]

No other case in which a corporation was clearly given authority to act as trustee can be identified until 1847. Between that date and 1875, however, sixty-five savings institutions were authorized by express provisions in their charters to execute trusts of every description.[39] About twenty miscellaneous financial corporations chartered between 1869 and 1875 were empowered to execute trusts,[40] and nine others were given trust powers by supplementary legislation during the eighteen seventies.[41]

The general incorporation laws enacted in New Jersey before 1875 embraced almost every field of business activity. It will be recalled from the discussion in Part I of this study that most of the general laws provided only for rather specialized enterprises.[42] The laws of 1846 and 1849 together with their amendments were exceptional, however. The 1846 law authorized companies to incorporate "to carry on any branch or branches of lawful manufactures within this state . . ." [43] The privileges of the act were extended to mining companies in 1848.[44] The general law of 1849 provided for the incorporation of companies "to carry on any kind of manufacturing, mining, mechanical, agricultural, or chemical business, within this state, and also for purposes of inland navigation . . ." [45] The coverage of this law was extended gradually by a series of amendments,[46] and finally in 1865 the act was amended to embrace all persons

[38] "By this means, more, perhaps, than by any other, capital from a distance is invited to, and employed at home, and powerfully invigorates the local industry. By authorizing Companies entrusted with similar powers, other States have favored this policy, and are now reaping the advantages." *Votes and Proceedings of the General Assembly,* 60 sess., 2 sit. (1836), p. 259. Cf. also *Journal of the Legislative Council,* 60 sess., 2 sit. (1836), p. 185.

[39] E.g., *N. J. Laws,* 1857, Ch. 71, p. 219, Ch. 202, p. 512.

[40] E.g., *N. J. Laws,* 1869, Ch. 331, p. 901; 1873, Ch. 459, p. 1373.

[41] E.g., *N. J. Laws,* 1870, Ch. 129, p. 344.

[42] Cf. *supra,* pp. 23, 121–122, 153–154.

[43] *N. J. Laws,* 1846, p. 64.

[44] *N. J. Laws,* 1848, p. 9.

[45] *N. J. Laws,* 1849, p. 300.

[46] *N. J. Laws,* 1852, Ch. 44, p. 87; 1853, Ch. 184, p. 427; 1860, Ch. 117, p. 267.

who wished to incorporate "for the purpose of carrying on any lawful business whatever." [47] It is significant that another supplement was also passed in 1865 to permit any company incorporated under the authority of the 1849 law to carry on a part of its business outside New Jersey, providing "a majority of the persons associated in the organization of such company shall be citizens and residents of this state." [48]

In the remaining portion of this chapter, attention will be directed to a few of the major special powers and privileges that were granted to certain New Jersey corporations to assist them in the prosecution of their business and to some of the principal restrictions placed upon them. It would be neither feasible nor profitable to attempt in this study an analysis of the thousands of minor provisions to be found in special charters, charter amendments, general incorporation laws, and general regulatory legislation that had a bearing on what New Jersey's corporations could or could not do or on what they were required to do in the conduct of their business affairs. Most of the minor regulations about business operations applied to special types of corporations such as banks or other financial institutions and to companies such as those chartered to construct bridges, canals, turnpikes, railroads, and gas and water works, and they can be more satisfactorily treated in specialized studies in which companies of each particular type are grouped together.[49]

[47] *N. J. Laws,* 1865, Ch. 491, p. 913. [48] *Ibid.,* Ch. 201, p. 354.

[49] An excellent example of such a study is J. A. Durrenberger's *Turnpikes.* A few examples of the kind of regulatory provisions that are not given detailed consideration in the present study might well be mentioned. Turnpike companies were subject to numerous rules as to the location, width, surface, and grading of their roads as well as to regulations concerning the bridges, railings, milestones, toll gates, and sign boards that were to be erected along the route. They were also permitted to collect penalties from persons who willfully destroyed their toll gates or milestones, from those who disregarded the traffic regulations of the company, and from persons who forcibly passed the toll gates or used a "shun pike" to avoid paying the toll.

Bridge companies were generally subject to regulations concerning the width of their structures and of the spans provided for the passage of boats, to rules about keeping bridge tenders on duty and about lights for the guidance of vessels. They were also subject to penalties for failing to keep the bridges in repair or for charging illegal tolls.

One of the most valuable special privileges granted to business corporations to assist them in the enjoyment of their franchises was the power to take property by condemnation. In legal theory, when a state permits a corporation to take private property by condemnation, it is designating an agent to exercise the state's power of eminent domain. New Jersey was frequently willing to delegate this important power to private corporations. The S. U. M., the state's first business corporation, was allowed ample power to take the land necessary for building its canals and improving river navigation.[50] In this instance, as in all later cases where the right of taking property by condemnation was granted, a procedure to be followed in establishing the price was set forth in the charter.[51] From 1791 to 1830, the power of eminent domain was delegated to a large number of companies whose contemplated projects clearly involved the public necessity or convenience. This group was composed of companies chartered to build bridges,[52] canals,[53] turnpikes,[54] and railroads,[55] companies to improve the navigation on rivers or other streams,[56] and water companies.[57]

The propriety of giving private corporations the right to take land by condemnation does not appear to have been seriously challenged in New Jersey until 1831 when the legislature gave the right to the Trenton Delaware Falls Company, a corporation chartered to build a raceway to supply water power for manufacturing.[58] The right of the legislature to grant such a

Banks and other financial institutions were usually restricted as to the nature of the investments they might make, were frequently required to submit periodic reports to a designated state official, and were subject in varying degrees to governmental inspection.

[50] *N. J. Laws,* 16 sess., 1 sit. (1791), Ch. 356, p. 730.

[51] The rules of procedure varied widely from charter to charter. Corporations allowed to take land were frequently also empowered to use gravel, sand, or similar materials found near their works and, if no agreement as to the price could be made with the owner, to have the price established according to a prescribed procedure.

[52] E.g., *N. J. Laws,* 17 sess., 1 sit. (1792), Ch. 406, p. 806.

[53] E.g., *N. J. Laws,* 44 sess., 2 sit. (1820, public), p. 55.

[54] E.g., *N. J. Laws,* 25 sess., 2 sit. (1801), Ch. 38, p. 80.

[55] E.g., *N. J. Laws,* 39 sess., 2 sit. (1815, private), p. 68.

[56] E.g., *N. J. Laws,* 19 sess., 2 sit. (1795), Ch. 544, p. 1041.

[57] E.g., *N. J. Laws,* 25 sess., 1 sit. (1800), Ch. 5, p. 10.

[58] *N. J. Laws,* 55 sess., 2 sit. (1831), p. 131.

company the power to condemn private property was questioned in a case brought into the court of chancery, and in 1832 the chancellor wrote a decision upholding the action of the legislature.[59] The principal issue as expressed by the chancellor was whether the water power works could be considered to be of a public nature in the same sense as canals, turnpikes, or railroads.[60] The jurist thought the issue could not be decided on the narrow grounds of whether the public were to participate directly in the benefits but on the broad grounds of whether or not the contemplated project would prove of general benefit to the community. He believed the water power company would sufficiently benefit the community to justify its power to condemn land:

The great principle remains. There must be a public use or benefit; that is indisputable: but what that shall consist of, or how extensive it shall be to authorize an appropriation of private property, is not easily reducible to general rule . . . [The legislature] have authorized a company to do what the state itself might have done without having their right questioned. They have in this pursued the ordinary mode. All great improvements in our state are made through private incorporated companies, and perhaps better accomplished in that way than any other.[61]

In subsequent years, not only were corporations allowed to take land for the traditional purposes of constructing turnpikes, bridges, and the like, but the legislature permitted private prop-

[59] *Scudder* v. *Trenton Delaware Falls Company,* 1 New Jersey Equity, 694 (1832).

[60] "It has been seen, that turnpike roads and canals are considered of a public nature, so far as to authorize the taking of private property for their construction. Railroads have lately been added to this class of public improvements . . . It is contended, however, that the present case is going a step further than has yet been done. Turnpike roads have been considered as public, or as appropriated to public uses, because every one has a right to travel them on paying the regular toll. Railroads have been considered public, because they facilitate the conveyance of passengers and the transportation of merchandize, and thereby benefit the community; whereas the object of the present franchise is to create a water power, and erect thereon extensive manufacturing establishments. These will be under the control of individuals . . . under no obligation to let the public participate in the immediate profits of their undertaking." *Ibid.,* pp. 727–28.

[61] *Ibid.,* pp. 729–30.

erty to be appropriated for other water power developments,[62] for ferry docks,[63] and for several miscellaneous purposes such as the construction of pneumatic tubes intended to be used for transportation.[64]

Protection from competition was, of course, greatly desired by business corporations, and some New Jersey companies enjoyed a degree of monopoly privilege by definite legislative grant. The most important monopoly privilege in New Jersey was enjoyed by the Joint Companies. The significant details of their agreement with the legislature that no other railroad would be authorized for the purpose of transporting passengers or merchandise between New York and Philadelphia have been given in Part I of this study and need not be recounted here.[65]

Bridge companies were the first type of New Jersey corporations to be expressly protected from competition. The first two bridge companies possessing definite monopoly privileges were the Proprietors of the Bridges over the rivers Passaic and Hackinsack and the Proprietors of the New-Brunswick Bridge, incorporated in 1797 and 1799 respectively. These companies, however, did not enjoy their protected status by virtue of the terms of their charters of incorporation but by virtue of legislative acts passed in 1790.[66] In 1801, the New Jersey legislature passed an amendment to the charter of a company that had been incorporated in 1798 to build a bridge across the Delaware at Trenton forbidding the construction of any other bridge within a distance of three miles.[67] Nearly sixty years later, the court of chancery held the monopoly grant of 1801 void on the ground that it could not be given by New Jersey alone but only with the concurrence of Pennsylvania.[68] A company chartered by New Jersey in 1819 to operate a part-bridge, part-ferry crossing between Camden and Philadelphia was to be protected, if Pennsylvania concurred, by the following

[62] E.g., *N. J. Laws,* 1853, Ch. 188, p. 431.

[63] E.g., *N. J. Laws,* 1869, Ch. 455, p. 1136.

[64] E.g., *N. J. Laws,* 1867, Ch. 191, p. 417.

[65] Cf. *supra,* pp. 54–59.

[66] *N. J. Laws,* 15 sess., 1 sit. (1790), Ch. 333, p. 685, Ch. 335, p. 694.

[67] *N. J. Laws,* 25 sess., 2 sit. (1801), Ch. 26, p. 58.

[68] *President, Managers, and Company for Erecting a Bridge over the River Delaware at or near Trenton* v. *Trenton City Bridge Company,* 13 New Jersey Equity, 46 (1860).

clause in its charter: ". . . to afford the said company a reasonable prospect of advantage from the investment of their funds, to the extent necessary for the erection of a permanent bridge and ferries . . . no other authority shall hereafter be given to any person or persons to erect . . . a bridge over any part of the river Delaware, within three miles of the city of Philadelphia, for the term of twenty years . . ." [69] A company chartered in 1869 to construct a bridge over the upper Delaware was protected by a provision that no one could operate a public ferry within one and a half miles of the bridge.[70]

The two companies incorporated in 1824 to construct major canals were afforded limited protection. In one of those cases, no canals over ten miles long were to be constructed within ten miles of the company's main trunk without the company's permission.[71] In the other case, no canal or railroad could be built within ten miles of the canal or feeder unless the company consented.[72] By the terms of its charter, the Delaware and Raritan Canal Company of 1830 enjoyed protection against other canals for a distance of five miles from its works,[73] but it gained its impregnable monopoly position as a result of its alliance with the Camden and Amboy to form the Joint Companies. Two ferry companies were also protected from competition by the terms of their charters. One, chartered for twenty years in 1849 to operate ferries to Staten Island, was granted exclusive privileges for a distance of one-half mile on either side for three years and one-quarter mile thereafter "for the purpose of insuring success to the undertaking, which in its establishment and first efforts must be hazardous, and for the purpose of protecting

[69] *N. J. Laws,* 43 sess., 2 sit. (1819, private), p. 45.

[70] *N. J. Laws,* 1869, Ch. 452, p. 1134. This charter had been passed previously by Pennsylvania but required the agreement of New Jersey. It should be noted that the charters of many bridge companies that gave express permission to purchase ferry privileges at the places where the bridges were to be constructed also provided that no one was to receive compensation for ferrying at those points once the bridges were built and the ferries paid for. E.g., *ibid.,* 60 sess., 2 sit. (1836), pp. 79, 299.

[71] The Morris Canal and Banking Company. *N. J. Laws,* 49 sess., 1 sit. (1824), p. 158.

[72] The Delaware and Raritan Canal Company. *N. J. Laws,* 49 sess., 1 sit. (1824), p. 175.

[73] *N. J. Laws,* 54 sess., 2 sit. (1830), p. 73.

the enterprise when established . . ." [74] The other was granted a thirty-year charter in 1868 to operate a ferry at the same point as the older company and was given a guarantee that no competing ferry should be established within one-half mile.[75] In the same year, however, the governor vetoed the charter of a ferry company on the ground that it granted monopoly privileges along an eight-mile stretch of well-populated territory and appeared to be a "perpetual exclusive ferry privilege." [76]

The vast majority of corporations operating transportation facilities, however, had no express guarantee of exclusive privileges. The legal question as to whether monopoly privileges would be implied in such cases need not be examined here.[77] It is sufficient to say that the New Jersey legislators appear to have been cautious about chartering public utility companies when they would compete with companies already established.

Although cases in which the legislature may actually have chartered corporations in the utility field to compete with companies already established are difficult to detect, one clear case can be found. In 1810, a group of persons sought a charter for the Trenton Aqueduct Company to compete with the Trenton Water Works that had been incorporated in 1804. Petitions for and against a second water company were sent to the legislature. The proponents of the new project maintained that the old company was unable to provide an adequate and dependable supply of water to the residents of Trenton and that a second company was needed to assure a sufficient supply "on moderate terms, and to prevent a Monopoly of that most useful and Necessary article":

> Your Petitioners have no intention of violating the rights of others, but they know no principle of right or justice which will prohibit them from obtaining so useful and necessary an article as water as abundantly & at as low a rate as they can with propriety. They

[74] *N. J. Laws,* 1849, p. 230. [75] *N. J. Laws,* 1868, Ch. 165, p. 371.

[76] *Votes and Proceedings of the General Assembly,* 1868, p. 1025. The veto was sustained. *Ibid.,* p. 1026.

[77] For a brief account of this question as it concerned early American turnpike and bridge companies see C. J. Evans, "Private Turnpikes and Bridges," *American Law Review,* L (July–August 1916), pp. 527–535.

think that it is for the security of the City and the Convenience of the Inhabitants that both Institutions should exist, and that a reasonable prospect is afforded to the Stock holders of each to reap an handsome interest on the Capital stock of the Company. Your Petitioners disclaim any intention of speculating upon the ruin of the other Company . . . Their Charter gives them no exclusive right to supply the City with water, and as it can be obtained from other sources, purer & cooler cheaper & more abundantly than from theirs, your Petitioners humbly hope that your honorable body who are at all times disposed to encourage any undertaking for the public good will extend your aid to their association.[78]

The existing company countered with petitions of its own in which it pointed out the reasonableness of its rates and profits. Some of the arguments employed to defeat the charter bill are worthy of reproduction:

We presume we address a just, wise and enlightened Legislature, who will act for the good of Society. We ask then, Can it be for the good of Society that a company, who have risen under Legislative countenance, who have risked their money, who have expended their labor, and who, by these risks and by that labor, have procured a great and acknowledged benefit to their neighbors: — a benefit, which, but for them, would probably never have been procured, should see their reasonable hopes and expectations blasted by a rival company who cannot add one single additional benefit? . . . We conceive not; and therefore flatter ourselves we shall be justified in praying that no act of incorporation shall be granted to them.[79]

Nor can a competition be useful — Where the whole profits of an undertaking afford not more than an adequate compensation to those who embark in it, a division or competition is always prejudicial. Such must here be the inevitable consequence — The supply of the whole city upon moderate terms will not yield more than a fair remuneration for the expense and risk of the undertaking — The necessary result therefore of the establishment of a new company must be that the profit, when divided will become an object not worth attention and thus both fall into neglect and ruin and so valuable an

[78] Two manuscript petitions, dated October 26, 1810. These and the other petitions referred to here are preserved in the collection of the New Jersey State Library.

[79] Manuscript petition, dated November 1, 1810.

institution be defeated, or otherwise both companies by common consent must demand from those they supply with water an unreasonable compensation.[80]

Apparently the legislators felt that the Trenton Water Works did not possess any implied monopoly, for they acted favorably on the charter of the new company.[81] It is interesting in contrast to this episode that the general incorporation law for gas companies enacted over sixty years later did not authorize "the building of gas works or laying of gas pipes in any city or town which is already being supplied with gas." [82]

Finally, one other form of special privilege will be treated here — the right of one corporation to hold stock in another corporation. Clauses that clearly legalized intercorporate stockholding can be found only rarely in New Jersey charters or charter amendments before 1848. The first was in a law of 1804 authorizing the governor to exercise the state's right to purchase stock in the Newark Banking and Insurance Company when he found individuals or corporate bodies to which he could resell the shares.[83] The 1812 act of the legislature creating the six so-called state banks provided that the capital stock not reserved for the state could be subscribed by any individuals or "bodies corporate." [84] Subscriptions were open to the United States, any "body corporate," or individual in the case of the New-Jersey Delaware and Raritan Canal Company chartered in 1820.[85]

[80] Manuscript petition, dated 1811. These petitions did not overlook any argument that could be used to defeat the proposed charter. For example: "The cruelty of this proceeding will be more apparent, when it is known that one of the original members of our company, who exerted himself most, and took the greatest number of shares with a view to encourage the undertaking, is since dead, and has left a helpless orphan with little else to depend upon for support, besides the income from those shares." This "unoffending orphan" it was maintained was "not likely for reasons unnecessary here to detail ever to be able to support or provide for himself."

[81] *N. J. Laws,* 35 sess., 2 sit. (1811), p. 437. Apparently the episode was not soon forgotten. A letter by "Justice" in the *Trenton Federalist,* June 8, 1818, made reference to the fact that the Trenton Water Works company had been deprived of the fair fruits of its enterprise by the violated faith of the legislature.

[82] *N. J. Laws,* 1874, Ch. 509, p. 124.

[83] *N. J. Laws,* 29 sess., 1 sit. (1804), Ch. 165, p. 482.

[84] *N. J. Laws,* 36 sess., 2 sit. (1812, public), p. 3.

[85] *N. J. Laws,* 44 sess., 2 sit. (1820, public), p. 55.

Stock in the Orange and Sussex Canal Company of 1823 could be subscribed by "either individual or corporate" persons.[86] When the New Jersey Railroad and Transportation Company was chartered in 1832, it was authorized to purchase bridges and turnpikes necessary for its project or to purchase "any and all of the shares of the capital stock of such roads and bridge companies, and to hold the same as shareholders therein . . ."[87] An 1836 amendment to the charter of the State Bank at Newark permitted the directors to sell any part of a newly authorized stock issue that was not taken up by existing stockholders to any person or "corporation."[88] Two land development companies incorporated in 1838 were allowed to take stock in any canal, railroad, turnpike, or other highway already chartered or that might be chartered in the future by New Jersey if their facilities led to or passed through the land companies' property.[89]

Although this handful of cases constitutes the whole list of instances in which intercorporate stockholding was expressly and clearly authorized before 1848, there are bits of evidence in the statutes to indicate that it may not have been uncommon in the early years for one corporation to hold the stock of another corporation. The right to subscribe to the stock of the S. U. M. was open to "any Person, Copartnership or Body Politic."[90] In the charters of most early banks and some other companies the sections dealing with the payment of installments on the capital stock provided for forfeiture of the shares of any individual, copartnership, or "body politic" that was delinquent.[91] Professor Davis, encountering similar phraseology in the eighteenth century charters of some other states, thought it might "imply that subscriptions by corporations (whether business or public) would not be unexpected."[92] It seems highly uncertain, however, whether legislators actually intended to

[86] *N. J. Laws,* 48 sess., 1 sit. (1823, private), p. 166.
[87] *N. J. Laws,* 56 sess., 2 sit. (1832), p. 96.
[88] *N. J. Laws,* 60 sess., 2 sit. (1836), p. 351.
[89] *N. J. Laws,* 62 sess., 2 sit. (1838), pp. 92, 157.
[90] *N. J. Laws,* 16 sess., 1 sit. (1791), Ch. 356, p. 730.
[91] E.g., *N. J. Laws,* 29 sess., 1 sit. (1804), Ch. 154, p. 449.
[92] Davis, *Essays in the Earlier History of American Corporations,* II, 325.

include private corporations as well as governmental units within the purview of the term "body politic."

From 1848 on, however, there were over one hundred separate instances in which intercorporate stockholding was expressly authorized. The authorizations can be divided into two principal types. First, there were the cases in which the stock of a corporation was declared eligible for purchase by other corporations. Second, there were the cases in which a corporation was authorized to hold stock in other corporations.

By the terms of their special charters, the stock of forty-seven corporations was made eligible for purchase by other corporations. Several examples will suffice to show that there was no uniformity within this group. Some of the charters merely stated that any other corporation could hold the stock.[93] Others restricted the privilege to New Jersey corporations.[94] In a number of instances, only certain types of corporations could own the stock.[95] Only companies designated by name could take the stock in a few cases.[96] Occasionally the percentage of the stock that could be bought by another corporation was limited.[97] In several instances it was expressly provided that the corporation purchasing the stock would enjoy the voting privilege.[98]

A different approach was taken in twenty-four charters. In these cases the companies being incorporated were allowed to hold stock in other corporations. Again there was a great variety of provisions. A number of charters conferred authority to hold the stock of corporations created by any state.[99] Others allowed stock to be held in New Jersey corporations only.[100] Many designated the type or types of corporations in which stock could be owned.[101] Three additional companies received even more liberal treatment. Their stock could be held by certain

[93] E.g., *N. J. Laws*, 1867, Ch. 160, p. 301.
[94] E.g., *N. J. Laws*, 1866, Ch. 169, p. 358.
[95] E.g., *N. J. Laws*, 1852, Ch. 83, p. 186.
[96] E.g., *N. J. Laws*, 1854, Ch. 66, p. 144.
[97] E.g., *N. J. Laws*, 1872, Ch. 445, p. 1009.
[98] E.g., *N. J. Laws*, 1866, Ch. 7, p. 11.
[99] E.g., *ibid.*, Ch. 249, p. 595.
[100] E.g., *N. J. Laws*, 1873, Ch. 699, p. 1591.
[101] E.g., *N. J. Laws*, 1860, Ch. 137, p. 385; 1867, Ch. 331, p. 764.

corporations, and in addition they were allowed to purchase the stock of other corporations.[102]

The thirty remaining cases in which intercorporate stockholding was legalized are to be found in charter amendments. Some made the stocks of certain companies eligible for purchase by corporations,[103] while others authorized designated companies to hold the stock of any corporation or of specified corporations.[104] There was no uniformity within either group.

It is noteworthy that railroad companies were involved one way or another in a substantial number of the instances in which intercorporate stockholding was authorized after 1848. The period was one of extensive railroad construction and of the development of railroad systems. Newly projected railroads doubtless had an improved chance of marketing their shares if the roads to which they would be tributary were able to subscribe.[105]

Many New Jersey business corporations were subjected to various regulations that definitely restricted them in the conduct of their business affairs. Although there were many kinds

[102] *N. J. Laws,* 1872, Ch. 304, p. 673; 1873, Ch. 631, p. 1496; 1874, Ch. 345, p. 1183.

[103] E.g., *N. J. Laws,* 1868, Ch. 422, p. 984.

[104] E.g., *N. J. Laws,* 1854, Ch. 26, p. 61; 1861, Ch. 13, p. 24.

[105] The Belvidere Delaware Railroad's experience is a good illustration of the manner in which a railroad venture might be saved from failure by a stock subscription from another road. In 1848, when the already extended time for completing the Belvidere Delaware was nearing expiration, the Joint Companies were authorized to subscribe to any amount of its stock. *N. J. Laws,* 1848, p. 114. A joint resolution of the legislature the following year declared that the charter would not be forfeited if just a specified portion of the road was completed by the expiration of the time, provided no dividends were paid to stockholders until the whole line was completed. *Ibid.,* 1849, p. 333. The resolution was defended by the *State Gazette* of February 28, 1849, with the following argument: "When it is remembered, that almost the only subscription to this stock is that of the joint companies ($500,000) and that the people along the route have almost entirely failed to join in the enterprise, it will be obvious to all, that the passage of the joint resolution will be of much more advantage to the community than to the company, on which it imposes such conditions."

The Joint Companies, operating the state's principal transportation system, were frequently empowered to purchase stock in connecting railroads. E.g., *N. J. Laws,* 1852, Ch. 118, p. 255; 1853, Joint Resolution IX, p. 489.

of restrictive provisions in corporate charters, only the two that appear to be most significant will be treated here. They are provisions as to the maximum amount of real estate that might be owned and limitations on the tolls or prices that could be charged.

As a general rule the corporations of New Jersey were authorized by express language in their charters to hold whatever real and personal property was necessary to enable them to carry on the business for which they had been created. In many cases a clause was added to permit the companies to hold additional real estate if it had been mortgaged to them as security, conveyed to them in satisfaction of debts, or purchased at sales by virtue of an execution.[106] Although there was a distinct feeling on the part of early nineteenth century legislators that it was undesirable to permit large amounts of land to come into corporate hands, it was generally assumed sufficient protection merely to limit the amount of land a corporation could hold to what was necessary for the purposes of the business. In certain instances, however, the legislators went further and placed a definite limit on the amount of land that could be held when it was thought the companies might get control of an excessive amount of real estate. Definite limits were established most often in the case of land development, manufacturing, mining, and railroad companies.[107]

Almost every corporation chartered before 1860 for the purpose of developing real estate was forbidden to hold over a designated amount of land.[108] Only about a dozen of the many land companies chartered after 1860, however, were limited in the amount of land they could hold.[109]

The lawmakers seem to have been apprehensive at times that manufacturing company charters would be perverted by un-

[106] E.g., *N. J. Laws,* 60 sess., 2 sit. (1836), p. 333. The frequency with which this special privilege was given bears testimony to the fact that many early nineteenth century business firms found it necessary to take land in payment of debts owed them.

[107] Ferries, steamboat lines, hotels, and telegraph companies were also subjected to definite limits in a very few cases.

[108] E.g., *N. J. Laws,* 62 sess., 2 sit. (1838), p. 92.

[109] When limits were expressed, they averaged about five hundred acres. E.g., *N. J. Laws,* 1870, Ch. 364, p. 760.

scrupulous operators and used for the primary purpose of land holding. Only 5 manufacturing companies chartered before 1836 were limited in the amount of land they could hold, and in these cases the maximum was expressed in terms of the value of the land.[110] Between 1836 and 1844, however, a period when manufacturing corporations were regarded with suspicion, definite limits on the amount of land that could be held were put into twenty-nine manufacturing company charters. They represented one-half the total number of manufacturing company charters enacted during those years. The number of acres that could be held varied widely from charter to charter. In some instances the figure was as low as 1, 3, or 4 acres,[111] but in the case of silk manufacturing companies that intended to plant mulberry trees and raise silk worms it was set as high as several hundred acres.[112] Occasionally the maximum amount was expressed in terms of value.[113] In the years following 1844, only 19 manufacturing companies were subjected to absolute limitations on the amount of their land. That was a small number compared to the total of 374 manufacturing companies that were chartered by special acts after 1844. It should also be noted that the general manufacturing company laws of 1846 and 1849 did not fix any absolute limit on the amount of land a corporation might hold.

The land holdings of mining companies were definitely limited in only about twelve cases during the whole period under study. In general the limits set for mining companies were more generous than those imposed upon manufacturing companies, running in some cases as high as several thousand acres.[114]

Railroad companies found it necessary to hold land in addition to what was necessary for their roadbeds in order to construct stations, freight handling and storage facilities, and shops. Practically every railroad company chartered by New Jersey was strictly limited in the amount of land it could hold for the accommodation of such appurtenances. Since most rail-

[110] E.g., *N. J. Laws,* 34 sess., 1 sit. (1809), Ch. 38, p. 137.
[111] E.g., *N. J. Laws,* 60 sess., 2 sit. (1836), p. 339.
[112] E.g., *N. J. Laws,* 61 sess., 2 sit. (1837), p. 393.
[113] E.g., *N. J. Laws,* 60 sess., 2 sit. (1836), p. 399.
[114] E.g., *N. J. Laws,* 59 sess., 2 sit. (1835), p. 138.

road companies were taxed according to special rules, some caution had to be exercised to avoid the removal of an inordinate amount of land from local assessment rolls.[115] Many early charters limited the land a railroad company could own in addition to its roadbed to two acres at each terminus.[116] Others allowed extra land to be held at intermediate points along the line up to two acres at each place.[117] In later charters, the limit was usually four or five acres at each place.[118] Since the parcels of land allowed by the terms of the charters frequently proved insufficient, a law was enacted in 1855 permitting railroad companies to hold as much land at stations as was "strictly necessary . . . for station and railroad purposes," but the land in excess of the amount set in the various charters was to be subject to the same taxes as other land in the same places.[119] The general railroad law of 1873 permitted up to ten acres to be held at each terminus and at individual points along the line.[120]

Certain types of corporations were strictly regulated as to the charges they could make for their services. The most important representatives of this group were companies chartered to construct and operate transportation facilities.

Most bridge, turnpike and plank road, canal and inland waterway, railroad, and ferry companies were subject to some form of limitation on the tolls they could take. In a number of the earliest charters, the legislators endeavored to introduce an element of flexibility in the tolls so that once the companies had actual operating experience the earnings could be made to bear a definite relationship to the investment. The directors of the S. U. M. could charge any tolls on their canals, but the returns to the company were not to exceed 15 per cent on the investment in the waterways over and above the costs of maintenance. The directors were to present triennial reports on canal operations to the assembly, and if it appeared that the net income was over 15 per cent in any three-year period the excess was to be turned over to the legislature to be used by them for

[115] Cf. *infra*, pp. 396–403.

[116] E.g., *N. J. Laws*, 60 sess., 2 sit. (1836), pp. 60, 119.

[117] E.g., *ibid.*, pp. 204, 226.

[118] E.g., *N. J. Laws*, 1849, pp. 93, 289.

[119] *N. J. Laws*, 1855, Ch. 52, p. 118.

[120] *N. J. Laws*, 1873, Ch. 413, p. 88.

the "Encouragement of Literature, Arts and Sciences," and the tolls were then to be reduced.[121] The tolls of a 1792 bridge company were to be lowered if any decennial report showed the net income of the previous five-year period to be in excess of 12 per cent.[122] A company created in 1802 to improve navigation on the Raritan River was to report to the assembly every seven years, and if the net income was shown to be over 15 per cent the tolls were to be reduced to bring future earnings down to that level.[123] Somewhat similar schemes were adopted in a turnpike company charter of 1804 and in the charter of the company that was incorporated in the same year to open inland navigation between the Delaware and Raritan rivers, and in both cases the tolls were not to return a net income of over 12 per cent.[124] In the case of another turnpike company chartered in 1804, all profits over 12 per cent were to be used by the governor of the state to purchase and extinguish the privately owned stock of the company.[125]

A more elaborate formula for the determination of tolls was adopted in the charters of five bridge companies, two turnpike companies, and one inland navigation company. The net income was to be computed at set intervals, and provision was made for lowering the established tolls if the net income was over a designated percentage on the investment and for raising them if the profit fell below a prescribed minimum.[126]

In the charters of the 1815 railroad company and of four canal companies incorporated during the eighteen twenties and thirties, the legislature reserved the right to appoint commissioners to regulate the tolls in the light of the companies' operating experience. A minimum below which the tolls were not to

[121] *N. J. Laws,* 16 sess., 1 sit. (1791), Ch. 356, p. 730.

[122] *N. J. Laws,* 17 sess., 1 sit. (1792), Ch. 406, p. 806.

[123] *N. J. Laws,* 27 sess., 1 sit. (1802), Ch. 86, p. 196.

[124] *N. J. Laws,* 28 sess., 2 sit. (1804), Ch. 113, p. 287; 29 sess., 1 sit. (1804), Ch. 153, p. 433.

[125] *N. J. Laws,* 29 sess., 1 sit. (1804), Ch. 151, p. 419.

[126] E.g., *N. J. Laws,* 19 sess., 2 sit. (1795), Ch. 554, p. 1067; 25 sess., 2 sit. (1801), Ch. 38, p. 80; 36 sess., 2 sit. (1812, private), p. 47. The maximum net income was set at fifteen per cent in six instances and at twelve and ten in the other two; the minimum was fixed at six per cent in five cases and at eight per cent in three.

be set was provided in each case, and there was an additional requirement in the four canal company charters that the commissioners fix the tolls "with due regard to the interests of the company and of the citizens of the state." [127]

The legislature reserved the right in several charters to alter the rates of toll by amendatory legislation. Maximum tolls were set in the 1796 charter of an inland waterway company, but they were "subject nevertheless to be regulated by the legislature . . . at least once in every fifty years." [128] The lawmakers also reserved the right to alter at any time the tolls of a ferry company incorporated in 1818,[129] and in the 1828 charter of a road and ferry company they retained the power to "reduce and regulate the toll, in such manner as they shall deem proper" at the expiration of every twenty-year period.[130]

The cases in which the legislators endeavored to make special provisions for maintaining some continuing control over tolls were, however, the exception rather than the rule. In all turnpike company charters, except the three very early ones mentioned above, a schedule of maximum rates was set forth with no provision for later changes, and the same was true of the charters of many other companies incorporated during the early years to build transportation facilities. By the middle of the eighteen thirties, the lawmakers had completely abandoned the earlier practice of enacting elaborate formulas for rate regulation and were content merely to establish in each charter the maximum tolls that could be charged. Perhaps the most cogent reason for the change in policy was that the right to alter any of the terms of charters of incorporation was reserved by the legislature as a regular practice after 1835.[131] Moreover, experience had probably proved reports on operations prepared by the companies themselves to be of no value in determining whether the tolls should be changed, and the state government had no adequate machinery for making independent findings.

[127] E.g., *N. J. Laws,* 49 sess., 1 sit. (1824), pp. 158, 175.
[128] *N. J. Laws,* 20 sess., 2 sit. (1796), Ch. 586, p. 57.
[129] *N. J. Laws,* 42 sess., 2 sit. (1818, private), p. 88.
[130] *N. J. Laws,* 52 sess., 2 sit. (1828), p. 15.
[131] Cf. *infra,* pp. 381–384.

It is likely too that the operations of the early companies were so unprofitable that there seemed little necessity of attempting a continuing regulation of tolls with a view to limiting the earnings to some such figure as 12 or 15 per cent.[132]

The problem of the rate structure was not given much attention in most charters. Although rather elaborate schedules of maximum tolls for a number of classes of persons, beasts, and vehicles were written into the charters of some ferry companies,[133] the schedules of maximum rates for bridges, turnpikes, plank roads, canals, and inland waterways were very simple.[134] In the case of railroads, the charters usually established the maximum rate per mile for passengers and the maximum rate per ton-mile for property. Since in the early days of railroading the roads were thought of as public highways, it was usual in early charters to find separate and lower maximum rates for passengers and property carried in cars that were not owned by the railroad companies.[135] Sometimes certain commodity rates that were not to be quoted by the ton were singled out for special mention, as for example the rate per mile for a cord of wood, thousand feet of lumber, or bushel of grain.[136] Railroads operating in farming districts were occasionally required to quote rates on fertilizers at not over one-half the maxi-

[132] In fact, in a number of instances the legislature increased the maximum tolls because earnings had proved to be so low. E.g., *N. J. Laws,* 22 sess., 2 sit. (1798), Ch. 632, p. 263.

[133] E.g., *N. J. Laws,* 65 sess., 2 sit. (1841), p. 20.

[134] Bridge and turnpike companies were generally directed to allow free passage to certain individuals. Among the persons frequently exempted from bridge tolls were those on their way to or from church, school children, and militia trainees. E.g., *N. J. Laws,* 60 sess., 2 sit. (1836), p. 79. Those allowed free passage on turnpikes included persons en route to or from church services or funerals, militiamen called to active duty, farmers traveling on the ordinary business of their farms, and persons going to or from mills at which they had grain ground for the use of their families. E.g., *ibid.,* 1855, Ch. 132, p. 356.

[135] E.g., *N. J. Laws,* 60 sess., 2 sit. (1836), p. 60. Early railroad company charters commonly stated that the roads were public highways "free for the passage of any rail road carriage thereon, with passengers or property, upon payment of the tolls prescribed." The cars used were to be of the same general description as those belonging to the company, and the time of starting and the rate of speed were to be regulated by the company. So that people could actually make use of the roads, many early charters required that there be a track for one or more horses. E.g., *ibid.,* p. 226.

[136] E.g., *ibid.,* p. 204.

mum rates set for other commodities.[137] Charter provisions regulating the tolls of horse railroads were frequently similar in form to those of the steam roads,[138] but many horse roads that were to operate in the streets of cities and towns were limited to a maximum fare for passenger trips anywhere on the line.[139] In a substantial number of instances, the tolls of horse railroads were not limited at all.[140]

The New Jersey lawmakers attempted very little rate fixing outside the transportation field during the period under investigation. Water companies were free in all but two cases to fix whatever prices they wished. The exceptions were the Trenton Aqueduct Company chartered in 1811 that could not charge rates to yield over 12 per cent on the capital expended[141] and the Hudson County Aqueduct Company of 1865 that was not to charge more for water than was then paid by residents of Hoboken and Hudson City.[142] Five gas company charters passed between 1853 and 1871 established maximum prices at which gas could be sold ranging from three to six dollars per 1000 cubic feet.[143] A telegraph company chartered in 1859 with power to lease existing lines or to purchase their stock was forbidden to increase rates in its New Jersey offices beyond what was then charged.[144] An 1861 telegraph company charter merely stated that the company was not to charge more than other companies then operating in New Jersey.[145]

The foregoing account of the nature and scope of corporate business in New Jersey necessarily leaves many aspects of the story untold. The crude statistics of corporate charters give us no idea of the number of stillbirths included among them. Yet, as has been indicated, that figure was undoubtedly large. Simi-

[137] E.g., *N. J. Laws,* 1851, pp. 78 and 201.
[138] E.g., *N. J. Laws,* 1868, Ch. 169, p. 378.
[139] Five cents was the usual maximum fare. E.g., *N. J. Laws,* 1866, Ch. 366, p. 830.
[140] E.g., *N. J. Laws,* 1854, Ch. 204, p. 496.
[141] *N. J. Laws,* 35 sess., 2 sit. (1811), p. 437.
[142] *N. J. Laws,* 1865, Ch. 463, p. 837.
[143] E.g., *N. J. Laws,* 1853, Ch. 108, p. 271; 1868, Ch. 457, p. 1052.
[144] *N. J. Laws,* 1859, Ch. 208, p. 611.
[145] *N. J. Laws,* 1861, Ch. 174, p. 518.

larly the rate of infant mortality among business corporations must have been high. One would also wish to know much about the actual operating experience of companies that survived for any length of time: How much capital they actually succeeded in raising and from what sources it was derived, whether they enjoyed financial success and how their operating results compared with those of unincorporated firms doing a similar type of business, how widespread the activities of industrial and financial corporations were, the average life span of corporations in various fields and the factors that contributed to the demise of those that disappeared from the scene, as well as many other facts about their life histories. It would likewise be pertinent to the story to know even within a wide margin of error how significant corporate enterprise was in the total economy at various periods. Except for areas such as bridge, turnpike, canal, and railroad operations where the nature of the business practically necessitated the corporate form of organization and the field of commercial banking where individual enterprise was early ruled out by statute, the available data give us little idea as to the proportions in which any particular field was shared by corporate and noncorporate organizations. To have such information about various branches of manufacturing and mining for different periods during the nineteenth century would be of immense value in assessing the contribution made by corporations to our early economic development.

CHAPTER VIII

Capital Structure

It is the purpose of the present and the succeeding chapter to present the principal facts about the capital structures of the business corporations chartered by New Jersey during the entire period under investigation in this study. The information presented must necessarily be restricted to what can be gleaned from the state statutes. Rules and regulations concerning the capital structure of the business corporations of the state are to be found in acts granting special charters, in acts supplementing special charters, in general regulating laws, and in general incorporation laws. The present chapter deals with all forms of capital stock — common stock, preferred stock, and several unusual forms of stock. Chapter IX is concerned with the borrowed capital of business corporations.

COMMON STOCK

Common stock was, of course, an indispensable feature in the capital structures of all business corporations created either by special or general acts except in the case of the relatively few purely mutual concerns.[1] In fact, until the middle part of the nineteenth century it was expected that the business corporations of New Jersey would raise the principal part of the capital funds they required through the issue of common stock, and it was not until the latter half of the century that the legislature specifically empowered large numbers of companies to issue preferred stock or bonds. There was, however, an utter lack of consistency in the requirements set forth by the New Jersey legislature with respect to the common stock of business corporations, and much of the ensuing discussion of the more im-

[1] 2148 of the 2318 business corporations chartered by special act between 1791 and 1875 were stock companies.

portant aspects of the subject of common stock must necessarily be confined to general statements.[2]

It was only rarely that special charters failed to express some definite figures for the amount of capital stock that was to be issued. Twelve charters enacted before 1810 did not specify the amount of stock to be issued,[3] but in later years only a very few charters were silent on this important point. Most charters that failed to specify the size of the capital stock appear to have been enacted for the purpose of incorporating existing business enterprises where it was anticipated that the property of the corporation would be essentially that of the predecessor association.

Four principal types of formulas were employed by the New Jersey legislature in stating the amount of capital stock that might be issued by specially chartered corporations.[4] The least frequently used of the four was one that forbade the issuance of more than a stated amount of capital stock for each mile of turnpike or telegraph lines constructed. The charters of twelve early turnpike companies and one telegraph company were so worded.[5] In a much larger number of charters, the total capital stock was merely set at a definite figure, although in most such cases the companies were allowed to commence operations when only a small part of the total capital stock was sold.[6] The great majority of charters, however, explicitly permitted considerable latitude as to the amount of stock that might be issued. A form of statement very commonly employed throughout the era of special chartering was one setting a maximum limit on the amount of the total capital stock.[7] Another type, and the one

[2] Any exact analysis of the statutory provisions regulating common stock issuance is impossible not only because of the complexity and infinite variety of the statutory provisions but also because of frequent ambiguities that make the intent of the legislature doubtful.

[3] E.g., *N. J. Laws*, 21 sess., 2 sit. (1797), Ch. 653, p. 201; 23 sess., 3 sit. (1799), Ch. 794, p. 528; 29 sess., 1 sit. (1804), Ch. 133, p. 363.

[4] It is necessary here to omit discussion of a number of unusual cases that may have appeared only once or twice each.

[5] E.g., *N. J. Laws*, 25 sess., 2 sit. (1801), Ch. 38, p. 80; 1855, Ch. 248, p. 724.

[6] E.g., *N. J. Laws*, 35 sess., 2 sit. (1811), pp. 331, 351; 52 sess., 2 sit. (1828), pp. 107, 209; 1860, Ch. 88, p. 206.

[7] E.g., *ibid.*, pp. 437, 476; 1849, pp. 81, 318.

appearing most frequently of all toward the end of the period under study, set a definite figure for the capital stock but provided in addition for an increase in the amount of the stock at the option of the corporation. When charters thus permitted the stock to be increased over the original figure, the amount of the increase was generally limited.[8] In over fifty charters, however, no maximum limit was placed on the amount by which the stock might be increased, the capital requirements of the companies in carrying out their contemplated objects being the only limiting factor in these instances.[9]

Even though the nominal amount of the capital stock was generally expressed in one of the above forms, most charters included additional requirements concerning the number of shares of stock for which subscribers must be found or the amount of capital that must actually be paid up, or both, before the corporations could go into full and effective operation. The amounts of capital that had to be subscribed for or paid up before operations could begin were usually only a small fraction of the nominal capital. In setting minimum capital requirements, the New Jersey legislature did not follow any consistent policy but throughout the period of special chartering enacted a bewildering variety of rules. The examples given below will illustrate the capriciousness of the legislature in this matter.

The fifteen early charters that required the governor to issue his "letters patent" before the companies were officially incorporated made the governor's action contingent upon subscribers having been found for a certain percentage of the shares of stock.[10] Although the practice of incorporation by the issuing of "letters patent" was not followed in any case after 1819, a large number of charters enacted at various times up to 1875 required that a minimum of shares be subscribed before the companies should be considered to be incorporated.[11] While most

[8] E.g., *N. J. Laws,* 1856, Ch. 2, p. 5, Ch. 177, p. 387; 1867, Ch. 7, p. 9, Ch. 314, p. 702.

[9] Most of these cases appeared either near the beginning or the end of the period under investigation. E.g., *N. J. Laws,* 19 sess., 2 sit. (1795), Ch. 554, p. 1067; 40 sess., 2 sit. (1816, private), p. 98; 1867, Ch. 160, p. 301.

[10] E.g., *N. J. Laws,* 20 sess., 2 sit. (1796), Ch. 586, p. 57; 34 sess., 1 sit. (1809), Ch. 47, p. 164. Also cf. *supra,* pp. 12–13.

[11] E.g., *N. J. Laws,* 55 sess., 2 sit. (1831), pp. 95, 106; 1847, pp. 93, 150.

charters did not state explicitly that the companies were not incorporated until a certain number of subscriptions had been obtained, the majority of them did include provisions that made an effective corporate organization impossible until a specified number of shares had been subscribed. Hundreds of charters, for example, set forth the number of shares that were to be subscribed before the first election of directors could be held and the companies fully organized.[12]

Since only a part of the special charters required that original subscribers to the capital stock make a payment at the time they agreed to purchase shares,[13] the above regulations did not always guarantee that any money would actually be paid in by subscribers before the corporations were fully organized. It was a common practice of the legislature, however, to require the payment of a definite amount of capital before corporations could actively pursue the business for which they were established. In regulating the minimum amount of paid-in capital with which a corporation might begin business, the legislators again did not adhere to any consistent policy, but some general observations can be made from a study of the special charters. Most commercial banking companies were not permitted to begin discounting notes and bills and issuing bank notes until a minimum amount had been paid in on the capital stock.[14] Other types of corporations were not subjected to the requirement that a minimum capital be paid in before commencing business until the eighteen twenties.[15] From that time until the eighteen fifties, a substantial number of charters for all types of business required a minimum capital to be paid in before business might

[12] The amounts to be subscribed before the initial meeting and election could be held were generally only a small percentage of the total number of shares authorized. E.g., *N. J. Laws,* 29 sess., 1 sit. (1804), Ch. 137, p. 382, Ch. 154, p. 449; 61 sess., 2 sit. (1837), pp. 160, 221, 421; 1864, Ch. 270, p. 429.

[13] Cf. *infra,* p. 250.

[14] E.g., *N. J. Laws,* 36 sess., 2 sit. (1812, public), p. 3; 55 sess., 2 sit. (1831), p. 41; 1859, Ch. 84, p. 224, Ch. 206, p. 599.

[15] There were earlier examples where the requirement that a designated number of shares be subscribed before a corporation could be fully organized was coupled with the provision that a nominal sum per share be paid at the time of subscription to assure a modest paid-in capital, but no separate provisions demanding a more substantial capital before beginning business. E.g., *N. J. Laws,* 39 sess., 2 sit. (1815, private), pp. 41, 104.

begin.[16] After 1850, such provisions were included in a constantly decreasing proportion of the special charters enacted, and by the eighteen seventies the legislature for the most part confined minimum paid-in capital requirements to commercial banks, insurance companies, and other financial institutions.[17] The effectiveness of many minimum capital requirements was weakened by clauses permitting companies to begin operations either when the stipulated minimum amount was paid or when it was "secured to be paid." [18] Most bank charters were more strictly drawn and required that the minimum capital be paid in specie and that an affidavit be filed with an appropriate public official certifying that the designated amount was actually paid in.[19] During the decade of the eighteen forties, the Democrats, in an effort to protect the creditors of business corporations, included similar clauses in many charters for manufacturing, mining, and other types of corporations.[20] After the middle of the century, special charters for most nonfinancial business corporations were enacted with the same loosely drawn minimum capital requirements as charters passed before the Democrats' attempts at reform, or with no minimum requirements at all.[21]

[16] E.g., *N. J. Laws,* 49 sess., 1 sit. (1824), p. 64; 56 sess., 2 sit. (1832), pp. 170, 189; 1845, pp. 205, 221, 245.

[17] E.g., *N. J. Laws,* 1870, Ch. 132, p. 347, Ch. 174, p. 425; 1872, Ch. 444, p. 1007.

[18] E.g., *N. J. Laws,* 48 sess., 1 sit. (1823, private), p. 124; 60 sess., 2 sit. (1836), pp. 176, 259. Occasionally the legislators denied the request of corporators for the right to begin business when the minimum capital was merely "secured to be paid." Cf. *Votes and Proceedings of the General Assembly,* 1861, pp. 915–16.

[19] E.g., *N. J. Laws,* 49 sess., 1 sit. (1824), pp. 35, 99.

[20] E.g., *N. J. Laws,* 66 sess., 2 sit. (1842), p. 100; 68 sess., 2 sit. (1844), pp. 55, 265; 1848, pp. 20, 30.

[21] After 1836, some charters contained both provisions for a minimum subscription before organizing the corporation and minimum paid-in capital requirements before beginning business. When such was the case, the amount to be subscribed before formal organization took place was often larger than the amount to be paid in before business was begun. E.g., *N. J. Laws,* 61 sess., 2 sit. (1837), pp. 262, 265; 1846, p. 88. It is doubtful whether any of the requirements for the subscription or payment of a certain amount of capital stock proved to be an obstacle to newly chartered corporations. In the first place, the requirements were generally modest. Secondly, if a new company had difficulty fulfilling them, the legislators appear to have been willing to moderate their demands by passing new legislation. E.g., *N. J. Laws,* 59 sess., 1 sit. (1834), p. 6; 68 sess., 2 sit. (1844), p. 127.

The capital stock of all business corporations was apparently to be divided into shares, each share having a par value. It is true that forty-seven special charters did not lay down any requirements as to the par value of the shares, but this is not to be interpreted to mean that no-par value shares in the modern sense were permitted. Many early charters that failed to specify the par value of the shares of stock were either definitely or apparently charters to incorporate business ventures that were already in operation, and probably it was anticipated that the outstanding shares of the unincorporated associations would become the corporate stock.[22] Toward the end of the period of special chartering, a number of charters for what were evidently new ventures made no specification as to the par value of the stock, and they appear to have given the corporators or corporate officials a free hand in determining what the par value should be.[23] Seven other charters passed at the end of the period merely stated minimum figures below which the par should not be set.[24] One further one allowed the par value to be put at any figure between $5 and $50.[25]

The remaining 2093 charters established definite par values for the capital stock. A statistical analysis reveals that while the extreme limits of par were represented by one case each at $1 and $2000,[26] the most popular range was between $25 and $100, inclusive.[27] The majority of the par values were below $100, 57.0 per cent falling below $100 and only 43.0 per cent being $100 or more. It is an interesting fact that par values of less than $100 were by far the most frequently used denominations before 1860, and it was only after that date that $100 par value shares overtook $25 and $50 shares in popularity. Companies such as those for the construction of turnpikes and railroads

[22] E.g., *N. J. Laws,* 21 sess., 2 sit. (1797), Ch. 653, p. 201; 27 sess., 1 sit. (1802), Ch. 75, p. 157.

[23] E.g., *N. J. Laws,* 1871, Ch. 116, p. 363; 1872, Ch. 370, p. 872, Ch. 467, p. 1078.

[24] The minimum par values ranged between $5 and $50. E.g., *N. J. Laws,* 1870, Ch. 90, p. 254, Ch. 248, p. 562; 1872, Ch. 40, p. 193.

[25] *N. J. Laws,* 1866, Ch. 410, p. 937.

[26] Par value was $1 in the case of a quarrying company. *N. J. Laws,* 1867, Ch. 264, p. 559. It was set at $2000 in a land company's charter. *Ibid.,* 1872, Ch. 164, p. 387.

[27] 88.5 per cent fell within this range.

that needed to appeal to a large number of small investors in order to raise the capital necessary for the construction of their works nearly always issued stock with par values of $20, $25, or $50.[28] The same was true of most water and gas companies.[29] Even in the case of commercial banks, the stock of which was not difficult to sell, par values were with few exceptions set at $50 or below.[30] After 1870, $100 became the more popular figure for bank shares.[31] Generally speaking, $100 shares were more frequently employed by manufacturing companies than by other types of corporations.[32]

There is evidence that some legislators were reluctant to permit the issuance of low par value shares, their reluctance being based perhaps on a fear that persons of modest means would be encouraged to buy speculative securities if the par value was too low. For example, in 1854 an attempt was made in the senate to set the par value of the shares of a mining company at $100 in stead of at $10 as requested by the applicants for the charter.[33] Yet in a surprisingly large number of cases par values were set as low as $5 and $10. The $5 figure appeared in thirty-three charters and the $10 figure in seventy-six, the majority of such cases occurring after 1850. In the earlier years, low par value shares were employed by such concerns as water and gas companies.[34] In later years, however, they found their greatest popularity with mining and petroleum companies, most of which ventures appear to have been highly speculative in nature.[35]

At the opposite end of the scale were found fifty-four charters that established the par value of the capital stock at figures in excess of $100. In these upper reaches, $500 and $1000 stocks

[28] E.g., *N. J. Laws,* 60 sess., 2 sit. (1836), pp. 60, 141; 1870, Ch. 349, p. 979.

[29] E.g., *N. J. Laws,* 63 sess., 2 sit. (1839), p. 98; 1849, pp. 47, 235, 279.

[30] E.g., *N. J. Laws,* 49 sess., 1 sit. (1824), pp. 35, 99, 118; 1855, Ch. 190, p. 519.

[31] E.g., *N. J. Laws,* 1871, Ch. 266, p. 659; 1872, Ch. 3, p. 140.

[32] E.g., *N. J. Laws,* 61 sess., 2 sit. (1837), pp. 262, 486; 1846, pp. 53, 77, 85.

[33] *Journal of the Senate,* 1854, p. 417. When the charter was finally passed, however, the par value remained at the $10 figure. *N. J. Laws,* 1854, Ch. 110, p. 271.

[34] E.g., *N. J. Laws,* 50 sess., 1 sit. (1825), pp. 102, 105.

[35] E.g., *N. J. Laws,* 1861, Ch. 73, p. 158; 1865, Ch. 160, p. 290, Ch. 327, p. 622, and Ch. 437, p. 792.

were in the majority, occurring in twenty-eight and twelve cases respectively.[36]

On a number of occasions the legislature enacted charter amendments permitting changes in the par value of shares of capital stock. The cases in which the par was reduced in order to effect a reduction in the amount of the capital stock account will be discussed later, but in about a dozen instances the reduction in par was made apparently either to achieve an ordinary stock split or to assist newly chartered companies that were having difficulty marketing shares of high par value.[37] Increases in par value designed to effect reverse splits were authorized on seven occasions.[38]

In setting forth the regulations governing the original sale of capital stock in those cases where stock was to be offered for public subscription, the New Jersey legislature employed a wide variety of plans to secure what was considered a desirable distribution of the shares. Very often public notices were required to be given in designated places a certain time before the subscription books were to be opened, and charters frequently specified the period of time during which the books were to remain open.[39] Such provisions were supplemented by more direct controls, however, in approximately 300 charters. Most of the controls were designed either to assure at least some participation on the part of all who wished to subscribe to the stock, to restrict the right to subscribe to citizens of New Jersey or to residents of particular political subdivisions of the state, or to guarantee the right of the state government itself to subscribe. In over ninety per cent of the cases in which the legislature evidenced some concern as to the manner in which the stock was

[36] Such high par values were frequently employed in the formation of corporations that were to take over assets already owned by the corporators in exchange for the stock. E.g., *N. J. Laws,* 1849, p. 7; 1852, Ch. 4, p. 19, Ch. 89, p. 208.

[37] E.g., *N. J. Laws,* 1848, p. 15; 1859, Ch. 51, p. 92. Sometimes the reduction in par was made simultaneously with a grant of authority to increase the capital by issuing more shares. Presumably new shares of $500 or $1000 par value would have had a limited market appeal. E.g., *ibid.,* 62 sess., 2 sit. (1838), p. 87; 1866, Ch. 16, p. 38.

[38] E.g., *N. J. Laws,* 1854, Ch. 216, p. 524; 1859, Ch. 65, p. 167.

[39] E.g., *N. J. Laws,* 1845, pp. 38, 55, 133; 1860, Ch. 25, p. 59, Ch. 184, p. 479.

distributed, the companies involved were chartered for the purpose of conducting a banking business or constructing works of general public utility such as bridges, turnpikes, canals, railroads, or gas manufacturing and distributing systems.

The earliest device used to achieve wide distribution of the capital stock was to put a limit on the number of shares to which any one person could subscribe on the first days during which the subscription books were open.[40] Restrictions of this type were put into twenty-two charters. Some of the formulas developed were quite detailed, as, for example, one in the 1792 charter of a bridge company permitting anyone over twenty-one years of age to subscribe for one share on the first day, for one or two shares on the second day, for one, two, or three shares on the third day, and for any number thereafter.[41] Later and more simple rules forbade anyone from subscribing over a specified amount on the first few days.[42] Two charters merely stated that no one was to own more than a given number of shares.[43]

Another plan was to permit anyone to subscribe for as many shares as he wished, and, if an oversubscription resulted, the allotment of shares to each subscriber would be reduced below the amount for which he had subscribed. There were various schemes for apportioning the stock. Nearly eighty charters required that the shares be distributed among the subscribers in proportion to the amounts for which they had subscribed, or, as it was sometimes expressed, in a fair and equitable manner.[44] In order to protect small subscribers from being left without any shares as the result of an apportionment, an additional ninety charters provided that individual subscriptions could not be reduced below a specified number of shares.[45] Citizens of New

[40] It should be recalled also that in eleven of the fifteen early charters that required the governor to incorporate the companies by issuing his "letters patent" the governor was not to act until the required number of shares had been subscribed by a minimum number of persons. Cf. *supra*, pp. 12–13.

[41] *N. J. Laws*, 17 sess., 1 sit. (1792), Ch. 406, p. 806. See also *ibid.*, 20 sess., 2 sit. (1796), Ch. 586, p. 57; 38 sess., 2 sit. (1814, private), p. 169.

[42] E.g., *N. J. Laws*, 1851, pp. 245, 295.

[43] *N. J. Laws*, 1866, Ch. 335, p. 775; 1868, Ch. 378, p. 849.

[44] E.g., *N. J. Laws*, 57 sess., 2 sit. (1833), pp. 75, 128; 1849, pp. 13, 230, 312.

[45] The number of shares below which a subscription could not be reduced ranged anywhere from one to twenty, but the average was about six. E.g., *N. J. Laws*, 36 sess., 2 sit. (1812, private), p. 87; 1849, pp. 121, 157, 171.

Jersey were to be given preferential treatment in allotting shares among subscribers according to the terms of fourteen charters.[46] In thirty-nine charters enacted after 1830 the corporators were expressly given a free hand in apportioning the stock among subscribers. They were simply directed to distribute the shares in such a manner as they deemed "expedient and conducive to the object of the incorporation," in a way that would "secure the speedy construction" of the contemplated works, or as they thought "proper." [47]

The New Jersey lawmakers sometimes took measures to give certain groups of persons an advantage in subscribing to the capital stock of newly chartered corporations. The preference to be given to New Jersey citizens in distributing the stock of fourteen companies has been mentioned in the preceding paragraph. Twelve bank charters and one other charter permitted only residents of New Jersey to subscribe to the stock.[48] Citizens of New Jersey were awarded the exclusive right to subscribe for the stock of ten banks and one water power company for a specified number of days.[49] Two other charters gave Jerseymen the privilege of taking a designated part of the stock before others could subscribe.[50] Twenty-three bank charters enacted during and after 1855 required that the majority of the capital stock must be held by residents of New Jersey or that the majority of the stockholders be residents of the state, and one required that Jerseymen hold three-fourths of the capital stock.[51] Four gas company charters gave the first right to subscribe to residents of cities in which the firms were to operate. After a time, any citizen of New Jersey could subscribe, and then anyone.[52] One bank charter similarly gave prior subscription rights to residents of three designated counties.[53]

[46] These were all either bank or railroad charters. E.g., *N. J. Laws,* 56 sess., 2 sit. (1832), pp. 59, 65; 1866, Ch. 169, p. 358, Ch. 376, p. 845.

[47] Most such provisions were found in railroad charters. E.g., *N. J. Laws,* 55 sess., 2 sit. (1831), pp. 24, 66; 1850, p. 41.

[48] E.g., *N. J. Laws,* 54 sess., 2 sit. (1830), pp. 42, 59; 1859, Ch. 84, p. 224.

[49] E.g., *N. J. Laws,* 36 sess., 2 sit. (1812, public), p. 3; 1860, Ch. 246, p. 632.

[50] *N. J. Laws,* 49 sess., 1 sit. (1824), p. 99; 52 sess., 2 sit. (1828), p. 87.

[51] E.g., *N. J. Laws,* 1855, Ch. 247, p. 718; 1860, Ch. 247, p. 640.

[52] E.g., *N. J. Laws,* 1851, p. 460; 1854, Ch. 15, p. 31.

[53] *N. J. Laws,* 1855, Ch. 222, p. 632.

A final group of charter provisions concerned with the distribution of corporate stock includes those that reserved a definite portion of stock for purchase by the state of New Jersey. The first twelve bank charters provided that the state could subscribe to substantial amounts of stock if it desired.[54] In thus providing for state participation in early banks, the New Jersey legislators were in accord with the practice of most other states.[55] During the early years of the nineteenth century, the legislature also reserved the right to subscribe to the stock of two canal companies, one turnpike company, and one water power concern.[56] The lawmakers likewise reserved rights for the state to purchase stock in eight railroad corporations.[57]

It was not generally expected that when persons subscribed to corporate stock they would make immediate payment for the entire amount of the purchase price. In fact, a majority of the New Jersey charters made no requirement that anything at all be paid at the time of subscription. On the other hand, approximately 850 charters enacted by the New Jersey legislature did require designated amounts per share to be paid at the time of subscription. The sums that were to be paid per share when subscriptions were made varied widely, but amounts representing 5 or 10 per cent of the par values were quite common.[58] Apparently the payments were to be made in cash, although only a few charters were explicit in this respect.[59] A small number of early charters also established the amounts that were to be paid before subscribers received their stock certificates.[60]

The principal part of the stockholders' contribution was ordi-

[54] E.g., *N. J. Laws,* 28 sess., 2 sit. (1804), Ch. 109, p. 268; 36 sess., 2 sit. (1812, public), p. 3. In most instances, the time during which the state might subscribe was unlimited.

[55] Cf. D. R. Dewey, *State Banking Before the Civil War,* pp. 33–40.

[56] *N. J. Laws,* 29 sess., 1 sit. (1804), Ch. 151, p. 419; 49 sess., 1 sit. (1824), p. 175; 54 sess., 2 sit. (1830), p. 73; 55 sess., 2 sit. (1831), p. 131.

[57] E.g., *N. J. Laws,* 54 sess., 2 sit. (1830), p. 83; 1851, pp. 5, 37. In most instances, the state's privileges did not expire until a definite time after the railroad had been completed.

[58] E.g., *N. J. Laws,* 30 sess., 2 sit. (1806), Ch. 189, p. 577; 1845, pp. 198, 211, 258.

[59] E.g., *N. J. Laws,* 58 sess., 2 sit. (1834), p. 55; 60 sess., 2 sit. (1836), pp. 37, 204, 270.

[60] E.g., *N. J. Laws,* 20 sess., 2 sit. (1796), Ch. 586, p. 57; 34 sess., 1 sit. (1809), Ch. 47, p. 164, Ch. 49, p. 176.

narily made at a time subsequent to the date of subscription and was paid in at such times and in such amounts as the affairs of the corporations demanded. Nearly all New Jersey charters had something to say about the manner in which calls upon stockholders for payment of their shares were to be made. Some merely stated that the calls were to be made by the board of directors and left the determination of the manner and amount of the calls to the discretion of that body.[61] A good many charters specified how far in advance of the date the payments were due the stockholders should be notified and also designated the form in which notice was to be given.[62] Other charters went further and regulated the amount of the payments that could be demanded at any one time and the frequency with which calls could be made. In about 250 cases, upper limits were put upon the amount of each individual payment per share demanded from the stockholders.[63] A slightly larger number of charters offered greater protection to stockholders by setting a maximum amount on each payment and in addition specifying the interval of time that must elapse between calls.[64] In about a score of charters, including those for the earliest banks, the matter of payments on the capital stock was approached in a positive manner, and the amounts of the payments and the intervals at which they were to be paid were specified.[65]

The usual penalty on stockholders for nonpayment of installments on the capital stock was forfeiture of the shares and of the payments already made. Specific monthly penalties for nonpayment were written into sixteen charters enacted before 1823, and in a majority of these cases the directors were permitted to declare shares forfeited only after the fines, or in some instances,

[61] E.g., *N. J. Laws,* 25 sess., 2 sit. (1801), Ch. 38, p. 80; 1860, Ch. 37, p. 87.

[62] E.g., *N. J. Laws,* 48 sess., 1 sit. (1823, private), pp. 124, 157; 1860, Ch. 56, p. 130, Ch. 78, p. 188.

[63] E.g., *N. J. Laws,* 37 sess., 2 sit. (1813, private), pp. 22, 54; 1849, pp. 55, 105.

[64] E.g., *N. J. Laws,* 56 sess., 2 sit. (1832), pp. 96, 121; 1869, Ch. 183, p. 472, Ch. 533, p. 1280.

[65] E.g., *N. J. Laws,* 28 sess., 2 sit. (1804), Ch. 109, p. 268; 29 sess., 1 sit. (1804), Ch. 154, p. 449. Since they apparently did not need the capital at as fast a rate as it was scheduled to be paid in, two banks were granted amendments to their charters permitting them to call for payments at their discretion. *Ibid.,* 30 sess., 1 sit. (1805), Ch. 167, p. 488; 33 sess., 1 sit. (1808), Ch. 6, p. 11.

the fines plus the payment then due, equalled the amount that had already been paid.[66] In most instances, however, the directors were empowered to declare shares forfeited if payments were not made within a designated time after they were due or after the required notice had been served, and sometimes the directors' action in this matter was not restricted in any way.[67] As a general rule, corporate directors were seemingly powerless to compel stockholders to pay installments on the shares for which they had subscribed, but thirty-six charters and two charter amendments departed from the usual pattern and invested directors with authority to bring legal action against stockholders to force them to pay installments that were owing.[68] Five additional charters declared that even if a stockholder had forfeited his shares for nonpayment he was not thereby relieved from liability to pay up the amount of stock for which he had subscribed.[69]

It was by no means an invariable rule that the stock of New Jersey's business corporations was to be paid for in the form of cash, and the statutes are replete with grants of authority to issue stock for a consideration other than cash.[70] Payment for the stock of Alexander Hamilton's S. U. M., if subscribed for in advance of the first election, could be made either in specie or in designated issues of United States stock. In the case of stock subscribed for later, the directors had full power to determine the form of payment.[71] The stock of a bank chartered in 1816 could be paid one-fifth in United States stock and four-fifths in cash.[72] Then there were many cases where the principal assets

[66] E.g., *N. J. Laws,* 17 sess., 1 sit. (1792), Ch. 406, p. 806; 22 sess., 2 sit. (1798), Ch. 708, p. 321; 34 sess., 1 sit. (1809), Ch. 47, p. 164.

[67] E.g., *N. J. Laws,* 27 sess., 1 sit. (1802), Ch. 81, p. 172; 57 sess., 2 sit. (1833), pp. 15, 37, 121.

[68] E.g., *N. J. Laws,* 48 sess., 1 sit. (1823, private), p. 166; 1866, Ch. 32, p. 67, Ch. 141, p. 305.

[69] E.g., *N. J. Laws,* 1867, Ch. 130, p. 233.

[70] Even when no explicit authority to issue stock in exchange for property or services was given, the New Jersey charters, with few exceptions, did not expressly state that payment must be made in cash. In this respect they differed from most Maryland charters. Cf. J. G. Blandi, *Maryland Business Corporations: 1783–1852,* p. 34.

[71] *N. J. Laws,* 16 sess., 1 sit. (1791), Ch. 356, p. 730.

[72] *N. J. Laws,* 40 sess., 2 sit. (1816, private), p. 48.

of newly chartered corporations were expected to consist of designated property held by the corporators, by other specified individuals, or by a predecessor business association. In such situations, the owners of the property were to receive stock in the corporations as payment.[73] If charters were granted to existing business associations that already had shares outstanding, they commonly provided that the old shareholders should receive an equivalent amount of the corporate stock in exchange for their holdings.[74]

A practice that originated very early in connection with turnpike companies permitted subscribers to pay for their stock by providing services to the companies. A number of turnpike company charters enacted during the first decade of the nineteenth century stipulated that no stockholders should be compelled to forfeit their shares for nonpayment of installments if they had agreed to build portions of the roads and had given "security" that they would do so.[75] Such provisions did not appear again until 1858, but between that year and 1875 there were forty-three instances in which subscribers to the stock of turnpike companies were expressly given the right to pay all their installments except the first by performing work on the roads. Ten of these charters made the qualification that the stockholders must be willing to do the work "as cheaply as it otherwise can be done," [76] and three set eight shares as the maximum number that one stockholder could pay for in this manner.[77] During the eighteen seventies, two other companies were given authority by their charters to issue stock in exchange for services performed, and three railroad companies received similar privileges by charter amendments.[78]

Corporation officials sometimes found the right to issue stock in exchange for property a useful privilege. Although from the

[73] All such cases cannot, of course, be detected from the sketchy information contained in the charters, but a number of corporations clearly fall within this category. E.g., *N. J. Laws*, 1847, pp. 61, 126.

[74] E.g., *N. J. Laws*, 64 sess., 2 sit. (1840), p. 51; 1845, pp. 29, 186.

[75] E.g., *N. J. Laws*, 30 sess., 2 sit. (1806), Ch. 186, p. 526; 32 sess., 1 sit. (1807), Ch. 6, p. 26.

[76] E.g., *N. J. Laws*, 1860, Ch. 60, p. 137; 1862, Ch. 84, p. 151.

[77] E.g., *N. J. Laws*, 1868, Ch. 297, p. 681.

[78] E.g., *N. J. Laws*, 1870, Ch. 63, p. 201; 1873, Ch. 550, p. 1444.

earliest years many charters authorized the issue of stock in payment for certain specified properties, corporations were not given a free hand in issuing stock in return for property until after 1848. But after that date, a constantly increasing number of corporations were favored with blanket authority to purchase property and give their stock in payment.[79] Between 1848 and 1875, the privilege was bestowed on 344 corporations, by the terms of the original charters in 332 of these cases and by charter amendments in the remaining twelve. Companies for manufacturing, mining, and land development were most frequently favored, accounting respectively for 43.9, 19.2, and 16.3 per cent of the whole group of 344 cases.[80]

The various clauses permitting stock to be issued in payment for property were not standardized. In a few cases it appears that only real property was to be paid for in stock.[81] Most charters conferred a more broad authority, for the type of property to be taken in exchange for stock was usually not restricted,[82] and frequently even patents and sometimes franchises were specifically mentioned as kinds of property for which stock could be given.[83] In many instances, especially when mining companies were involved, stock could be used to pay for property whether it was purchased or merely leased.[84] The charters were equally inconsistent in the matter of the valuation of property paid for in shares of stock. Most were completely silent about the problem.[85] Nearly fifty designated the directors as the persons to approve the valuation,[86] some thirty required the

[79] During the eighteen fifties, however, some legislators attempted to defeat clauses in special charter legislation allowing the issuance of stock in return for contributions of property. E.g., *Journal of the Senate*, 1854, p. 417; *ibid.*, 1858, pp. 179–180.

[80] Seven manufacturing companies were allowed to give stock for property only after a stated minimum amount of capital had been paid in in the ordinary manner. E.g., *N. J. Laws*, 1860, Ch. 88, p. 206.

[81] E.g., *N. J. Laws*, 1855, Ch. 142, p. 397.

[82] E.g., *N. J. Laws*, 1865, Ch. 450, p. 812; 1872, Ch. 47, p. 201, Ch. 359, p. 849.

[83] E.g., *N. J. Laws*, 1869, Ch. 52, p. 81, Ch. 568, p. 1443; 1874, Ch. 81, p. 940.

[84] E.g., *N. J. Laws*, 1860, Ch. 93, p. 226; 1874, Ch. 530, p. 1291.

[85] E.g., *N. J. Laws*, 1865, Ch. 450, p. 812; 1869, Ch. 127, p. 303, Ch. 459, p. 1145.

[86] E.g., *N. J. Laws*, 1865, Ch. 378, p. 704; 1872, Ch. 104, p. 297.

valuation to have the approval of a specified proportion of the stockholders,[87] and a few stated that the valuation should be made either by stockholders or directors, or by both groups.[88] In some cases the requirements concerning the valuation of the property seem to have been very loose, and stock could be issued for property "at a valuation to be agreed upon," on "terms as may be deemed best for its [the company's] interests," or according to some equally indefinite rule.[89] Little further care seems to have been taken in framing the clauses to avoid possible stock watering when shares were issued for property, but very occasionally corporations were expressly forbidden to issue the stock at less than par value or at less than the actual cash or bona fide value of the property received.[90] In only one case was stock issued for property required to be distinguished on the books and in official reports from stock paid for in cash.[91]

Three ways in which common stock could be issued during the period under study without involving contributions of new cash, services, or property were by means of stock dividends, by the exchange of stock for convertible bonds, and by giving stock in payment of corporate debts. Each case can be treated very briefly. So far as the language of the statutes is concerned, it is a moot question whether New Jersey corporations could distribute stock dividends in the absence of express authority to do so. There were, however, at least three special charters and nine charter amendments, all enacted after 1850, in which companies were explictly empowered to make stock dividends. In a majority of the dozen cases it was made perfectly clear that the stock dividends were to represent earnings that had been reinvested to improve or extend the companies' works.[92] Bonds that could be made convertible into stock were expressly authorized by the legislature in twenty-one cases between 1853

[87] E.g., *N. J. Laws,* 1866, Ch. 249, p. 595, Ch. 411, p. 938; 1874, Ch. 123, p. 967.

[88] E.g., *N. J. Laws,* 1864, Ch. 26, p. 47; 1869, Ch. 143, p. 359.

[89] E.g., *N. J. Laws,* 1855, Ch. 142, p. 397; 1865, Ch. 309, p. 579.

[90] E.g., *N. J. Laws,* 1873, Ch. 181, p. 1040, Ch. 670, p. 1587.

[91] *Ibid.,* Ch. 642, p. 1516.

[92] E.g., *N. J. Laws,* 1857, Ch. 106, p. 303; 1868, Ch. 362, p. 816, and Ch. 562, p. 1203; 1873, Ch. 15, p. 914.

and 1875. The details of these authorizations are presented in the following chapter.[93] Eight corporations were given the right to issue shares of stock in payment of the corporate debts. The privilege was not qualified in any way.[94]

A few words remain to be said concerning the general conditions on which specially chartered corporations were permitted to increase or decrease the amount of their capital stock. Earlier in the present chapter it was pointed out that special charters frequently set forth a definite figure for the capital stock but provided at the same time for the issue of either a definite or indeterminate amount of additional stock.[95] In such cases there was no fixed rule as to what parties were to decide whether or not to exercise the privilege of increasing the capital stock. Most charters merely stated that the "company" was at liberty to increase the stock, language that would presumably leave the decision to be made as directed by the stockholders in the bylaws.[96] A relatively few charters empowered the directors to decide upon the increase.[97] Express provision was made in about 120 charters, nearly all of which were passed after 1850, for stockholder approval before the stock could be increased to the maximum authorized amount. There was no uniformity in the requirements in such cases. For example, among the charters were some that required the affirmative votes of "a majority of the stockholders," [98] others that required the approval of a majority in interest of the stockholders,[99] and a number that established two-thirds in interest of the stockholders as the vote necessary to approve the increase.[100] When corporations were permitted by the terms of their charters to increase their capital stock, they were not as a rule subject to statutory limitations as to the manner of distributing the new shares. In only thirty-five cases, a small percentage of the total, were

[93] Cf. *infra*, pp. 293–294.

[94] E.g., *N. J. Laws*, 1869, Ch. 29, p. 34; 1871, Ch. 143, p. 422.

[95] Cf. *supra*, pp. 241–242.

[96] E.g., *N. J. Laws*, 57 sess., 2 sit. (1833), pp. 15, 37; 1860, Ch. 36, p. 83, Ch. 218, p. 571.

[97] E.g., *N. J. Laws*, 1865, Ch. 74, p. 132, Ch. 257, p. 451; 1872, Ch. 135, p. 347.

[98] E.g., *N. J. Laws*, 1865, Ch. 7, p. 17.

[99] E.g., *N. J. Laws*, 1868, Ch. 249, p. 555, Ch. 384, p. 867.

[100] E.g., *N. J. Laws*, 1867, Ch. 234, p. 488; 1873, Ch. 344, p. 1283.

there explicit directions to give present shareholders the first opportunity to subscribe.[101]

As might be expected, many companies found it desirable or necessary to request supplementary legislation empowering them to increase their capital stock beyond the maximum amount authorized by their original charters. The New Jersey statute books contain nearly three hundred charter amendments permitting corporations to increase their capital for the purpose of extending the scope of their business, for improving, completing, or enlarging their works, or for paying off their debts. Such amendments were apt to be silent as to who should decide whether and when the privilege of increasing the stock was to be exercised,[102] but in a number of instances the decision was put squarely in the hands of the directors.[103] Only thirty-one amendments provided for approval of the increase by some proportion of the stockholders.[104] In regard to the distribution of the new shares, only sixteen of the supplementary acts stated explicitly that stockholders were to be given a prior right to subscribe before subscriptions were taken from other persons.[105] It is an interesting thing that in four of the sixteen cases the preëmptive right was abridged and applied only to one-third or one-half of the new shares.[106] Although each amendment authorizing increases in the capital stock made the par value of the new shares equal to that of the existing stock, only a few amendments made mention of the price at which the new shares were to be sold. In three cases where banks were involved, the directors were to "equalize the value of the new stock to the old, by requiring payment on the new stock of the rateable proportion of the expenses of said bank in its organization and establishment, and an amount equal to the surplus profits on

[101] Twenty-four of the cases in which preëmptive rights were explicitly safeguarded were charters for banks and insurance companies. E.g., *N. J. Laws*, 28 sess., 2 sit. (1804), Ch. 109, p. 268; 1868, Ch. 17, p. 38, Ch. 515, p. 1126.

[102] E.g., *N. J. Laws*, 1855, Ch. 127, p. 341; 1867, Ch. 143, p. 265.

[103] E.g., *N. J. Laws*, 1855, Ch. 122, p. 326; 1865, Ch. 133, p. 326, Ch. 220, p. 391.

[104] E.g., *N. J. Laws*, 58 sess., 2 sit. (1834), p. 142; 1857, Ch. 86, p. 259.

[105] E.g., *N. J. Laws*, 1848, p. 13; 1862, Ch. 119, p. 237.

[106] *N. J. Laws*, 60 sess., 2 sit. (1836), pp. 171, 173, 239; 61 sess., 2 sit. (1837), p. 91.

hand." [107] Another amendment to a bank charter stated that the two-thirds of the new stock on which the stockholders had no preëmptive rights "shall be subject to . . . reasonable and equitable allowance for any surplus profits that may exist in the said company . . ." [108] Five bank charter amendments empowered the directors to sell to anyone the shares not subscribed for by the existing stockholders "for the best price or prices that can be obtained, not less than their par value, and the overplus, if any, be credited to the account of the profits of the said bank." [109]

Permission to reduce the capital stock was granted in only eleven special charters of incorporation, all of which were enacted after 1860. Of this group, the charters of three mining companies and four manufacturing companies allowed the stock to be decreased without apparent limit upon a vote of the stockholders.[110] The four other companies were permitted to decrease their capital, but not below stipulated minimum figures.[111]

Twenty-seven corporations had their charters amended to allow them to reduce their capital stock. Minimum figures below which the capital was not to be reduced were generally established in these cases,[112] but in three instances no minima seem to have been set.[113] In some cases, the capital reduction was to be effected by a reduction in the par value of the outstanding shares,[114] and in others by a decrease in the number of shares outstanding.[115] Occasionally the amendments expressly permitted a choice between reducing the par value or the number of shares,[116] but in several instances the acts did not make any

[107] *N. J. Laws,* 60 sess., 2 sit. (1836), pp. 173, 239; 1849, p. 5. According to the 1849 amendment, the amount necessary to "equalize" the new stock was to be "added to the undivided profits of the bank."

[108] *N. J. Laws,* 60 sess., 2 sit. (1836), p. 171.

[109] E.g., *ibid.,* p. 351; 1855, Ch. 88, p. 210.

[110] E.g., *N. J. Laws,* 1865, Ch. 154, p. 276; 1867, Ch. 360, p. 820.

[111] E.g., *N. J. Laws,* 1862, Ch. 51, p. 70.

[112] E.g., *N. J. Laws,* 1864, Ch. 224, p. 336; 1873, Ch. 59, p. 956.

[113] E.g., *N. J. Laws,* 1873, Ch. 63, p. 961.

[114] E.g., *N. J. Laws,* 1867, Ch. 343, p. 788; 1873, Ch. 59, p. 956.

[115] E.g., *N. J. Laws,* 1864, Ch. 219, p. 332; 1872, Ch. 174, p. 411.

[116] E.g., *N. J. Laws,* 1865, Ch. 30, p. 62; 1869, Ch. 45, p. 71.

statement as to the manner in which the reduction in capital was to be accomplished.[117] A majority of the amendments required the approval of a stated proportion of the stockholders before the capital could be reduced.[118] Unfortunately there are very few clues in the statutes to indicate why amendments permitting reductions in the capital stock were requested, although the bare fact that business losses had been sustained or that the corporate property had greatly depreciated in value was frequently mentioned in the amendments. In each of the two earliest cases, the banks requesting authority to decrease their capital stock represented that their capital had become "impaired by losses, which, under the existing charter, prevents a division of the interest or profits of the remaining capital among the stockholders . . ." [119] On the third occasion that the legislators permitted a corporation to reduce its capital, the directors of the bank concerned had maintained that because of the establishment of other banks their whole paid-in capital could no longer be employed.[120] Although other acts made no mention of the reasons for reducing the capital stock, it is quite likely that the desire to wipe out an accumulated deficit so that dividends could be paid was the incentive in many cases. It is also quite likely that certain savings in taxes could be realized by reducing the amount of the capital stock.[121]

[117] E.g., *N. J. Laws,* 1860, Ch. 6, p. 24; 1867, Ch. 205, p. 438.

[118] E.g., *N. J. Laws,* 67 sess., 2 sit. (1843), p. 62; 1874, Ch. 226, p. 1082.

[119] *N. J. Laws,* 45 sess., 1 sit. (1820, private), p. 150; 46 sess., 1 sit. (1821, private), p. 21. In the second instance, the stockholders had sent a petition to the legislature "praying for a reduction of the par value of the shares in said bank, so as to enable them to declare dividends." *Votes and Proceedings of the General Assembly,* 46 sess., 1 sit. (1821), p. 14.

[120] *N. J. Laws,* 47 sess., 1 sit. (1822, private), p. 91.

[121] Although it is not possible here to analyze the tax aspects thoroughly, it seems probable that tax considerations were of some significance. After 1810, banks were subject to a special tax on their paid-in capital stock, and the first eight amendments reducing capital stock were passed on behalf of banking companies. In 1862, the state tax laws were modified to change the basis of the taxation of non-banking corporations so that they were assessed and taxed "at the full amount of their capital stock paid in, and accumulated surplus . . ." *N. J. Laws,* 1862, Ch. 194, p. 344. This change may explain the fact that beginning in 1864 manufacturing and other non-banking corporations appeared for the first time among the companies seeking capital reductions.

Most of the twenty general incorporation laws enacted in New Jersey during the period under study contained some provisions concerning the capital stock of the companies organized under their authority. The provisions of the general laws, however, varied widely. It is the purpose of the concluding paragraphs of this section to treat the most important ways in which the general incorporation laws sought to deal with the matter of the common stock.

Three general laws established both minimum and maximum limits on the amount of the capital stock. They were the banking law of 1850, the general law of 1854 for companies engaged in transportation by water, and an 1865 law for land development companies, wherein the amounts were set respectively at $50,000 to $500,000, $50,000 to $1,000,000, and $100,000 to $500,000.[122] The 1849 law for manufacturing and other types of companies, the 1852 insurance law, and the gas company law of 1874 merely established minimum limits of $10,000, $50,000, and $10,000, respectively.[123] The minimum amount of capital stock for railroad companies organized under the 1873 railroad act was set at $10,000 per mile of road.[124] Three general laws imposed only upper limits on the amount of the capital. They were the 1816 general law for certain types of manufacturing companies where $100,000 was the maximum, the 1857 law for the incorporation of companies to build factory buildings with a limit of $300,000 on the capital, and the law of 1869 for the formation of companies to cut peat or stone in which $200,000 was the established maximum.[125]

Regulations as to the amount of capital that had to be subscribed or paid in before effective organization could be completed were found in four general laws. The 1849 manufacturing company law required a paid-in capital of $6000 be-

[122] *N. J. Laws*, 1850, p. 140; 1854, Ch. 201, p. 470; 1865, Ch. 379, p. 707. In 1866, the minimum capital for the water carriers was reduced to $10,000. *Ibid.*, 1866, Ch. 153, p. 343.

[123] *N. J. Laws*, 1849, p. 300; 1852, Ch. 74, p. 159; 1874, Ch. 509, p. 124. In 1875, the general law of 1849 was amended to permit certain companies handling dairy products to be organized with a capital of only $5000. *Ibid.*, 1875, Ch. 173, p. 35.

[124] *N. J. Laws*, 1873, Ch. 413, p. 88.

[125] *N. J. Laws*, 40 sess., 2 sit. (1816, public), p. 17; 1857, Ch. 130, p. 373; 1869, Ch. 374, p. 1001.

fore business could begin.[126] The telegraph company law of 1853 did not permit corporations to be organized until two or more persons had subscribed one-third of the capital necessary to build the lines in New Jersey.[127] Companies that were organized under the general law of 1854 for water carriers were not to exercise corporate powers until 20 per cent of the capital stock was paid in,[128] and those being organized under the 1873 railroad law were not to file their certificates of incorporation until $2000 per mile of the proposed road was subscribed and 10 per cent paid in cash.[129]

With one exception, the general laws seem to have allowed the corporators to fix the par value of the shares of capital stock at any figure. The ordinary rule was that the certificates of incorporation must state the amount of the capital stock and the number of shares into which it was divided. The exceptional case was an 1867 general law for land companies that required the capital stock to be divided into $50 shares.[130]

The general railroad law was the only one in which subscribers were required to make a payment at the time of subscription, and the amount to be paid in that case was 10 per cent in cash.[131] Ten of the general laws, however, laid down rules respecting the manner in which installments on the capital stock should be called. There was little unusual about these regulations. It should be noted, however, that the important 1846 and 1849 general laws allowed two-thirds in interest of the stockholders to decide at a special meeting when to call for payments on the stock. If payments were not forthcoming after a thirty-day notice, the same proportion of stockholders could order the sale at public auction of enough of a delinquent stockholder's shares to pay the assessment then owing.[132] The general railroad law of 1873 stated that if a company did not declare shares forfeited for nonpayment, a delinquent stockholder would be individually liable to the company for the

[126] *N. J. Laws,* 1849, p. 300. In 1874 and 1875, the minimum paid-in capital was reduced to $1000 for companies engaged in manufacturing and selling certain dairy products. *Ibid.,* 1874, Ch. 314, p. 59; 1875, Ch. 173, p. 35.

[127] *N. J. Laws,* 1853, Ch. 122, p. 304.

[128] *N. J. Laws,* 1854, Ch. 201, p. 470.

[129] *N. J. Laws,* 1873, Ch. 413, p. 88.

[130] *N. J. Laws,* 1867, Ch. 378, p. 855.

[131] *N. J. Laws,* 1873, Ch. 413, p. 88.

[132] *N. J. Laws,* 1846, p. 64; 1849, p. 300.

amount of stock he held until the whole amount was paid in.[133]

In the matter of the form in which payment for stock was to be made, the general laws were decidedly illiberal. The 1846 and 1849 general laws for manufacturing and other companies and the 1874 gas company law contained definite language to the effect that no note or obligation, whether secured by pledge or otherwise, should be considered as payment for any part of the capital stock.[134] Only two unimportant general laws made express provision for the issue of stock in return for property. One was an 1867 law for land development companies that permitted stock to be paid for in money or land. If the stock was issued in exchange for land, the value of the land was to be appraised by the directors.[135] The other was the general law of 1869 authorizing the formation of corporations for cutting peat or stone. In this case, the directors could vote to issue stock for property required for the business, but the stock was not to be issued for less than its par value.[136]

There is no doubt that the failure of the important general incorporation laws to provide for the issue of stock for a consideration other than money was one of the factors that help to explain why these laws were so little used. It has been pointed out previously in the present chapter that after 1848 several hundred specially chartered corporations were empowered to issue stock in return for property. Most of these companies, it will be recalled, were engaged in manufacturing or mining, exactly the type of companies that might have been expected to file certificates of incorporation under the terms of the 1849 general law. An unsuccessful attempt was made in the New Jersey senate to remedy this shortcoming of the law of 1849 by permitting any company that had been organized under the authority of that law to issue stock in exchange for real or personal property "suitable and proper" for business

[133] *N. J. Laws,* 1873, Ch. 413, p. 88.

[134] In each case, the effect of the clause was strengthened by prohibiting all loans of money by the company to stockholders. *N. J. Laws,* 1846, p. 64; 1849, p. 300; 1874, Ch. 509, p. 124.

[135] *N. J. Laws,* 1867, Ch. 378, p. 855.

[136] *N. J. Laws,* 1869, Ch. 374, p. 1001.

purposes.[137] It is significant that the general incorporation law appearing in the revised statutes of 1875 permitted companies to purchase necessary property and to issue in payment stock to the amount of its value.[138]

Twelve of the general laws provided for companies that wished to increase the amount of their capital stock, and five allowed the capital stock to be reduced. Reductions had to be voted on by the stockholders, in every case, but only seven of the laws permitting the stock to be increased expressly required the increases to be approved by the stockholders. In its original form, the manufacturing company law of 1846 had not allowed increases that brought the total capital beyond the amount contemplated by the original certificates of incorporation,[139] but the law was amended in 1848 to permit the stock to be increased to double the amount set forth in the certificates.[140] The general law of 1849 was more liberal in that no limit was put upon the amount by which the stock could be increased.[141] Only one general law specifically awarded the existing stockholders the privilege of subscribing first to new stock.[142]

PREFERRED STOCK

Dr. George H. Evans, Jr., in a study of the beginnings of the use of preference shares in the United States, declares that preferred stock appeared in this country at a date earlier than has been generally supposed. Yet he cites as the earliest examples certain issues made in 1836 by Maryland railroad and canal corporations, issues that were unusual in that the state was the subscriber to the preferred shares.[143] Dr. Evans places the

[137] It was proposed that two "indifferent persons" appraise the property. *Newark Daily Advertiser,* March 1, 1870.

[138] Shares paid for in property were to be stamped as "issued for property purchased," and such stock was to be distinguished in all published statements and reports. *Revised Statutes of New Jersey* (1875), pp. 20–21.

[139] *N. J. Laws,* 1846, p. 64.

[140] *N. J. Laws,* 1848, p. 9.

[141] *N. J. Laws,* 1849, p. 300.

[142] *N. J. Laws,* 1856, Ch. 156, p. 312. This was an amendment to the insurance company law of 1852.

[143] G. H. Evans, Jr., "The Early History of Preferred Stock in the United States," *American Economic Review,* XIX (March 1929), pp. 43–50.

date of the earliest issues of preferred stock to be held by individuals as late as the eighteen forties.[144]

The statutes of New Jersey, however, reveal some earlier, perhaps they are the first, cases in which corporations were given authority to depart from a simple structure of capital stock wherein each ownership share participated equally in the profits. As in other jurisdictions, the earliest preferred stock authorizations in New Jersey were not included in original charters but were granted by the legislature in the form of amendments to charters. The early cases in which New Jersey corporations were allowed to issue shares with a preferred status have been overlooked in the literature of the history of American corporation finance.

In the year 1830, the Newark and Pompton Turnpike Company, a corporation chartered by New Jersey in 1806, was in financial difficulty. In January of 1830, the legislature passed a supplement to the act of incorporation permitting the company to open a stock subscription of $25,000 "to liquidate the debts of the said company." [145] If the stock was not sold after sixty days, the creditors of the company could subscribe for as many shares as would equal the debts owed to them respectively. The shares, if subscribed by the creditors, were to be called "new or preferred stock," and the net revenues of the company were to be applied "in the first place" to the payment of "lawful interest" [146] to the holders of the preferred stock. The remaining provisions departed from the present-day conception of preferred stock, for profits remaining after the "interest" payments were to be employed "to pay off the said debts, and so far to extinguish the said new or preferred stock." The company further had the right to pay the debts and thereby extinguish the preferred stock at any time. The special stock could be transferred in the same manner as the original shares, and the owners were entitled to "all the rights and privileges" to which the ordinary shareholders were entitled. Perhaps the most important of these was the right to vote for directors.

This 1830 charter supplement is unusual in several respects.

[144] *Ibid.*, p. 50. [145] *N. J. Laws,* 54 sess., 2 sit. (1830), p. 25.

[146] The legal interest rate in New Jersey at this time was 6 per cent.

Not only does it appear to be at least one of the earliest departures in American corporation finance in the direction of differentiation of stockholders, but unlike the Maryland examples it legalized a preferred issue that was to be held by individuals rather than by the state. Another interesting feature is the inclusion of the term "preferred stock." This is contradictory to Dr. Evans' statement that the "earliest statutes permitting the use of stock with prior dividend rights did not use the expression preferred stock." [147] That author finds the term used in newspaper accounts in 1836, but he cites no occurrence of the expression in legislative acts before 1848.[148] Finally, the New Jersey case is interesting in that it links the preferred stock so directly to the matter of corporate indebtedness. Support is thus found here for the generally accepted view that the earliest issues of preferred stock resulted from financial embarrassment on the part of the issuing corporations. In fact, the very language of the statute shows that the preferred stock was regarded almost as a debt, and a debt that should be discharged as soon as possible.

The Newark and Pompton Turnpike case assumes proportions greater than a mere historical accident, for the next three years afforded three further examples of the authorization of preferred stock by the New Jersey legislature. In 1831, the New-Jersey Turnpike Company received permission to liquidate its indebtedness by issuing $16,000 of stock on terms identical with those of the previous case.[149] A company that had been chartered in 1800 to shorten the navigation of Salem Creek was authorized in 1831 to sell publicly a stock issue of $5,000, the certificates of which were to be marked "New Stock." [150] The managers were directed to declare dividends "not exceeding four per centum on the money called in on the new stock, before any dividend shall be paid to the holders of shares of the old stock; and, after the payment of four per centum to the holders of the new stock, it shall be the duty of the said president and managers, to declare a dividend of the

[147] G. H. Evans, Jr., "The Early History of Preferred Stock," p. 52.
[148] *Loc. cit.* [149] *N. J. Laws,* 55 sess., 2 sit. (1831), p. 142.
[150] *N. J. Laws,* 55 sess., 2 sit. (1831), p. 155.

surplus, if any, to be paid to the holders of the old stock . . ." Holders of the preferred stock were to enjoy all the rights and privileges of the original issue. The financial difficulty in this case seems to have been the inability of the company to raise sufficient funds to cut its canal. The final example of the early period occurred in 1834 and is more nearly like the Maryland cases, for the state was to benefit from the dividend preference. The legislative act in this instance directed the trustees of the state school fund to exchange 250 turnpike shares held by them for an equal number of shares in the New-Jersey Railroad and Transportation Company.[151] In the event that the dividends on the railroad stock failed to amount to 8 per cent of the par value each year, the company was bound to pay the deficiency to the state trustees out of company funds "before any dividend is made to the other stockholders." This case amounted to a guarantee of dividends rather than an ordinary preference, for until the railroad began to pay regular dividends on its stock or at any subsequent period when dividends were not paid the road was obligated to pay 8 per cent on the state-owned stock.[152] This guarantee was solely for the benefit of the state, for if the state sold its railroad stock the company was released from any guarantee of dividends.

No further authorizations of preferred shares appeared in the New Jersey statute books until 1849, but between that date and the end of the period under investigation there were twelve instances in which the legislature passed charter amendments permitting preferred stock issues. Perhaps the most interesting fact about the group of amendments is that exactly one-half the corporations empowered to issue preferred stock were engaged outside the field of transportation. Preferred stock appears to have become after 1850 a device for aiding in the financing of New Jersey's manufacturing and mining enterprises.[153]

[151] *N. J. Laws,* 58 sess., 2 sit. (1834), p. 163.

[152] As a further guarantee, the exchanged turnpike stock was to be hypothecated to the school fund trustees with authority to receive dividends on it as security for the faithful compliance of the railroad with the terms of the act.

[153] For a description of some early industrial preferred stocks, including an issue of the New Jersey Zinc Company, see G. H. Evans, Jr., "Early Industrial Preferred Stocks in the United States," *Journal of Political Economy,* XL (April 1932), pp. 227–243.

There was little uniformity in this group of supplements authorizing preferred stock issues. In only five cases was the consent of a stated proportion of the ordinary stockholders required before the preferred stock could be issued.[154] In four cases the existing stockholders enjoyed a prior right to subscribe to the preferred stock at the time of its issue.[155] The rate of preferred dividends was restricted in five instances.[156] Several of the issues of preferred stock were expressly stated to enjoy what has in more recent times come to be known as a "participating" feature. The first such example appeared in 1855 in connection with a mining company whose 8 per cent preferred stock was made participating by a proviso establishing the right of the preferred stockholders to share equally with holders of the original stock in all profits remaining after 8 per cent had been divided on the whole capital stock.[157] In two other cases the preferred issues were required to be participating on terms established in the amendments,[158] and in another the issue could be made participating.[159]

A few miscellaneous provisions are worthy of mention. In one case the preferred stock could be issued in payment for mines and other real estate,[160] while in another the special stock could be given to creditors in exchange for the debts of the company on any terms agreed upon.[161] The preferred stock of a sugar refinery was not to entitle the holders to vote.[162] The other eleven supplements were silent on the subject of voting rights. In only one case did the supplements authorizing preferred stock indicate the position the holders were to enjoy in the final distribution of assets. In that instance, preferred shareholders were to have first claim up to the par value of their shares and then they were to share equally with the holders of

[154] *N. J. Laws,* 1849, p. 33; 1853, Ch. 68, p. 165; 1857, Ch. 104, p. 300; 1868, Ch. 35, p. 69; 1870, Ch. 13, p. 113.

[155] *N. J. Laws,* 1849, p. 33; 1855, Ch. 208, p. 579; 1857, Ch. 104, p. 300, Ch. 122, p. 362.

[156] The rates ranged from 4 to 8 per cent. E.g., *N. J. Laws,* 1853, Ch. 68, p. 165; 1856, Ch. 10, p. 12.

[157] *N. J. Laws,* 1855, Ch. 208, p. 579.

[158] *N. J. Laws,* 1857, Ch. 104, p. 300, Ch. 122, p. 362.

[159] *N. J. Laws,* 1865, Ch. 46, p. 86.

[160] *N. J. Laws,* 1853, Ch. 68, p. 165.

[161] *N. J. Laws,* 1856, Ch. 10, p. 12.

[162] *N. J. Laws,* 1870, Ch. 13, p. 113.

the original stock after the latter had been compensated up to the par value of their shares.[163] In one case, a building company was merely prohibited from issuing special stock except in the manner provided in an act of 1860 that permitted manufacturing companies to create preferred stock.[164] The form of the phraseology suggests that it may have been the practice of some New Jersey corporations to issue preferred stock without express statutory authority.[165]

The next way in which the New Jersey legislature gave authority for preferred stock issues was more general in its application than the above supplementary acts. In 1860, the legislature authorized any manufacturing corporation existing by virtue of New Jersey law to issue preferred stock.[166] Manufacturing companies were permitted to create special stock up to one-half the paid-in capital. On this stock they were required to pay a half-yearly dividend, not to exceed 4 per cent, "before any dividend shall be set apart or paid on the said general stock." The preferred stockholders were not to be individually liable for any debts of the corporation. Apparently the preferred stock was viewed as a temporary feature in the capital structure, for it was to be made subject to redemption at par "at a fixed time to be expressed in the certificates." No special stock, however, could be created unless the directors were given the authority by at least two-thirds of the stock voted at a meeting called for the purpose of considering the question. The existence of this 1860 statute adds further evidence in support of the contention that it was companies outside the

[163] *N. J. Laws,* 1857, Ch. 104, p. 300.

[164] For details of the 1860 statute see below.

[165] There is evidence that such a practice was indulged in in some other states. Cf. G. H. Evans, Jr., "The Early History of Preferred Stock," pp. 53–55. The New Jersey legislators were not prepared to authorize an issue of preferred stock every time such action was requested. For example, a petition of the stockholders of the New Jersey Zinc Company for authority to make the unissued stock of their company preferred stock "for the purpose of raising additional cash working capital" was laid on the table in the assembly in 1855 and not subsequently acted upon. *Votes and Proceedings of the General Assembly,* 1855, p. 938.

[166] *N. J. Laws,* 1860, Ch. 228, p. 603.

transportation industry that had become most interested in issuing preferred stock by the eighteen fifties.[167]

In 1871, a supplement to the 1846 general regulating act opened the door for any New Jersey corporation to issue preferred shares.[168] The directors of any corporation were permitted to declare a part of the stock, up to two-thirds of the total amount authorized, to be preferred stock, and they were allowed to issue preferred stock certificates to all who gave "valuable consideration" in exchange. The legislature apparently attempted to give more protection to the common stockholder than in previous authorizations by requiring the written consent of all the stockholders before the preferred share issue was legalized. Definite rules were established regulating the dividend rights of the preferred stockholders. They were entitled to receive half-yearly shares in the earnings remaining after payment of expenses and taxes until they received 7 per cent on their shares during a year. Until such time, the common stockholders were prohibited from receiving dividends. In the event that the profits were sufficient to pay 7 per cent on the preferred stock and 7 per cent on the common stock, the remaining profits were to be divided proportionally among the stockholders of both classes. The preferred stock was differentiated from the ordinary shares in one further and important respect. The 1871 statute declared that the "holders of said preferred stock shall not be authorized to vote thereon for directors or managers of said corporation." Although previous to this date preferred stockholders had been expressly deprived of a vote in only one minor instance, the way was now opened for the wholesale disfranchisement of large numbers of stock-

[167] Some other states passed similar "special stock acts" for the benefit of manufacturing corporations at about the same time. Massachusetts had enacted one in 1855, and, although its terms were less liberal than those of the New Jersey act, it had perhaps served the Trenton lawmakers as a model. *Acts and Resolves Passed by the General Court of Massachusetts,* 1855, Ch. 290, p. 702. A similar law passed in Ohio a decade after the New Jersey statute is mentioned by G. H. Evans, Jr., in "Preferred Stock in the United States: 1850–1878," *American Economic Review,* XXI (March 1931), p. 59.

[168] *N. J. Laws,* 1871, Ch. 284, p. 58.

holders that has become a major concern in more recent times.[169]

A more generous warrant to issue preferred stock was granted in 1875 to certain transportation companies. A law enacted at that time declared that when railroads, canals, bridges, and roads were sold under court decree or by virtue of a mortgage, the successor company established by the purchasers could issue any preferred stock deemed necessary.[170] In the same year, a more explicit statute was passed to cover the case of railroads sold under mortgage.[171] The successor company was authorized to divide its stock into "classes" and establish preferences with respect to payment of dividends in favor of any portion of the capital stock if such a procedure was desirable in order to effectuate a plan for the readjustment of the claims of mortgage creditors, other creditors, and stockholders.

Finally, the authority to issue preferred stock was sometimes included in special charters of incorporation at the time of the original grant. This did not happen in New Jersey until 1868 and occurred in only five instances, all of which concerned transportation or communication agencies. The Nicaragua Railway Company, chartered in New Jersey in 1868 for establishing a trans-Isthmian railroad and telegraph system, was the first such case. The corporation was authorized to issue 8 per cent preferred stock, the holders of which could participate in further profits after 8 per cent was paid on the common stock.[172] In the same year, a company chartered to operate telegraph lines in Peru was permitted to issue a 7 per cent preferred stock with the same type of provisions as the above for further participation in the profits.[173] In subsequent years, a canal company, a railroad holding and management company, and a transportation company were given broad authority in their

[169] The 1871 New Jersey statute is of broader scope than those reported from other jurisdictions by Dr. Evans in his study of preferred stock. He makes no mention of the New Jersey statute. Cf. G. H. Evans, Jr., "Preferred Stock in the United States," pp. 58–59.

[170] *N. J. Laws,* 1875, Ch. 235, p. 41.

[171] *Ibid.,* Ch. 429, p. 101.

[172] *N. J. Laws,* 1868, Ch. 362, p. 816.

[173] *Ibid.,* Ch. 562, p. 1203.

original charters to issue preferred stock.[174] The relative paucity of cases in which preferred stock was authorized at the time special charters were enacted, combined with the fact that none of the general incorporation laws of New Jersey during the period under study touched on the subject of preferred stock issues, makes it quite clear that preferred stock was not viewed as a form of security that would normally be included in the initial capital structures of the state's corporations.

Several general observations can be made from the foregoing survey of preferred stock authorizations in New Jersey. In the first place, the investigation reveals four cases in which corporations were allowed to issue preferred stock that antedate by as much as six years those instances that have been noted in other states. The New Jersey examples assume even greater historical importance in the rather significant particular that the preferred stock was intended, in all but one case, to be held by individuals rather than by the state. The study of New Jersey experience bears out the general belief that early preferred stock issues were viewed as expedients to raise capital at a time subsequent to the inauguration of an enterprise in case sufficient capital to complete a contemplated project could not be raised by sales of ordinary shares or in case a corporation became embarrassed by heavy indebtedness.

The present writer finds New Jersey experience to be at variance with the general impression that preferred stock played a significant role outside the field of transportation only after 1875.[175] It is true that the four very early examples of preferred stock were confined to the transportation industry, but in the group of charter amendments passed during and after 1849 nontransportation companies are represented as frequently as the transportation group. Moreover, the passage in 1860 of a

[174] *N. J. Laws,* 1871, Ch. 625, p. 1541; 1872, Ch. 329, p. 772; 1874, Ch. 82, p. 943.

[175] Dr. Evans declares that until about 1875 "preferred stock was confined . . . almost entirely to the transportation industry," and he notes only eleven cases of the existence of such stock in other fields before 1878. He points out, however, that his conclusion is in contrast to the situation in Germany and England. G. H. Evans, Jr., "Preferred Stock in the United States," p. 56.

general authorization for the issuance of preferred stock by manufacturing companies, suggests that companies of that type had become increasingly interested in preferred stock. Since the legislature departed in this instance from its established practice of providing for such stock only by special supplement, it would appear that there was some pressure from the manufacturing community for an easier method of securing permission to issue stock with prior dividend rights. Unfortunately it is impossible to determine the degree to which manufacturing companies availed themselves of the privileges of the statute.

Certainly it is clear that the New Jersey railroads evidenced much less interest in preferred stock than might have been expected. It will be shown in the succeeding chapter that the mortgage bond as a device for raising capital appeared at about the same time as preferred stock and that the mortgage bond surged far ahead of preferred stock in popularity in railroad finance in the middle of the nineteenth century.[176] The general railroad law of 1873 made no special provision for preferred shares, and the statutes of 1875 authorizing railroads to issue preferred shares were applicable only in cases where roads had been sold under duress and had been taken over by new companies. It may be that the common notion that only transportation companies were very much interested in preferred issues before 1875 arises from the fact that investigators of the subject have usually arrived at their conclusions after studies of stock market quotations. Undoubtedly the preferred issues of railroad companies were larger and more widely held and traded than those of other concerns.

CLASSIFIED STOCK

There remain to be examined several unusual variations in the types of capital stock that New Jersey corporations were allowed to issue before 1875. The first among these were special issues of stock intended for financing railroad extensions. In the eighteen thirties, when railroad companies completed or anticipated completion of their lines, the aspirations of the managers turned in the direction of expansion. When the first

[176] Cf. *infra*, pp. 284–285.

two railroad extensions were authorized, the roads were granted the privilege of issuing additional stock similar to the original stock and standing on an equal footing with it.[177] Beginning in 1836, however, a number of railroads were allowed to finance extensions by issues of stock that were, either by legal requirement or at the option of the corporations, to be differentiated from the original stock. By a supplementary act of 1836, the New Jersey, Hudson and Delaware Rail Road Company was allowed to create a new stock issue to construct a lateral road. The conditions of the authorization were that "the said capital stock of the said lateral road . . . and the dividends and profits thereof, shall be held and enjoyed separate, apart, and distinct from the stock of the main road, and not be subject to any contracts or liabilities for the same." [178] A few weeks later, the Morris and Essex Rail Road Company was given power to construct several branch lines. This company had a choice of procedures, for the terms of its authorization were that "separate subscriptions may be opened, separate stock may be created, and accounts be opened and kept for each road, or the whole be blended in one general fund, as the company by their officers shall direct." [179]

There were eight additional charter supplements scattered over the statute books during the next thirty years permitting the creation of similar separate stocks. Whether the new stock would be kept separate or would be "blended" was left at the option of the issuing corporation in seven of the cases.[180] In the eighth instance, the stock had to be kept separate until a specified part of the extension was complete, and then dividends were to be paid equally on the whole stock.[181]

Companies that financed extensions by the creation of such separate stocks were neither increasing their common stock in ordinary fashion nor were they issuing preferred shares. The separate stocks were common stock but represented ownership in only one particular section of the enterprise. Separate books

[177] *N. J. Laws,* 57 sess., 2 sit. (1833), p. 69; 58 sess., 2 sit. (1834), p. 22.
[178] *N. J. Laws,* 60 sess., 2 sit. (1836), p. 98.
[179] *N. J. Laws,* 60 sess., 2 sit. (1836), p. 223.
[180] E.g., *N. J. Laws,* 62 sess., 2 sit. (1838), p. 154; 1851, p. 28.
[181] *N. J. Laws,* 1857, Ch. 144, p. 400.

of account could be kept for the separately owned sections, and separate dividend distributions could be made.[182]

Since the railroad companies presumably sought permission to create the separate stocks, some attempt should be made to explain the usefulness of such issues. In the absence of contemporary testimony, perhaps the best conjecture is that in the early cases the original stockholders, while anxious to see branches built as feeders to the main line, did not wish to see the profitableness of their investment diluted by dividends to new stockholders and by charges for construction and operation in the event the branch lines proved financial failures. In later years, it may have been possible in this way to prevent the mortgage bondholders from claiming liens on branches and extensions by virtue of mortgages on the original property and thus destroy the opportunity of laying a new first mortgage on the newly constructed line.[183] An alternative method of accomplishing the same purposes would have been to obtain, as was sometimes done, a charter for a separate company that would construct the extension. This was an elaborate procedure compared with getting a mere charter supplement, and the existence of two separate corporate entities might cause difficulty if it was later desired to unite the sections of the road.

There was one additional and somewhat different case in which a corporation was allowed by charter supplement to divide its stock into separate parts. The Central American Transit Company, chartered in 1862, was granted by an act of 1865 broad powers to divide the various parts of its business and to keep separate books, maintain separate management,

[182] Although, for want of a better term to include several variations, this section is headed "Classified Stock," the special stock issues described above depart from the modern use of that expression. Classified stock has come to refer to stock with varying degrees of preference in dividend and asset distributions in the identical corporate property. To invent a term for the special issues discussed here, "segmented stock" might be more descriptive.

[183] One authorization specifically stated that separate stock and accounts were to be kept, that the branch and its rolling stock were not liable for the payment of company debts, and that debts of the spur were liens only on the spur just as if it was owned by a separate and distinct company. *N. J. Laws,* 1863, Ch. 5, p. 7.

issue separate and distinct stocks, and pay dividends "as if each was conducted by different companies." [184]

In only two instances was the privilege of classifying the stock granted to corporations by their original charters. The first and most interesting case is that of the Lodi Manufacturing Company, a concern chartered in 1840 to manufacture fertilizer.[185] Perhaps to interest farmers in the products of the concern, the charter permitted the directors, after five hundred regular shares had been subscribed, to authorize a further subscription of five hundred shares to be subscribed for "by farmers or gardeners exclusively," to not over five shares per person. In the distribution of the special stock, preference was to be given to New Jersey agriculturalists. If the special stock was not all subscribed in sixty days, persons other than farmers could buy it. The directors were empowered to declare on each share of the special stock an annual dividend of fifty bushels of poudrette for the first five years. After that time the stock was to receive the same dividends as ordinary shares. In the second case, the 1865 charter of the New Jersey Oil Company authorized a $1,000,000 increase in the capital stock and permitted the company to "classify the said stock." [186] This indefinite language might have been intended to authorize special shares of the type discussed in this section, to permit classes of common stock differing in dividend priority, in voting rights, or in other respects, or to allow ordinary preferred stock.

[184] *N. J. Laws,* 1865, Ch. 46, p. 86.

[185] *N. J. Laws,* 64 sess., 2 sit. (1840), p. 23.

[186] *N. J. Laws,* 1865, Ch. 154, p. 276.

CHAPTER IX

Capital Structure (Continued)

BORROWED CAPITAL

NO DEFINITIVE account of the importance of borrowed funds in the financial structures of New Jersey corporations before 1875 could be written without access to the books of account of the companies themselves. In view of the impossibility of assembling such data, the most authoritative and informative sources of material are the legislative enactments on the subject of corporate borrowing. By tracing legislation aimed at restricting the power of corporations to incur debts, one can determine when corporate borrowing became a problem significant enough to claim the critical attention of the legislature. By studying the statutes, one can also establish with some certainty the period when borrowed capital became such an important and permanent feature of financial plans that corporation officials sought special favors in its behalf.

The subject of borrowed capital can be divided into two phases. There are the miscellaneous and temporary obligations incurred by corporations in the ordinary course of business, and, on the other hand, there is the funded debt that assumes a formal and permanent place in financial structures. It is the funded debt that concerns us most directly here, and a major part of the discussion will consider that phase of the problem. Historically, however, the floating debt takes precedence and will be treated first.

A significant bit of negative evidence is found in the fact that in no case was a corporation expressly forbidden to borrow. Without doubt, incorporated concerns followed the ordinary business practice of financing a part of their working capital by obtaining credit from those with whom they did business. Since the power to mortgage the corporate property was not expressed in charters until relatively late, it is probable that the early debts were generally secured not by pledges of specific property but merely by the general credit of the borrowing corporations.

It was not until the eighteen forties that the New Jersey solons made an effort to limit the general borrowing power of non-banking corporations,[1] except in the unique case of a ferry company whose 1817 charter declared that the "trustees" could not bind the stockholders beyond the amount of the "joint stock" and that if debts were contracted "beyond the funds" of the company the trustees were liable in their individual estates.[2] By 1840, great concern was evidenced over the question of the relation of corporations to their creditors.[3] A water power company and a manufacturing company chartered in 1840 were enjoined from incurring debts and obligations for the payment of money to an amount exceeding the capital actually paid in. Violation of the provisions incurred a forfeiture of the charters and made the managers severally liable for all debts and contracts.[4] During the decade of the eighteen forties, similar debt limitations were included in sixteen additional charters.[5] In each case, the debt limit was put at the amount of the paid-in capital (sometimes expressed as the "cash capital"), but the penalties for exceeding the maximum varied widely. In four instances, the directors were made jointly

[1] It was customary from the first to limit the total debts of commercial banks, but the purpose was primarily to limit the note issues. Such limitations were quite different in nature from those designed to regulate the amount of capital that could be raised by borrowing.

[2] *N. J. Laws,* 41 sess., 2 sit. (1817, private), p. 45. The language suggests that the aim of this provision was rather to protect the stockholders from any danger of liability beyond their respective shares than primarily to protect creditors.

[3] As previously stated, this concern was the outgrowth of agitation by Jacksonian Democrats against the privilege of limited liability enjoyed by corporation stockholders, and it was intensified because of losses suffered by creditors during the business depression after 1837.

[4] *N. J. Laws,* 64 sess., 2 sit. (1840), pp. 112, 121.

[5] Nine were charters for manufacturing companies, four for steamboat and ferry companies, two for bridge companies, and one for a mining concern. In addition, debt limits were included in two amendments to manufacturing company charters. In one, the charter was forfeited if the debts exceeded the capital stock paid in. *N. J. Laws,* 65 sess., 2 sit. (1841), p. 38. In the other, a similar offence made the directors liable for all debts. *Ibid.,* p. 48.

and severally liable for debts if the limit was exceeded.[6] One charter passed in 1842 and three passed in 1844 made both directors and stockholders liable.[7] In one case, only the stockholders were declared liable.[8] Two companies were to forfeit their charters if they exceeded their debt limits.[9] In six cases, no penalties were expressly provided.[10]

The two general incorporation laws for manufacturing companies that were enacted during the eighteen forties contained provisions limiting the debts of companies organized under their authority to the amount of the paid-in capital stock. In both cases, those who were directors at the time the debts were incurred were liable to the amount of any excess. The directors could escape liability if they voted against incurring the illegal debts and notified the stockholders of their dissent at a meeting called for the purpose.[11]

Over-all debt limitations, like many restrictive provisions designed to protect creditors, waned sharply in importance after 1850 and were for the most part confined to a few classes of corporations. In spite of the tremendous increase in the number of charters, such debt limits were found in only fifty instances during the twenty-five years after 1850.[12] The debt limit was set in thirteen of these charters at the amount of the paid-in capital stock,[13] but in thirty it was more liberal, being

[6] E.g., *N. J. Laws,* 65 sess., 2 sit. (1841), pp. 54, 70.

[7] E.g., *N. J. Laws,* 68 sess., 2 sit. (1844), pp. 55, 265.

[8] *N. J. Laws,* 66 sess., 2 sit. (1842), p. 100.

[9] *N. J. Laws,* 65 sess., 2 sit. (1841), p. 122; 1849, p. 230.

[10] Debt limitations were frequently proposed from the floor while charters were under discussion in the legislature. Cf. *Votes and Proceedings of the General Assembly,* 64 sess., 2 sit. (1840), p. 357; *ibid.,* 66 sess., 2 sit. (1842), p. 367. After 1844, the legislators showed increasing unwillingness to impose debt limitations. In 1845, for example, several attempts to include debt limitations in charters were defeated in the assembly. *Ibid.,* 1845, pp. 463, 467, 668.

[11] *N. J. Laws,* 1846, p. 64; 1849, p. 300. These general laws also contained a provision for publicity to protect creditors. Statements were to be published every January setting forth the capital stock paid in, the assets deemed "good," and the existing debts. In the event the statements were not published at the required time, the 1846 law made stockholders liable for all debts. For similar neglect, the law of 1849 made directors liable for all debts.

[12] Of these cases, thirty concerned hotel companies and ten concerned hall associations.

[13] E.g., *N. J. Laws,* 1860, Ch. 36, p. 83.

the amount of the capital subscribed.[14] In six examples, the debt limits were expressed as fractions of the paid-in or subscribed capital.[15] One hotel company charter was unique in limiting debts to the "ability of the said company to pay, from the proceeds of the sale of its stock and the income of the said hotel." [16] Comparison of the fifty limiting clauses passed after 1850 with those of the eighteen forties reveals a decreasing disposition on the part of the legislators to invoke penalties when the debt limits were exceeded. Only six of the fifty involved penalties, and these were all in charters passed before 1864. Two of the six made directors liable for all debts[17] and four for debts to the amount by which the limits were exceeded.[18] Dissenting directors could escape liability in four of the six cases by filing notice of their dissent.[19] None threatened forfeiture of the charter.

Only two of the numerous general incorporation laws passed after 1850 contained over-all debt limitations. The first was the general law of 1852 for plank roads in which debts were limited to the money actually in the treasury or due on the remaining installments on the capital stock.[20] The 1874 general law for gas companies established the debt limit at the amount of the paid-in capital. Those persons who were directors when the limit was exceeded were made liable to the amount of the excess until the debts were reduced to the permitted amount. Dissenting directors could escape liability by notifying the stockholders of their dissent.[21]

The writer does not wish to give the impression that after

[14] E.g., *N. J. Laws*, 1856, Ch. 58, p. 125.

[15] E.g., *N. J. Laws*, 1854, Ch. 167, p. 413.

[16] *N. J. Laws*, 1857, Ch. 32, p. 73.

[17] *N. J. Laws*, 1854, Ch. 167, p. 413; 1863, Ch. 230, p. 448.

[18] E.g., *N. J. Laws*, 1851, p. 15; 1854, Ch. 64, p. 140.

[19] In all but one of the cases, the dissents had to be filed with the clerk of the county.

[20] *N. J. Laws*, 1852, Ch. 51, p. 95.

[21] *N. J. Laws*, 1874, Ch. 509, p. 124. At least one unsuccessful attempt was made to establish a maximum limit on the debts of all New Jersey corporations. A bill introduced in the senate in 1858 proposed to amend the 1846 general regulating act by limiting debt to the amount of the paid-in capital stock and by making directors liable for debts in excess of the allowed maximum. *Journal of the Senate*, 1858, pp. 144, 720–21.

1850 there were few limits of any kind on the power of corporations to borrow. There were, indeed, numerous limitations. They were, however, combined with the express power to borrow money, to issue bonds, and to mortgage the corporate property and were apparently designed to limit only the funded debt. They were thus quite different from the general debt limitations of the type discussed above.[22]

Turning to the subject of debt that was a formal part of the capital structures of corporations, the late eighteen forties arise from the obscurity of the statute books as the years when long-term debt assumed wide importance. A sharp line between casual and funded debt is hard to establish from the meager information of the statutes, but it is reasonable to trace the increasing use of long-term debt by referring to charter and supplemental provisions giving corporations the power to mortgage their property. It is unlikely that any large amount of funded debt could have existed in the early years of the nineteenth century without mortgage security. In the absence of express authority, the right of a private corporation to mortgage its real and personal estate was a moot question in New Jersey, and a charter amendment was regarded as necessary to assure the validity of a mortgage if the mortgaging power had not been expressly stated in the original grant.[23] When authority to mortgage was given, it was usually accompanied by

[22] A similar interpretation was expressed by a chief justice of the state supreme court in discussing the meaning of an express grant in a railroad charter of power to borrow a fixed amount of money and secure repayment by a mortgage. It was clear to the justice that the section was designed not to limit general indebtedness but to grant additional power that the company would not otherwise have had. He declared that every corporation, unless specifically restrained, had power to incur debts in the course of legitimate business and of making and endorsing negotiable paper in payment of such debts. *Lucas* v. *Pitney*, 27 New Jersey Law, 221 (1858). Further supporting evidence for this view is found in occasional charters that contained separate limits for bonds and for total debt. E.g., *N. J. Laws*, 1872, Ch. 95, p. 284.

[23] In one early case, however, the chancellor upheld the legality of a mortgage on a banking house on the ground that the right of the corporation to mortgage its property was implied in the power to hold real estate. *Leggett* v. *The New Jersey Manufacturing and Banking Company*, 1 New Jersey Equity, 541 (1832). There is also evidence that some corporations issued bonds secured

positive statements of the right to borrow money and by one or more of the following provisions: the terms on which money could be borrowed, the amount that could be borrowed, and express authority to issue bonds. Clauses of this type thus differ from the over-all debt limitations discussed previously, and when such positively expressed borrowing rights were included among the corporate powers, it is reasonably certain that the corporators intended to obtain part of their long-term capital from creditors.

Although positively expressed borrowing provisions did not become numerous until 1847, several examples appeared before that time. The 1815 charter of a steamboat company included the right to mortgage the corporate land and other property,[24] and similar power was expressed in a manufacturing company charter of 1829.[25] In 1838, a land company was authorized in its charter to borrow money on mortgage.[26]

These three were the only instances in which borrowing rights were positively expressed in original charters before 1847. It is necessary to turn to the charter amendments to find most of the early examples. In the early period of its employment, long-term debt was not viewed as a feature of an initial capital structure but rather as an expedient to be used in the event of financial difficulty.

First among the various charter amendments providing for borrowing was one passed in 1829 for the benefit of the Morris Canal and Banking Company that was having difficulty in raising the funds requisite for construction.[27] The company was allowed to borrow $500,000 and to issue to any person or corporation 6 per cent "post notes" in denominations of not less than $300. To secure payment of interest and principal, the company was authorized to mortgage the whole property and the chartered rights and privileges. If the chancellor was convinced that a default occurred, the assignees might operate

by mortgage in advance of express authorization. A gas company and a manufacturing concern had such actions legalized by supplements passed after the bonds had been issued. *N. J. Laws,* 1867, Ch. 4, p. 6; 1868, Ch. 215, p. 476.

[24] *N. J. Laws,* 39 sess., 2 sit. (1815, private), p. 91.

[25] *N. J. Laws,* 54 sess., 1 sit. (1829), p. 6.

[26] *N. J. Laws,* 62 sess., 2 sit. (1838), p. 230.

[27] *N. J. Laws,* 53 sess., 2 sit. (1829), p. 86.

the works in trust for the owners of the notes during the term of the charter; but if the interest and redemption agreements were carried out, the conveyance should cease and become void.

In the following year, the same company was granted the right to borrow any sum of money appearing to the directors to be "necessary and proper," without any express limitation as to the interest rate or the denomination of the notes.[28] The same power to mortgage was repeated, but with the provision that nothing should impair prior liens on the property and that persons or corporations with claims by virtue of pledges made pursuant to the supplement should have no right except according to the priority of their respective encumbrances. These supplements make it possible for New Jersey to claim another "first" in the realm of corporation finance, for according to an exhaustive study of the development of trust companies in the United States the "earliest trust deed by a corporation which has been found was dated March 29, 1830, and was entered into by the Morris Canal and Banking Company with a single individual as trustee." [29]

A small wave of borrowing authorizations appeared after the panic of 1837. In 1838, the directors of the Morris and Essex Rail Road Company were granted the right to borrow any sum of money necessary to complete their works and purchase rolling stock. Hypothecation of the property, franchises, and any unsubscribed or forfeited shares in the possession of the company was authorized to secure the payment of interest and principal.[30] The Trenton Delaware Falls Company, a water power concern, was allowed by an 1839 amendment to its charter to borrow money and secure the loan by mortgage.[31] A turnpike corporation, "in order to relieve the company from their embarrassments, in consequence of the destruction of their bridge," was permitted in 1842 to borrow $2000 and give mortgage security.[32] In the same year, the Morris and Essex

[28] *N. J. Laws,* 54 sess., 2 sit. (1830), p. 17.

[29] "Wilhelm Willink, Jr., was the trustee, and he negotiated a loan of $750,000 in the city of Amsterdam." J. G. Smith, *The Development of Trust Companies in the United States,* p. 273.

[30] *N. J. Laws,* 62 sess., 2 sit. (1838), p. 125.

[31] *N. J. Laws,* 63 sess., 2 sit. (1839), p. 168.

[32] *N. J. Laws,* 66 sess., 2 sit. (1842), p. 16.

Rail Road Company, if allowed by two-thirds of the stock voted at a general meeting, was authorized to borrow by giving a mortgage on the whole road.[33] This grant was unusual in providing that if the road should be sold by virtue of court decree, any stockholders could recover it by paying within forty days the amount for which it was sold plus interest. The mortgages of another railroad company were declared valid if two-thirds of the stockholders represented at a meeting called for the purpose gave their assent.[34] In the event of a sale of the road, the stockholders were allowed to recover the property by paying the amount of the judgment and interest within six months.

Two other corporations were expressly allowed by charter supplements before 1847 to borrow on mortgage security. The Belvidere Delaware Bridge Company suffered destruction of its property by a freshet immediately after construction and owed debts in consequence of having replaced the bridge. The charter supplement authorizing the company to borrow money was the earliest to include a direct statement to the effect that it was doubtful whether a corporation could mortgage its property to secure the payment of debts without express permission. The supplement gave the company the right to mortgage its bridge to secure the payment of debts incurred in building and rebuilding, "but for no other purpose." [35] A railroad company petitioned the legislature in 1844 for authority to issue mortgage bonds in order to purchase iron for their road, since "doubts have arisen whether they have sufficient powers to make such bonds and mortgages; and they thereupon having requested legislative aid in the premises." The legislature granted the company power to issue 6 per cent bonds of not less than $500 denomination to the total sum of $100,000 and permitted the company to mortgage its property and chartered rights to secure execution of the contract.[36]

[33] *Ibid.*, p. 83.

[34] The wording of the supplement indicates that a mortgage had already been given. *N. J. Laws*, 66 sess., 2 sit. (1842), p. 155.

[35] To insure proper use of the authority given, the act prohibited the president and directors from mortgaging the bridge for any part of their own indebtedness to the company for "stock which they have not paid up to an equal amount with other stockholders." *N. J. Laws*, 67 sess., 2 sit. (1843), p. 118.

[36] *N. J. Laws*, 68 sess., 2 sit. (1844), p. 17.

Beginning in 1847, many New Jersey business corporations were expressly authorized at the time of their incorporation to mortgage their property. In the single year 1847, for example, there were five such cases.[37] It should be emphasized that before this date only a very few charters had contained similar authority. Since even railroad companies, later the most important single group of borrowers, had not previously been granted the right of mortgage in their initial charters, the writer feels secure in asserting that long-term debt did not loom important in the original financial plans of New Jersey corporations until the end of the eighteen forties.[38]

That there was a new interest in corporate borrowing is evidenced by the fact that 808 special charters passed between 1847 and 1875, inclusive, contained positive provisions with respect to incurring and securing debts. During the same years, 147 charter supplements concerning the borrowing rights of particular business corporations were enacted. Only 4 general incorporation laws, however, expressly authorized companies organized under them to borrow funds by mortgaging their property. Three of these were general laws for the formation of land companies,[39] and the fourth was the general railroad law of 1873.[40]

A study of the 808 special charters indicates that nearly every type of business corporation was interested in the possibility of raising funds by loan. Borrowing rights were expressed most frequently in the charters of manufacturing, steam railroad, land, horse railroad, and mining corporations, occurring in 218, 127, 115, 63, and 56 cases respectively. Inclusion of such provisions was not, however, an invariable rule, for the figures above represent respectively only 60.3, 75.1, 69.6, 36.8, and 49.5 per cent of the total number of corporations of the

[37] *N. J. Laws,* 1847, pp. 61, 92, 98, 128, 136. Two were railroad companies, two manufacturing companies, and one a hall company.

[38] It is, of course, probable that in earlier years some corporations mortgaged their property without express authority. Furthermore, some corporations may have enjoyed long-term loans without mortgaging their property, but European lenders who purchased the large American bond issues generally demanded the security of a mortgage.

[39] *N. J. Laws,* 1855, Ch. 256, p. 754; 1865, Ch. 379, p. 707; 1867, Ch. 378, p. 855.

[40] *N. J. Laws,* 1873, Ch. 413, p. 88.

same types created by special charter during the period. The 147 charter supplements also evidence a disposition on the part of a wide variety of business corporations to issue debt securities, but in the supplementary authorizations the steam railroads play a greater part, 35 per cent of the supplements concerning corporations of this type. All the supplements do not represent entirely new borrowing authority. A number merely relaxed the limits or terms in the case of corporations that already possessed certain borrowing rights. Two of the supplements were passed for the benefit of companies organized under general laws that did not give adequate borrowing privileges; instead of seeking special charters, the corporations merely requested charter amendments to increase their authority in certain respects.[41]

The statutes afford an incomplete record of the purposes that businessmen hoped to serve by borrowing, but there is sufficient evidence to indicate a wide variety of incentives. Those enterprises that sought borrowing sanctions at the time of their incorporation probably intended to raise part of their necessary capital funds through loans in case the authorized proprietary capital was insufficient or in case not enough subscribers willing to take ownership securities could be found. The terms of a few railroad charters made borrowing privileges something to be exercised only in the event that the funds raised through the sale of stock were inadequate, the right to borrow being contingent on a failure to sell all the common stock.[42] A number of railroad charters specified the right to borrow for building, repairing, and equipping the roads.[43]

The charter amendments are more illuminating, although even these afford relatively few glimpses into the reasons for which borrowing privileges were sought. Supplements to railroad company charters authorizing extensions of original lines often conferred borrowing privileges, and the frequency with

[41] One, a steamship company, was allowed to borrow on mortgage bonds since "doubts have arisen as to the power of said corporation to mortgage under the general law . . ." *N. J. Laws,* 1875 (private), Ch. 204, p. 168. The other, a corporation under the 1867 general law for land companies, was granted broader borrowing privileges than the terms of the general law allowed. *Ibid.,* 1875 (private), Ch. 299, p. 239.

[42] E.g., *N. J. Laws,* 1864, Ch. 281, p. 452; 1866, Ch. 233, p. 561.

[43] E.g., *N. J. Laws,* 1847, p. 128; 1849, pp. 93, 272.

which such cases occurred indicates that a desire to expand was one of the most common reasons for seeking loans.[44] In the case of non-railroad companies, it was not usually apparent when borrowing privileges were sought for expansion, since express authority to expand ordinary businesses was unnecessary. Near the end of the period under discussion, however, a gas company was allowed to borrow because of an expressed desire to extend its works without increasing the capital stock,[45] and a manufacturing company was given positive borrowing rights in order to enable it to raise additional capital.[46] The supplementary enactments show also that an important need for borrowed funds arose from the difficulties of corporations whose proceeds from stock issues proved inadequate either because of overestimation of the prospective subscriptions or underestimation of the cost of the projected works. The Belvidere Delaware Rail Road Company, on the ground that it had nearly exhausted the funds raised from the sale of capital stock, was allowed to float convertible bonds to complete and equip the road.[47] Several supplements granted borrowing privileges to other railroads in the same predicament. The supplements also reveal the fact that corporations having difficulty with existing debts sometimes requested legislation to make long-term borrowing possible. The twelve supplements that mentioned paying or funding of existing debts as a motive for issuing formal debt instruments concerned turnpike companies in five instances,[48] railroads in five,[49] and gas and transportation companies in one each.[50]

[44] E.g., *N. J. Laws,* 1851, pp. 28, 386. In many cases, the supplements also conferred the right to issue additional stock.

[45] *N. J. Laws,* 1868, Ch. 423, p. 985.

[46] *N. J. Laws,* 1873, Ch. 28, p. 929.

[47] *N. J. Laws,* 1853, Joint Resolution II, p. 484.

[48] E.g., *N. J. Laws,* 1854, Ch. 210, p. 518; 1859, Ch. 26, p. 55. The difficulty that turnpike companies had with their floating debt can be explained by the depressed condition of that business after the middle of the nineteenth century. It is also interesting that only three turnpike companies were given definite borrowing privileges at the time of incorporation.

[49] E.g., *N. J. Laws,* 1867, Ch. 90, p. 148; 1873, Ch. 391, p. 1302. One supplement merely explained that a previous authorization of bonds of the Joint Companies was to be interpreted to permit use of the proceeds to pay debts as well as to make physical improvements. *Ibid.,* 1874, Ch. 155, p. 997.

[50] *N. J. Laws,* 1868, Ch. 141, p. 302; 1871, Ch. 517, p. 1339.

In the three general land company laws, it was made clear that the borrowing power was to be used principally to assist in purchasing the required land. The law of 1865 permitted companies organized under it to issue mortgage bonds up to one-fourth the purchase price of the land when it was not "convenient" to pay cash,[51] and the law of 1867 allowed mortgages to be given in case the companies found their capital inadequate to buy and improve the necessary land.[52] The general railroad law authorized the use of the proceeds of loans to aid construction and to purchase equipment.[53]

Of the whole group of charters and charter amendments conferring specific borrowing powers enacted between 1847 and 1875, only a few made mention of what parties were to determine when and to what extent the privileges should be employed.[54] Seventeen grants, however, indicated a disposition on the part of the lawmakers to protect stockholders against reckless exercise of the borrowing power. Of these, eleven required the consent of a specified proportion of the owners before mortgages could be executed or bonds issued.[55] Stockholder consent was required in the remaining six cases only if the bonds were to be sold at less than a specified percentage of the face value.[56] Since most of the grants were silent on the question of what persons were to make decisions on borrowing policy, it is to be presumed that such matters were usually regulated by the bylaws.

In some instances, borrowing rights were made contingent upon special circumstances. The cases where borrowing was permitted only if the whole capital stock was not subscribed have already been mentioned.[57] In sixteen cases, no borrowing

[51] *N. J. Laws*, 1865, Ch. 379, p. 707. [52] *N. J. Laws*, 1867, Ch. 378, p. 855.

[53] *N. J. Laws*, 1873, Ch. 413, p. 88.

[54] In analyzing the terms on which borrowing privileges could be exercised, the charters, charter amendments, and general statutes will be considered together.

[55] E.g., *N. J. Laws*, 1855, Ch. 13, p. 23; 1867, Ch. 20, p. 23; 1868, Ch. 542, p. 1168.

[56] E.g., *N. J. Laws*, 1866, Ch. 226, p. 546, Ch. 452, p. 1001. The consent required in these and the above instances ranged from a majority in interest of the stockholders to unanimous consent.

[57] Cf. *supra*, p. 285.

was to be undertaken until a specified amount of capital stock had actually been paid in cash.[58]

Between 1847 and 1875, New Jersey lawmakers were disposed to place maximum limits on the amount of money that corporations might raise under their borrowing privileges. While the limits may have afforded some protection to stockholders, the main intent of the legislators was probably to protect creditors. The governor, in an 1866 message vetoing a bill that endowed a transit company with unlimited authority to issue bonds, expressed the prevailing attitude when he declared: "Believing . . . that the public should be protected from an unlimited issue of bonds . . . by a corporation of this State, I am constrained to withhold from the bill my approval." [59]

In 41 charters[60] and 51 supplements[61] the maximum limits were expressed in absolute dollar figures. A more popular type of provision was one relating the borrowing limit to the capital stock. Borrowing was limited in this manner in 188 charters and charter supplements, but the limiting clauses were not uniform. The upper limit was expressed in terms of paid-in capital in 146 instances and merely in terms of the "capital" in 42 cases.[62] Of the total 188 cases, in 38 companies were permitted to borrow up to 100 per cent of their paid-in capital or their "capital," [63] three-fourths was the limit in 6 cases,[64] two-thirds in 66,[65] and one-half in 78.[66] The 1865 and 1867 general land company laws limited mortgages respectively to one-fourth the purchase price of the land bought and to the capital stock.[67]

[58] E.g., *N. J. Laws*, 1860, Ch. 225, p. 588; 1864, Ch. 332, p. 578, Ch. 352, p. 619.

[59] *Journal of the Senate*, 1866, p. 169. The senators unanimously sustained the veto. *Ibid.*, p. 223.

[60] E.g., *N. J. Laws*, 1853, Ch. 28, p. 67; 1864, Ch. 335, p. 583.

[61] E.g., *N. J. Laws*, 1854, Ch. 11, p. 22, Ch. 210, p. 518.

[62] The meaning of "capital" in the latter cases is uncertain. In two instances, it was expressly declared to be the authorized capital and hence had little protective value to creditors. *N. J. Laws*, 1870, Ch. 390, p. 815; 1871, Ch. 289, p. 706.

[63] E.g., *N. J. Laws*, 1851, p. 78; 1859, Ch. 178, p. 516.

[64] E.g., *N. J. Laws*, 1869, Ch. 162, p. 427.

[65] E.g., *N. J. Laws*, 1857, Ch. 203, p. 517; 1866, Ch. 376, p. 845.

[66] E.g., *N. J. Laws*, 1856, Ch. 34, p. 60; 1867, Ch. 200, p. 433.

[67] *N. J. Laws*, 1865, Ch. 379, p. 707; 1867, Ch. 378, p. 855.

The general railroad law of 1873 limited the bonds issued to the amount of the capital stock.[68] Other forms of limitation were employed, but they were used too infrequently to warrant special analysis.[69]

One should not put too much emphasis on the importance of the above limitations. In the first place, less than one-fourth of the charters and charter supplements granting express borrowing privileges that were enacted between 1847 and 1875 contained any limit on the amount of money to be borrowed. Furthermore, the fact that there were relatively few requests for relief from maximum limits on borrowing indicates that even when limits were specified they were generous enough to permit a volume of borrowing adequate for business demands.[70]

The statutes throw very little light on the nature of the credit instruments actually employed by borrowing corporations. In many cases the corporations received express authority to issue bonds,[71] but in a majority of cases no specific reference to bonds was made. The absence of specific mention of the power to issue bonds cannot, however, be interpreted as precluding bond issues, for in 1863 the chancellor of New Jersey held that a corporation possessing the power to borrow money had as a necessary power and legal right the authority to give its obligations in any form not expressly forbidden by law.[72]

Probably in most cases the credit instruments given to lenders who supplied long-term funds to corporations were secured by mortgages on the corporate property. Only rarely did the

[68] *N. J. Laws,* 1873, Ch. 413, p. 88.

[69] One type limited borrowing to a proportion of the actual value of the real estate owned. E.g., *N. J. Laws,* 1868, Ch. 9, p. 17. Another type found in three railroad charter supplements limited borrowing to a fixed amount per mile of road. *Ibid.,* 1851, p. 386; 1868, Ch. 122, p. 258; 1874, Ch. 489, p. 1247.

[70] A few expanding railroad companies requested and were given increased borrowing power. E.g., *N. J. Laws,* 1862, Ch. 1, p. 3. A hotel company's limit was raised to a specific dollar figure in place of the former limit of the paid-in capital stock. *Ibid.,* 1870, Ch. 356, p. 738. A railroad company was relieved entirely of its borrowing limit upon application to the legislature. *Ibid.,* 1872, Ch. 20, p. 158. The writer found no evidence of refusals to raise maximum borrowing limits.

[71] E.g., *N. J. Laws,* 1859, Ch. 202, p. 585; 1866, Ch. 393, p. 900.

[72] *Stratton* v. *Allen,* 16 New Jersey Equity, 229 (1863).

positive borrowing authorizations of New Jersey corporations fail to include the power of giving mortgages,[73] and in over one-third of the charters and supplements bestowing borrowing privileges the sole provision was the right to mortgage the corporate property.[74] The usual clause authorizing mortgages permitted pledging both real and personal property, and occasionally the franchise privileges were specifically included as a part of the property that might be mortgaged.[75] The position of purchasers of railroad, canal, and turnpike properties sold under court decree had been given definite statutory expression in 1842. The purchasers of such properties were to enjoy the rights, privileges, and franchises of the corporations for the duration of the charters.[76] In 1858, purchasers of similar properties sold under court decree to satisfy a mortgage debt were allowed the further privilege, if they numbered at least fifteen, of becoming a new corporation subject to the terms of the former charter by filing a certificate with the secretary of state.[77]

The statutes were generally silent as to the type of mortgage to be given and as to the priority enjoyed by various mortgagees. In twenty-five cases, most of them concerning railroad companies, the mortgages were required to be first liens on the company property.[78] In three such instances, when the mortgaging power was granted to railroad companies about to construct branches, the mortgagees of the main lines were prohibited from claiming a first lien on the branches by virtue of their existing mortgages.[79] Specific authorizations of second mortgage bonds appeared only three times.[80]

Statutory provision was made in only two cases for issues of

[73] E.g., *N. J. Laws,* 1867, Ch. 349, p. 801.

[74] E.g., *N. J. Laws,* 1847, pp. 61, 92; 1864, Ch. 4, p. 8.

[75] E.g., *N. J. Laws,* 1847, p. 98; 1853, Ch. 28, p. 67.

[76] *N. J. Laws,* 66 sess., 2 sit. (1842), p. 164.

[77] *N. J. Laws,* 1858, Ch. 91, p. 215.

[78] E.g., *N. J. Laws,* 1865, Ch. 291, p. 541; 1870, Ch. 517, p. 1265. The mortgage lien was usually declared to extend to the rolling stock in the case of railroad companies.

[79] E.g., *N. J. Laws,* 1872, Ch. 230, p. 578.

[80] *N. J. Laws,* 1869, Ch. 18, p. 22; 1871, Ch. 299, p. 733; 1872, Ch. 176, p. 413.

other than ordinary mortgage bonds. A real-estate loan company of 1871 and a similar concern of 1875 were authorized to issue a type of bond somewhat similar to modern collateral trust bonds. The loan companies were to surrender mortgages they took on New Jersey real estate to a panel of three trustees, after which the companies could, with the trustees' consent, issue bonds to the amount of the mortgages pledged as security.[81]

During the railroad building era, many small or secondary roads were unable to furnish adequate security on the strength of their own property or general credit to encourage lenders to purchase their debt securities on terms favorable to the borrowing companies. In some states, such roads sought and received state guarantees of their bonds. While no railroad bonds were guaranteed by the state of New Jersey, the legislature made numerous provisions for the guarantee of bonds by private corporations. The first authorizations of guaranteed bonds appeared in the New Jersey laws in 1854 in the form of supplements to corporate charters, and between that date and 1875 such bonds were authorized in nineteen charters and twenty supplements.[82] That bond endorsements were still unfamiliar in the eighteen fifties is attested by the need for a joint resolution of the legislature in 1855 to explain that the term "endorse" in one of the 1854 authorizations was to be taken to mean guar-

[81] *N. J. Laws,* 1871, Ch. 515, p. 1333; 1875 (private), Ch. 420, p. 272. The expressed purpose of the two charters was the creation of a type of bond that "foreign" capitalists would purchase, thereby encouraging out-of-state funds to be invested in New Jersey real estate.

[82] It is to be presumed that both principal and interest payments were to be guaranteed, although definite language to that effect was used in only a few instances. E.g., *N. J. Laws,* 1868, Ch. 122, p. 258, Ch. 422, p. 984. It is not possible to determine how many guarantees were made without express authority. The validity of unauthorized guarantees, however, was open to question, and a land company that had guaranteed the bonds of a railroad with which its business had become "somewhat connected" successfully sought legislative authorization for its act on the ground that the power to make the guarantee was doubtful and the bonds hence insecure in the hands of the holders. *Ibid.,* 1855, Ch. 207, p. 578. The guarantee of $2,000,000 of horse railroad company bonds given by the New Jersey Railroad and Transportation Company in 1870 was similarly validated by special act in 1871. *Ibid.,* 1871, Ch. 354, p. 942.

antee and to explain further that the state of New Jersey was not responsible for the payment of the bonds.[83]

The device of the guaranteed bond was developed and employed in New Jersey almost entirely within the field of railroading, and the bonds made eligible for endorsement were with few exceptions those of railroad companies.[84] It is apparent that the practice of endorsing bonds developed when railroad companies became conscious of the advantage that would accrue to them if they encouraged the construction of subsidiary lines to serve as traffic feeders.[85] Construction of the shorter lines could in many cases be assured only if the bonds were guaranteed by an established company. One authorization for the guarantee of bonds was granted on the ground that the road whose bonds were to be endorsed was having difficulty in getting funds by ordinary methods of mortgaging and had to furnish security adequate to encourage capitalists to invest.[86] When authority to guarantee bonds was given, limits were not put on the amount of the bonds that might be so secured except in five cases.[87] No requirement of consent by the stockholders of the guaranteeing corporation was included save in two cases in which railroad companies were permitted to endorse bonds of non-railroad corporations.[88] In a number of cases, the authority to guarantee railroad bonds was accompanied by permission to aid construction in any other way.[89]

It appears that a rather close community of interest existed between the companies whose bonds were guaranteed and the guarantors. One authorization permitted the Joint Companies

[83] *N. J. Laws,* 1855, Joint Resolution I, p. 799.

[84] The exceptions were the bonds of coal mining companies in Pennsylvania and of a water company that could be endorsed by railroad companies. *N. J. Laws,* 1874, Ch. 341, p. 1176; 1875 (private), Ch. 225, p. 202.

[85] Three companies that were expanding into important railway "systems" were mentioned most frequently as prospective guarantors: namely, the Joint Companies, the Morris and Essex, and the West Jersey.

[86] *N. J. Laws,* 1854, Joint Resolution III, p. 543.

[87] For examples of the exceptions see *N. J. Laws,* 1854, Ch. 114, p. 301; 1861, Ch. 13, p. 24.

[88] In both cases, the consent of a majority in interest of the stockholders of the guaranteeing railroads was required. *N. J. Laws,* 1874, Ch. 341, p. 1176; 1875 (private), Ch. 225, p. 202.

[89] E.g., *N. J. Laws,* 1870, Ch. 462, p. 1011; 1872, Ch. 597, p. 1359.

to endorse the bonds of any railroad company in which they owned one-half the capital stock,[90] occasionally a road was allowed to endorse bonds issued by any connecting line,[91] and sometimes the authorizations were restricted to the bonds of leased roads[92] or to roads with lines in the same counties.[93] In cases where the two roads involved were specifically named, they were generally companies operating in the same territory. Many of the "railroads" whose bonds were to be guaranteed were probably mere extensions or branches that the established roads would own or control. A first-lien construction mortgage could be put on the new road to secure the bonds, and their salability would be improved by the guarantee of the parent company. Such a device might have been useful to avoid the reach of an after-acquired property clause in an old mortgage that would have extended to the branch if it were constructed by the existing company.

It was realized rather early that corporation bonds could be made attractive to prospective lenders if the right of conversion into stock of the corporation was included in the bond contract. Between 1853 and 1875, twenty-one companies were permitted to issue convertible bonds if they so desired. Twelve of the authorizations appeared in charter supplements[94] and nine in original charters.[95] In four of these cases, only part of the total authorized bonds could be made convertible, the amount being limited to an absolute figure of $200,000 in three instances[96] and to one-half the total authorized bonds in one instance.[97] The legislature seems to have intended in all cases to leave the

[90] *N. J. Laws*, 1854, Joint Resolution III, p. 543.

[91] E.g., *N. J. Laws*, 1854, Ch. 216, p. 524.

[92] E.g., *N. J. Laws*, 1873, Ch. 154, p. 1021.

[93] E.g., *N. J. Laws*, 1854, Ch. 39, p. 100, Ch. 114, p. 301.

[94] E.g., *N. J. Laws*, 1853, Joint Resolution II, p. 484; 1858, Ch. 21, p. 37.

[95] E.g., *N. J. Laws*, 1866, Ch. 7, p. 11; 1868, Ch. 562, p. 1203. One company was allowed to make its bonds convertible into either common or preferred stock. *Ibid.*, 1874, Ch. 82, p. 943. It is impossible to estimate the extent to which convertible bonds were issued without statutory authority. A supplement to the Morris and Essex charter refers to an issue of convertible bonds, yet at no time was the company given express permission to issue such bonds. *Ibid.*, 1867, Ch. 88, p. 144.

[96] E.g., *N. J. Laws*, 1867, Ch. 356, p. 810.

[97] *N. J. Laws*, 1855, Ch. 3, p. 4.

exercise of the conversion privilege at the option of the bondholders, and in the event of an exchange of bonds for stock it appears to have been generally assumed that the source of the stock given out would be the authorized but unissued shares. A unique case was one in which a company was allowed to increase its capital stock by the amount necessary to convert the bonds.[98]

Borrowing corporations were permitted considerable latitude in regard to the denominations in which they issued their bonds. In only fifteen special laws was any restriction expressed. Three of these required the bonds to be in denominations of at least $100,[99] ten at least $500,[100] one not less than $100 or more than $1000 each,[101] and one stipulated that "certificates of loan" issued under a mortgage be in denominations of at least $25.[102]

New Jersey legislators also evidenced little interest in regulating the time of maturity of credit instruments issued by corporations. Twenty-three charters and supplements, however, included a variety of clauses limiting the life of the bonds issued. Periods of twenty and thirty years were mentioned most frequently.[103]

Stipulations regarding the interest rate at which bonds could be written and the price at which they could be sold appeared more frequently in borrowing authorizations than any other type of provision except that giving the right to mortgage. The existence in New Jersey of stringent usury laws was responsible for this fact. The legal interest rate in colonial New Jersey

[98] *N. J. Laws,* 1874, Ch. 78, p. 933.

[99] E.g., *N. J. Laws,* 1867, Ch. 349, p. 801.

[100] E.g., *N. J. Laws,* 1868, Ch. 64, p. 145, Ch. 141, p. 302.

[101] *N. J. Laws,* 1873, Ch. 28, p. 929.

[102] *N. J. Laws,* 1855, Ch. 112, p. 283.

[103] In fourteen cases, the bonds could run for thirty years. E.g., *N. J. Laws,* 1863, Ch. 207, p. 416. In six cases, the limit was twenty years. E.g., *ibid.,* 1861, Ch. 83, p. 183. One of the latter cases concerned a gas company that was authorized to make serial bonds by dividing the issue into classes, one of which would be redeemed at the end of each year after ten years had passed. *Ibid.,* 1868, Ch. 141, p. 302. In one instance, the principal was to be made payable in fifteen to fifty years, in another in ten years. *Ibid.,* 1865, Ch. 463, p. 837; 1873, Ch. 28, p. 929. A gas company was prohibited from issuing bonds with a life exceeding the duration of the company. *Ibid.,* 1864, Ch. 174, p. 272.

had been established at 7 per cent.[104] The colonial limit of 7 per cent was retained after the Revolution, but in 1823 the legal interest rate was reduced to 6 per cent.[105] Beginning in 1852, the 6 per cent maximum was gradually whittled away. Between 1852 and 1865, eight amendments modified the "Act against Usury" by allowing 7 per cent to be taken in certain townships or counties.[106] A new state-wide limit of 7 per cent was adopted in 1866, and 7 per cent continued as the legal rate for the remainder of the period under investigation.[107] When corporations began to borrow extensively, they came directly against the difficulty of selling their bonds at a rate that came within the legal limit of 6 or 7 per cent. It is not surprising that when they requested authority to borrow, corporation officials asked for some degree of relief from the operation of the usury laws.

An analysis of the authorizations to borrow money given between 1847 and 1875 shows that relief from the usury laws was often granted. Historically, the first form of relief given concerned the rate of interest at which bonds could be written. Up to and including 1866, during which year the legal rate of interest was raised to 7 per cent, eighty-five charters and twenty-five charter supplements granted individual corporations the right to borrow at any rate not exceeding 7 per cent.[108] Such authorizations usually included the condition that the borrowing company could not plead any usury statute to obstruct enforcement of a bond contract. Thus at a time when

[104] Samuel Allinson, ed., *Acts of the General Assembly of the Province of New-Jersey . . .* , Ch. 161, p. 110 (1738–1739). Although an act to reduce the rate to 6 per cent was passed in 1774, royal consent to the reduction was not forthcoming. *Ibid.*, Ch. 593, p. 442 (1774).

[105] *N. J. Laws*, 48 sess., 1 sit. (1823, public), p. 49.

[106] E.g., *N. J. Laws*, 1852, Ch. 183, p. 447; 1854, Ch. 107, p. 260. The reason given for such increases in the rate was that in no other way could a large amount of funds be prevented from seeking investment in New York rather than in New Jersey. The business community may have been largely responsible for this gradual weakening of the usury law, for most of the localities where 7 per cent was permitted were in the industrial northern section of the state and the process began at the very time when corporate borrowing became common. See also the 1856 message of Governor Price in *Votes and Proceedings of the General Assembly*, 1856, p. 33.

[107] *N. J. Laws*, 1866, Ch. 171, p. 406.

[108] E.g., *N. J. Laws*, 1847, p. 128; 1851, p. 37; 1865, Ch. 225, p. 397.

the legal interest rate in most sections of New Jersey was 6 per cent, many corporations were benefited by permission to write bonds at an interest rate of 7 per cent.

Some corporations were awarded even more generous privileges. One was allowed to issue bonds at 8 per cent and another at 10 per cent.[109] The bonds of sixteen companies were specifically authorized to bear any interest without being invalidated by reason of the usury law.[110] Seven corporations were merely prohibited from making any defence of usury in connection with the enforcement of their bond contracts, but it is uncertain whether the intention of the legislature was to permit these companies to issue bonds at any rate of interest they desired.[111] When taxes on intangible property became relatively heavy in the years following the Civil War, corporations wishing to borrow funds found increasing difficulty in selling their bonds at the then legal rate of 7 per cent. In 1867, a Trenton hall company, needing more money than could be raised through stock issues, approached the legislature with the argument that they were unable to borrow at the legal rate because of the high property taxes in Trenton. The company was authorized either to make an agreement with the purchasers of the bonds to pay the taxes levied on the securities or to borrow at a rate over 7 per cent in lieu of paying the taxes.[112] Three manufacturing corporations received somewhat similar authority during the following few years.[113]

Equally important to corporations attempting to sell their bonds or give their mortgages on terms at once acceptable to lenders and within the restrictions of the usury laws was the price at which the credit instruments might be issued. It was realized at an early date that limitations on nominal rates of interest would be no obstacle in floating bonds if the securities could legally be issued at a price below their face value.

[109] *N. J. Laws,* 1859, Ch. 116, p. 320; 1869, Ch. 342, p. 926.

[110] E.g., *N. J. Laws,* 1854, Ch. 22, p. 45; 1864, Ch. 42, p. 72, Ch. 344, p. 603. Occasionally, ambiguous phrases appeared permitting sales of bonds at any "rate" or on any "terms," but since such provisions were sometimes combined with a limit on the interest at which the bonds could be written, they can be assumed to have applied merely to the selling price of the bonds.

[111] E.g., *N. J. Laws,* 1866, Ch. 173, p. 408.

[112] *N. J. Laws,* 1867, Ch. 192, p. 419.

[113] E.g., *N. J. Laws,* 1871, Ch. 458, p. 1206.

In 1855, the railroad and canal companies were able to secure the passage of the following supplement to the usury law:

> That no bond, mortgage, or other security for the payment of money, heretofore made or issued, or that may hereafter be made or issued, by any railroad or canal corporation, created by or under the laws of this state, shall be held, deemed, or considered invalid because such bond, mortgage, or other security may have been made, issued, sold, assigned, or otherwise disposed of, by such corporation below the par value thereof; *provided,* such bond, mortgage, or other security, shall be valid on its face . . .[114]

It is interesting that some railroad companies were partially denied the advantages of this supplement during later years. Eighteen railroad charters and supplements prohibited sales of bonds at less than 90 per cent of their face (usually referred to as "par") value,[115] and two railroad companies were not permitted to sell bonds at less than 80 per cent of their face value.[116] The apparent purpose of such abrogations of the general rule was to protect stockholders from the undesirable effects of reckless borrowing by the directors, for in five of the above cases the bonds could be sold for less than the 90 per cent figure with the consent of two-thirds of the stockholders.[117]

Railroad and canal companies were not alone in desiring legislation putting their borrowing activities beyond the operation of the usury laws. A glimpse of the effort made to liberalize the usury statute for the benefit of other corporations is afforded by an 1857 newspaper account of an attempt to secure the passage of a bill permitting manufacturing corporations to go beyond the restrictions of the usury statute by selling their bonds below "par." The bill failed to pass the senate.[118] Many corporations of various types, however, secured special acts

[114] *N. J. Laws,* 1855, Ch. 177, p. 500. The amendment did not affect suits then pending.

[115] E.g., *N. J. Laws,* 1859, Ch. 202, p. 585; 1865, Ch. 291, p. 541, Ch. 359, p. 675.

[116] *N. J. Laws,* 1870, Ch. 63, p. 201, Ch. 517, p. 1265.

[117] *N. J. Laws,* 1864, Ch. 291, p. 482; 1869, Ch. 538, p. 1297. It is not possible to tell in all cases whether consent had to be given by two-thirds in interest or two-thirds of the number of stockholders.

[118] *Newark Daily Advertiser,* February 25, 1857.

empowering them to sell their bonds at a discount. Eight were granted the right to issue bonds at not less than 90 per cent of face value[119] and one at not less than 80 per cent.[120] Forty-eight companies received still more generous terms in clauses that removed all limits to the price at which their bonds could be sold. Of the latter, thirty-seven were allowed to dispose of their bonds at any price.[121] Nine were given similarly broad power by clauses authorizing them to sell their bonds at the "market" price.[122] A unique case was that of a manufacturing company that was allowed to sell its bonds below face value if all the stockholders gave written consent.[123]

In spite of their evident willingness to give relief from the usury laws by acts of special application, the New Jersey lawmakers were not disposed to provide such relief by laws of general application to other than railroad and canal companies until 1874. Hence many of the state's corporations continued to be hampered by the usury laws. The ordinary business corporation, unless it was favored by special legislation, might encounter difficulty in selling its debt securities at a rate encompassed by the usury statute. This would have been particularly true if the borrowing was necessitated by financial embarrassment. In 1874, however, this disability was swept away by an amendment to the usury act providing that no bond or mortgage for payment of money issued previously or in the future by any corporation created by New Jersey was invalid or subject to deduction on the amount due because it was issued or sold below "par" value.[124]

The detailed material of the present chapter is of significance not merely as a catalogue of the over-all debt restrictions im-

[119] E.g., *N. J. Laws,* 1855, Ch. 3, p. 4; 1868, Ch. 260, p. 572.

[120] *N. J. Laws,* 1868, Ch. 388, p. 876. In this case, the price could be lower than 80 per cent if two-thirds of the stockholders consented.

[121] E.g., *N. J. Laws,* 1867, Ch. 50, p. 79, Ch. 137, p. 258.

[122] E.g., *N. J. Laws,* 1868, Ch. 9, p. 17, Ch. 185, p. 421.

[123] *N. J. Laws,* 1869, Ch. 62, p. 98.

[124] *N. J. Laws,* 1874, Ch. 359, p. 67. The amendment did not apply to suits then pending.

posed on New Jersey corporations and of the terms of the borrowing rights given to these artificial persons; nor does it have meaning only in establishing the period when business corporations evidenced general interest in raising capital by formal issues of debt securities. The facts presented are of particular interest in illustrating one phase of the special *versus* the general incorporation law controversy going on in New Jersey during most of the years between 1845 and 1875.

During those years, corporate borrowing was becoming important, and yet corporations organized under the general incorporation laws of the period were at a great disadvantage in regard to borrowing. The disadvantage in the case of the most important general laws was a double one: the obstacle of over-all debt limits and the absence of any positively expressed mortgaging or other borrowing rights. It has been shown that the general manufacturing company law of 1846 and its successor of 1849, the latter being subsequently broadened to cover all types of business, contained strict debt limits and imposed penalties if the limits were exceeded. Two other general laws contained similar restrictions on indebtedness. As regards positive expressions of borrowing rights, only three minor general laws for land companies and the general railroad law of 1873 made mention of the right to mortgage or to issue bonds.

On the other hand, over-all debt limits practically disappeared from special charters after 1846, and nearly one thousand special charters and charter supplements passed between 1846 and 1875 expressly permitted a wide variety of borrowing privileges. The disparity in borrowing provisions between the two types of laws can be explained by the fact that the persons interested in increased borrowing privileges pressed merely for legislation covering their own particular cases, while the proponents and guardians of general laws were the very persons who were concerned with restricting the rights of corporate bodies generally.[125]

[125] By way of contrast, it can be stated that the general incorporation laws of New York State were more lenient in the matter of borrowing than those of New Jersey. To consider a few of the more important general laws of New

It is impossible to determine how much of the lack of popularity of the general incorporation laws among the business community of New Jersey resulted from the failure of those laws to keep step with changing concepts of corporate debt. The evidence is strong, however, that a desire for broad borrowing powers was an important consideration in discouraging companies from filing certificates of incorporation under the general laws and in stimulating companies already organized under general laws to seek special charters or at least special supplements granting them broader privileges than the terms of the general laws allowed.

York, we find that companies organized under the general law of 1811 were permitted after 1822 to secure payment of debts contracted by them in the course of their business "by mortgaging all or any part of the real estate of such company" upon the consent of over two-thirds in interest of the stockholders. *N. Y. Laws,* 45 sess. (1822), Ch. 213, p. 217. Corporations under the general gaslight company law of 1848 were permitted in 1854 to issue bonds up to one-third of the paid-in capital stock for the purpose of business expansion. *Ibid.,* 1854, Ch. 312, p. 665. In 1867, the same companies were allowed to mortgage their real estate to secure bonds or other liabilities if the consent of two-thirds in interest of the stockholders could be obtained. *Ibid.,* 1867, Ch. 480, p. 1231. The general manufacturing law of 1848 was amended in 1864 to permit companies organized by virtue of its authority to secure debts by mortgaging their real estate if two-thirds in interest of the stockholders consented. *Ibid.,* 1864, Ch. 517, p. 1154.

The difference between the situations in New York and New Jersey can be explained in part by the fact that the New York constitution of 1846 required incorporation to be governed by general laws where possible. In New York, members of the business community seeking enlarged borrowing privileges had to concentrate their attention on securing relaxation of the terms of the general laws. An individual corporation in New Jersey could obtain favors by the more simple expedient of a special act to cover its individual case.

CHAPTER X

Stockholders and Directors

ALTHOUGH the stockholders of a business corporation are the proprietors of the business, it was not assumed in any New Jersey charter that the stockholders as a group should engage in the active management of corporate affairs. The special charters and general incorporation laws made provision for the selection of a group of individuals who were to undertake the managerial function as representatives of the stockholders. The stockholders' representatives were usually called directors, although occasionally they were legally designated "managers" [1] or "trustees." [2]

The purpose of the present chapter is to indicate the nature of the relationship between stockholders and directors in New Jersey corporations insofar as special charters, general regulating laws, and general incorporation laws provide the necessary information. Much of what is said must necessarily be very general and in some respects incomplete because many details of the relationship between stockholders and directors were left to be determined by the bylaws of each corporation. The legislators, nevertheless, imposed a sufficient number of regulations in special acts and in laws of general application to indicate the more important stockholder-director relationships, and it is these regulations that will be analysed here.

First, the election of directors will be discussed. Among the election details that were generally regulated by the lawmakers were the time, place, and notification for elections, the necessary qualifications for voting, the number of votes to which stockholders were entitled, the number of directors to be chosen, and the eligibility requirements for directors. Secondly, the division of authority as between stockholders and

[1] E.g., *N. J. Laws,* 25 sess., 1 sit. (1800), Ch. 10, p. 18.

[2] E.g., *N. J. Laws,* 39 sess., 2 sit. (1815, private), p. 172.

directors on certain matters of business policy will be investigated. Not a great deal of information can be gleaned from the statute books on this second point, but there is enough material to make possible some discussion of the stockholders' right to financial information, of the determination of dividend policy, and of the making of decisions about such matters as leasing the corporate assets, consolidating with other corporations, and voluntary dissolution.

The amount of attention that was given in nearly every special charter to the regulation of the election of directors bears testimony to the importance attached to the election procedure. Further evidence on this point is afforded by the fact that the earliest important piece of general legislation governing business corporation practices in New Jersey was an act, passed in 1825, "to prevent fraudulent elections by incorporated companies, and to facilitate proceedings against them." [3] There is no doubt that from the earliest years the election of directors was considered to be the primary managerial function of stockholders in business corporations and one that needed careful regulation in the interest of stockholders.

It should be stated at the beginning that no standard policy was adopted for the selection of the initial boards of directors. Although in the majority of instances the first directors were to be elected in the same manner as subsequent boards, a large number of special charters designated the men who were to form the first board, the names being drawn generally from the list of incorporators. Examples of charters in which the initial boards were designated appeared as early as the closing years of the eighteenth century,[4] and occurred with increasing frequency toward the end of the period under investigation.[5]

Most of the special charters and the various general incorporation laws contained explicit directions as to the time and place

[3] *N. J. Laws,* 50 sess., 1 sit. (1825), p. 81.

[4] E.g., *N. J. Laws,* 21 sess., 2 sit. (1797), Ch. 653, p. 201; 23 sess., 3 sit. (1799), Ch. 794, p. 528.

[5] E.g., *N. J. Laws,* 1851, pp. 25, 45, 67, 89, 214.

of holding elections and as to the advance notice to be given stockholders. The general rule was that elections should be held annually. In a very few special charters semi-annual elections were the rule.[6] A number of special charters left it to the bylaws to specify how frequently elections should be held.[7] In many instances in which annual elections were required by the charters, the entire board did not have to be elected annually. Beginning in 1836, considerable interest was shown in plans whereby the board was divided into separate classes, with only one class to be elected each year. The first such scheme was permitted by an amendment to the charter of the Morris Canal and Banking Company in 1836. The amendment permitted the company to divide its board into five classes and elect one class each year.[8] In succeeding years, similar plans were authorized in six other charter amendments[9] and in forty-three original charters.[10] Generally the directors were to be divided into three or four classes. Plans for classifying directors in this fashion were most frequently found in insurance company charters.

Some charters mentioned specific days on which elections were to be held,[11] while others did not.[12] A majority of the charters contained a clause to the effect that failure to hold an election on the appointed day did not work a dissolution of the corporation but that the election might be held at some later date.[13] The general law of 1825 regulating corporate elections

[6] E.g., *N. J. Laws*, 1871, Ch. 2, p. 164.

[7] E.g., *N. J. Laws*, 27 sess., 1 sit. (1802), Ch. 75, p. 157; 1855, Ch. 77, p. 175. A letter published in the *Emporium and True American* on January 30, 1836, is indicative of a feeling against permitting directors to be elected for long terms. The writer called attention to a petition reported to be before the legislature asking that directors of the Morris Canal and Banking Company be elected for life. He objected strongly to the example of a corporation thus creating an "aristocracy" in the form of a board of directors without the "usual amenability to the stockholders or the public, uniformly created in all existing acts of incorporation in New-Jersey."

[8] *N. J. Laws*, 60 sess., 2 sit. (1836), p. 262.

[9] E.g., *N. J. Laws*, 1862, Ch. 12, p. 16; 1871, Ch. 62, p. 286.

[10] E.g., *N. J. Laws*, 61 sess., 2 sit. (1837), p. 443; 1870, Ch. 217, p. 519, Ch. 292, p. 655.

[11] E.g., *N. J. Laws*, 34 sess., 1 sit. (1809), Ch. 38, p. 137; 1848, p. 222.

[12] E.g., *N. J. Laws*, 63 sess., 2 sit. (1839), p. 44; 1855, Ch. 66, p. 148.

[13] E.g., *N. J. Laws*, 40 sess., 2 sit. (1816, private), p. 158; 1845, p. 205.

declared it to be the duty of the president and directors to hold an election within thirty days if for any reason the election had not been held on the regular date.[14] Beginning in the eighteen thirties, additional provisions were sometimes written into special charters empowering a designated proportion of stockholders to issue a notice for the annual election if it was not done by the directors.[15] The general incorporation laws of 1846 and 1849 also made provision for any three or more stockholders to call a meeting if the officers refused or neglected to do so.[16]

The special charters were not uniform in their provisions as to the places where elections should be held. Some specified the name of the town or county,[17] some merely required that elections be held in New Jersey,[18] while many were silent about this matter.[19] The general regulating law of 1846 was amended in 1849 to require that all New Jersey corporations whose charters did not specify the place where they were to hold their meetings should hold them within the state.[20] Some special charters passed during the eighteen sixties and seventies, however, expressly permitted all corporate meetings to be held outside New Jersey.[21]

In order to protect stockholders in the exercise of their voting privilege, a large number of special charters required that definite notice of forthcoming elections be given by the directors. The general practice in such cases was to specify the amount of time that should elapse between the notification and the election and to prescribe the form in which the notice should be given.[22] In many instances, the charters said nothing about giving stock-

[14] *N. J. Laws,* 50 sess., 1 sit. (1825), p. 81.

[15] Such provisions appeared most frequently in manufacturing company charters. E.g., *N. J. Laws,* 60 sess., 2 sit. (1836), pp. 256, 339, 388.

[16] *N. J. Laws,* 1846, p. 64; 1849, p. 300. [17] E.g., *N. J. Laws,* 1847, p. 126.

[18] E.g., *N. J. Laws,* 25 sess., 2 sit. (1801), Ch. 38, p. 80; 61 sess., 2 sit. (1837), p. 157.

[19] E.g., *N. J. Laws,* 58 sess., 1 sit. (1833), p. 8; 1847, p. 71.

[20] *N. J. Laws,* 1849, p. 215. Companies whose charters were not subject to amendment and steamboat and ferry companies operating on the waters between New Jersey and the adjoining states were exempt.

[21] E.g., *N. J. Laws,* 1867, Ch. 186, p. 398; 1873, Ch. 86, p. 971.

[22] E.g., *N. J. Laws,* 25 sess., 2 sit. (1801), Ch. 38, p. 80; 1847, pp. 10, 32. In most cases notification was to be given by means of newspaper advertisements, but in some instances notices were to be mailed to stockholders.

holders advance notice of elections, and in such cases the bylaws would rule.[23]

The 1825 statute designed to regulate corporate elections stated that the books of a company in which transfers of stock were recorded were to be the sole evidence of who were stockholders and of what persons were entitled to vote at elections. It provided further that the transfer books were to be open to the examination of every stockholder for thirty days previous to any election.[24] The law was strengthened in 1841 by an amendment requiring the officer in charge of the transfer book to prepare, ten days before the election, a correct list in alphabetical order of all stockholders entitled to vote at that election with the number of shares held by each, to exhibit the list to any stockholder asking to see it, and to produce it at the election. Since the same amendment forbade anyone from voting shares that had been transferred within a period of twenty days preceding an election, the list prepared ten days beforehand was the final and authoritative word on who could vote and on how many votes each person could cast.[25]

As Angell and Ames pointed out in 1832 in their treatise on the law of corporations, the right of voting by proxy was not a general right and could be claimed only by parties who could prove special authority for the privilege.[26] From the earliest years, the New Jersey legislators wrote into nearly every charter a clause allowing stockholders the privilege of voting by proxy.[27] In 1841, the right of voting by proxy was made practically universal in New Jersey corporations by an amendment to the 1825 law regulating corporate elections. The amendment declared that stockholders were to enjoy the privilege of voting by proxy in every corporation unless the charter contained definite language to the contrary. The only limitation was that no proxy

[23] E.g., *N. J. Laws,* 58 sess., 2 sit. (1834), p. 44; 1860, Ch. 8, p. 30.

[24] *N. J. Laws,* 50 sess. 1 sit. (1825), p. 81. Severe penalties were imposed on the officer having custody of the transfer book if he refused to exhibit the book to any stockholder who asked to examine it.

[25] *N. J. Laws,* 65 sess., 2 sit. (1841), p. 116 .

[26] Joseph K. Angell and Samuel Ames, *A Treatise on the Law of Private Corporations Aggregate* (1st ed., 1832), p. 67.

[27] E.g., *N. J. Laws,* 16 sess., 1 sit. (1791), Ch. 356, p. 730; 17 sess., 1 sit. (1792), Ch. 406, p. 806; 19 sess., 2 sit. (1795), Ch. 544, p. 1041.

could be allowed if it had been given more than three years before the date of the election.[28]

Citizenship or residence requirements were sometimes imposed on stockholders as prerequisites to voting in corporate elections. Shareholders in the six so-called "state" banks chartered in 1812 were required to be citizens of the United States in order to qualify as voting stockholders,[29] and the charters of two 1815 banks made residence in the United States a necessary qualification for voting by proxy.[30] The charters of eight insurance companies passed between 1824 and 1837 also required that shareholders be citizens of the United States in order to vote in corporate elections.[31] According to the terms of a bank charter of 1834, no stockholder was permitted to vote unless he was a citizen of New Jersey.[32] An 1849 bank charter allowed only those stockholders who resided in New Jersey to cast votes,[33] but a month after it was passed the legislature enacted an amendment to the general regulating act of 1846 repealing all parts of any act of incorporation that prohibited stockholders residing out of the state from voting.[34] The charter of a bank passed in 1855 was the only later case in which residence in New Jersey was made a qualification for voting.[35]

Many special charters specified a period of time previous to corporate elections during which a shareholder must own his stock if he wished to participate in the voting. Nine bank char-

[28] *N. J. Laws,* 65 sess., 2 sit. (1841), p. 116.

[29] *N. J. Laws,* 36 sess., 2 sit. (1812, public), p. 3.

[30] *N. J. Laws,* 39 sess., 2 sit. (1815, private), pp. 21, 32.

[31] E.g., *N. J. Laws,* 49 sess., 1 sit. (1824), p. 74; 61 sess., 2 sit. (1837), p. 176.

[32] *N. J. Laws,* 58 sess., 2 sit. (1834), p. 144.

[33] *N. J. Laws,* 1849, p. 13.

[34] *N. J. Laws,* 1849, p. 310. Jonathan Pickel opposed the measure on the ground that the "'aristocratic' citizens" of other states should not be allowed to vote in the elections of New Jersey corporations merely because they owned stock in them. The argument that to deprive out-of-state shareholders of votes would drive much capital out of New Jersey, however, was the one that prevailed. *Sentinal of Freedom,* March 2, 1849.

[35] *N. J. Laws,* 1865, Ch. 251, p. 736. It should be recalled that another device frequently employed to keep control of business corporations in the hands of New Jersey residents was the requirement that either all or a majority of the stockholders be Jerseymen. Such rules were found in many bank charters. Cf. *supra,* p. 249. In only one instance was a charter explicit as to what would happen if a stockholder removed from New Jersey, and in that case the stock was not to be forfeited but the holder was disqualified from voting. *N. J. Laws,* 1848, p. 130.

ters passed between 1812 and 1823 required that stock be owned at least three months before election time to entitle the holder to vote.[36] Between 1824 and 1840, 52 charters, including 18 for banks, specified varying minimum periods during which shares had to be held if their owners were to vote in corporate elections.[37] The legislators apparently believed in the salutary effect of this type of regulation, for when the 1825 general law regulating corporate elections was amended in 1841 they adopted the rule that no share could be voted in any corporate election if it had been transferred on the books of the company within a period of 20 days preceding the election.[38] Either the existence of this 20-day rule was later overlooked or there was a desire on the part of incorporating groups to change the rule by special charter provisions, because 101 charters passed between 1842 and 1875 specified periods either shorter or longer than 20 days during which a stockholder must hold his shares in order to qualify for voting. Fifty-six of this group provided for periods of less than 20 days,[39] and 45 specified longer periods.[40]

There were in addition nine charters that forbade shareholders to vote unless all the installments due on their shares had been paid[41] and two that allowed votes to be cast only by virtue of full-paid shares.[42]

The New Jersey legislators generally set forth definite rules for the determination of the number of votes to which stockholders of business corporations were entitled. When they made no explicit provision in this matter, the common law rule of one vote per stockholder prevailed, a situation that was usually unacceptable to the principal shareholders.[43]

The most commonly used formula permitted stockholders to

[36] E.g., *N. J. Laws,* 39 sess., 2 sit. (1815, private), pp. 21, 32.

[37] E.g., *N. J. Laws,* 49 sess., 1 sit. (1824), pp. 74, 99, 140.

[38] *N. J. Laws,* 65 sess., 2 sit. (1841), p. 116.

[39] E.g., *N. J. Laws,* 1860, Ch. 93, p. 226, Ch. 189, p. 486.

[40] E.g., *N. J. Laws,* 1860, Ch. 37, p. 87, Ch. 246, p. 632.

[41] E.g., *N. J. Laws,* 62 sess., 2 sit. (1838), pp. 92, 157.

[42] *N. J. Laws,* 1867, Ch. 12, p. 14; 1869, Ch. 564, p. 1374.

[43] In 1834, the New Jersey supreme court held that a bridge company whose charter was silent on the matter of the voting ratio could not adopt a one-vote-per-share voting scheme even if it made a bylaw to that effect. *Taylor* v. *Griswold,* 14 New Jersey Law, 224 (1834).

cast one vote for each share of stock in their possession. In the early years, this rule was written into each charter to which it was to apply, but in 1841 the general act governing corporate elections was amended so that every stockholder in an incorporated company should be entitled to one vote per share unless the charter contained some contrary stipulation.[44]

Although 1 vote per share was the rule in the vast majority of corporations, certain significant exceptions should be noted. The most frequently used variation was the regressive voting scheme in which the number of votes a stockholder could cast did not increase in proportion to his stockholdings. Such schemes were written into 123 charters between 1796 and 1867, inclusive. The voting arrangements varied widely. Some took the form of very elaborate schedules of which the following formula found in the 1807 charter of a banking company may be taken as typical: 1 vote per share for the first 2 shares, 1 vote for every 2 shares between 3 and 8, 1 vote for every 4 shares between 9 and 20, 1 vote for every 6 shares between 21 and 50, and 1 vote for every 10 shares over 50.[45] Many of the formulas were more simple, as for example the stipulations in 2 1825 turnpike company charters permitting stockholders 1 vote per share for the first 10 shares owned and 1 vote per 5 shares for all in excess of 10.[46] In 17 instances, the regressive schemes were supplemented by absolute maximum limits on the number of votes an individual stockholder could cast.[47]

Although regressive voting schemes appeared in the charters of many different types of concerns, they were most frequently inserted in bank charters. Forty-two special bank charters, one-half the total number passed by the New Jersey legislature, contained regressive voting arrangements. This group included nearly every bank charter passed before 1850 and several passed after that date.[48] In not making the voting power of

[44] *N. J. Laws,* 65 sess., 2 sit. (1841), p. 116.

[45] *N. J. Laws,* 32 sess., 1 sit. (1807), Ch. 30, p. 80.

[46] *N. J. Laws,* 50 sess., 1 sit. (1825), pp. 20, 28.

[47] E.g., *N. J. Laws,* 20 sess., 2 sit. (1796), Ch. 586, p. 57; 60 sess., 2 sit. (1836), p. 333.

[48] E.g., *N. J. Laws,* 28 sess., 2 sit. (1804), Ch. 109, p. 268; 36 sess., 2 sit. (1812, public), p. 3; 1855, Ch. 222, p. 632, Ch. 240, p. 682.

bank stockholders proportional to the number of shares held, New Jersey practice was consistent with that of many other states during the early nineteenth century.[49] There were also, however, fifteen manufacturing companies,[50] twelve turnpike companies,[51] ten railroad companies,[52] and a large miscellaneous group of concerns whose charters provided for regressive voting arrangements.[53]

In addition to the 123 charters with regressive voting schemes, there were 90 in which stockholders were allowed 1 vote per share with an upper limit on the number of votes any single stockholder might cast. This type of provision was most frequently inserted in the charters of turnpike companies. Limits on the number of votes which one stockholder could have were written into the charters of 56 turnpike companies,[54] 14 bridge companies,[55] and 20 companies of various types.[56] The maximum number of votes allowed in such cases was usually 10 or 20, although 3 manufacturing company charters permitted 100 votes per shareholder.[57] In the charters of 3 ferry companies and 1 telegraph company the maximum number of votes that any one stockholder could cast was expressed as a proportion of the total number of votes to which all the stockholders were entitled, the proportions being established at one-sixth, one-fourth, or one-half.[58] There was one further and unique case in which the maximum limit applied only to a particular class of stockholders. This was the charter of the S. U.

[49] Cf. D. R. Dewey, *State Banking Before the Civil War,* pp. 112–115.

[50] E.g., *N. J. Laws,* 39 sess., 2 sit. (1815, private), pp. 108, 112, 115.

[51] E.g., *N. J. Laws,* 52 sess., 2 sit. (1828), p. 25.

[52] E.g., *N. J. Laws,* 60 sess., 2 sit. (1836), pp. 86, 226, 370.

[53] The miscellaneous group included among others bridge, canal, ferry, steamboat, and water companies.

[54] E.g., *N. J. Laws,* 30 sess., 2 sit. (1806), Ch. 188, p. 567, Ch. 195, p. 622; 1849, pp. 145, 194.

[55] E.g., *N. J. Laws,* 17 sess., 1 sit. (1792), Ch. 406, p. 806; 56 sess., 2 sit. (1832), p. 82.

[56] These included manufacturing, canal, and ferry companies.

[57] E.g., *N. J. Laws,* 1867, Ch. 20, p. 23.

[58] E.g., *N. J. Laws,* 1850, p. 260; 1869, Ch. 455, p. 1136. The 1853 general incorporation law for telegraph companies limited the votes of any one stockholder to one-third of the total votes represented at the meeting. *Ibid.,* 1853, Ch. 122, p. 304.

M. in which the United States government or any state that might subscribe to the shares was limited to a maximum of 100 votes.[59]

There may also have been some cases in which corporations provided in their bylaws for unusual voting arrangements. A few special charters[60] and the general incorporation laws of 1846 and 1849[61] left the voting ratios to be governed by rules set forth in the bylaws.

Regressive voting schemes and limitations on the number of votes that a stockholder might enjoy were originally adopted as measures to prohibit the concentration of corporate control in the hands of one or a few large stockholders. Such plans were more or less ineffective because a large holder could spread the nominal ownership of his shares among relatives or friends and thus enjoy a voting power in proportion to his holdings. They were consequently abandoned in some states in the early years of the nineteenth century, yet they appeared with surprising frequency in the special charters of New Jersey up through the decade of the eighteen fifties and in a number of instances after that time. Beginning about the middle of the nineteenth century, however, some New Jersey corporations requested the legislature to relieve them of such charter provisions, and from 1849 onward eight charter amendments were passed to put the voting in particular corporations on an unrestricted one-vote-per-share basis.[62]

It is interesting that eleven charters passed in the last two decades of the period under investigation specifically restricted each stockholder to only one vote. Six of the eleven were charters for coöperative associations,[63] three were manufacturing company charters,[64] one a hotel company charter,[65] and one the charter of an insurance company.[66] The insurance company

[59] *N. J. Laws,* 16 sess., 1 sit. (1791), Ch. 356, p. 730.
[60] E.g., *N. J. Laws,* 1864, Ch. 137, p. 220.
[61] *N. J. Laws,* 1846, p. 64; 1849, p. 300.
[62] E.g., *N. J. Laws,* 1849, p. 51; 1860, Ch. 7, p. 26, Ch. 33, p. 80.
[63] E.g., *N. J. Laws,* 1868, Ch. 240, p. 529, Ch. 462, p. 1065.
[64] *N. J. Laws,* 1857, Ch. 48, p. 106, Ch. 217, p. 554; 1872, Ch. 67, p. 239.
[65] *N. J. Laws,* 1853, Ch. 98, p. 245.
[66] *N. J. Laws,* 1870, Ch. 206, p. 500.

and one of the manufacturing corporations were by later amendments put on a one-vote-per-share basis.[67]

By the eighteen seventies, there was considerable interest in the United States in the problem of securing representation on corporate directorates for minority stockholder groups. Although several states actually amended their constitutions to require cumulative voting in corporate elections,[68] there was apparently little concern in New Jersey over the problem of minority representation. As early as 1851, a group of minority stockholders of a manufacturing company had asked the New Jersey legislature to provide for their representation on the board of directors, but the charter amendment they requested was not passed.[69] An 1853 railroad company charter, however, permitted a particular ferry company to subscribe to $10,000 of the stock with the privilege of appointing one director for each $5,000 subscribed.[70] In 1872, a bill was offered in the senate that would have required corporate elections to be conducted according to a cumulative arrangement whenever the holders of one-fifth of the total stock so requested. The proposal, however, was not acted upon.[71] Only one special charter passed in New Jersey during the period under study made cumulative voting compulsory. This was an 1872 railroad company charter according to the terms of which each share of stock entitled the holder to as many votes as there were directors to be elected. The votes could be concentrated upon one candidate or distributed as the stockholder desired.[72]

The lawmakers frequently provided, however, for the direct appointment of directors by the state government or by local governmental units in the event these units became corporate stockholders. During the first third of the nineteenth century, the legislature reserved to the state the right to appoint a cer-

[67] *N. J. Laws*, 1872, Ch. 14, p. 153; 1873, Ch. 455, p. 1363.

[68] Cf. *supra*, p. 194.

[69] *Newark Daily Advertiser*, January 31, 1851. The minority stockholders were disgruntled because the directors had not issued a stock dividend on the basis of retained earnings.

[70] *N. J. Laws*, 1853, Ch. 120, p. 287.

[71] *Newark Daily Advertiser*, March 14, 1872.

[72] *N. J. Laws*, 1872, Ch. 587, p. 1297.

tain number of directors in ten banking and transportation companies if the state subscribed to specified amounts of the stock.[73] The 1836 charter of a ferry company provided for the appointment of one director by the city of Camden should that municipality take a specified number of shares.[74] By virtue of two later laws, the cities of Trenton and New Brunswick were permitted to purchase stock in the water companies operating within their confines. When they had bought stock, they were to appoint a proportion of the boards of directors equal to the proportion they owned of the total stock.[75]

A word should be added concerning the election of the boards of directors of mutual companies. Although the directors of mutual savings institutions appear to have been self-perpetuating groups, the directors of mutual insurance companies were to be elected by the insured persons or "members." The earliest charters of mutual insurance companies merely stated that directors were to be elected by the members, in which case the rule of one vote per member probably prevailed.[76] In 1835, the charter of a mutual insurance company was amended to allow the members a number of votes proportional to the amounts they had paid into the company, with a maximum of five votes for any member.[77] The charters of twenty-two mutual insurance companies passed between 1839 and 1875 granted members one vote for each $100 or $500 of insurance they carried. In fourteen of these cases there was no qualification as to how many or how few votes any one member might possess,[78] but eight of the charters guaranteed each member at least one vote and established either five or ten votes as the maximum number any one member might cast.[79]

[73] E.g., *N. J. Laws,* 29 sess., 1 sit. (1804), Ch. 154, p. 449; 54 sess., 2 sit. (1830), pp. 73, 83. The six so-called state banks chartered in 1812 have not been included in this count. These cases were different, for the legislature retained the right to appoint a majority of the directors of each institution whether the state subscribed to the stock or not. The arrangement was altered in the following year. Cf. *supra,* pp. 64–66.

[74] *N. J. Laws,* 60 sess., 2 sit. (1836), p. 265.

[75] *N. J. Laws,* 1855, Ch. 63, p. 141; 1861, Ch. 164, p. 475.

[76] E.g., *N. J. Laws,* 36 sess., 1 sit. (1811, private), p. 23.

[77] *N. J. Laws,* 59 sess., 2 sit. (1835), p. 71.

[78] E.g., *N. J. Laws,* 63 sess., 2 sit. (1839), p. 118.

[79] E.g., *N. J. Laws,* 65 sess., 1 sit. (1840), p. 7; 1867, Ch. 394, p. 886.

The exact number of persons to be elected to the board of directors of a business corporation was set forth in nearly every special charter passed in New Jersey. Generally an odd number was selected. While the size of the boards of directors varied widely from charter to charter, five, seven, and nine were popular numbers.[80] A few charters left the number of directors to be determined by the companies,[81] although when the stockholders were allowed to fix the number of directors their freedom of action was usually restricted by a minimum or maximum number or both expressed in the charters.[82] Most of the general incorporation laws allowed the corporators considerable latitude in choosing the number of directors to be entered in the certificate of incorporation. For example, the 1816 general law permitted any number not over nine,[83] the general laws of 1846 and 1849 allowed any number not less than three,[84] and the general banking law of 1850 did not limit in any way the number of directors a bank might have.[85]

There were two principal types of eligibility requirements imposed on corporate directors from time to time in New Jersey during the period under investigation. They were, first, a requirement that directors be holders of stock in order to qualify for directorships and, second, a specific residence or citizenship requirement. Both of these tests made their initial appearance in New Jersey in an 1800 water company charter,[86] and they were applied either singly or in combination in hundreds of instances during subsequent years.

In considering the stock ownership requirement, the record between 1800 and 1872, inclusive, must first be examined.[87] During that period, the requirement that persons must own

[80] E.g., *N. J. Laws,* 30 sess., 2 sit. (1806), Ch. 186, p. 526; 50 sess., 1 sit. (1825), pp. 58, 74, 83; 1850, pp. 18, 52, 80, 173.

[81] E.g., *N. J. Laws,* 61 sess., 2 sit. (1837), p. 411.

[82] E.g., *N. J. Laws,* 49 sess., 1 sit. (1824), p. 49; 59 sess., 2 sit. (1835), p. 121; 1860, Ch. 8, p. 30, Ch. 56, p. 130.

[83] *N. J. Laws,* 40 sess., 2 sit. (1816, public), p. 17.

[84] *N. J. Laws,* 1846, p. 64; 1849, p. 300.

[85] *N. J. Laws,* 1850, p. 140.

[86] *N. J. Laws,* 25 sess., 1 sit. (1800), Ch. 5, p. 10.

[87] 1872 is chosen as the terminal date because at the end of that year's session the legislature passed a law requiring all corporate directors to be stockholders.

stock before they were eligible for directorships was written into 956 special charters, slightly over one-half the total number of stock-company charters passed in New Jersey during those years.[88] In 43 of the 956 cases, the minimum amounts of stock that directors should own were specified. Minima of 5 or 10 shares were most frequently stipulated,[89] although in a few instances the figures were set as high as 50 or 100 shares.[90] In addition, the general incorporation law of 1816,[91] the general law of 1849,[92] and the 1854 general law for companies engaged in water transportation [93] made stock ownership a necessary qualification for directors. Finally in 1872, the general regulating act of 1846 was amended to require that no person could be elected a director of any stock-issuing corporation of New Jersey unless he was a bona fide owner of some of the stock. If a corporate director ceased to hold his stock at any time subsequent to the election, his seat on the board was to be vacant.[94]

Mention should also be made of the rule applied in the case of mutual insurance companies. The charters of fifty-eight mutual insurance concerns required directors to be members of the companies.[95] These fifty-eight cases accounted for the vast majority of mutual insurance companies chartered by the state.

During the nineteenth century, the New Jersey lawmakers frequently imposed citizenship or residence requirements on the directors and presidents of business corporations. Slightly over 1000 special charters, nearly one-half the total number granted in New Jersey, made some stipulation as to the citizenship or residence of either all or a part of the members of the boards of directors. Over one-fourth of this number included further rules as to the residence of the presidents. In addition, there were thirty-odd special charters that laid down residence re-

[88] E.g., *N. J. Laws,* 39 sess., 2 sit. (1815, private), pp. 108, 172; 1857, Ch. 65, p. 197, Ch. 115, p. 340.

[89] E.g., *N. J. Laws,* 52 sess., 2 sit. (1828), pp. 107, 209; 61 sess., 2 sit. (1837), pp. 66, 130.

[90] E.g., *N. J. Laws,* 1866, Ch. 393, p. 900; 1871, Ch. 365, p. 957.

[91] *N. J. Laws,* 40 sess., 2 sit. (1816, public), p. 17.

[92] *N. J. Laws,* 1849, p. 300.

[93] *N. J. Laws,* 1854, Ch. 201, p. 470.

[94] *N. J. Laws,* 1872, Ch. 537, p. 89.

[95] E.g., *N. J. Laws,* 36 sess., 1 sit. (1811, private), p. 23; 1846, pp. 39, 43, 58.

quirements for the presidents without any reference to the domicile of the other members of the boards of directors. There was no uniformity in the citizenship and residence requirements, but some general observations as to their nature are made in the following paragraphs.

In the early years of the nineteenth century, a popular charter provision was that all directors be citizens of the United States. Provisions of this type appeared in fifty-one New Jersey charters between 1804 and the early eighteen forties. They were found mainly in the charters of banks and manufacturing companies.[96]

A provision frequently embodied in charters during the whole period under study required that a certain proportion of the directors be residents of New Jersey.[97] Nearly 150 special charters for various types of business concerns contained the requirement that all directors should be residents of New Jersey.[98] About 25 charters established some proportion less than all but more than a bare majority as the minimum number of directors who must be New Jersey residents.[99] Nearly 700 charters provided that a majority of the boards of directors be composed of Jerseymen,[100] while 15 others demanded that some number less than a majority have New Jersey residence.[101]

Sometimes the residence tests were more exacting and required that a certain number of directors be residents of particular New Jersey counties, townships, or municipalities. Although rules of this type were applied to many different types of concerns, they occurred most frequently in the charters of banks, insurance companies, and local utility enterprises such as gas and water companies where it appeared desirable to keep the control of the business in local hands. According to the

[96] E.g., *N. J. Laws,* 28 sess., 2 sit. (1804), Ch. 109, p. 268; 39 sess., 2 sit. (1815, private), pp. 21, 172; 52 sess., 2 sit. (1828), pp. 107, 168, 209.

[97] Sometimes the expression "citizen of New Jersey" was employed, but for the purposes of this discussion it will be considered as synonymous with "resident of New Jersey."

[98] E.g., *N. J. Laws,* 49 sess., 1 sit. (1824), p. 74; 58 sess., 2 sit. (1834), pp. 47, 55, 150; 1862, Ch. 103, p. 209, Ch. 182, p. 319.

[99] E.g., *N. J. Laws,* 1847, pp. 36, 39; 1862, Ch. 51, p. 70, Ch. 61, p. 103.

[100] E.g., *N. J. Laws,* 63 sess., 2 sit. (1839), pp. 57, 127; 1866, Ch. 95, p. 226.

[101] E.g., *N. J. Laws,* 1861, Ch. 68, p. 148; 1870, Ch. 81, p. 230.

terms of about 30 charters, all directors were to be residents of designated sections of New Jersey.[102] Some 70 charters required only a majority to be residents of specified localities,[103] and about a dozen more required either slightly more or less than a majority.[104]

From time to time attempts were made to secure passage of a law making residence within New Jersey a universal requirement for directors of all the state's corporations.[105] At no time during the period under investigation, however, was the rule made general, but it is notable that several of the general incorporation laws required a majority of the directors to be residents of New Jersey. These were the law of 1849,[106] the banking law of 1850 as amended in 1851,[107] the general plank road and insurance laws of 1852,[108] the general law of 1854 for companies engaged in water transportation,[109] the general land company law of 1867,[110] the 1869 general law for companies cutting peat and stone,[111] and the gas company law of 1874.[112] The rule in the 1853 general law for telegraph companies was that at least one-third of the directors must reside in New Jersey.[113]

Clauses regulating the place of residence of the presidents of business corporations were embodied in many special charters. In most such cases, the rules concerning the residence of the presidents were found in combination with residence requirements for directors, but there were some instances in which the residence rules applied to the presidents alone. All the cases can be considered together here. Over one hundred charters required the presidents to reside in counties, townships, or munic-

[102] E.g., *N. J. Laws,* 50 sess., 1 sit. (1825), p. 105; 1853, Ch. 6, p. 9, Ch. 108, p. 271.

[103] E.g., *N. J. Laws,* 1847, p. 71; 1857, Ch. 59, p. 185.

[104] E.g., *N. J. Laws,* 1857, Ch. 115, p. 340; 1863, Ch. 93, p. 180.

[105] E.g., *Newark Daily Advertiser,* February 6, 1850. The newspaper reported that it had been "ascertained that the worst failures that have taken place in this state were companies managed by directors residing out of the state."

[106] *N. J. Laws,* 1849, p. 300.

[107] *N. J. Laws,* 1851, p. 292.

[108] *N. J. Laws,* 1852, Ch. 51, p. 95, Ch. 74, p. 159.

[109] *N. J. Laws,* 1854, Ch. 201, p. 470.

[110] *N. J. Laws,* 1867, Ch. 378, p. 855.

[111] *N. J. Laws,* 1869, Ch. 374, p. 1001.

[112] *N. J. Laws,* 1874, Ch. 509, p. 124.

[113] *N. J. Laws,* 1853, Ch. 122, p. 304.

ipalities that were specifically designated.[114] After the middle of the nineteenth century, the more commonly adopted rule was that the presidents merely be residents of New Jersey. More than two hundred charters contained the latter requirement.[115] The general law of 1849 also required the presidents of corporations organized under its authority to reside in New Jersey.[116]

Toward the end of the period under investigation, an increasingly smaller proportion of special charters imposed residence qualifications on corporate directors or presidents. Undoubtedly most groups seeking charters resisted any such restrictive provisions, and the increasingly interstate nature of business made it less feasible for the lawmakers to insist upon them. About twenty-five companies were granted charter amendments either repealing or relaxing the residence requirements that had been established in their original charters.[117] In no case, however, were the residence requirements of the general incorporation laws relaxed.

A few miscellaneous provisions concerning the composition of the boards of directors were found among the special charters and will be considered briefly. The first was a provision occurring in the charters of three banks incorporated between 1804 and 1807 and the first mutual insurance company incorporated in 1811 whereby rotation in office was required for a part of the board of directors.[118] In these cases, only about five-sixths of the directors were eligible each year for reëlection.[119] Rotation in office was not required in any New Jersey charter after 1811.

The ownership of property as a qualification for directors appears to have been imposed in only two New Jersey charters.

[114] E.g., *N. J. Laws,* 39 sess., 2 sit. (1815, private), pp. 21, 32; 54 sess., 2 sit. (1830), p. 59.

[115] E.g., *N. J. Laws,* 1856, Ch. 89, p. 186, Ch. 143, p. 267.

[116] *N. J. Laws,* 1849, p. 300.

[117] E.g., *N. J. Laws,* 57 sess., 2 sit. (1833), p. 106; 1853, Ch. 10, p. 20; 1869, Ch. 27, p. 32, Ch. 49, p. 78.

[118] Similar provisions were to be found in earlier bank and insurance company charters in other states. Cf. J. S. Davis, *Essays in the Earlier History of American Corporations,* II, 324–25.

[119] E.g., *N. J. Laws,* 28 sess., 2 sit. (1804), Ch. 109, p. 268; 36 sess., 1 sit. (1811, private), p. 23.

These were two bank charters of 1818 that required directors to own at least $1000 worth of real estate.[120]

The New Jersey lawmakers sometimes attempted to prohibit interlocking directorates.[121] The charter of the first mutual insurance company declared that no director might be president or a director of any other fire insurance company.[122] The act passed during the same session of the legislature creating the six so-called "state" banks did not permit directors to hold the office of president or director in any other bank.[123] Provisions of like nature were embodied in the charters of twenty-five mutual insurance companies passed between 1833 and 1872.[124] After 1860, a few insurance companies were granted amendments to their charters repealing the provisions against interlocking directorates.[125]

A number of circumstances in which directors sometimes were required to go to the stockholders for approval of their plans before they could act were pointed out in the two preceding chapters. All those instances were concerned with capital structure changes. They included such measures as issuing stock that was authorized but unissued, increasing or decreasing the authorized capital, issuing preferred stock, and mortgaging the corporate assets and issuing bonds. The final section of the present chapter deals with several other aspects of the division of rights and duties as between stockholders and directors.

Among the various provisions found in New Jersey charters regulating the relationship of stockholders and management,

[120] *N. J. Laws,* 42 sess., 2 sit. (1818, private), pp. 49, 75. A charter amendment passed the following year relieved the directors of one of the banks from the property qualification. *Ibid.,* 43 sess., 2 sit. (1819, private), p. 16.

[121] Precedents for this action can be found in other states as early as the eighteenth century. Cf. Davis, II, 325.

[122] *N. J. Laws,* 36 sess., 1 sit. (1811, private), p. 23.

[123] *N. J. Laws,* 36 sess., 2 sit. (1812, public), p. 3.

[124] E.g., *N. J. Laws,* 57 sess., 2 sit. (1833), p. 137; 1856, Ch. 53, p. 105, Ch. 85, p. 166.

[125] E.g., *N. J. Laws,* 1862, Ch. 114, p. 227.

one that occurred very frequently concerned the duty of the directors to make information about corporate financial affairs available to stockholders. Over 900 special charters contained some stipulation to assure stockholders an opportunity to inform themselves as to the financial results of the operations of their companies.

In practically every case before the eighteen twenties and in many thereafter, the stockholders' right to information was restricted to an annual review. Altogether there were about 430 such instances. In cases of this type, the annual meeting of the company was generally designated as the occasion for informing stockholders about business operations. Many early charters merely stipulated that the books containing the company's accounts and a record of the proceedings of the board of directors were to be submitted to the stockholders at the election meetings.[126] After 1820, the usual form of the requirement was that at the annual meeting the directors should submit a financial report.[127] A few bank charters required that the annual statement be available to stockholders several weeks before the election of directors.[128] In some other cases, the directors were not only to submit their annual report at the corporate meetings but were also obligated to produce the account books if the holders of a designated number of shares should so require.[129]

A form of requirement that made information continuously available to stockholders appeared in many special charters in New Jersey after 1820. In these cases, the management was directed to keep books of account in which all business transactions should be recorded and to make the books available to stockholders at all times. Nearly 340 special charters merely guaranteed stockholders access to the account books and did not require the directors to submit annual reports. Although the right of stockholders to examine the accounts was found in many different types of charters, it was expressed most fre-

[126] E.g., *N. J. Laws,* 32 sess., 1 sit. (1807), Ch. 1, p. 3, Ch. 6, p. 26.
[127] E.g., *N. J. Laws,* 49 sess., 1 sit. (1824), p. 158; 1856, Ch. 52, p. 102.
[128] E.g., *N. J. Laws,* 58 sess., 2 sit. (1834), p. 150.
[129] E.g., *N. J. Laws,* 60 sess., 2 sit. (1836), p. 265.

quently in the charters of manufacturing companies[130] and gas companies.[131]

Beginning about 1830, the legislators occasionally combined in a single charter a provision for annual reports to stockholders and a requirement that the books of account be open to stockholders. Altogether there were over 140 instances in which stockholders were afforded both sources of information. A majority of these were charters for manufacturing companies.[132] When both provisions were included in bank charters, the time during which the books were to be open to inspection by stockholders was sometimes restricted to a designated number of days prior to the election of directors.[133]

The subject of dividends was always of special concern to stockholders, and clauses regulating the authority of directors in the matter of dividend policy were found in a great many special charters in New Jersey.[134] In the dividend sections of the charters there was generally a passage indicating what was to be the test of the legality of a dividend. The wording varied widely, and at no time during the entire period under study did New Jersey lawmakers adopt standard language to describe what constituted a legal dividend. Many special charters stated that dividends were to be paid only from what was variously described as clear profits, net profits, actual profits, or income.[135] Other charters merely said that dividends must not be paid out of any part of the capital stock or, as it was sometimes expressed, that the capital must not be impaired by dividend payments.[136] Frequently both rules were included in a single charter.[137]

130 E.g., *N. J. Laws,* 49 sess., 1 sit. (1824), p. 8; 59 sess., 2 sit. (1835), pp. 44, 121.

131 E.g., *N. J. Laws,* 1849, pp. 235, 257.

132 E.g., *N. J. Laws,* 1855, Ch. 21, p. 50; 1860, Ch. 88, p. 206.

133 E.g., *N. J. Laws,* 61 sess., 2 sit. (1837), pp. 243, 413.

134 The evolution of dividend law in several other jurisdictions has been described by Donald Kehl in "The Origin and Early Development of American Dividend Law," *Harvard Law Review,* LIII (November 1939), pp. 36–67.

135 E.g., *N. J. Laws,* 17 sess., 1 sit. (1792), Ch. 406, p. 806; 21 sess., 2 sit. (1797), Ch. 627, p. 157; 1857, Ch. 6, p. 15, Ch. 141, p. 393.

136 E.g., *N. J. Laws,* 1855, Ch. 50, p. 114.

137 E.g., *N. J. Laws,* 28 sess., 2 sit. (1804), Ch. 109, p. 268; 58 sess., 2 sit. (1834), pp. 55, 73, 84.

The general regulating act of 1846 contained a clause making it illegal for the directors of any bank or manufacturing or "moneyed" corporation of New Jersey to pay dividends "except from the surplus profits arising from the business of the corporation . . ." or "to divide, withdraw, or in any way pay to the stockholders . . . any part of the capital stock . . ." [138] The general incorporation laws of 1846 and 1849 provided that the directors of a company organized by virtue of their authority were not to "declare and pay any dividend when the company is unable to pay its debts, or any dividend, the payment of which would render it so unable . . ." [139] The rule in the general insurance company law of 1852 was that no dividend could be paid by a company "when its capital stock is impaired, or when the making of such dividend would have the effect of impairing its capital stock . . ." [140] According to the 1874 general law for gas companies, the directors could not declare a dividend "when the company is insolvent, or when the payment thereof would render it insolvent . . ." [141] These examples are sufficient to illustrate the diverse ways in which the New Jersey legislators described what constituted legal and illegal dividends.[142]

While the tests of the legality of dividends were important, of even more significance to stockholders was the amount of discretion directors were allowed in the matter of paying out or retaining earnings that were legally available for dividends. The charter of the S. U. M. specified "That there shall be a yearly Dividend for the first Five Years immediately ensuing the last Day of December next, and thenceforth a half yearly Dividend, of so much of the Profits of the said Society as to the Directors thereof shall seem expedient." [143] The directors of New Jersey's first business corporation were thus afforded complete control over the disposition of corporate earnings. Five of the

[138] *N. J. Laws,* 1846, p. 16. [139] *N. J. Laws,* 1846, p. 64; 1849, p. 300.

[140] *N. J. Laws,* 1852, Ch. 74, p. 159. [141] *N. J. Laws,* 1874, Ch. 509, p. 124.

[142] A number of charters imposed severe penalties on directors who paid illegal dividends. The penalties took the form of personal liability for all or a part of the corporate debts. The penalties are discussed in detail in the following chapter. Cf. *infra,* pp. 330–331, 340, 357–358, 359–360.

[143] *N. J. Laws,* 16 sess., 1 sit. (1791), Ch. 356, p. 730.

charters passed during the ensuing decade, however, contained dividend rules that suggest an intent on the part of the lawmakers to force directors to distribute among the stockholders all earnings legally available for dividends. Typical of such provisions is one found in a 1792 charter directing that the management "shall make and declare a Dividend of the clear Profits and Income thereof (all contingent Costs and Charges being first deducted) among all the Subscribers to the said Company's Stock, and shall, on every the first Monday in January in every Year, publish the yearly Dividend to be made of the clear Profits among the Stockholders, and of the Time and Place when and where the same will be paid, and shall cause the same to be paid accordingly." [144] Despite the mandatory tone of such provisions, it is probable that directors were able to retain earnings since the exact nature and amount of the "contingent Costs and Charges" were presumably to be decided by them. A number of early bridge company charters were more specific in permitting directors considerable latitude in the matter of dividend payments. The following example of the type of provision found in many bridge company charters was taken from an act of incorporation passed in 1795. It provided that the directors "shall make and declare a dividend of the profits and income thereof among all the subscribers to the said company's stock, deducting first therefrom all contingent costs and charges, and such proportion of the said income as may be deemed necessary for a growing fund to provide against the decay, and for the rebuilding and repairing of the said bridge . . ." [145]

The New Jersey legislators very soon reverted to the use of dividend clauses similar in tone to that in the charter of the S. U. M. giving directors clearly expressed authority either to

[144] *N. J. Laws,* 17 sess., 1 sit. (1792), Ch. 406, p. 806.

[145] *N. J. Laws,* 19 sess., 2 sit. (1795), Ch. 554, p. 1067. Similar clauses were found in twenty-three later bridge company charters. Apparently the lawmakers conceived of the "growing fund" as a fund of liquid assets, for in two charters they required that the fund be loaned out with other surplus money in the treasury in such manner as seemed most in the interest of the company. *Ibid.,* 36 sess., 2 sit. (1812, private), pp. 47, 102.

pay out or retain earnings at their discretion. The change began with the charter of the Newark Banking and Insurance Company passed in 1804. This charter and some other bank charters passed during the first decade of the nineteenth century stated that the directors should make semi-annual dividends of as much of the profits as they thought "advisable." [146] The same full freedom of action was given to directors in many subsequent charters. The language employed, however, varied from charter to charter. The charters of several ferry companies authorized the retention of profits "as a contingent fund at the discretion of the said president and trustees," [147] others variously permitted directors to declare dividends of as much of the profits as they thought "proper," [148] "expedient," [149] "just and reasonable," [150] or "prudent and proper," [151] and there were cases in which still different expressions were employed.

It is not to be inferred, however, that the directors of all New Jersey's nineteenth century corporations were allowed a free hand in making decisions as to dividend policy. Clauses that might be interpreted to require distribution of the whole net income appeared in charters from time to time.[152] Also two canal company charters passed in 1820 and 1823 provided for annual distribution of all profits except such amounts as the stockholders determined to leave in the hands of the treasurer for repairs and contingent charges.[153] Three manufacturing company charters passed during the eighteen thirties forbade the directors to retain total surplus funds in excess of desig-

[146] E.g., *N. J. Laws,* 28 sess., 2 sit. (1804), Ch. 109, p. 268; 32 sess., 1 sit. (1807), Ch. 30, p. 80.

[147] E.g., *N. J. Laws,* 39 sess., 2 sit. (1815, private), p. 91.

[148] E.g., *N. J. Laws,* 49 sess., 1 sit. (1824), p. 175.

[149] E.g., *N. J. Laws,* 49 sess., 1 sit. (1824), p. 140.

[150] E.g., *N. J. Laws,* 51 sess., 1 sit. (1826), p. 81.

[151] E.g., *N. J. Laws,* 55 sess., 2 sit. (1831), p. 66.

[152] For example: "That annual dividends of the profits arising from the investment and employ of the capital stock of this company shall be made . . ." *N. J. Laws,* 50 sess., 1 sit. (1825), p. 50. "That the directors . . . shall make annual dividends of the profits of the said company among the stockholders . . ." *Ibid.,* 63 sess., 2 sit. (1839), p. 44.

[153] *N. J. Laws,* 44 sess., 2 sit. (1820, public), p. 55; 48 sess., 1 sit. (1823, private), p. 166.

nated amounts.[154] A type of clause that appeared in the charters of seven canal and six railroad companies between 1830 and 1869 should also be noted. In these cases, the directors were to pay semi-annual dividends of only as much of the profits as they deemed prudent, but if they did not pay a dividend they were required to "assign their reasons to the stockholders, in writing, for not doing so." [155] While the directors were not forced by such clauses to pay dividends, they at least had to justify their failure to divide a part of the profits. When in 1832 the state received a second block of 1000 shares of the stock of the Joint Companies, the legislators, for obvious reasons, required that the directors of the companies pay dividends equal to the whole amount of the net profit, "retaining only such surplus funds as may be deemed requisite to meet unexpected and extraordinary damages to the works respectively, which surplus fund shall in no case exceed, in the whole, the sum of one hundred thousand dollars." [156] The most striking instance of statutory interference with the freedom of directors of New Jersey corporations to regulate dividend policy, however, occurred in 1866. In that year, the 1846 general regulating act was amended to prohibit the directors of any manufacturing company from retaining a surplus of more than one-half the amount of the capital stock. Accumulated profits over that amount had to be distributed annually to all stockholders who so demanded.[157]

No general statutes were enacted in New Jersey during the period under study to regulate lease or consolidation agreements

[154] *N. J. Laws,* 59 sess., 2 sit. (1835), p. 99; 60 sess., 2 sit. (1836), p. 388; 61 sess., 2 sit. (1837), p. 484. The maximum amounts that could be retained in the form of a "surplus fund" were $10,000, $5,000, and $7,000, respectively.

[155] E.g., *N. J. Laws,* 60 sess., 2 sit. (1836), pp. 102, 284.

[156] *N. J. Laws,* 56 sess., 2 sit. (1832), p. 79.

[157] "That all manufacturing corporations within this state shall, on the first day of August in each and every year . . . after reserving over and above their capital stock paid in as a working capital for said corporation a sum to be specified by their board of directors, and not exceeding the amount of one-half of the capital stock paid or secured to be paid, declare a dividend of the whole of their accumulated profits exceeding the amount so reserved as working capital, and pass the share or dividend of each stockholder of such profits to the credit of their respective stockholders, and pay the same to such stockholders on demand." *N. J. Laws,* 1866, Ch. 442, p. 1034.

made between corporations. Laws authorizing particular railroad companies to enter lease or consolidation arrangements appeared, however, in considerable number after 1850. Between that date and 1875, twenty-six railroads were authorized by charter amendments and thirteen were allowed by the terms of their original charters to enter into some sort of lease or consolidation arrangement. A few of these were merely authorized to lease their assets to other railroad companies, a number were granted only the right to consolidate with other, and usually connecting, railroad companies, while some were authorized to take either step.

In such cases, the directors were given no final authority. The lawmakers generally required specifically that a stated proportion of the stockholders must give their consent before any agreement made by the directors to lease or consolidate the corporate assets would be effective. Usually the consent of a majority or two-thirds of the stockholders in interest was sufficient. If the directors were contemplating a lease arrangement, consent was required only of the stockholders in the company whose assets were to be leased.[158] In cases of consolidation, a certain proportion of the stockholders of each corporation generally had to approve.[159] In a few of the early authorizations, no provision was made for compensating dissenting stockholders. In the eighteen sixties and seventies, however, the equity court of New Jersey ruled that a corporation could not make a radical change in its objectives or in the nature of its business without the unanimous consent of the stockholders even though it had obtained a charter amendment from the legislature authorizing the change. The court held, nevertheless, that the legislators could justifiably eliminate dissenting stockholders by providing a means of compensating them for their shares in view of the fact that the dissenters were obstructing an action considered by the lawmakers to be in the public interest.[160] In accordance with this position, later charter amend-

[158] E.g., *N. J. Laws*, 1856, Ch. 37, p. 65; 1857, Ch. 111, p. 313.

[159] E.g., *N. J. Laws*, 1866, Ch. 10, p. 15; 1872, Ch. 450, p. 1017.

[160] E.g., *Zabriskie* v. *The Hackensack and New York Railroad Company*, 18 New Jersey Equity, 178 (1867); *Black* v. *The Delaware and Raritan Canal Company*, 24 New Jersey Equity, 455 (1873).

ments authorizing leases or consolidations usually provided rules for compensating dissenting stockholders.[161]

The stockholders of New Jersey corporations also had the final word as to whether a company should be dissolved voluntarily. The vast majority of special charters were silent on the matter of voluntary dissolution. Nearly three hundred special charters, however, specified the procedure to be followed when the question of dissolution came up.[162] In each of these cases, dissolution came up.[162] In each of these cases, dissolution was to be voted on at a general stockholders' meeting specially summoned for the purpose. The usual requirement was that some proportion such as two-thirds or three-fourths of the stockholders in interest had to be present or represented if the question was voted on.[163] In a few instances, the consent of two-thirds or three-fourths of the stockholders in interest was required before dissolution could be effected.[164] The clauses dealing with dissolution generally stated that the directors would become trustees to supervise the liquidation procedure unless the stockholders wished to appoint other persons for the purpose. The general incorporation laws of New Jersey failed to provide rules governing the dissolution of corporations organized by virtue of their authority. This shortcoming was rectified in the case of the 1849 general law by an amendment of 1870. The amendment permitted the directors, at their option, to call a special meeting of the stockholders, and if two-thirds in interest of the stockholders gave their consent in writing the corporation could be dissolved.[165]

[161] E.g., *N. J. Laws,* 1873, Ch. 23, p. 924.

[162] Such provisions were found most frequently in the charters of manufacturing, mining, and land development companies.

[163] E.g., *N. J. Laws,* 52 sess., 2 sit. (1828), p. 146; 1857, Ch. 90, p. 268.

[164] E.g., *N. J. Laws,* 1867, Ch. 11, p. 13.

[165] *N. J. Laws,* 1870, Ch. 29, p. 8.

CHAPTER XI

Liability of Stockholders and Directors

IT HAS been pointed out in Part I of the present study that persons seeking charters of incorporation regarded the privilege of limiting their liability for the business debts as one of the principal advantages of doing business under the corporate form of organization.[1] Since most eighteenth and nineteenth century charters were silent on the matter of liability, it is to be presumed that stockholders and directors in the majority of American business corporations were not liable personally for the business debts. As early as 1832, the American legal writers Joseph K. Angell and Samuel Ames were able to state:

> No rule of law we believe is better settled, than that, in general, the individual members of a private corporate body are not liable for the debts, either in their persons or in their property, beyond the amount of property which they have in the stock.[2]

At the same time, however, these writers took cognizance of the fact that there existed a tendency on the part of several of the principal incorporating jurisdictions to write a certain measure of personal liability into the charters of some of their business corporations:

> The statute books of many of the states will show that an opinion has strongly and extensively prevailed, that the common law relative to commercial corporations, is not adequate to their proper regulation and government. One of the most material alterations of the common law introduced for the better regulation of such corporations, and for the security of their creditors, is that of making each

[1] Cf. *supra*, pp. 39–41.

[2] Joseph K. Angell and Samuel Ames, *A Treatise on the Law of Private Corporations Aggregate* (1st ed., 1832), p. 349.

member personally liable in his private estate for the company debts . . .

The practice of making the members of a corporation personally liable for the debts of the company, originated in a general distrust of the community of companies incorporated for carrying on trade.[3]

Present-day students of the history of the American business corporation have also noted numerous cases in which the states during the first half of the nineteenth century departed from the common law rule on the matter of individual liability and imposed liability for corporate debts on stockholders or directors by legislative action.[4]

It is the purpose of the present chapter to examine in detail the subject of the personal liability of directors and stockholders in New Jersey business corporations before 1875. Beginning shortly after 1800, New Jersey lawmakers saw fit to include in certain charters clauses depriving either the stockholders or directors of all or a part of the immunity from personal liability for business debts that they enjoyed in the absence of express language to the contrary. The clauses imposing personal responsibility for business debts were, with slight exception, of three general types. First, those making corporate stockholders liable for an amount beyond what they invested or agreed to invest in the enterprise. In such cases liability was imposed either unconditionally or in the event of some contingency such as the failure to file certain required certificates or to pay in the agreed amount of capital before commencing business. Second, those declaring directors liable for the notes circulated by banking companies. Third, those imposing a de-

[3] *Ibid.*, pp. 357, 370. Angell and Ames expressed the opinion that the practice of establishing personal liability by definite legislative action was further proof of their contention that individual members of a corporation were not answerable for the business debts under the common law. *Ibid.*, p. 370.

[4] Cf. Shaw Livermore, "Unlimited Liability in Early American Corporations," *Journal of Political Economy*, XLIII (October 1935), pp. 674–687, and *Early American Land Companies* . . . , pp. 258–271; E. M. Dodd, Jr., "The First Half Century of Statutory Regulation of Business Corporations in Massachusetts," *Harvard Legal Essays*, pp. 89–95, and "The Evolution of Limited Liability in American Industry: Massachusetts," *Harvard Law Review*, LXI (September 1948), p. 1352; J. G. Blandi, *Maryland Business Corporations: 1783–1852*, pp. 39–55.

gree of liability on directors in the event of the declaration of illegal dividends, of exceeding a stipulated debt limit, or of failing to file certain required reports.

During the whole period under discussion here, the New Jersey legislature singled out commercial banks for special treatment in the matter of the liability of stockholders and directors. Although the precise policy varied from time to time, the charters of nearly all banking companies contained some form of liability provision affecting stockholders or directors, or both. No clear line of development can be discerned in the case of companies chartered for the purpose of carrying on ordinary business enterprises. For several decades after 1813, the stockholders and directors of numerous corporations, most notably those in the fields of manufacturing and mining, were subjected to special liability provisions. The legislators' policy in this regard, however, varied widely from charter to charter. The whole question of imposing personal liability on the directors and stockholders of ordinary business corporations became a critical issue in the decade of the eighteen forties. The determined group of Democrats who favored rather stringent liability provisions in the charters of manufacturing and mining companies was routed after 1850, and there were very few liability clauses of any kind in the special charters of ordinary business corporations enacted after that date. As concerns corporations engaged in the transportation and communication industries, only a very few were hampered by liability clauses of any type.

The ensuing discussion will treat first the liability provisions incorporated by the New Jersey legislature into the charters of commercial banking companies. Since such "monied" corporations were treated generally as forming a special class of enterprises and were subject to more strict liability provisions than other types of corporations, they can best be dealt with separately. The second half of the discussion will be concerned with the vacillating policy of the New Jersey legislature in the matter of the liability of stockholders and directors of non-banking corporations.

The year 1850 marks the dividing line between two distinct periods in the development of director and stockholder liability in New Jersey's commercial banks. During the years before 1850, special liability was imposed upon the directors of most banks, but no liability was provided for bank stockholders beyond what they invested or agreed to invest in the stock. After 1850, the stockholders as well as the directors of New Jersey banks were subject to special liability provisions.

Between 1804, the date of the charter of New Jersey's first bank, and 1850, the New Jersey legislature passed charters for forty-five companies with banking privileges and by supplementary acts awarded banking privileges to two other corporations. In every case but two, the legislators endeavored to secure a high standard of performance by bank directors by making them subject to special liability provisions.[5] In so doing, the New Jersey lawmakers were following a practice that had developed in America in the eighteenth century and that was common in the early years of the nineteenth century.[6]

All fifteen New Jersey bank charters enacted before 1822 imposed personal liability on the presidents and directors if they incurred debts in excess of an amount specified in the charters or if they declared illegal dividends.[7] Such clauses, however, invariably provided for the exoneration of directors from liability if they were absent from the meeting at which the proscribed action was taken or if they dissented and registered their dissent in the manner specified.[8]

Between 1822 and 1850, New Jersey did not follow a consistent policy with respect to the liability of bank directors. In

[5] The exceptions were The President and Directors of the New Jersey Protection and Lombard Bank, and The Morris Canal and Banking Company. *N. J. Laws,* 49 sess., 1 sit. (1824), pp. 140, 158.

[6] Cf. D. R. Dewey, *State Banking Before the Civil War,* pp. 115–117, and Blandi, pp. 47–48.

[7] E.g., *N. J. Laws,* 28 sess., 2 sit. (1804), Ch. 109, p. 268; 32 sess., 1 sit. (1807), Ch. 30, p. 80. Professor Dewey's account of early American bank charters is in error in stating that the directors of New Jersey banks were made personally liable in the event of declaring illegal dividends only in charters passed during and after 1812. Cf. Dewey, p. 117.

[8] In order to escape liability, a dissenting director was required to notify the stockholders of his action and also in most cases to serve notice on the governor or some other state official. E.g., *N. J. Laws,* 36 sess., 2 sit. (1812, public), p. 3.

eleven cases, acts conferring banking privileges followed the traditional pattern and specified liability for declaring illegal dividends and for exceeding the established debt limits.[9] Five bank charters enacted during these years made no reference to personal liability if the banks' debt limits were exceeded but did contain the usual liability clauses for declaring illegal dividends.[10] Two charters omitted reference to liability for illegal dividends but made the directors liable for debts in excess of the legal maxima.[11] Fourteen of the acts conferring banking privileges passed between 1824 and 1838 made no provision for director liability either for declaring dividends that impaired the capital stock or for exceeding the legal debt limit.[12]

The New Jersey legislators also subjected the directors of many banks to a liability provision much more stringent than those discussed above. This was one making bank directors personally liable for the notes and bills issued and circulated. Since bank notes formed the principal part of the circulating medium of the society and in the ordinary process of exchange came into the possession of persons who thereby became creditors of the issuing banks, the notes were considered to be a type of liability that demanded special safeguards. Two bank charters enacted in 1818, significantly a year of postwar depression, were the first to contain special provisions for securing the circulating notes. In case the companies acted in any respect contrary to their charters, the presidents and directors were to be liable in their private estates, if the corporate property was insufficient, for the payment of the circulating notes they issued.[13] In 1828, a more stringent liability clause appeared in the charters of two banks. The presidents and directors of the banking companies were made personally liable, jointly and severally, for the circulating notes they issued if payment was refused when demanded at the banking houses

[9] E.g., *N. J. Laws,* 54 sess., 2 sit. (1830), pp. 42, 59.
[10] E.g., *N. J. Laws,* 47 sess., 1 sit. (1822, private), p. 48.
[11] *N. J. Laws,* 48 sess., 1 sit. (1823, private), p. 157; 49 sess., 1 sit. (1824), p. 99.
[12] E.g., *N. J. Laws,* 56 sess., 2 sit. (1832), pp. 59, 65.
[13] *N. J. Laws,* 42 sess., 2 sit. (1818, private), pp. 49, 75.

during the usual business hours.[14] This harsh liability provision was repeated in the charters of all twenty companies that were granted banking privileges between 1830 and 1850.[15] Thus during the years when New Jersey lawmakers were relaxing the general provisions concerning the liability of bank directors when illegal dividends were declared and when legal debt limits were exceeded, they were imposing in new bank charters full personal liability on directors for the bank notes issued by their institutions.[16] Clearly the legislators had come to consider note holders to be a class of bank creditors deserving special security.

An important fact emerges from the investigation of the special liability provisions in pre-1850 New Jersey bank charters. While the legislators hoped to control banking practices by subjecting bank directors to some measure of personal liability, in not a single case were bank stockholders subjected to any form of extended liability. In not imposing additional liability on bank stockholders during this period, the New Jersey legislature was again acting in accord with the legislatures of many other states.[17] It has been suggested that extended stock-

[14] *N. J. Laws,* 52 sess., 2 sit. (1828), pp. 54, 128. The liability clause read as follows: ". . . the president and directors of said corporation shall individually, and jointly, and severally, be, and continue liable to every creditor for the payment of any bills obligatory or of credit, note or notes, that they or any of them may issue and circulate, and upon demand of payment being made at the bank during the usual hours of business, and refusal thereof, an action may be brought against the said persons then acting as president and directors of the said company, jointly or severally, and it shall be lawful for the plaintiff or plaintiffs to declare therein generally for money had and received, with a specification of the dates, sums, payees, and numbers of the said bills or notes so demanded, and payment whereof hath been neglected or refused, and, upon judgment being rendered, execution shall issue thereon."

[15] E.g., *N. J. Laws,* 61 sess., 2 sit. (1837), pp. 203, 215, 254, 413. It would appear from the account in Dewey, pp. 115–117, that this was an unusually stringent provision. Professor Dewey's account of directors' liability for the notes of New Jersey banks, however, is itself incomplete and in error.

[16] The legislators were not prepared, however, to subject directors to unlimited liability for bank notes at the time of renewing the charters of existing banks. Of twenty-three bank charter extensions granted between 1828 and 1850, only two imposed personal liability for notes on directors. On some occasions opposition was expressed in the legislature to giving consideration to petitioners who sought charter extensions but who would not submit to making the directors personally liable for the bank notes. E.g., *Emporium and True American,* January 29, 1841.

[17] Cf. Dewey, pp. 117–120; Blandi, pp. 42–43.

holder liability in banking companies developed late in most incorporating jurisdictions for two principal reasons. In the first place, many early bank charters reserved to the states the right to subscribe to a part of the stock and hence the state governments would not wish to be subject to any liability as stockholders. Secondly, there was a fear that people would not invest in banks in which they would be subject to personal liability and that economic development would thus be discouraged.[18]

There is evidence, however, that during the eighteen twenties some Jerseymen were of the opinion that bank stockholders should be personally liable at least for the payment of circulating bank notes. In 1825, for example, a number of residents of the agricultural county of Hunterdon sent a petition to the assembly "praying that in all banks, hereafter to be chartered, the stockholders of such banks may be made responsible in their individual capacities, for the payment of their notes put in circulation." [19] The Democratic *True American* reported in 1826 that the petitioners for a charter for a bank at Rahway had offered if necessary "to be responsible in their individual capacities to twice the amount of their stock." [20]

The question of extended liability for bank stockholders arose again in the late eighteen thirties and in the eighteen forties at the same time that the Democrats were declaring themselves in favor of subjecting all corporation stockholders to additional liability. A Democratic newspaper stated in 1841 that when the matter of liability for bank stockholders arose in the legislature all the Democrats were in favor of imposing liability but nearly all the "Federalists" were against it.[21] It will be recalled that heated debate on the question of bank stockholder liability occurred during New Jersey's 1844 constitutional con-

[18] Blandi, pp. 44–47.

[19] *Votes and Proceedings of the General Assembly,* 50 sess., 1 sit. (1825), pp. 13–14, 89. The *True American* stated on November 5, 1825: "The proposition for making the Stockholders of banks hereafter to be chartered, responsible individually for the payment of the notes they issue, lies inactive on the table, and is a very insufficient check upon the ardor of the new petitioners."

[20] *True American,* December 2, 1826.

[21] *Emporium and True American,* February 5, 1841. The editor was convinced that the "Federalists" were not willing to protect the people from worthless bank paper.

vention. All the proposals made for constitutional provisions requiring unlimited or double liability for bank stockholders were, however, ultimately rejected by the convention.[22]

Influenced by a group of articulate Democrats who favored imposing liability on bank stockholders and perhaps by the example of other states that were adopting constitutional provisions requiring some liability for the holders of bank stock, the New Jersey legislators made stockholders in banks chartered from 1850 on subject to some degree of personal liability. The first stockholder liability provision to be enacted into law was that written into the general incorporation law for banks passed in 1850 under the sponsorship of the Democrats. The law provided

> That whenever default shall be made in the payment of any debt or liability of any association under this act, the stockholders of such association shall be individually responsible, equally and ratably; such responsibility to be enforced as herein after provided for the amount of such debt or liability, with interest, to the extent of the amount of their respective shares of stock in any such association.[23]

Provision was made for any stockholder who was forced because of this double liability provision to pay debts of a bank to file a claim against the property of the corporation and also to file a bill for contribution against the other stockholders.

Beginning in 1850, the Democrats began their campaign, discussed in a previous chapter, to force all new banks and banks seeking recharter to organize under the general act.[24] Applicants for bank charters voiced so many objections to the provisions of the general law that in 1851 certain modifications were made, the most significant being the repeal of the stockholder liability section.[25] There was apparently little effective opposition in the legislature to making this change in the gen-

[22] Cf. *supra*, pp. 102–104. Although only two states had adopted constitutional provisions requiring extended liability for bank stockholders before 1844, many states were soon to take such a step. Cf. *supra*, pp. 190–191.

[23] *N. J. Laws*, 1850, p. 140.

[24] Cf. *supra*, pp. 127–142.

[25] *N. J. Laws*, 1851, p. 292.

eral law.[26] Most Democrats were willing to make certain alterations in the law in order to meet some of the objections raised against it by persons who continued to put pressure on the legislature to pass special bank charters, and the stockholder liability clause may not have seemed especially necessary since the circulating notes of general-law banks were safeguarded by 100 per cent deposits of securities with the state treasurer.[27] During debate on the question of repealing the liability sections, several positive arguments were presented in favor of repeal. They were that personal liability of stockholders was a "humbug" in that nothing was ever collected from stockholders anyway, that it held out "illusory prospects of security to the people," and that irresponsible men were never deterred by a liability provision.[28]

Because of the obvious advantage to a bank of having a special charter of the traditional type as compared with organizing under the general banking law with its requirement of full security deposits for the circulating notes, the friends of the general act found it difficult and ultimately impossible to resist the pressure for special charters. While no new special charters for banks were enacted from the year of the passage of the general banking law until 1855, the legislature extended the charters of three old banks.[29] In none of these cases was any provision made for stockholder liability, although an attempt was made in the legislature to make the stockholders of one of the banks subject to double liability for all the debts.[30] George F. Fort, a Democratic governor and staunch advocate of requiring all banks to come eventually under the general law, recommended in his messages in 1851, 1852, and 1853 the immediate passage of a law making the stockholders of existing specially chartered

[26] *Newark Daily Advertiser,* March 5, 12, 13, 1851.

[27] Cf. *ibid.,* January 25, 1851.

[28] *Ibid.,* March 12, 1851. The editor of this Whig paper, in a leading editorial in opposition to the general law, had declared: "The personal liability of the stockholders of a General Banking company will probably not be found upon experiment to be of any considerable importance." *Ibid.,* January 24, 1851.

[29] *N. J. Laws,* 1850, p. 291; 1851, pp. 275, 281.

[30] *Votes and Proceedings of the General Assembly,* 1850, p. 438. The proposal was narrowly defeated.

banks liable for the banks' debts at least to the extent of their respective stockholdings.[31] Two bills designed to make the stockholders and directors of existing banks responsible for the payment of bank notes were defeated in the legislature in 1854.[32]

Petitioners for new special bank charters and renewals of existing charters put increased pressure on the legislature during the sessions of 1853 and 1854. When several bills for the renewal of existing charters were being entertained by the legislators in 1853, the more moderate Democrats were willing to support the measures if the stockholders were made liable up to the amount of their stock for all claims on the banks. Apparently they would have preferred unlimited liability for bank stockholders but were willing to accept double liability as a

[31] "When a member of the convention which framed the constitution of this state, I had the honor of voting in a minority upon a proposition asserting the principle of personal liability of stockholders in banks and other chartered companies . . . The application of this rule seems to be especially required in regard to banking institutions." *Ibid.*, 1851, pp. 127, 128.

In referring to the liability of directors for the notes of many banks, Fort declared: "That this provision for public security can, and will be often evaded, is very obvious. Besides it puts the bank creditor to the trouble and hazard of a suit at law, and will generally prove inoperative from the inability and unwillingness of those who usually suffer most from bank failures to seek redress. Though not a thorough preventive of the evils of vicious banking, it operates as a check, and should be made more effectual by extending that liability to the stockholders to an amount, at least equal to the stock held by them, respectively." *Appendix to the House Journal*, 1852, p. 12.

"Heretofore, in my official communications to the legislature, I have recommended that the *stockholders*, as well as the officers of banks, should be held responsible for the liabilities of these corporations. I can see no propriety in making a distinction in favor of the business of banking, by granting it exemptions which have no application and cannot be adduced in regard to the indebtedness of ordinary partnerships or associations engaged in other pursuits. The greater the privilege the more danger results from its abuse . . . Each stockholder should therefore be held responsible for the whole amount of debts due by the company." *Ibid.*, 1853, p. 9.

[32] Cf. *supra*, p. 135. The committee that reported one of these bills to the assembly was of the opinion that to enact it into law would be a breach of faith on the part of the state, but at the same time the committee emphasized the fact that the legislature "is inflexibly determined to maintain the system of security banking by forcing all of the old banks, at the expiration of their charters to re-organize under the free banking law, or close their business." *Votes and Proceedings of the General Assembly*, 1854, pp. 1039–40.

compromise.[33] No special bank bills were actually passed, however, during the session.

In 1854, the Democratic-controlled corporation committee of the assembly added provisions imposing unlimited liability on stockholders to all bills for new bank charters and for the renewal of old charters. On at least one occasion, the assembly recommitted a bill with the recommendation that the stockholders be made subject only to double liability, but the committee did not change it.[34] The Whig press decried the attitude of the Democrats by declaring that not only would the resulting bills be unacceptable to the applicants but that bank shares would become worthless if bill holders could sue any stockholder for all his property, leaving him as his only redress a suit against the other stockholders for contribution. Another favorite Whig argument was that banking capital would be driven out of New Jersey if bank stockholders were treated so harshly.[35] By the time the session of 1854 had come to an end, the legislators had not taken favorable action on any special bank bills.

A new legislative policy on the matter of banking corporations was established in 1855. Many new bank charters were being sought in that year, a number of specially chartered banks were about to expire, and some banks that had come to the end of their charters and had organized under the general law were anxious to return to their former status. In spite of the fact that the Democratic governor, Rodman M. Price, strongly recommended that no special bank bills be passed[36] and although taking favorable action on special bank charters was contrary to the expressed opinion of many Democrats,[37] the

[33] *Newark Daily Advertiser*, February 4, 1853. The newspaper thought their idea was to extend the banks for the present with the hope of making them come under the general law at a later date.

[34] *Ibid.*, January 25, 1854. In reporting the special bank bills, the committee expressed a conviction that even with stringent liability clauses the bills should not be favorably considered. Their report declared that no special bank bill should pass so long as the general banking law was still on the statute books. *Votes and Proceedings of the General Assembly*, 1854, pp. 75–79.

[35] *Newark Daily Advertiser*, January 25 and February 1, 1854.

[36] *Appendix to the House Journal*, 1855, pp. 9, 12.

[37] Cf. *supra*, pp. 136–137.

pressure for bank acts was too strong for the legislators to resist. During the session, discussions about banking policy revolved around the question of finding some suitable formula for imposing liability on directors and stockholders in specially chartered banks. Although many Democrats favored unlimited liability of stockholders as well as of directors for payment of the circulating notes and the Whigs were generally against imposing any extended liability on stockholders, a compromise was finally reached.[38] It was agreed that in new bank charters and in laws extending existing charters the holders of circulating notes and bills would be given a preference over all other creditors in the distribution of the corporate assets. Bank directors were to be unlimitedly liable, jointly and severally, for the circulating bills and notes of their institutions. If the corporate assets and the property of the directors were insufficient to pay the note holders in full, then stockholders were to be liable up to the par value of the shares held by them at the time the corporation became insolvent.[39] Once the legislators

[38] *Votes and Proceedings of the General Assembly*, 1855, pp. 365, 370ff; *Newark Daily Advertiser*, March 15, 1855.

[39] This formula was first applied in the act extending the charter of the Farmers Bank of New Jersey. Since the liability provisions became the model followed in subsequent bank charters, it is desirable to quote from them at some length:

"That if the said corporation shall at any time hereafter become insolvent, the whole assets of the said corporation, at the time of its becoming insolvent, shall be first liable for its bills or notes then in circulation, and shall be first applied to the payment thereof; and in case of a distribution of the assets of said corporation among the creditors thereof, under the order or decree of the court of chancery or other court, the holders of such bills or notes shall be equal in priority, and shall have a preference over all the other creditors . . .

"That all the directors of said corporation . . . shall be jointly and severally liable for the payment of all the bills or notes of said corporation which may be in circulation at the time of its becoming insolvent, and may be jointly or severally prosecuted, at law or in equity, by any receiver or receivers that shall or may be appointed, for the payment of any such bills or notes, as if the same were their joint and several bills or notes executed by them in their individual capacity; and it shall not be lawful for any director of said corporation to resign his office to avoid such liability; and if any director shall so attempt to resign his office, he shall be and continue liable the same as if no such resignation had been attempted; and such liability of directors shall continue after they cease to be directors, either by resignation or otherwise, if the said corporation was insolvent when they ceased to be directors; and it shall not be lawful for any director to assign or transfer his stock or other property to avoid such liability; and in case of the payment of any such bills or notes by any of said directors,

had agreed upon a compromise in the matter of director and stockholder liability for bank notes, they proceeded to extend the special charters of eight banks and enacted twelve new special bank charters.[40] The new formula for director and stockholder liability was applied in each instance. Governor Price objected strenuously to this reversion to the practice of enacting special banking legislation. He vetoed five of the bank bills, but his vetoes were overridden in every case.[41]

The new prescription for director and stockholder liability, since it represented a compromise, did not completely satisfy either of the parties to the dispute. The more radical Democrats favored a policy either of refusing absolutely to charter or recharter any banks by special act or of passing special bank acts only if stockholders were subjected to unlimited liability.[42] The Whigs, on the other hand, raised objections to imposing even double liability on bank stockholders. They argued that banks were necessary to the economic development of the state and that investment in them would be hampered if stockholders were liable in their personal estates. They maintained that it was bad policy to make stockholders liable for losses since much bank stock was held by "women and orphans," and they

---

the other directors who may be liable shall account in the same way as other joint debtors are accountable to each other . . .

"That if the assets of said corporation and the property of said directors shall prove insufficient to redeem the whole of the said bills and notes, then the amount that shall or may be realized from said assets and property shall be distributed ratably among the holders of the said bills and notes . . .

"That the stockholders of said corporation at the time of its becoming insolvent, other than said directors, shall be jointly and severally liable to any receiver or receivers that shall or may be appointed as aforesaid to an amount sufficient to redeem the said bills and notes, after the assets of said corporation and the property of said directors shall have been distributed as aforesaid; *provided,* that no stockholder, other than said directors, shall be made liable to an amount exceeding the par value of the stock held by him at the time said corporation becomes insolvent; and if that amount shall not be required for the full redemption of said bills and notes, then the said stockholders shall be liable in the ratio of the said stock so held by them . . ." *N. J. Laws,* 1855, Ch. 163, p. 483.

40 Several of the new charters were for banks that had been organized under the general banking act of 1850.

41 Cf. *supra,* pp. 137–138.

42 E.g., *Newark Daily Advertiser,* March 15 and 22, 1855.

held it to be preferable that "the Directors who have the control of the Bank should bear the full responsibility." [43]

Nevertheless, as a New Jersey newspaper reported, the "policy of the State in relation to banking is determined." [44] The general banking law became virtually a forgotten issue. The liability provisions that were formulated in 1855 were inserted in all bank charters passed after 1855 and before 1875.[45] Also when bank charters were extended by the legislature, the identical liability provisions were made an integral part of the renewed charters.[46] Occasionally the old controversy flared up in the legislature in the years following 1855. In 1864, for example, the banking committee of the assembly reported a bill extending the existence of a bank. The committee had made the stockholders unlimitedly liable for all debts of the bank, and all the time-worn arguments were revived on both sides of the question. When the bill to extend the charter was finally passed, however, it contained the liability clauses that had been adopted in 1855.[47]

A word remains to be said in regard to the liability of bank directors for declaring illegal dividends and for exceeding specified debt limits. It will be recalled that most bank charters of the period before 1850 had contained some such provisions. As concerns liability for illegal dividends, the directors of all banks chartered after 1846 were liable personally, jointly and severally, for any amount paid out or returned to the stockholders that did not come from "the surplus profits arising from the business . . ." This liability was not written into each individual charter but was expressed in the general regulating act of 1846.[48] Bank charters enacted after 1850 did not contain debt

[43] E.g., *ibid.*, February 15 and March 20, 1855. [44] *Ibid.*, March 30, 1855.

[45] E.g., *N. J. Laws*, 1860, Ch. 246, p. 632, Ch. 247, p. 640; 1871, Ch. 124, p. 549.

[46] E.g., *N. J. Laws*, 1859, Ch. 45, p. 83; 1864, Ch. 65, p. 110. The legislature, in 1857, also voted to add the new liability provisions to the charter of a bank that was seeking merely the authority to increase its capital stock. *Votes and Proceedings of the General Assembly*, 1857, pp. 417–420; *N. J. Laws*, 1857, Ch. 86, p. 259.

[47] *Newark Daily Advertiser*, February 4, 10, 11, and 24, 1864; *N. J. Laws*, 1864, Ch. 78, p. 129.

[48] *N. J. Laws*, 1846, p. 16. The usual provision by which absent or dissenting directors could avoid liability was included here.

limitations of the old type wherein directors had been held liable when debts beyond a specified amount were incurred. The charters did, however, limit the size of the note issue of the banks, and they generally made bank presidents and cashiers who knowingly issued notes in excess of the allowed amount guilty of a misdemeanor punishable by imprisonment for a term of one to five years.[49]

When the liability provisions of New Jersey's non-banking corporations are examined, the interesting fact is disclosed that the earliest form of liability clause employed in such charters was one appearing frequently after 1813 subjecting stockholders to extended liability for the corporate debts. Since additional stockholder liability was not imposed in New Jersey bank charters until the middle of the nineteenth century, the liability provisions of banking and certain non-banking corporations thus stand in clear contrast.

The first New Jersey charter to impose upon stockholders personal liability in addition to the amount they had invested or agreed to invest in the stock was one passed in 1813 for a textile concern at Paterson.[50] The charter expressly declared that in the event of the dissolution of the corporation the stockholders were responsible in their individual and private capacities for all the debts then owing "to the extent of their respective shares, and no further, on any suit or action to be brought or prosecuted after such dissolution of the said corporation . . ." The language employed in this section is ambiguous. Considered by itself, it might be interpreted to have been included in the charter as an assurance that the stockholders would not be held responsible for business debts beyond their obligation to pay the full par value of the shares to which they subscribed, in other words to be certain they would enjoy what is commonly called limited liability. On the other hand, it might be interpreted to have imposed double liability on the stockholders of the corporation, that is to have made them personally liable

[49] E.g., *N. J. Laws,* 1859, Ch. 13, p. 23; 1870, Ch. 132, p. 347.

[50] The Beaver Woollen Factory at Paterson. *N. J. Laws,* 37 sess., 2 sit, (1813, private), p. 109.

beyond their obligation to make full payment for their shares to a further amount equal to the par value of the stock they held. When the clause is considered in its proper historical setting, there remains little doubt that the New Jersey lawmakers intended to impose double liability on the stockholders of this corporation.

In the first place, seventy-seven business corporations of various types had been created by New Jersey legislatures before this particular charter was granted, and in no case had it been considered necessary to insert definite language in a charter in order to guarantee the stockholders limited liability. This was true even in cases when the charters had been sought for the express purpose of limiting the liability of owners.[51] Stockholders in these corporations must have been assumed to have had no liability beyond what they had agreed to invest in the stock. Nor is it likely that the clause was inserted merely to make sure that the stockholders had an obligation to pay the full par value of their shares. This obligation would have been desired in the case of any type of corporation, yet the clause in question, or a closely similar counterpart, was used subsequently only in the charters of manufacturing or mining companies. This fact would indicate that the legislators intended to subject the stockholders of corporations engaged in these particular fields of activity to a greater measure of personal responsibility than that imposed on the stockholders in other types of corporations. Manufacturing establishments and mining enterprises had traditionally been financed by individual proprietors or partners, and corporations operating in the manufacturing or mining industries came into direct competition with firms whose owners were personally liable for the business debts. The same thing was not true in other fields of endeavor in which corporations were engaged, for example in the construction of local utilities or of transportation facilities, where the large amount of capital required made the corporate form of organization an indispensable engine of finance.

A consideration of the policy of other states during this period affords further substantiation for the belief that the New Jersey legislators intended the clause in question to subject

[51] Cf. *supra*, p. 39.

stockholders to double liability. It has been mentioned in the opening paragraphs of the present chapter that there was a movement in America during the first decades of the nineteenth century to deprive the stockholders in certain corporations of full limited liability. Stockholders in manufacturing corporations were treated most harshly in this respect. It seems most likely that in 1813 the New Jersey lawmakers were participating in the general movement to impose some measure of personal responsibility on stockholders in manufacturing corporations. More specifically, it should be pointed out that the general incorporation law for manufacturing companies enacted by New York in 1811 had contained a closely similar liability clause.[52] While the same ambiguity of language created a difference of opinion in New York as to what the legislature had intended, the courts of that state ultimately held that stockholders in corporations organized under the act were subject to double liability.[53] The terms of the New York act were known to the New Jersey lawmakers as early as 1812, for in that year a general incorporation law with an identical title was introduced at Trenton.[54] It should also be noted that the 1813 charter for the textile concern at Paterson was the first manufacturing company charter to be passed in New Jersey after the date when New York had adopted its general incorporation law. It thus appears logical to assume that when the New Jersey lawmakers wrote into that charter a liability clause similar to the one contained in the 1811 act of New York, they were intending to follow the example of their neighbor and impose a measure of personal liability on the stockholders in manufacturing corporations. Double liability represented a compromise between those persons who might

[52] ". . . for all debts which shall be due and owing by the company at the time of its dissolution, the persons then composing such company shall be individually responsible to the extent of their respective shares of stock in the said company and no further . . ." *N. Y. Laws,* 34 sess. (1811), Ch. 67, p. 111.

[53] The question of the liability of stockholders under the 1811 corporation law of New York has been fully explored by S. E. Howard in "Stockholders' Liability under the New York Act of March 22, 1811," *Journal of Political Economy,* XLVI (August 1938), pp. 499–514. Some students of the history of business corporations have assumed without investigation that the 1811 law afforded full limited liability to the stockholders of corporations organized under its authority. Cf. *ibid.,* p. 500n.

[54] Cf. *supra,* p. 19.

wish to make the stockholders in manufacturing corporations subject to full partnership liability, a policy that had been followed, for example, in Massachusetts after 1809, and those who did not wish to subject stockholders in manufacturing corporations to any form of extended liability.

The policy of making stockholders in manufacturing corporations subject to double liability must have seemed a wise one to New Jersey legislators, for each of the twelve manufacturing company charters enacted during the subsequent ten-year period contained a liability clause similar to the one inserted in the 1813 charter.[55] In most of these later cases the personal liability of stockholders was increased beyond "the extent of their respective shares" to a further amount equal to "the dividends and profits they may receive thereon . . ." [56] A similar liability clause was also inserted in the charter of a steamboat company granted in 1815.[57] When the New Jersey legislators enacted the 1816 general incorporation act for certain types of manufacturing concerns, they included in it the double liability clause found in the New York act of 1811 which served as their model. They altered the clause slightly, however, by adding a further liability equal to "the dividend and profits" the stockholders might have received on their stock, just as had been done in several special charters for manufacturing concerns.[58]

[55] E.g., *N. J. Laws,* 38 sess., 2 sit. (1814, private), pp. 148, 240; 48 sess., 1 sit. (1823, private), p. 124.

[56] Although the wording varied slightly from charter to charter, the following is a typical example: ". . . for all debts which, in case of the dissolution of the said company, shall then be due and owing by said company, the stockholders for the time being, shall be responsible in their individual capacity, to the extent of their respective shares, and the dividends and profits they may receive thereon, together with all the corporate stock of the said corporation, of whatever nature or kind the same may be, and no further, on any suit or action to be brought, or prosecuted, after such dissolution of the said corporation . . ." *N. J. Laws,* 40 sess., 2 sit. (1816, private), p. 158.

[57] *N. J. Laws,* 39 sess., 2 sit. (1815, private), p. 99.

[58] ". . . for all debts which shall be due and owing by the company at the time of its dissolution; the persons then composing such company, shall be individually responsible to the extent of their respective shares of stock in the said company, *and of the dividend and profits they may have received thereon,* and no further . . ." *N. J. Laws,* 40 sess., 2 sit. (1816, public), p. 17. The italics have been supplied by the author to indicate words that were not in the 1811 New York act.

Beginning in 1824, the New Jersey lawmakers wavered in their determination to make stockholders in all manufacturing corporations subject to double liability. Although thirty-two manufacturing company charters were granted between 1824 and 1834, inclusive, the double liability clause was written into only six.[59] Stockholders in corporations engaged in mining were more frequently subjected to extended liability during these years. Seven of the thirteen mining corporations created between 1824 and 1834 had charters with provisions for double liability.[60] Another mining company charter passed in 1834 made stockholders unlimitedly liable for the corporate debts,[61] but this provision was removed by a supplementary act the following year.[62] In one of the two charters for fishing companies enacted during this period, the legislators also went all the way in the direction of depriving the stockholders of limited liability and made them "jointly and severally liable in their individual capacities for any and all debts which may be due and owing by said company" at the time of dissolution or if the charter was surrendered.[63]

The period from approximately 1834 to about 1850 was

[59] *N. J. Laws,* 49 sess., 1 sit. (1824), p. 8; 50 sess., 1 sit. (1825), p. 58; 52 sess., 2 sit. (1828), pp. 103, 123, 149; 53 sess., 2 sit. (1829), p. 54. No mention was made in any of these cases of liability for dividends and profits received.

[60] E.g., *N. J. Laws,* 50 sess., 1 sit. (1825), p. 83; 52 sess., 2 sit. (1828), pp. 166, 188. The double liability clauses in some mining company charters were much more explicit as to the intention of the legislature than those in the charters of manufacturing companies. For example: "That for all debts due and owing by the said company, the persons composing the company at the time of contracting such debt shall be individually responsible, to an amount over and above their respective shares in the stock of said company equal to the amount of said shares; but nothing herein contained shall be so construed as to exempt the said company, or any estate, real or personal, which they may hold in their corporate capacity from liability for such debts." *Ibid.,* 52 sess., 2 sit. (1828), p. 93.

[61] *N. J. Laws,* 58 sess., 2 sit. (1834), p. 44.

[62] *N. J. Laws,* 59 sess., 2 sit. (1835), p. 130.

[63] *N. J. Laws,* 51 sess., 1 sit. (1826), p. 75. This was the first instance in which the stockholders in any New Jersey corporation were made unlimitedly liable for the company debts. The case was unusual, however, in that each of the twenty-four incorporators held a lease on two acres of state oyster lands and they wished incorporation in order that the entire plot of forty-eight acres might be leased to them as a company. The charter was undoubtedly sought, as stated in the preamble, merely "for the more easy management of their business."

marked by considerable agitation to impose a large measure of personal liability on stockholders in business corporations. The movement originated among the members of the radical wing of the Democratic party, and a determined group of these men carried on their crusade for about fifteen years. The original aim of the Democrats appears to have been to make the stockholders of corporations unlimitedly liable for the business debts. In 1834, during legislative debate on a bill to charter a manufacturing corporation, an amendment was offered making the stockholders "individually responsible for all debts which might at any time be due, and owing by the company." [64] Unlimited liability for corporate stockholders was also advocated occasionally in the Democratic press, as, for example, in 1836 when the *Emporium and True American* recommended that in all future charters stockholders be made fully liable for the business debts.[65] In spite of their expressed sentiments on the matter of liability, the Democrats could point to little in the way of solid accomplishment during the latter part of the eighteen thirties. One mining company charter of 1837 subjected stockholders to double liability.[66] In the same year, another mining company charter and a manufacturing company charter held stockholders liable to repay any part of the corporate capital that might have been distributed to them if the remaining property of the corporations proved insufficient to pay the corporate debts.[67]

The number of business corporation charters sought in New Jersey dropped sharply for several years following the panic of 1837, and for a time little was heard from the proponents of extended liability for corporate stockholders. When the full effects of the business depression had been felt, however, there was a revival of interest in measures to protect corporate credi-

[64] *Votes and Proceedings of the General Assembly,* 58 sess., 2 sit. (1834), p. 505. A substitute amendment providing double liability was offered as a compromise, but it was not accepted and consideration of the bill was postponed until the next session. *Loc. cit.* When the bill was finally passed, no extended liability at all was imposed on stockholders. *N. J. Laws,* 59 sess., 2 sit. (1835), p. 111.

[65] *Emporium and True American,* December 24, 1836.

[66] *N. J. Laws,* 61 sess., 2 sit. (1837), p. 157.

[67] *N. J. Laws,* 61 sess., 2 sit. (1837), pp. 76, 147.

tors from losses in the future. Shortly after 1840, the radical Democrats took up the cudgels once again and fought for their cause with intensified vigor during the ensuing decade. The issue came to the forefront of legislative and public attention early in 1842 when the legislators were considering three bills for the incorporation of manufacturing companies. A Democratic newspaper declared that the question of the responsibility of these companies for their debts was a matter of great importance to the public:

> There can be no question — certainly not at this late day, with the volumes of experience before us, and with the explosions of broken down and rotten institutions still sounding in our ears — of the importance of imposing certain restrictions, in order to protect the people from the frauds and villainies of incorporated companies . . . The amount which the mechanics, laborers and merchants have lost by the failures of large incorporated companies, must be immense . . . Should an incorporation [*sic*], simply because it is an incorporation, have the privilege to contract debts, squander their capital, and leave the community to suffer, while, individually, the persons interested are in affluence? Should they have privileges which are denied to individuals? [68]

When one of the bills came up for discussion in the assembly, a member moved to add certain clauses making any stockholder liable in his personal estate for the business debts if creditors having executions or judgments against the company were unable to collect from the company.[69] This proposal was defeated by a vote of thirty to twelve.[70] The same legislator immediately proposed another clause declaring stockholders jointly and severally liable for all the business debts until the whole amount of the capital stock authorized by the charter was actually paid in and a sworn statement to that effect filed in the office of the county clerk.[71] This more moderate proposal was

[68] *Emporium and True American*, February 11, 1842.

[69] *Votes and Proceedings of the General Assembly*, 66 sess., 2 sit. (1842), pp. 374–75. Stockholders who paid the corporate debts either voluntarily or under compulsion could enforce a claim against the other stockholders to contribute in proportion to their stockholdings and could also make a claim against the corporate property.

[70] *Ibid.*, pp. 375–76. [71] *Ibid.*, p. 376.

also rejected, the vote on the proposition being twenty-eight to sixteen.[72] A similar test case was made of another of the bills in the legislative council, and amendments identical with those suggested in the assembly were voted down.[73] Another move was made later on when the third bill was under consideration in the legislative council to require the capital stock to be "paid *bona-fide,* and not in notes or obligations" before the company could go into operation, and also to make the stockholders jointly and severally liable for all debts if any part of the capital was withdrawn before all liabilities were paid. These proposals were also turned down.[74] Some suggestions for making stockholders liable in certain circumstances in order to protect creditors were adopted, and in their final form two of the manufacturing company charters contained a variety of liability provisions. Both declared the stockholders liable for all the business debts if any dividend was declared that made the company insolvent, if any part of the capital was refunded before all the liabilities were discharged, if debts were contracted in excess of the paid-in capital, or if required annual statements of the capital paid in and of the existing debts were not published.[75] The third manufacturing company charter contained no provision for stockholder liability.[76]

During the legislative session of 1843–44, the Democrats were again active in their efforts to impose safeguards designed to make certain that the capital of business corporations was actually paid in, that the capital was not dissipated through refunds or dividends, that the established debt limits were not exceeded, and that public statements of the paid-in capital and of the existing debts were made annually. To secure the enforcement of such regulations, the Democrats continued to advocate stockholder liability as the penalty for their violation. Jonathan Pickel, Hunterdon County Democrat and proponent of general incorporation laws and of stringent forms of stockholder liability, was a prime mover in the effort during this session. The

[72] *Ibid.,* p. 377.

[73] *Journal of the Legislature Council,* 66 sess., 2 sit. (1842), pp. 157–159.

[74] *Ibid.,* p. 308.

[75] *N. J. Laws,* 66 sess., 2 sit. (1842), pp. 100, 150.

[76] *Ibid.,* p. 105.

Democratic campaign had some tangible results as three charters enacted during the session testify. These charters, two for manufacturing companies and one for a steamboat company, made stockholders, along with the presidents and directors, liable for all the business debts if the debts exceeded the paid-in capital, if any dividend that was declared made the company insolvent, if any capital was refunded when debts were outstanding, or if the directors did not submit to the stockholders an annual statement of the amount of capital paid in and of debts owing.[77] In addition, a supplementary act to increase the capital of an existing manufacturing corporation imposed personal liability on the president, directors, and stockholders for the same offenses.[78]

Although Jonathan Pickel and other radical Democrats were unsuccessful in their efforts during the 1844 constitutional convention to secure the adoption of constitutional clauses imposing some measure of liability on stockholders in New Jersey corporations,[79] they did not abandon their campaign in the legislature. Pickel was again a member of the assembly during the 1845 session, the first under the new constitution, and was the spokesman for the group advocating stockholder liability. Early in the session, the assembly had a steamboat company charter under consideration, and Pickel offered the following amendment providing for proportional liability of stockholders:

> For the security and payment of all the debts, contracts and liabilities of this company, the president, directors and stockholders shall be personally liable, both in all their real as well as personal estate, for all debts, contracts and liabilities, during the time they were stockholders, and in proportion to the amount of stock owned; and there shall be no transfer of any of the shares of the said company, except by and with the consent of the board of directors, whose

[77] *N. J. Laws,* 68 sess., 2 sit. (1844), pp. 55, 57, 265.

[78] *Ibid.,* p. 155. In another case, however, the Democrats failed in their effort to include similar protective provisions in an act authorizing a manufacturing company to extend the scope of its operations. *Votes and Proceedings of the General Assembly,* 68 sess., 2 sit. (1844), pp. 350, 356; *Journal of the Legislative Council,* 68 sess., 2 sit. (1844), pp. 234–35; *N. J. Laws,* 68 sess., 2 sit. (1844), p. 79.

[79] Cf. *supra,* pp. 102–104.

duty it shall be to register the names of all the stockholders, with the number of shares owned, and the date when they became owners of said stock; and it shall be the duty of the board of directors, at least one month before their annual meeting, to advertise and publish a list of all the persons names, as stockholders, and the number of shares owned by each, in one or more of the newspapers published in the county where the meeting of the board of directors is held.[80]

When Pickel introduced the above clause, he commented that "he did not expect his amendment would pass, but he thought these corporate Companies should be made more safe to the public, by making the stockholders personally liable." He also admitted that he "feared the effects of these corporations, which come always dressed in one guise, viz., the 'public good.' "[81] Assemblyman Pickel was quite correct in assuming that his amendment would not be acceptable, for the assembly speedily rejected it by a vote of thirty-five to fifteen.[82]

Mr. Pickel was not content to let the matter of stockholder liability die after the first test case. During the remainder of the session, he continued to insist that his liability clause be inserted in various business corporation charters when the charters came up for discussion in the assembly. He moved that it be included in two other steamboat company charters,[83] in eight charters for manufacturing companies,[84] in one for a dry dock concern,[85] and in one bank charter.[86] Because of his persistence, Pickel received wide attention in the New Jersey press. The *Newark Daily Advertiser,* a Whig paper that was opposed to Pickel's views, referred repeatedly in columns entitled "Pickelania" or "Pickel scriptum" to his attempts to secure the adoption of "his stereotyped 'personal responsibility' " clause.[87] The public also took notice, and on at least one occasion a petition in support of the principle of stockholder liability was sent to

[80] *Votes and Proceedings of the General Assembly,* 1845, p. 198.
[81] *Newark Daily Advertiser,* January 29, 1845.
[82] *Votes and Proceedings of the General Assembly,* 1845, pp. 198–99.
[83] *Ibid.,* pp. 240, 722–23. [84] *Ibid.,* pp. 411, 442, 499, 588, 609, 641, 801, 818.
[85] *Ibid.,* pp. 241–42. [86] *Ibid.,* p. 269.
[87] E.g., *Newark Daily Advertiser,* March 6 and 12, 1845.

Pickel so that he might submit it to the legislature.[88] The efforts of Pickel to impose proportional liability on stockholders were, however, unavailing. In every instance, his motions to insert the liability clause in charters received the support of only about one-third of the members of the assembly.[89]

Undismayed by their lack of success in promoting the proportional liability clause, Pickel and his associates attempted during the 1845 session to secure the adoption of other types of provisions for stockholder liability. They proposed unlimited liability for stockholders in a gas manufacturing company,[90] but most of their alternative proposals were of milder form. For example, they suggested in connection with various charters that stockholders be made liable for all debts if a stipulated part of the capital stock was not paid in in cash, if dividends were paid out of capital, or if capital was withdrawn when liabilities were unpaid.[91] Other suggestions were that stockholders be made liable if dividends were paid when "any debts" were outstanding and that limits be placed on the permissible corporate debts with stockholders becoming unlimitedly liable if the limits were exceeded.[92] The final fruits of all these efforts were, however, quite meager. Of the twenty-two charters granted in 1845, provisions for stockholder liability appeared in but four. The four were charters for manufacturing companies, and they contained provisions declaring stockholders jointly and severally liable for all debts until specified amounts of the capital stock had been "paid in or satisfactorily secured." These four charters also made the presidents, directors, and stockholders jointly and severally liable for all debts if, in the

[88] The memorial from citizens of Middlesex County, "setting forth, that the granting of charters is a violation of equal rights, and praying the legislature if such charters are granted, to make the stockholder personally liable," was read and laid on the table. *Votes and Proceedings of the General Assembly*, 1845, p. 501.

[89] His support came principally from members representing agricultural counties. It is interesting that George F. Fort, a Democrat who had been a delegate to the 1844 constitutional convention and who was to be governor from 1851 to 1854, supported Pickel in most instances. Throughout his career, Fort was an advocate of increased stockholder liability and of general incorporation laws.

[90] *Votes and Proceedings of the General Assembly*, 1845, p. 667.

[91] E.g., *ibid.*, pp. 443–44.

[92] *Ibid.*, pp. 463, 467, 523, 668.

event of dissolution, any part of the capital was withdrawn before all obligations were discharged.[93]

It will be recalled that during the 1846 session of the legislature a general regulating act for all corporations and a general incorporation act for manufacturing corporations were enacted. The regulating act made no provision for any form of extended stockholder liability but merely stated that stockholders were required to pay for their shares in full if the corporate property proved insufficient to discharge the debts.[94] Before it had been adopted, however, the assembly had had under consideration a more stringent form of regulating act applying merely to manufacturing corporations that included a number of liability provisions for which many Democrats had contended for a decade.[95] Approaching the problem on the assumption that when the members of a manufacturing company sought to incorporate they wished "to substitute for personal liability, a *cash capital*," the suggested law gave stockholders limited liability only after the capital was actually paid in and deprived them of the privilege if any part of the capital was withdrawn for their benefit.[96] Although this particular regulating act did not receive the approval of the assembly,[97] its liability features were incorporated in the general incorporation law for manufacturing companies enacted later in the session.

The 1846 general incorporation law for manufacturing companies[98] required that the capital stock specified in the certificate of incorporation as the amount with which a company would begin business must be paid in and a sworn statement to that effect filed and published before the stockholders would enjoy the privilege of limited liability. Likewise stockholders were unlimitedly liable for debts if, when the capital stock was reduced, any capital was withdrawn before the payment of all previously contracted debts. Stockholders were also fully liable for the debts if an annual statement of the capital stock paid in, the assets of the company "deemed good," and the existing debts

[93] *N. J. Laws,* 1845, pp. 129, 173, 205, 221.
[94] *N. J. Laws,* 1846, p. 16.
[95] *Votes and Proceedings of the General Assembly,* 1846, pp. 142–43, 155.
[96] *State Gazette,* January 30, 1846.
[97] Cf. *supra,* pp. 114–115.
[98] *N. J. Laws,* 1846, p. 64.

was not published.[99] Some opposition had been expressed in the assembly to the liability provisions of this bill when it was up for discussion,[100] but the provisions were acceptable to those who felt that creditors could be too easily defrauded by the average corporation. The views of the latter group were expressed in a letter written to the *Newark Daily Advertiser* shortly after the general incorporation law was in force:

> The duties and liabilities of the companies thus authorized, their managers and stockholders, are well guarded. Corporations under this act cannot be formed as *substitutes* for capital. Individual liability is preserved until the capital is put in actually and bona fide — then individual liability ceases, until that capital is wrongfully taken away. Thus honest enterprise, by means of companies, is allowed; but the public are protected against kiting and humbuggery. How many companies have been formed, with large sounding capitals, when in fact there was no capital at all, and the community have been swindled by trusting to appearances, which had nothing substantial to rest on? This cannot be done under the present law. Those who desire to form a company, can only do so safely by furnishing an actual capital. If they are unfortunate in the honest management of this, they have no further loss than the sum advanced. But if they think to establish a company without means, they will have to make good out of their personal pockets what should have been advanced at first. This is the main feature of the act.[101]

Because the 1846 general law proved inadequate in a number of respects, the legislators replaced it in 1849 by a new general incorporation act of increased coverage that altered the provisions for stockholder liability in several important particulars.[102] In the 1849 act, stockholders were no longer unlimitedly

[99] Any stockholder who became liable under the terms of the act and who either voluntarily or by compulsion paid the debts could file a bill against other stockholders for contribution in proportion to their stockholdings.

[100] Cf. *supra*, p. 118.

[101] *Newark Daily Advertiser*, March 2, 1846. The writer of the letter also pointed out that these principles had long been in successful operation in connection with manufacturing corporations in Massachusetts. "And the effect of the law there has been to make such institutions popular as instruments of public benefit; instead of being, as has been too often the case here, scourges to the community where located, and engines for swindlers to plunder with."

[102] *N. J. Laws*, 1849, p. 300.

liable for the debts before the amount of capital with which the corporation was to begin business was fully paid in, nor were they made liable if the company did not publish the required annual statement of its financial condition. Furthermore, stockholders were no longer fully liable for the debts when any capital was withdrawn before all debts were discharged, but they were liable for the return of any withdrawals made for their benefit before public notice of the capital reduction was given or before all previously contracted debts were paid. On the other hand, stockholders were made responsible for the return of any illegal dividends whereas they had not been thus liable under the 1846 act.[103]

It will be useful at this point to mention the provisions for stockholder liability that appeared in subsequent general laws.[104] The 1852 general law for plank road companies made stockholders liable individually to an amount equal to their stock for debts in excess of the amount of money actually in the treasury or owing to the company in the form of remaining installments on the stock.[105] The general insurance company law of the same year made the corporators and those entitled to participation in profits liable jointly and severally until the whole capital was paid in and a certificate to that effect was filed.[106] In the 1854 general law for the formation of companies to carry on ocean and inland waterway transportation, stockholders were subject to double liability until the whole capital was paid in and that fact made a matter of public record. The same law made stockholders jointly and severally liable for all debts owing to laborers and mechanics if such debts could not be satisfied out of the corporate assets.[107] The general incorpora-

[103] It should be stated parenthetically that the 1849 act gave laborers in the employ of the corporations organized under its authority the status of preferred creditors. They were to enjoy a lien on the assets ahead of all other creditors for the wages owing to them. The Democrats had for some time favored giving laborers this special status.

[104] Discussion of the 1850 general banking law will be omitted here since it appears in the earlier section of the present chapter.

[105] *N. J. Laws,* 1852, Ch. 51, p. 95.

[106] *N. J. Laws,* 1852, Ch. 74, p. 159. Two years later they were relieved of this liability if $50,000 of capital was paid in. *Ibid.,* 1854, Ch. 194, p. 455.

[107] *N. J. Laws,* 1854, Ch. 201, p. 470.

tion law of 1849 was amended in 1865 to impose double liability on stockholders until the whole amount of the capital stock was paid in.[108] The gas company general incorporation law of 1874 provided that stockholders should refund any illegal dividends paid to them.[109]

Thus New Jersey's general incorporation law of widest coverage, the one passed in 1849, and several other important general laws enacted in the period between 1846 and 1875 contained rather harsh stockholder liability provisions of the type the Democrats had advocated during the early eighteen forties when private acts of incorporation were under consideration in the legislature. Yet the special acts of incorporation that were passed from 1846 onward made provision for stockholder liability in relatively few instances. For example, stockholders were not held liable in any special charter enacted between 1846 and 1875 for corporate debts when specified debt limits were exceeded.[110] In only one case, a special charter for a manufacturing company granted in 1847, were stockholders made liable for the business debts when capital funds were distributed before all debts were paid.[111] The 1867 charter of a company organized to promote immigration made stockholders liable for debts until the capital was paid in.[112] In the same year, stockholders in two commercial loan companies were subjected to double liability until their stock was fully paid for, and similar stipulations appeared in the charters of two other loan companies in 1868 and 1873 and in a market company charter in 1873.[113]

A number of special charters passed during and after 1846 did provide for ordinary double liability.[114] The charters of ten

108 *N. J. Laws*, 1865, Ch. 201, p. 354.

109 *N. J. Laws*, 1874, Ch. 509, p. 124.

110 In fact, few debt limits were expressed in special charters after the eighteen forties. The debt limit was distinctly a feature of that particular decade. Cf. *supra*, pp. 278–279.

111 *N. J. Laws*, 1847, p. 160.

112 *N. J. Laws*, 1867, Ch. 471, p. 992. Suits against stockholders had to be brought within two years and after execution was made against the corporate property.

113 E.g., *N. J. Laws*, 1867, Ch. 266, p. 563; 1873, Ch. 295, p. 1225.

114 Liability clauses in particular charters were sometimes ambiguous. A few cases where it is not certain that a form of extended liability was intended have been omitted here.

mining companies enacted in 1846, 1848, and 1865 were among these cases.[115] Double liability was also provided in the charters of an express company of 1868 and a manufacturing company of 1869.[116] After 1869, however, double liability was imposed, outside the field of commercial banking, only upon stockholders in building and loan associations and savings banks with capital stocks. Stockholders in seven such institutions were subjected to double liability.[117]

It is clear, therefore, that after 1850 the tendency in New Jersey was away from imposing extended liability on stockholders in non-banking corporations chartered by special act. In 1851 and 1853, the legislature went so far as to remove by supplementary acts the double liability provisions in the charters of an 1848 mining company and an 1823 manufacturing company.[118] The efforts of the Democrats in the eighteen thirties and forties to make stockholders in specially chartered business corporations liable for business debts thus went largely unrewarded. Stockholder liability provisions of various types remained in some of the general incorporation laws, however, and this circumstance helps to explain why persons seeking to incorporate their business enterprises preferred special acts of incorporation.

The story of the liability of directors in non-banking corporations in New Jersey can be told in relatively few words. Directors in non-banking corporations were not subjected to any form of liability until many years after it was the generally accepted practice to impose certain forms of liability upon bank directors. The first charter in which the directors of a non-banking corporation were subject to liability was enacted in 1817.[119] In this instance, the president and "trustees" of a ferry boat company were made liable in their individual estates for the business debts if they contracted debts "beyond the funds" of the company. Directors of ordinary business corporations were

[115] *N. J. Laws,* 1846, pp. 55, 100, 151, 153; 1848, pp. 76, 81, 180, 209; 1865, Ch. 264, p. 460, Ch. 283, p. 484.

[116] *N. J. Laws,* 1868, Ch. 231, p. 505; 1869, Ch. 333, p. 907.

[117] E.g., *N. J. Laws,* 1872, Ch. 222, p. 563; 1873, Ch. 395, p. 1316.

[118] *N. J. Laws,* 1851, p. 343; 1853, Ch. 45, p. 120.

[119] *N. J. Laws,* 41 sess., 2 sit. (1817, private), p. 45.

not again made liable in the event of incurring debts in excess of a specified amount until 1840, but between that date and 1863 they were held liable for exceeding established debt limits in fifteen special charters and one supplement to a special charter.[120] In nine of these cases the directors were liable for all debts if the limit was exceeded,[121] but only for the amount of the excess in the remaining seven.[122] After 1863, no special charters imposed liability on directors or officers when debt limits were exceeded.

It was not until 1824 that directors of any non-banking corporation were made liable when illegal dividends were declared. Between that date and 1846, inclusive, twenty-six special charters and one special supplement imposed varying degrees of liability on directors of non-banking corporations for impairing the capital stock by payments to stockholders.[123] By the terms of the general regulating act of 1846, directors in any "bank, or moneyed or manufacturing corporation" were made jointly and severally liable for sums returned or paid to stockholders that did not represent "surplus profits arising from the business . . ." [124] After 1846, directors of other types of specially

[120] The sixteen cases included six manufacturing, one mining, two bridge, two water power, one steamboat, one hall, and three hotel companies. Usually directors could avoid liability on the ground that they were absent from the meeting at which it was decided to incur the illegal debt or that they had registered their dissent in the prescribed fashion. In four instances, stockholders were liable along with directors.

[121] E.g., *N. J. Laws,* 64 sess., 2 sit. (1840), pp. 112, 121.

[122] E.g., *N. J. Laws,* 1854, Ch. 64, p. 140; 1860, Ch. 184, p. 479.

[123] Eleven pertained to insurance companies and eleven to manufacturing companies. The remainder included one canal, one land improvement, one steamboat, and two mining companies. In a few cases, directors were made liable for all debts if capital was illegally distributed. E.g., *N. J. Laws,* 68 sess., 2 sit. (1844), pp. 55, 265. Usually, however, the directors were liable only for the amount of capital illegally divided. E.g., *ibid.,* 61 sess., 2 sit. (1837), pp. 176, 438. In most instances, absent or dissenting directors could escape liability, and generally the capital had to be impaired "knowingly." In three cases, stockholders also were liable.

[124] *N. J. Laws,* 1846, p. 16. Provision was made here for absent or dissenting directors to escape liability. In only one manufacturing company charter enacted after 1846 was the directors' liability provision made more stringent than that imposed by the general regulating act. That charter was passed in 1847 and made directors and stockholders liable for all debts if the capital was divided before all debts were paid. *Ibid.,* 1847, p. 160.

chartered corporations were very seldom liable in connection with illegal dividends. There were only thirteen special charters between 1847 and 1874 in which directors were specifically made liable for debts when illegal dividends were paid, of which eleven were charters for insurance companies.[125]

During the eighteen thirties and forties, the proposal was sometimes made by the more radical Democrats that directors of ordinary business corporations be made fully liable without qualification for company debts. Yet this principle was adopted by the New Jersey legislature in only two instances. The first example was an 1830 charter that stated that the president and directors of a steamboat company would "jointly and severally be holden and liable for all debts of the said company, in their private and individual capacities . . ." [126] In the second case, the 1834 charter of a mining company made the directors and stockholders "responsible in their private capacity" for all corporate debts.[127] Later attempts to make the directors of ordinary business corporations chartered by special act liable at all times for the business debts were defeated.[128]

Several of the general incorporation laws of New Jersey laid down conditions under which corporate directors or officers were liable for all or a specified part of the debts of corporations organized under their authority. The most severe liability provisions were those imposed for failure to file certain required certificates, for failure to publish required statements, or for material misrepresentations in the certificates or public notices. The general incorporation laws of 1846 and 1849 required the filing and publishing of a certificate within thirty days after the original capital stock was paid up. They also required the filing and publishing of certificates if the capital stock was increased or decreased, within thirty days after collecting the final installment in case of an increase or within thirty days after a vote of the stockholders in case of a decrease. Failure to perform these

[125] E.g., *N. J. Laws,* 1857, Ch. 36, p. 78, Ch. 119, p. 356.

[126] *N. J. Laws,* 54 sess., 2 sit. (1830), p. 92.

[127] *N. J. Laws,* 58 sess., 2 sit. (1834), p. 44. A supplementary act passed the following year relieved the stockholders of liability but not the directors. *Ibid.,* 59 sess., 2 sit. (1835), p. 130.

[128] E.g., *Journal of the Legislative Council,* 60 sess., 2 sit. (1836), pp. 159–161.

duties made the directors and officers jointly and severally liable for all debts contracted after the thirty-day period and before filing the certificates.[129] The directors of corporations under the 1849 law were liable for all debts if they did not publish each January a statement of the capital stock paid in, the assets "deemed good," and the existing debts.[130] Both the 1846 and 1849 laws made the officers who signed any of the required certificates or public notices liable jointly and severally for all debts contracted while they were stockholders or officers if the certificates or notices were "false in any material representation." The 1854 general law for companies engaged in water transportation required a certificate to be filed when the capital stock was paid up, and declared the officers signing the certificate to be jointly and severally liable for all debts contracted while they were stockholders or officers if the certificate was untrue.[131] The general law for gas companies enacted in 1874 made officers liable for all debts if they neglected or refused to file a certificate when the stockholders had voted to increase or decrease the capital stock.[132]

According to the terms of three general laws, directors were subjected to liability for exceeding established debt limits. In the 1846 and 1849 laws and in the 1874 gas company law they were liable for the debts up to the amount by which the corporate debts exceeded the legal limits.[133] Directors who were absent when it was decided to contract the illegal debts and those who dissented and notified the stockholders of their dissent could avoid liability.

Four of the general laws imposed liability on directors for declaring illegal dividends. Directors of corporations organized under the 1846 law were liable for debts only to the amount of such dividend,[134] but the 1849 law made them liable for all debts existing at the time the illegal dividend was declared and for

[129] *N. J. Laws,* 1846, p. 64; 1849, p. 300.

[130] The section of the 1849 law requiring publication of an annual statement was repealed in 1875. *N. J. Laws,* 1875 (public), Ch. 101, p. 24.

[131] *N. J. Laws,* 1854, Ch. 201, p. 470.

[132] *N. J. Laws,* 1874, Ch. 509, p. 124.

[133] *N. J. Laws,* 1846, p. 64; 1849, p. 300; 1874, Ch. 509, p. 124.

[134] *N. J. Laws,* 1846, p. 64.

all debts contracted during the time they should remain in office.[135] The 1854 general law for the formation of water transportation companies made directors liable for all outstanding debts when declaring an illegal dividend and for all debts contracted thereafter so long as they remained in office.[136] Directors of corporations under the gas company law of 1874 were liable for the debts in case they declared an illegal dividend, but their liability was not to exceed the amount of such dividend.[137] In each of the above cases, provision was made to enable directors who were absent or in dissent at the time the illegal actions were taken to escape liability.

The general laws of 1846 and 1849 and the gas company general law of 1874 also imposed liability on officers who were responsible for making loans of money to stockholders. The officers were held liable for debts to the amount of the loans plus interest.[138]

The principal facts that emerge from the foregoing discussion of the liability of stockholders and directors of New Jersey corporations before 1875 may be summarized here by way of conclusion. In the field of commercial banking, directors were from the beginning subjected to special liability provisions. Before 1822, directors in all banks were made liable for incurring debts beyond the limits fixed in the charters and for declaring illegal dividends. Between 1822 and the late eighteen forties, directors in only some of the banks were subjected to such provisions. After the eighteen forties, total debt limitations were not included in bank charters. All bank directors were liable for corporate debts to the amount of any illegal dividends they might declare after the passage of the general regulating act of 1846. Beginning in 1828, the directors of all specially chartered banks were made unlimitedly liable for the circulating notes of their institutions.

The most significant fact about the bank charters is that no

135 *N. J. Laws,* 1849, p. 300.

136 *N. J. Laws,* 1854, Ch. 201, p. 470.

137 *N. J. Laws,* 1874, Ch. 509, p. 124.

138 *N. J. Laws,* 1846, p. 64; 1849, p. 300; 1874, Ch. 509, p. 124.

form of extended liability was imposed on stockholders until the middle of the nineteenth century. The general banking law of 1850 made stockholders unlimitedly liable for the corporate debts, but this provision was repealed in 1851. When in 1855 the legislature, after five years during which no new banks were chartered by special act, resumed the traditional practice of granting special bank charters, they imposed double liability on stockholders for the payment of the circulating bills and notes. This policy was adhered to for the remainder of the period under investigation in this study each time a new special bank charter was granted or an existing bank charter was renewed.

The policy of New Jersey with respect to the liability of stockholders and directors in non-banking corporations was quite different from that followed in the case of banking companies. The principal point of variance was in the matter of the liability of stockholders. Double liability provisions appeared in manufacturing company charters as early as 1813 and were included in each such charter enacted up to the year 1824. Provision for double liability was also made in the general manufacturing law of 1816. Stockholders were subjected to double liability in some of the manufacturing and mining companies chartered during the ten years after 1824. For fifteen years before 1850, the radical Democrats endeavored to secure acceptance of their belief that stockholders in ordinary business corporations should be personally responsible for corporate debts. They struggled to insert clauses calling for unlimited liability, proportional liability, or double liability in corporate charters, particularly in charters for companies that would be in direct competition with unincorporated enterprises. Although the Democrats fought a constantly intensified battle for stockholder liability until the middle of the century, they were sponsoring a losing cause. They were able to secure the adoption of only a few mild liability clauses during the years between 1834 and 1850. After 1850, provisions for stockholder liability appeared in special charters for non-banking corporations only upon rare occasions.

Between 1824 and 1846, directors of a small number of non-banking companies were made liable to varying degrees if they declared illegal dividends. After 1846, the directors of all manufacturing companies were liable to the amount of an illegal dividend by the terms of the general regulating act of that year; but this liability provision was seldom imposed on directors in other types of corporations after the eighteen forties. Provisions making directors liable when debts were contracted beyond an established maximum limit became popular between 1840 and 1850 but were only rarely employed in special charters after the latter date.

Considerable emphasis should be given to the fact that although the New Jersey legislators were very little inclined after 1850 to impose stockholder or director liability in the special charters they granted to non-banking concerns, several of the general incorporation laws contained a variety of liability provisions. This was particularly true of the general law of widest application, the law of 1849. That law provided a number of harsh rules in the matter of liability that represented vestiges of the attitude of the Democrats toward the business corporation during the eighteen forties. The presence of such provisions helps to explain why this law of wide coverage was rejected as unacceptable by businessmen who sought to incorporate their enterprises.

CHAPTER XII

State Control

VIRTUALLY every provision of a special charter of incorporation represents a form of control by the state over the corporation created by the charter. In the same manner, each stipulation in a general incorporation law can be considered to represent state control over the companies that file certificates of incorporation under the terms of the general law. Charter provisions such as those stating the type of business in which a corporation might engage, rules concerning the capital structure, the dividend policy, the liability of stockholders, and the election of directors and officers, provisions as to the tolls and charges that might be made, and stipulations about the taxes that were to be paid are treated in appropriate sections of this study. The present chapter is concerned with a number of the most important ways in which the New Jersey legislature sought to retain a measure of control over the very existence of its business corporations or to reserve the right to change the terms of the charters it granted. The charter provisions that receive attention in this chapter are those limiting the duration of the corporations, those setting forth either positive duties or prohibitions the neglect or disregard of which would render charters void, those reserving to the legislature the right to alter or repeal charters, and those in which the state retained the right either for itself or its political subdivisions to assume ownership and control of the corporate properties at some future date.

The problem of control by the state over incorporated groups occupied the attention of New Jersey lawmakers from the earliest years of their charter granting activity. Of the various devices employed to maintain a measure of control, one of the most widely discussed was the scheme of establishing in corporation charters a definite time during which the privileges granted should continue. If a charter expired after a definite period of time, the legislature was afforded an opportunity to reëxamine its terms before renewing the grant.

The very earliest New Jersey charters were silent as to the terms of life of the companies created, and the presumption was that the charters were perpetual. In some later cases all doubt was removed by definite language to the effect that the grants continued "forever hereafter."[1] Only two eighteenth century New Jersey business corporations were limited in duration.[2] There is evidence, however, that some early legislators desired to include such limitations in other charters.[3] The opposition of the promoters of internal improvement companies to any limitation and the willingness of a majority of the legislators to grant whatever terms were necessary to get such projects under way were probably responsible for the fact that most early companies were awarded perpetual charters.

Beginning in 1801, the New Jersey legislature followed the practice of limiting the duration of many of its business corpo-

[1] This was the case, for example, in the first two turnpike charters passed in New Jersey. *N. J. Laws,* 25 sess., 2 sit. (1801), Ch. 38, p. 80; 27 sess., 1 sit. (1802), Ch. 81, p. 172.

[2] *N. J. Laws,* 21 sess., 2 sit. (1797), Ch. 653, p. 201; 23 sess., 3 sit. (1799), Ch. 794, p. 528. The two were bridge companies, and they were unusual because they were incorporated for the terms of years during which they were entitled by earlier agreements with the legislature to hold their bridges and take tolls. Their power to take tolls expired in 1889 and 1892 respectively.

[3] In 1796, when a charter for a company to improve navigation on the Assunpink Creek was under discussion in the legislative council, a clause was proposed limiting to ninety-nine years the period during which the company could hold title to its proposed works. James Ewing, mayor of Trenton and a member of the committee seeking the charter, sent to the council a long petition opposing any such limitation. He declared "that the Section in question will be wholly destructive of the undertaking . . . It is not contemplated by the Section objected to, that at the end of the ninety-nine years the Company shall in any way be reimbursed [for] their original expenditures, if this was contemplated it would have more the appearance of Justice, though it would then be only the appearance, unless they were likewise to be reimbursed if the Scheme should prove unsuccessful." (The petition, dated March 15, 1796, is in the manuscript collection of the New Jersey State Library.) The charter as finally passed contained no statement as to the term of corporate existence or the period during which the company might hold title to its property. *N. J. Laws,* 20 sess., 2 sit. (1796), Ch. 586, p. 57.

ration charters,[4] and for the next sixty years a majority of the special charters contained clauses limiting their lives to a definite period of years. Bank charters were most strictly and consistently limited, no corporation being given banking powers for an indefinite time. Most banks established before 1844 were chartered for twenty years,[5] but in a few cases the duration varied somewhat.[6] The 1844 constitution limited all bank charters to a term of twenty years.[7]

Non-banking companies did not receive such consistent treatment in the matter of the duration of their corporate existences. Turnpike companies chartered between 1804 and 1838 were limited to terms of ninety-nine years,[8] with the exception of five that were chartered in 1811 for a period of fifty years.[9] Until the eighteen fifties, insurance companies were generally of limited duration, the most frequently stipulated terms being twenty-five and thirty years.[10] Governor Fort, in 1852, vetoed a charter establishing an insurance company because it had no twenty-year clause as required by the 1844 constitution for "money corporations," which phrase the governor interpreted to include nonmutual insurance companies.[11] This interpreta-

[4] The first case in which a charter itself contained an absolute expiration date was the fifty-year charter granted to New Jersey's first mining corporation in 1801. *N. J. Laws,* 26 sess., 1 sit. (1801), Ch. 52, p. 116.

[5] E.g., *N. J. Laws,* 28 sess., 2 sit. (1804), Ch. 109, p. 268; 49 sess., 1 sit. (1824), p. 35.

[6] A land company was given banking privileges for only fifteen years. *N. J. Laws,* 47 sess., 1 sit. (1822), p. 64. A few banks were chartered for twenty-one years. E.g., *ibid.,* 42 sess., 2 sit. (1818, private), p. 75. The banking privileges of the Morris Canal and Banking Company were the longest of all and continued for thirty-one years. *Ibid.,* 49 sess., 1 sit. (1824), p. 158. An assembly committee recommended in 1811 that new banks be "incorporated for the term of only fourteen years." *Votes and Proceedings of the General Assembly,* 35 sess., 2 sit. (1811), p. 410. The six new banks created the following year, however, were granted twenty-year charters.

[7] B. P. Poore, *The Federal and State Constitutions* (2nd ed., 1878), II, 1318.

[8] E.g., *N. J. Laws,* 28 sess., 2 sit. (1804), Ch. 113, p. 287; 41 sess., 2 sit. (1817, private), p. 67.

[9] E.g., *N. J. Laws,* 35 sess, 2 sit. (1811), pp. 351, 369.

[10] E.g., *N. J. Laws,* 37 sess., 1 sit. (1812, private), p. 6; 56 sess., 2 sit. (1832), p. 189.

[11] *Journal of the Senate,* 1852, p. 651–653; *Votes and Proceedings of the General Assembly,* 1852, pp. 838–39.

tion did not prevail, and only a fraction of the insurance charters subsequently enacted were limited in duration.

Except for the S. U. M., New Jersey's first manufacturing corporation, all manufacturing corporations chartered before 1823 were to endure only for limited periods. Twenty and twenty-one years were generally stipulated,[12] but five charters granted during the War of 1812 were effective for only fifteen years.[13] Beginning in 1823, a few perpetual manufacturing company charters were enacted by the legislature,[14] although most charters for manufacturing companies continued to be limited. When time limits were mentioned, however, they were usually for longer periods than those in earlier manufacturing company charters, limits of thirty and fifty years occurring most frequently.[15] The situation continued relatively unchanged until the end of the eighteen fifties when a somewhat larger number of perpetual charters was given to manufacturing concerns. After 1862, the great majority of manufacturing company charters contained no time limits.[16]

Time limits were seldom imposed on certain types of corporations. The principal representatives of this group were railroads. Although the 1815 charter of the New-Jersey Rail-Road Company was to last for a term of only fifty years,[17] the railroads chartered during the railroad era beginning in 1830 were for the most part given perpetual charters. The very few exceptions were limited to terms of between twenty-five and fifty years.[18] Canal and water companies were likewise seldom limited.

Slightly over one-third of all the corporations granted special

[12] E.g., *N. J. Laws,* 34 sess., 1 sit. (1809), Ch. 38, p. 137; 46 sess., 1 sit. (1821, private), p. 26.

[13] E.g., *N. J. Laws,* 39 sess., 1 sit. (1814, private), pp. 8, 13.

[14] E.g., *N. J. Laws,* 48 sess., 1 sit. (1823, private), p. 124; 52 sess., 2 sit. (1827), pp. 103, 107.

[15] E.g., *N. J. Laws,* 52 sess., 2 sit. (1827), pp. 123, 168, 209; 61 sess., 2 sit. (1837), pp. 36, 51, 55.

[16] For example, of the nine manufacturing charters passed in 1863, only three were limited; of the twenty-eight passed in 1868, all but seven were perpetual.

[17] *N. J. Laws,* 39 sess., 2 sit. (1815, private), p. 68.

[18] E.g., *N. J. Laws,* 58 sess., 2 sit. (1834), p. 55; 60 sess., 2 sit. (1836), p. 102.

charters by New Jersey were limited in duration.[19] It is interesting to note that the limited charters were, for the most part, passed between 1800 and 1860. After 1860, there was a noticeable decrease in the proportion of charters that were limited in duration. To cite a few examples, it was found that less than 30 per cent of the special charters granted in 1867 were so limited, only 15 per cent of those enacted in 1870, and less than 10 per cent in 1873, 1874, and 1875.

The practice of limiting charters to a fixed period of years necessitated numerous special amendments to extend corporations beyond the period initially established. It had been foreseen that such would be the case, for a number of early clauses that set time limits of a definite number of years also specified that the corporations were to continue to the end of the next legislative session.[20] The obvious intent of such provisions was to give the companies additional opportunity to secure extensions of their charters before their corporate existences ended. The first legislative act for extending the life of a corporate body was passed in 1821. It provided for the continuation of two banks that were to have expired in 1824.[21] By the close of 1875, 102 acts had been passed for the purpose of extending charters for definite periods of time,[22] and twenty-two supplements had been enacted to repeal the time limits in charters that had originally been intended to run for only a definite period of years.[23]

The time limits expressed in special acts of incorporation had little real significance. There is no evidence that non-banking institutions encountered any difficulty in securing renewals

[19] Out of a total of 2318 special charters, 851 were granted for limited periods.

[20] E.g., *N. J. Laws,* 29 sess., 1 sit. (1804), Ch. 154, p. 449; 32 sess., 1 sit. (1807), Ch. 30, p. 80.

[21] *N. J. Laws,* 46 sess., 1 sit. (1821, private), p. 24. The banks were rechartered for only fifteen years.

[22] Forty-six of these acts applied to banks.

[23] The first occasion on which an existing time limit was repealed was in 1835 in the case of a life insurance company. *N. J. Laws,* 59 sess., 2 sit. (1835), p. 23. The second case concerned a similar company in 1848. *Ibid.,* 1848, p. 4. The remaining twenty cases occurred during and after 1857. Eleven of the twenty were passed for the benefit of insurance companies. E.g., *ibid.,* 1866, Ch. 62, p. 144, Ch. 125, p. 287.

of their charters. The situation was different, however, in the case of banks. When the charter of a bank was about to expire, the legislators frequently seized upon the opportunity to enforce new restrictions on banking operations as the price of rechartering the bank. This practice was particularly noticeable after 1855 when every bank charter renewal imposed an increased measure of liability on bank stockholders and directors.[24]

The general incorporation laws of New Jersey did not follow a well-defined policy in the matter of the duration of companies organized under their provisions. The more important ones, however, set maximum limits. Manufacturing companies were restricted to a life of twenty years by the general incorporation law of 1816.[25] The 1846 general law for manufacturing companies left to the corporators the decision as to how long a corporation should endure, but its successor of 1849 established a fifty-year limit.[26] The banking law of 1850 limited its corporations to twenty years as required by the 1844 constitution.[27] The general insurance law of 1852 fixed an upper limit of thirty years, except for life insurance companies which were not thus restricted.[28] Five other general laws limited the number of years for which charters obtained under their provisions should be valid, but the remaining ten were silent on this point. The limits set in the more important general laws and the lack of provisions for renewing corporate privileges by amending the certificates were calculated to deter corporations from organizing under them.[29]

Special charters frequently established definite periods within which the operations of the corporations were required

[24] Cf. *supra*, pp. 337–340. [25] *N. J. Laws*, 40 sess., 2 sit. (1816, public), p. 17.
[26] *N. J. Laws*, 1849, p. 300. [27] *N. J. Laws*, 1850, p. 140.
[28] *N. J. Laws*, 1852, Ch. 74, p. 159.
[29] A further difficulty was encountered when it appeared that even companies organized under general laws for periods shorter than the permitted maximum time could not amend their certificates if they decided to continue for a longer period than they had originally anticipated. On two occasions, the legislature passed special laws to permit companies under the manufacturing law of 1849 to file statements extending their charters twenty years beyond the expiration dates stated in their original certificates. *N. J. Laws*, 1856, Ch. 46, p. 85; 1859, Ch. 106, p. 284.

to begin or within which a stated proportion of the capital stock had to be either subscribed or paid in. The purpose of these limitations was to prevent charters from becoming the mere objects of speculation, for noncompliance with the requirements rendered the charters void.

The first charter to designate a definite period within which the contemplated project was to be begun and completed was one enacted in 1795 for a bridge company. It required that the work must proceed "with all convenient speed," and if it was not commenced within three years and completed within seven, the state was to resume all the rights granted.[30] One other eighteenth century bridge company charter made a similar stipulation,[31] and bridge companies of the nineteenth century were occasionally required to complete their projects in a certain time on pain of forfeiting their charters.[32] This type of time limit was imposed most frequently, however, in turnpike company charters, appearing in every one enacted up to 1838 and in most passed after that date.[33] Railroads were also usually allowed only a certain time to begin and complete construction of their roads.[34] Numerous other corporations that were chartered for prosecuting works in the nature of public utilities were to lose their charters if their projects were not carried out within a definite time. The charters of eighteen canal companies[35] and of the same number of ferry companies[36] were

[30] *N. J. Laws,* 19 sess., 2 sit. (1795), Ch. 554, p. 1067.

[31] *N. J. Laws,* 22 sess., 2 sit. (1798), Ch. 708, p. 321.

[32] Fifteen post-1800 bridge charters were in this group. E.g., *N. J. Laws,* 34 sess., 1 sit. (1809), Ch. 47, p. 164; 1868, Ch. 520, p. 1136.

[33] Occasionally the time schedule was rather elaborate, the road to be commenced by a certain time, a specified amount to be done each year, and all to be finished by a definite date. E.g., *N. J. Laws,* 30 sess., 2 sit. (1806), Ch. 186, p. 526, Ch. 190, p. 586.

[34] E.g., *N. J. Laws,* 55 sess., 2 sit. (1831), pp. 24, 66. Railroad charters sometimes merely established the time by which the project must be completed and were silent as to the time of commencing work. E.g., *ibid.,* 60 sess., 2 sit. (1836), pp. 60, 158. Failure to complete the railroads within the stated time did not always mean forfeiture of the entire franchise but only insofar as it pertained to the unfinished sections. E.g., *ibid.,* 58 sess., 2 sit. (1834), p. 55.

[35] E.g., *N. J. Laws,* 40 sess., 2 sit. (1816, private), p. 185; 54 sess., 2 sit. (1830), p. 73.

[36] E.g., *N. J. Laws,* 1849, p. 189; 1868, Ch. 165, p. 371.

thus restricted, as were the charters of thirty-five other public utility concerns of various types.[37]

In addition to these cases of charters for public utility companies, fourteen manufacturing companies and one mining concern were required to begin operations within a definite time or lose their charters. The first of these were chartered in the eighteen twenties and were under the obligation to begin manufacturing operations within a limited time, in one instance within three years and in the other within two.[38] Six manufacturing companies incorporated in 1837 were to forfeit their charters unless business was carried on within five years,[39] and a seventh chartered the same year was required to begin within ten years' time.[40] The charters of two manufacturing companies and one mining firm passed between 1841 and 1843 were also to be void if business was not begun within a certain time.[41] It is noteworthy that most of the manufacturing company charters restricted in this fashion had been enacted during the decade after 1835 when there was an organized group of Democrats in the legislature urging circumspection in granting charters for ordinary business concerns. Of the numerous manufacturing firms chartered after that period, only two were under obligation to commence operations within a given time.[42]

A similar type of provision was sometimes put into charters requiring that a stated amount of capital stock be subscribed within a certain time if the charters were to continue in effect. This stipulation appeared first in 1824, and it is interesting that the first four charters to include it were those granting the most valuable franchises that New Jersey had to offer: namely, the charters of the Morris Canal and Banking Company, the Camden and Amboy Rail Road and Transportation Company, the

[37] These included twelve water companies, five gaslight, five harbor and land improvement, and thirteen miscellaneous concerns. Most of the water company charters merely specified the time by which work was to be commenced "in good faith."

[38] *N. J. Laws,* 49 sess., 1 sit. (1824), p. 64; 52 sess., 2 sit. (1828), p. 149.

[39] E.g., *N. J. Laws,* 61 sess., 2 sit. (1837), pp. 51, 66, 130.

[40] *N. J. Laws,* 61 sess., 2 sit. (1837), p. 80.

[41] *N. J. Laws,* 65 sess., 2 sit. (1841), p. 54; 66 sess., 2 sit. (1842), p. 150; 67 sess., 2 sit. (1843), p. 48.

[42] *N. J. Laws,* 1860, Ch. 25, p. 59; 1867, Ch. 265, p. 561.

Delaware and Raritan Canal Company, and the West-Jersey Rail Road and Transportation Company.[43] No other railroad charters contained this type of provision, but nearly every turnpike charter passed after 1838 was to be void if the number of shares necessary for incorporation or for calling the first meeting was not subscribed within a definite time.[44]

Nine manufacturing companies chartered around 1840 were subjected to strict rules regarding the payment of their capital stock. They could commence their operations only if specified amounts of capital were actually paid in within two years after the passage of the charters.[45] In later years, only three charters for manufacturing companies contained clauses requiring certain amounts of capital to be paid within designated periods.[46]

It was to be expected that many corporations would not be able to fulfill the requirement of completing their projects or of obtaining the required subscriptions in the allotted time, and the legislature was constantly besieged by requests for extensions of time. The petitioners usually represented that they could carry their projects to completion if allowed a few years of grace, and there is no evidence that the legislators were ever reluctant to grant this favor. The first two time extensions granted were passed in 1804 for the relief of bridge companies.[47] Two years later, the legislature extended the time for the completion of two turnpikes,[48] and numerous extensions were passed for the benefit of turnpike companies in later years.[49] Railroads also came to need increased time in which to complete construction, and many supplements for their relief appeared among the statutes, especially after the economic difficulties of

[43] *N. J. Laws,* 49 sess., 1 sit. (1824), p. 158; 54 sess., 2 sit. (1830), pp. 73, 83; 55 sess., 2 sit. (1831), p. 95.

[44] E.g., *N. J. Laws,* 63 sess., 2 sit. (1839), p. 172; 1849, pp. 145, 157, 171. Sometimes the time allowed was figured from the date of the act and sometimes from the date the books were first opened for subscription. In most cases the provision was accompanied by a definite time limit for completing the roads.

[45] E.g., *N. J. Laws,* 64 sess., 2 sit. (1840), pp. 23, 41, 112.

[46] *N. J. Laws,* 1855, Ch. 50, p. 114; 1856, Ch. 86, p. 172; 1864, Ch. 155, p. 245.

[47] *N. J. Laws,* 29 sess., 1 sit. (1804), Ch. 144, p. 404, Ch. 162, p. 478.

[48] *N. J. Laws,* 31 sess., 1 sit. (1806), Ch. 142, p. 745, Ch. 148, p. 757.

[49] Sometimes the same company received more than one extension. Cf. *N. J. Laws,* 48 sess., 1 sit. (1823, private), p. 129; 52 sess., 2 sit. (1828), p. 137.

the late eighteen thirties had set in.[50] Occasionally the legislature even responded favorably to appeals to revive the charters of turnpike, bridge, or water companies whose rights had already expired by reason of failure to complete their works in a given time.[51]

In an effort to assure the continued usefulness of transportation facilities constructed by private corporations, the New Jersey legislature sometimes included in charters a clause declaring the grants void if the facilities were abandoned or in disrepair for a stated period. This form of control was used only twice before 1830,[52] but beginning in that year it was employed frequently. Twenty-eight steam railroads,[53] twelve horse railroads,[54] three canals,[55] three dock companies,[56] and one plank road company[57] incorporated during and after 1830 were to lose their charters if their works were not kept in repair. The charters were to become void after periods of abandonment ranging between one and five years. If the charters became void, the lands occupied by the companies usually were to revert to the previous owners. In a few steam and horse railroad charters the superstructure was expressly declared to remain the property of the stockholders if removed within a stated or "reasonable" time. Only one other company was subject to forfeiture of its charter for discontinuing business. This was a steamboat company incorporated in 1852 that was to lose its

[50] E.g., *N. J. Laws,* 62 sess., 2 sit. (1838), p. 46; 67 sess., 2 sit. (1843), p. 76. In the latter case the corporators had not yet even opened the subscription books "on account of the depressed state of the money market."

[51] E.g., *N. J. Laws,* 49 sess., 1 sit. (1824), p. 82; 1855, Ch. 46, p. 104.

[52] A navigation company charter of 1804 was to be void if, after completion, the works were not usable for a period of five years. *N. J. Laws,* 29 sess., 1 sit. (1804), Ch. 153, p. 433. The first railroad charter, passed in 1815, was to become invalid if the road was allowed to decay and become impassible for two years. *Ibid.,* 39 sess., 2 sit. (1815, private), p. 68.

[53] E.g., *N. J. Laws,* 60 sess., 2 sit. (1836), pp. 141, 158, 245. Most of the steam railroads with clauses voiding their charters in case of failure to keep the roads in repair were chartered before 1860.

[54] E.g., *N. J. Laws,* 1871, Ch. 391, p. 1015, Ch. 524, p. 1361.

[55] E.g., *N. J. Laws,* 57 sess., 2 sit. (1833), p. 128.

[56] E.g., *N. J. Laws,* 1851, pp. 25, 67.

[57] *N. J. Laws,* 1854, Ch. 91, p. 210.

charter in the event that its service was discontinued for one year.[58]

Like the legislatures of other states, the governing body of New Jersey sought an effective means of forcing banking corporations to redeem their notes and other obligations in specie. Beginning in 1822, the New Jersey lawmakers included in nearly every bank charter some form of clause threatening forfeiture of the charter for failure to maintain specie redemption. The earliest provision required that no banking powers be exercised during the time that specie payments were refused on penalty of forfeiting the charter.[59] Equivalent provisions were included in five other bank charters before 1840.[60] The same provision reappeared in 1855 and became the most popular rule in the matter of note redemption, being written into thirty-four additional charters.[61] Thirteen bank charters were to become void if the companies failed to redeem in specie for longer than stated periods of time.[62] Eight banks received more harsh treatment than any of the above, their charters being declared forfeited "forever" if specie payments were suspended at any time.[63]

Over four hundred special acts of incorporation required

[58] *N. J. Laws,* 1852, Ch. 204, p. 527. If the charter became void, the directors were required to advertise and sell the real estate and to distribute the proceeds of the sale with the other assets.

[59] *N. J. Laws,* 47 sess., 1 sit. (1822, private), p. 70.

[60] E.g., *N. J. Laws,* 48 sess., 1 sit. (1823, private), p. 157; 63 sess., 2 sit. (1839), p. 131.

[61] E.g., *N. J. Laws,* 1855, Ch. 250, p. 728; 1871, Ch. 124, p. 549, Ch. 502, p. 1296.

[62] E.g., *N. J. Laws,* 61 sess., 2 sit. (1837), pp. 203, 215, 254, 413. The periods of suspension permitted ranged from seven days to three months.

[63] E.g., *N. J. Laws,* 52 sess., 2 sit. (1828), p. 128; 60 sess., 2 sit. (1836), p. 153. It became necessary for the legislature to suspend the operation of all the redemption rules in times of general financial crises. All such provisions then in force were suspended after November 1837 for several months unless the governor sooner proclaimed that the majority of banks in New York City and Philadelphia had resumed payments. *Ibid.,* 62 sess., 1 sit. (1837), p. 9. The suspension period was later extended indefinitely until the majority of New York City and Philadelphia banks were paying in specie. *Ibid.,* 62 sess., 2 sit. (1838), p. 244. Similar action was taken in 1862 to be effective for one year. *Ibid.,* 1862, Ch. 147, p. 273. The provisions of that law were extended indefinitely in 1863. *Ibid.,* 1863, Ch. 102, p. 195.

some form of periodic report to the legislature or to an agency of the state government. The reports were intended in some instances to be of assistance in regulating tolls,[64] in many to provide information about the cost of construction and revenues and operating expenses of public utility properties which the state had reserved the right to purchase,[65] in some to be used in connection with tax levies,[66] and in others to afford the legislators some knowledge of the condition of the reporting business units.[67] The general banking law, the general incorporation law for plank road companies, two general laws for land and building associations, the general incorporation law for insurance companies, and the general railroad law also provided for periodic reports from the companies organized under their authority.[68]

In most cases, no severe penalties were threatened for failure to submit reports, and probably the reports were frequently not filed. It was considered important, however, that the commercial banks report regularly. After 1823, virtually every bank was required to make periodic reports. In contrast to the other cases, the banks were generally subject to the loss of their charters if the required reports were overlooked. Frequently the bank charters were declared void only after the reports had been omitted for a period of two or three years,[69] but in a few cases the charters were declared to be forfeited for any

[64] This group included early bridge and turnpike companies. E.g., *N. J. Laws,* 19 sess., 2 sit. (1795), Ch. 554, p. 1067; 25 sess., 2 sit. (1801), Ch. 38, p. 80.

[65] This group included most turnpike companies chartered before 1830, many canal and most railroad companies. E.g., *N. J. Laws,* 29 sess., 1 sit. (1804), Ch. 137, p. 382; 49 sess., 1 sit. (1824), p. 175. A law of general application was enacted in 1852 requiring annual statements from all railroad and canal companies. *Ibid.,* 1852, Ch. 40, p. 82.

[66] The principal representatives of this group were railroad and canal companies. E.g., *N. J. Laws,* 54 sess., 2 sit. (1830), pp. 73, 83; 68 sess., 2 sit. (1844), p. 222.

[67] Commercial banks and savings institutions can be included in this group. E.g., *N. J. Laws,* 49 sess., 1 sit. (1824), p. 35; 52 sess., 2 sit. (1828), p. 76. In 1852, all insurance companies doing business in New Jersey, whether New Jersey or foreign corporations, were required to file annual financial reports. *Ibid.,* 1852, Ch. 79, p. 174.

[68] *N. J. Laws,* 1850, p. 140; 1852, Ch. 41, p. 83, Ch. 51, p. 95, Ch. 74, p. 159; 1865, Ch. 379, p. 707; 1873, Ch. 413, p. 88.

[69] E.g., *N. J. Laws,* 49 sess., 1 sit. (1824), p. 35; 1855, Ch. 190, p. 519.

failure to report as required.[70] In addition to the banking companies, one manufacturing corporation and one land improvement company were to forfeit their charters for failure to submit the reports required by the terms of their charters.[71]

It was common practice in New Jersey to include in special acts of incorporation a clause forbidding companies from conducting any type of business other than that clearly contemplated by their charters. Two charters of 1811 imposed the penalty of forfeiture in the event that the companies attempted to enter into fields of business not expressly permitted to them.[72] For about twenty-five years after 1830, the legislators wrote into many charters a similar penalty for engaging in unauthorized activities.[73]

Some corporations were granted the valuable banking privilege on the condition that they also engage in some other type of business. In a few of these cases the charters were to be forfeited unless the non-banking activities were undertaken within a stated time.[74] There was one further instance in which the legislature sought to control the future actions of a corporation by providing for charter forfeiture if certain conditions were not fulfilled. This was the case of a railroad charter that was declared to be void if the route as finally established failed to run close to certain designated towns.[75]

A far more flexible form of state control over corporations, and one that was gradually substituted for the controls previously discussed, was the reservation by the legislature of the right to alter, amend, or repeal charters. The advantages of this type of control are obvious. It was impossible for legislators to

[70] E.g., *N. J. Laws,* 1849, p. 13.

[71] *N. J. Laws,* 49 sess., 1 sit. (1824), p. 64; 61 sess., 2 sit. (1837), p. 443.

[72] *N. J. Laws,* 35 sess., 2 sit. (1811), p. 349; 36 sess., 1 sit. (1811), p. 23.

[73] E.g., *N. J. Laws,* 55 sess., 2 sit. (1831), p. 66; 58 sess., 2 sit. (1834), pp. 41, 47, 55.

[74] The charter of the Salem Steam-Mill and Banking Company, for example, was void if at least four pairs of millstones were not actually in operation within two years after the capital stock was subscribed. *N. J. Laws,* 47 sess., 1 sit. (1822, private), p. 48. The Commercial Bank of New-Jersey was to forfeit its charter unless a designated part of the capital stock was used to establish a fishing business to operate from the port of Perth Amboy within two years. *Ibid.,* 47 sess., 1 sit. (1822, private), p. 70.

[75] *N. J. Laws,* 1851, p. 78.

foresee all the problems that might arise in connection with any charter or to prophesy what restrictions might be rendered desirable in the future by changing economic and social conditions. If the legislature could modify or repeal a charter at will, it had continuing power to control its corporations in accord with revised notions of good public policy.

It is well known that until the United States Supreme Court gave a negative answer in the celebrated Dartmouth College decision in 1819, it was not definitely settled whether a state legislature could repeal or alter a corporate charter at will. It is less well known, however, that for many years previous to this decision, acts of incorporation had been widely held to be irrepealable contracts unless the power to repeal them had been expressly reserved.[76]

The earliest expression of opinion on the subject appearing in the published documents of New Jersey came from an assembly committee to which had been referred a petition requesting a law to prevent banks from issuing notes in small denominations. The committee's report made in 1806 declared

> That in the opinion of the committee the constitution of this state will not justify any measure which will go to destroy a charter right which has been granted to an incorporate body for a term of years without their consent; and even if such power had been reserved to this house by the acts of incorporation, the committee conceive it would not be good policy at this time to prohibit the banks of this state from issuing any notes of a smaller denomination than five dollars. . .[77]

In 1808, another assembly committee upheld the principle of the inviolability of charters. The committee reported as follows against a proposal to amend a turnpike company's charter:

[76] J. S. Davis, *Essays in the Earlier History of American Corporations,* II, 106, 310–316, outlines the debates on this point that occurred in several states during the eighteenth century and cites certain Connecticut charters, one enacted as early as 1789, in which the power of repeal or alteration was reserved. Shaw Livermore, *Early American Land Companies,* p. 260, states: "Advance reservation of the right to amend or repeal a charter thus antedated by a generation the doctrine of the Dartmouth College case."

[77] *Votes and Proceedings of the General Assembly,* 30 sess., 2 sit. (1806), p. 537. The bill was not passed.

> That in the opinion of the committee, the application of the memorialists is founded on a principle which ought never to be sanctioned by this house, namely, that the legislature have a right at their pleasure to alter and abridge any corporate body, of privileges previously granted, without their approbation or consent; a principle which if once acted upon by this house, would establish a precedent of very dangerous tendency, inasmuch as it would render insecure the chartered rights of every corporation in the state, and open a door for the most gross violations of public faith.[78]

A discussion over the right of the legislature to alter corporate charters flared up again in 1814. In that year, a bill was introduced in the legislature to force existing turnpike companies to open their gates without payment of toll if their roads were not in repair. Opponents of the measure declared it was against the constitution of the United States and the law of contracts. The principal speaker against the bill declared that the legislature could not destroy vested rights unless power to do so had been reserved in the charters, and he promised to take a "stand in favour of all incorporated bodies in this state" on that "solid ground." The same speaker thought that if this constitutional barrier was broken down the rights of corporations would never be secure and a "deadly blow" would be aimed at the enterprise and prosperity of the community. He concluded that since a contract was involved, any question over a company's fulfilling the contract should be made a matter for court action. Another speaker upheld the contract theory even though the state, like an individual, might easily make a bad bargain. The principal argument of those who favored the bill was that what one legislature could give another could take away. One declared that if the contract theory proved correct he would be more careful in the future in agreeing to corporations taking away *"the rights of the people."* [79]

A bill came before the assembly in 1817 that was designed to lay down rules regarding the election of bank directors and to impose certain liabilities on bank directors who declared dividends in the event that their institutions refused to redeem

[78] *Ibid.*, 33 sess., 1 sit. (1808), p. 43.
[79] The debate was fully reported in the *Trenton Federalist*, February 7, 1814.

their notes in specie once the banks of New York City and Philadelphia had resumed payments. Again it was objected that "the Legislature had no right to prescribe new conditions or regulations to bodies corporate, already created, without their consent . . ." One speaker declared that if there was a question of abuses or unlawful acts the judiciary should deal with it, and he suggested that although past legislative actions could not be changed, the lawmakers should be more careful in drawing up charters in the future. A speaker on the other side took the position that a general complaint was a subject for legislation without any petition from the banks themselves, and he "denied that these corporations, or any bodies corporate, possessed that high degree of inviolability, in the exercise of their corporate powers . . ." The same assemblyman thought that abuse of corporate powers should be subject to correction in America as in England and that a legislature had power "even to make void a charter of a body corporate under certain circumstances." [80]

An even more interesting debate occurred in the assembly early in 1819, the very year of the Dartmouth College decision. A turnpike company had been granted a supplement to its charter giving it power to erect a tollgate on a public road, and a bill for repeal of the supplement had been introduced. The supporters of the repeal bill said that the supplement had been obtained by "collusion, surprise or fraud, and [that the power it gave was one] which the legislature did not intend to grant . . ." The speaker of the assembly voted for the repeal with the explanation that "he considered the privileges granted in the supplement, as matters of favor, and therefore could, with propriety be resumed, or taken back, by the legislature . . ." The opponents of repeal argued in favor of the questioned supplement "as it granted charter rights and privileges, and was of the nature of a contract the Legislature could not repeal it; that if the supplement had been prosecuted by fraud, which was denied, (but rather through haste and inat-

[80] *Trenton Federalist,* February 3, 1817. The bill was finally indefinitely postponed. *True American,* February 10, 1817. It is interesting to recall that four years later when the next banks were chartered, provisions regulating the conduct of suspended banks under penalty of forfeiting their charters were included for the first time. Cf. *supra,* p. 373.

tention in the Legislature) the house was not a proper court to try the matter, and being a part in the contract could not lawfully and fairly decide thereon." [81]

Thus the doctrine that corporate charters were not subject to alteration or repeal at the discretion of the legislature was widely enough accepted in New Jersey during the first two decades of the nineteenth century to cause the defeat of several attempts to rescind or alter corporate privileges once they had been granted. The increasing acceptance of the contract theory undoubtedly explains why the legislature began after 1800 to grant corporate privileges only for definite periods, but it is surprising that the power to alter or repeal was so seldom reserved in charters before 1823. Before that date, the legislature had reserved the repeal power only in two charter supplements, and in those cases the power was very restricted in scope. A supplement of 1808 permitting a particular bank to issue notes in small denominations reserved to the legislature the right to reënact the original charter prohibition against such notes whenever the "public good" required.[82] Another supplement, enacted in 1813, gave the six "state" banks the right to issue notes of smaller denomination than those allowed by their charters, but with the proviso that the legislature "hereby reserve to themselves the right of repealing this supplement, whenever in their opinion the public good may require it." [83] The legislature had also reserved the right to alter legal rates of toll in two charters passed before 1823. The first case occurred in the charter of an inland waterway company passed in 1796. Maximum legal rates of toll were established by the charter, but they were "subject nevertheless to be regulated by the legislature . . . at least once in every fifty years." [84] The 1818 charter of a ferry company reserved to the legislature the right to alter the rates of toll at any time.[85]

Even after the Dartmouth College decision had definitely established the doctrine of the inviolability of corporate charters,

[81] *True American,* February 1, 1819. The repeal bill was defeated in the assembly by a vote of twenty-four to sixteen.
[82] *N. J. Laws,* 33 sess., 1 sit. (1808), Ch. 6, p. 11.
[83] *N. J. Laws,* 38 sess., 1 sit. (1813, public), p. 59.
[84] *N. J. Laws,* 20 sess., 2 sit. (1796), Ch. 586, p. 57.
[85] *N. J. Laws,* 42 sess., 2 sit. (1818, private), p. 88.

the New Jersey legislators did not immediately change their established policy and make charters subject to repeal. There is some evidence, however, that attempts were soon made by some legislators to reserve the right of amendment or repeal in charters, but the attempts were successfully resisted by those who sought acts of incorporation. As early as 1821, an assembly committee wrote into the charter of a manufacturing company a provision that the legislature might alter or repeal the act. By a vote of twenty-four to sixteen, the bill was recommitted for the express purpose of striking out this provision. The committee then reported the bill without any provision for amendment or repeal.[86]

Thus the first charter subject to repeal was one enacted in 1823 for a mutual fire insurance company wherein the legislature reserved the right of repeal in case they thought the grant "injurious to the public welfare." [87] During the succeeding decade, however, the legislators did not demonstrate any firm resolution to grant only repealable charters. Of the 130 charters enacted by the legislature from the session of 1824–25 to the session of 1834–35, inclusive, 54 were not subject to alteration or repeal, while some degree of continuing power was reserved by the lawmakers in the remaining 76. For a time, the legislature vacillated in its policy from year to year. For example, clauses providing for amendment or repeal were put into more than one-half the charters granted during the 1824–25 session, but the next legislature failed to include such clauses in any of its charters. Legislative policy was fairly well settled, however, by 1833, and the legislatures of 1833–34 and 1834–35 passed only one charter each in which the right of amendment or repeal was not included.[88] Whether or not the power to alter or repeal was included in a charter seems to have depended more upon the influence of individual applicants rather than upon the type of business for which an act of incorporation was sought. It is noteworthy, however, that all but one of the bank charters granted during the decade were made subject to altera-

[86] *True American,* November 17, 1821. The charter as finally passed was not subject to alteration or repeal. *N. J. Laws,* 46 sess., 1 sit. (1821, private), p. 26.

[87] *N. J. Laws,* 48 sess., 1 sit. (1823, private), p. 163.

[88] *N. J. Laws,* 58 sess., 2 sit. (1834), p. 133; 59 sess., 2 sit. (1835), p. 47.

tion or repeal and that all but 2 of the railroads chartered were free from legislative interference.

It is interesting to note that many of the clauses providing for amendment or repeal that were inserted in charters between 1826 and 1835 were strictly qualified. In the case of four manufacturing concerns, the legislature's reserved power could be exercised only if the companies violated or departed from the provisions of their charters.[89] Three other charters could be amended or repealed only for "good" or "just" cause.[90] The charter of one manufacturing company could be amended or repealed only after fifteen years, and then only for "just" cause.[91] In three cases, the legislators merely reserved the right to change the tolls allowed, and even this restricted power could be exercised only under certain conditions.[92]

A definite policy of making every charter subject at least to amendment was inaugurated by the legislature of 1835–36, and during the next ten years the only nonamendable charter granted was one for a small water company.[93] Two circumstances were responsible for this change in policy. In the first place, the legislators had become increasingly conscious of their inability to correct corporate abuses in the absence of power to repeal or amend the charters they granted. There had been, for example, an unfortunate experience in 1828 with the Salem and Philadelphia Manufacturing Company. This company had been chartered in 1825, and, although its charter expressly forbade the exercise of any banking powers, the company issued a number of circulating bills. Members of the assembly thought that the charter should be repealed, but a committee appointed to investigate the matter reported that since no power of repeal had been reserved in the charter, the only course to take, even in the event of clear abuse, was to institute legal proceedings.[94]

[89] *N. J. Laws,* 56 sess., 1 sit. (1831), p. 9; 56 sess., 2 sit. (1832), p. 49; 57 sess., 2 sit. (1833), p. 121; 59 sess., 2 sit. (1835), p. 99.

[90] *N. J. Laws,* 56th sess., 1 sit. (1831), p. 28; 56 sess., 2 sit. (1832), pp. 181, 184.

[91] *N. J. Laws,* 57 sess., 2 sit. (1833), p. 15.

[92] *N. J. Laws,* 51 sess., 1 sit. (1826), p. 81; 52 sess., 2 sit. (1828), pp. 15, 69.

[93] *N. J. Laws,* 1845, p. 258.

[94] The report read in part: "Upon looking into the act, no power is reserved, in express terms, in the Legislature, to repeal the charter, in case of its abuse; and according to the opinion of the Attorney General, contained in his report

The legislature then resolved that the attorney general be requested to start legal action against the company with a view to forfeiting the charter.[95]

More important, perhaps, than the lessons of experience in bringing about a change in policy was the Democratic campaign that got under way in New Jersey in about 1835 to see that corporations were held more strictly accountable to the public. The Democratic press was loud in its praise of the legislature of 1835–36, the first one to make all the charters it granted subject to amendment. The result of this policy, it was claimed, would be to put a "check" on corporations if they fell into bad hands, for they would be unlikely to venture their very existence on a "course of iniquity." [96] A program for future policy suggested by some Democrats in 1836 included a proposal to make the right of alteration or repeal an "inseparable reservation" in every charter so that the people might have a remedy against corporate abuse.[97]

The legislature showed less inclination to establish a definite policy of reserving the right of amendment or repeal in acts extending the lives or increasing the powers of existing corporations. In the important case of banks, the treatment was relatively uniform. Although in earlier years most efforts to reserve the right of repeal in supplements extending bank charters failed,[98] bank charters were extended after 1834 only with the express understanding that future legislatures could alter or repeal either the supplements or the original charters.[99] Supple-

at the last session, on the subject of the Jersey Bank and others, the right to repeal in such case, by an act of the Legislature seems to be questioned, and at all events, he recommends in such case, that legal proceedings be adopted in the Supreme Court." *Votes and Proceedings of the General Assembly,* 53 sess., 1 sit. (1828), p. 70.

[95] *N. J. Laws,* 53 sess., 1 sit. (1828), Joint Resolution, pp. 137–38.

[96] *Emporium and True American,* April 2, 1836.

[97] *Ibid.,* December 24, 1836. The policy actually adopted by the legislature was not quite uniform in its application, for nearly every railroad charter granted between 1835 and 1845 and the charters of a few other corporations merely reserved the right to "alter, amend, or modify" without expressly mentioning the power to repeal. E.g., *N. J. Laws,* 60 sess., 2 sit. (1836), p. 226.

[98] For an example see *Journal of the Legislative Council,* 56 sess., 2 sit. (1832), pp. 126–27.

[99] E.g., *N. J. Laws,* 65 sess., 2 sit. (1841), pp. 54, 59.

ments enacted for other types of business corporations, however, showed less uniformity in this particular.[100]

It will be recalled that in 1844 the New Jersey constitutional convention had turned down a proposal to require the legislature to make all future charters subject to amendment and repeal.[101] In 1846, however, the legislature enacted, without apparent opposition, the general regulating law for corporations which contained among its provisions the following clause:

> That the charter of every corporation which shall hereafter be granted by the legislature, shall be subject to alteration, suspension, and repeal, in the discretion of the legislature.[102]

Possibly the legislators thought the provision would apply only to charters that were made expressly subject to the general regulating act, but the courts subsequently took the opposite position. In cases concerning the status of post-1846 charters, it was ultimately held by the New Jersey courts that every charter passed after 1846 could be amended or repealed unless it contained definite language to the contrary. Thus in 1863 the chancery court, in a case involving a charter that had not been expressly declared to be subject to the 1846 regulating act, held that the effect of the 1846 law was to make all charters passed while it was in force subject to alteration and repeal as fully as if language to that effect had been included in every charter.[103] The same position was taken by the state supreme court in a case decided in 1866.[104] This doctrine was further strengthened in 1874 when the state supreme court held that an act of 1865

[100] Attempts were sometimes made in vain to reserve the power of repeal or amendment at a time when new privileges were about to be added to irrepealable charters. Thus when a railroad was given generous new powers by a supplementary act in 1835, the assembly voted down a motion to make the supplement subject to repeal or amendment. *Votes and Proceedings of the General Assembly,* 59 sess., 2 sit. (1835), p. 465. Jonathan Pickel, in 1844, tried to add a similar stipulation to a supplement that increased the list of goods that could be made by a certain manufacturing corporation. *Ibid.,* 68 sess., 2 sit. (1844), pp. 350, 356.

[101] Cf. *supra,* pp. 93–97.

[102] *N. J. Laws,* 1846, p. 16.

[103] *Story* v. *Jersey City and Bergen Point Plank Road Company,* 16 New Jersey Equity, 13 (1863).

[104] *The State, The Warren Railroad Company* v. *Person,* 32 New Jersey Law, 134 (1866).

authorizing the construction of a railroad branch line and giving the branch special tax status could be repealed even though it was merely a supplement to a charter. The court decided that every franchise granted to a corporation was equivalent to a charter and declared:

> The sixth section of the corporation act is a general provision, applicable to all grants of franchises to corporations thereafter made. The object the legislature had in view in its adoption was to retain control over legislative grants, that rights hastily granted, and without consideration, might be resumed when found to be impolitic . . . Its provisions became incorporated into every grant of that kind subsequently made, unless the contrary intent clearly appears.[105]

Thus the general regulating act of 1846 had the effect of making all charters and charter supplements passed after that date automatically subject to alteration or repeal.[106] The continuing control that the legislature henceforth held over the majority of its corporations was of great significance. It was to prove particularly valuable when the legislature decided to impose uniform regulations on banks and a system of uniform taxation on railroads.

At no time, however, does the legislature appear to have made significant use of the repealing power reserved in many charters passed before 1846 and in all passed after that date. When bank charters or the banking privileges of other corporations were repealed at various times, the institutions involved appear to have been already insolvent,[107] and one manufacturing company dissolved by formal legislative action was insolvent and had discontinued business.[108] The prevailing attitude

[105] *The State, The Morris and Essex Railroad Company* v. *Commissioner of Railroad Taxation,* 37 New Jersey Law, 238–39 (1874).

[106] A few curious exceptions appear among the charter supplements. For instance, an act of 1853 reviving a railroad charter originally enacted in 1837 expressly repealed a section in the original charter that had reserved the right of alteration or amendment. *N. J. Laws,* 1853, Ch. 110, p. 276. There was also a case in 1866 when a supplement to an 1845 gas company charter repealed a similar reservation that had been included in the original charter. *Ibid.,* 1866, Ch. 172, p. 407.

[107] E.g., *N. J. Laws,* 67 sess., 2 sit. (1843), p. 81; 1847, p. 43.

[108] *N. J. Laws,* 1860, Ch. 106, p. 246.

on the question of repealing charters was expressed in the 1841 report of a council committee appointed to consider the petition of numerous residents of Hoboken requesting repeal of the charter of the Hoboken Land and Improvement Company. This corporation had been chartered in 1838 for ninety-nine years and the right of repeal had been reserved in its charter.[109] The committee's report expressed the view

> That legislative action ought not further to be had on the subject, and that any interference by the legislature at this time would be a violation of public and of private faith, an invasion of vested rights, and an injury irreparable to certain of the parties and others, who have relied with confidence upon the certainty of our laws and their administration.[110]

No controversy occurred, however, when in 1858 the legislature declared all charters and charter supplements concerning turnpike companies that had failed to exercise their corporate rights and franchises for the preceding twenty years to be repealed.[111]

In numerous cases, the state reserved for itself or for its political subdivisions the privilege of purchasing the facilities of public utility companies. Reservation of the right to purchase such properties was a partial answer to the many persons who felt that works of public utility should be constructed and operated by the government and not by private companies. In this way the state was able to avoid risking public funds for the construction of projects that might prove impracticable or unprofitable while retaining the power to take ultimate possession of those works that proved successful.

The terms of the first New Jersey bridge company charter, enacted in 1792, gave the legislature the power to declare the bridge free at any time upon reimbursing the stockholders for the amount spent on construction and maintenance.[112] In 1801,

[109] *N. J. Laws,* 62 sess., 2 sit. (1838), p. 92.

[110] *Journal of the Legislative Council,* 65 sess., 2 sit. (1841), p. 245.

[111] *N. J. Laws,* 1858, Ch. 194, p. 460.

[112] *N. J. Laws,* 17 sess., 1 sit. (1792), Ch. 406, p. 806. The amount of the indemnification was to be determined according to the procedure outlined in the charter. In 1818, the legislature responded favorably to a petition from the public asking that the bridge be declared free. *Ibid.,* 42 sess., 2 sit. (1818, public), p. 5.

when the legislators amended the 1798 charter of a Delaware River bridge company to give the company a guarantee that no other bridge would be authorized within a distance of three miles from their bridge, they also provided that New Jersey or Pennsylvania, or both, could purchase the bridge after fifteen years from the time of its completion upon paying the value of the structure as determined by a group of appraisers.[113] Although the state did not reserve the right of purchase in any other bridge charters, it did so in most turnpike company charters passed in the early part of the nineteenth century. In all but six of the thirty-nine charters for turnpike companies granted between the session of 1804–05 and the session of 1815–16, the legislature inserted a clause empowering the state to buy the roads.[114] The time when the state might exercise its right to purchase was generally fifty years after the passage of the acts of incorporation, and the amount of the indemnification was generally established as the sums that had been spent by the companies on their roads.[115] In eleven turnpike charters, however, the cost to the state was to be computed by adding interest at the rate of 12 per cent a year to the amount spent by the companies and subtracting the "neat amount of toll received."[116] In one case, all the profit over 12 per cent was to be paid by the turnpike company to the state and was to be used by the state to extinguish the stock held by the public.[117] After 1816, the state reserved the privilege of purchasing a turnpike in only one instance.[118]

Beginning in 1849, the legislature adopted the policy of including in many charters a clause permitting counties to take

[113] *N. J. Laws,* 25 sess., 2 sit. (1801), Ch. 26, p. 58. The appraisers were to be appointed by the supreme court of New York State.

[114] Of the six charters where no right to purchase was reserved, five were limited to fifty years duration.

[115] E.g., *N. J. Laws,* 32 sess., 1 sit. (1807), Ch. 6, p. 26; 34 sess., 1 sit. (1809), Ch. 40, p. 141.

[116] E.g., *N. J. Laws,* 30 sess., 2 sit. (1806). Ch. 186, p. 526; 40 sess., 2 sit. (1816, private), p. 130.

[117] *N. J. Laws,* 29 sess., 1 sit. (1804), Ch. 151, p. 419.

[118] *N. J. Laws,* 52 sess., 2 sit. (1828), p. 25. The state could not purchase this turnpike until the end of ninety-nine years and was required to pay the amount spent by the company and 12 per cent a year, deducting the amount of tolls collected.

over turnpike roads located in their territory. Twenty-nine turnpike company charters and two charters for plank road companies enacted between 1849 and 1858 made some such provision. The county freeholders were authorized to pay the cost of the roads at any time and make them free of toll.[119] The 1852 general incorporation law for plank roads contained a similar provision affecting all companies organized under its authority.[120]

In five charters passed between 1820 and 1830 and in one enacted in 1869, the state reserved the privilege of purchasing canal properties. Before taking the canals, the state had to wait for designated periods, varying from twenty to ninety-nine years.[121] The indemnification to stockholders was to be determined with reference solely to the original cost,[122] except in one case where an additional amount was to be paid if that was necessary to afford the proprietors an average annual return of 12 per cent on their expenditures.[123]

During the era of railroad building, the legislature saw fit to reserve in many railroad charters the right to assume ownership of the roads. Between 1830 and 1873, clauses providing for state purchase were included in the charters of 104 steam and 4 horse railroad companies. In every instance, the state's right to purchase was not to be exercised until the end of a definite time, periods of 30, 35, and 50 years being most commonly specified.[124] In most of the cases where the state reserved the

[119] E.g., *N. J. Laws*, 1849, p. 133; 1854, Ch. 25, p. 51. In one case the county was to pay the cost of the road plus 6 per cent if that much had not been realized from the profits. *Ibid.*, 1852, Ch. 147, p. 328.

[120] *N. J. Laws*, 1852, Ch. 51, p. 95.

[121] In the case of the Morris Canal, if the state did not act within one year after the expiration of ninety-nine years, the charter was to continue for fifty more years, at the end of which time the works were to become the property of the state. *N. J. Laws*, 49 sess., 1 sit. (1824), p. 158. The thirty-year period established in the 1830 charter of the Delaware and Raritan Canal was extended in 1831 to fifty years on condition that the canal be constructed with a channel of specified dimensions. *Ibid.*, 55 sess., 2 sit. (1831). p. 64.

[122] E.g., *N. J. Laws*, 47 sess., 1 sit. (1822, private), p. 80; 49 sess., 1 sit. (1824), p. 175.

[123] *N. J. Laws*, 44 sess., 2 sit. (1820, public), p. 55.

[124] E.g., *N. J. Laws*, 60 sess., 2 sit. (1836), p. 245; 1848, p. 230; 1866, Ch. 486, p. 1068. In most cases the time was to be computed from the date of completion of the roads but in some from the date of the act of incorporation.

right to purchase railroad properties, the charters established procedures for the appointment of commissioners to determine the sums to be paid to the companies in the event that the state decided to purchase. The commissioners were generally instructed to consider only the original or "first" cost of the railroads in making their appraisals.[125] In a very few cases, however, the amount to be paid by the state was not restricted to the original cost but was to be determined by the "value" of the property.[126] In spite of the fact that such a large number of railroad charters provided for purchase of the roads by the state, the state government did not see fit to exercise its options. By the eighteen seventies, there was little expectation that the state would go into the railroad business, and the 1873 general law for railroads made no provision for state purchase of the roads organized under its authority.

A few miscellaneous instances in which charters of incorporation provided for state or municipal purchase of the corporate property remain to be mentioned. The 1865 charter of an ocean steamship company made provision for the purchase of the company's property by the state at a price to be established by commissioners appointed at any time after fifty years from the "completion" of the steamship line.[127] The property of a Delaware River bridge company that was chartered in 1869 could be purchased by the cities of Camden and Philadelphia after twenty years from the completion of the bridge if the cities paid the full cost of the structure.[128] Two charters of companies for the purpose of supplying water in Bordentown stipulated that the properties could be purchased by the borough of Bordentown after twenty years from the acts of incorporation if the companies were paid for their works at the original cost.[129]

[125] The following was a common form of statement: ". . . the aforesaid valuation shall be made without reference to the receipts or disbursements of the company, or advance of the stock, and the said valuation shall in no case exceed the first cost of the said rail road with the lands and appendages thereof." *N. J. Laws*, 55 sess., 2 sit. (1831), p. 24.

[126] E.g., *N. J. Laws*, 1851, p. 78.

[127] *N. J. Laws*, 1865, Ch. 446, p. 800.

[128] *N. J. Laws*, 1869, Ch. 121, p. 294.

[129] *N. J. Laws*, 59 sess., 2 sit. (1835), p. 47; 1849, p. 286.

CHAPTER XIII

Taxation

By the end of the nineteenth century, New Jersey had made itself nationally conspicuous because of its "liberal" corporation laws that were designed to attract companies from all over the country to file their certificates of incorporation at Trenton, and a large share of the public revenue of New Jersey was derived at that time from the incorporation fees and franchise taxes paid by companies incorporated in the state. The notion that business corporations might be made to provide the principal financial support of the state government was not, however, suddenly conceived by the lawmakers at the end of the eighteen hundreds, but had its roots deep in the state's financial experience throughout the whole of that century. The present chapter will present the significant facts concerning the relationship of New Jersey's corporation policy to the state revenues before 1875.

During the eighteenth century and the early part of the nineteenth century, no generally applicable principles or rules were developed in New Jersey to govern the taxation of ordinary business corporations, and most of the state's corporations paid their real estate and other taxes to local tax authorities in the same manner as individuals and unincorporated concerns. There were, nevertheless, certain types of business corporations that were singled out during the first half of the nineteenth century for special treatment in the matter of taxation. The principal representatives of the groups to which special rules of taxation were applied were commercial banks, insurance companies, canal and railroad corporations, and a few early telegraph companies.

It was in connection with bank charters that the New Jersey

lawmakers first realized how they might use their power to grant corporate charters in a way that would provide funds for the state treasury. This fact is not surprising, for the banking and note issuing privilege was the most valuable franchise the legislature had to offer during the early years of the nineteenth century. When New Jersey's first bank, the Newark Banking and Insurance Company, was chartered in 1804, the state reserved the right to subscribe to $25,000 of the capital stock within a limited period.[1] Rather than invest state funds in the stock of the bank, the legislators preferred instead to realize an immediate revenue from the state's subscription rights. Accordingly, the governor was authorized to exercise the right to subscribe to the stock when he had found persons who would agree to purchase the shares from the state for an amount equal at least to the current market.[2] Subsequent legislatures reserved to the state the right to subscribe to the stock of several other early banks and then sold the rights to provide funds for the state treasury. In the case of the Jersey Bank, the rights were ordered sold for $4,000.[3] The rights to subscribe to the stock of the New Brunswick bank were to be sold for a price that would yield at least $12 on each share to which the state was entitled to subscribe.[4] The subscription rights in the six "state" banks were to be sold for not less than designated amounts that ranged between $20,000 and $1,000 depending upon the bank involved.[5]

In two 1815 bank charters, the legislature not only reserved the right to subscribe to certain amounts of stock but in addition required "bonus" payments to be made into the state treasury as "consideration" for granting the charters. The amount of the "bonus" was $3,500 in one case and $6,000 in

[1] *N. J. Laws,* 28 sess., 2 sit. (1804), Ch. 109, p. 268.
[2] *N. J. Laws,* 29 sess., 1 sit. (1804), Ch. 165, p. 482.
[3] *N. J. Laws,* 32 sess., 1 sit. (1807), Ch. 26, p. 73.
[4] *N. J. Laws,* 34 sess., 1 sit. (1809), Ch. 54, p. 203.
[5] *N. J. Laws,* 37 sess., 2 sit. (1813, public), p. 19. The minimum selling prices came to a total of $30,000. Any person who bought the rights to subscribe to stock of the Camden bank for $20,000 was to agree to pay the state an additional $12,000 at the end of ten years if no other bank had been established in Gloucester County by that time. This provision was repealed later in the session, and the minimum selling price of the rights was raised to $25,000. *Ibid.,* p. 37.

the other.[6] For the next decade, the lawmakers demanded "bonus" payments in return for most of the bank charters they granted. A bank chartered in 1816 had to pay $2,000 in the form of forty full shares of stock issued in the name of the state as soon as it commenced business and was required to make a similar payment to the state when its whole capital had been subscribed.[7] One of the banks chartered in 1818 was to turn over to the state $1,000 worth of capital stock when its banking operations were begun and an additional $1,000 in stock when the whole amount of its capital stock had been issued.[8] In 1823, a bank was required to pay the state a "bonus" of $4,000 for its charter.[9] "Bonus" taxes were also imposed on five banks chartered in 1824. One of these banks had to pay $4,000 to the school fund, two were required to make payments of $25,000 each, another was to pay $5,000 and an additional $3,750 if the capital was later increased, and the final one had to pay an amount equal to 2 per cent of its capital.[10] The system of imposing "bonus" taxes in consideration for bank charters was discontinued after 1824.[11]

Proposals to levy an annual tax on bank capital were advanced in New Jersey in the early years of the nineteenth century. A bill designed to place a special tax on bank stock was introduced in the assembly in 1807, but consideration of it was postponed until the following year.[12] In 1808, the bill was defeated in the assembly,[13] and the following year it passed the assembly only to be rejected in the legislative council.[14] Writers in the Federalist press attacked the proposal to levy a special

[6] *N. J. Laws,* 39 sess., 2 sit. (1815, private), pp. 21, 32. In the first case, the legislature also reserved the right to borrow $50,000 for one year at 6 per cent upon giving the bank a thirty-day notice.

[7] *N. J. Laws,* 40 sess., 2 sit. (1816, private), p. 48.

[8] *N. J. Laws,* 42 sess., 2 sit. (1818, private), p. 49.

[9] *N. J. Laws,* 48 sess., 1 sit. (1823, private), p. 157.

[10] *N. J. Laws,* 49 sess., 1 sit. (1824), pp. 35, 99, 105, 118, 140.

[11] A listing of the bonus payments made to the state and of the actual revenue realized from the sale of subscription rights can be found in *Votes and Proceedings of the General Assembly,* 57 sess., 2 sit. (1833), pp. 178–180.

[12] *Ibid.,* 32 sess., 1 sit. (1807), pp. 150, 159.

[13] *Ibid.,* 33 sess., 1 sit. (1808), pp. 70–71.

[14] *Ibid.,* 34 sess., 1 sit. (1809), pp. 278–79; *Journal of the Legislative Council,* 34 sess., 1 sit. (1809), p. 891.

tax on banks as being a plan of the Democrats to raise revenue from *"aristocrats* and *foreigners."* They claimed the scheme was "nothing short of *forcing* the banks to pay *one half* of all the taxes of the State" and that it marked "the commencement, in New-Jersey, of a new system of taxation, levelled at *particular* holders of property, *supposed* to be *rich* and supposed to receive great profit from monied operations . . ." The main argument of the Democrats, on the other hand, was that residents of New York and Philadelphia owned most of the stock of New Jersey banks and that they should pay New Jersey for the protection they received from the state.[15]

In spite of Federalist opposition, the legislature passed a law in 1810 levying an annual tax on the banks equal to one-half of 1 per cent on the "whole amount of capital stock actually subscribed and paid in, and which shall hereafter be subscribed and paid in . . ." [16] Each time a new bank was chartered in subsequent years it was made subject to the tax, and the tax was also made to apply to banks that were organized under the general banking act of 1850. Extravagant expectations as to the revenue that would be derived from the special tax on bank stock were expressed soon after it was imposed. For example, an 1811 petition to the legislature requesting a charter for a bank at New Brunswick pointed out that the "revenue thence arising to the said state, would, in process of time, exonerate the good citizens of the state aforesaid from all taxes for supporting the government thereof . . ." [17] While the tax on banks never justified such optimistic predictions, it did provide a steady flow of income to the state government. After 1828, the revenue it yielded was allocated to the fund created for the support of free schools in New Jersey.[18] The reports of the state treasurer show that the school fund was receiving from the bank stock tax about $23,000 annually by 1837. The receipts

[15] *Trenton Federalist,* November 20, 1809.

[16] *N. J. Laws,* 35 sess., 1 sit. (1810), p. 244.

[17] Manuscript petition, dated 1811, in the collection of the New Jersey State Library.

[18] *N. J. Laws,* 52 sess., 2 sit. (1828), p. 172.

were only about $17,000 annually by 1847, but rose to approximately $31,000 by 1857.[19]

It can be seen from the above recital that the New Jersey lawmakers were not slow to discover the large revenues that could be derived by the state through the "sale" of bank charters. Nor were they slow in making the banks they chartered yield a continuing source of revenue by imposing an annual tax on them. The scheme of providing for the public purse through special levies on banks seemed wise to many Jerseymen because much of the capital stock of New Jersey banks was held by residents of other states.[20] It should also be noted that the action of the legislature in 1815 prohibiting all unincorporated banks was probably prompted by a desire to maintain the high value of bank charters.[21]

Insurance companies were also regarded as appropriate objects of special taxation. A fire insurance company incorporated in 1824 and one incorporated in 1826, the first stock companies chartered in New Jersey for the exclusive purpose of conducting an insurance business, were required to pay annual taxes of one-half of 1 per cent of their capital stock to the state treasurer after they had been in business for three years.[22] Special state taxes of one-quarter of 1 per cent of the capital stock were imposed in fourteen insurance company charters passed between 1831 and 1865.[23] The capital stock taxes on insurance

[19] Unsuccessful attempts were made from time to time to secure a general reduction in the rate of the bank tax. See, for example, *Votes and Proceedings of the General Assembly,* 47 sess., 1 sit. (1822), p. 100; *True American,* November 23, 1822. In 1859, the tax on general-law banks was reduced to one-quarter of 1 per cent in recognition of the fact that their profit opportunities were not equivalent to those of specially chartered banks. *N. J. Laws,* 1859, Ch. 185, p. 535.

[20] See, for example, communications in *True American,* February 28 and July 31, 1824.

[21] Many states during the early nineteenth century derived funds for their public schools through the use of special taxes on banks. Cf. J. A. Muscalus, *The Use of Banking Enterprises in the Financing of Public Education, 1796–1866.*

[22] *N. J. Laws,* 49 sess., 1 sit. (1824), p. 74; 51 sess., 1 sit. (1826), p. 70.

[23] E.g., *N. J. Laws,* 55 sess., 2 sit. (1831), p. 33; 1847, pp. 7, 39. In most cases, the tax was not to apply until three years after the companies had gone into operation.

companies apparently met with resistance, and four companies succeeded in securing amendments to their charters by which the special taxes imposed on them were repealed.[24]

The New Jersey legislators also undertook to levy taxes on the business done in New Jersey by out-of-state insurance companies. A law of 1826 designed to regulate "foreign" insurance companies operating in New Jersey required the New Jersey agents of such companies to file semiannual reports of the insurance premiums they collected and pay "by way of tax for the use of this state" 5 per cent of the gross premiums received.[25] In 1846, the tax was reduced to 2½ per cent.[26] It appears likely that the tax on out-of-state insurance companies was imposed in retaliation for taxes levied by other states on "foreign" companies, and in 1848 the New Jersey legislature declared that the tax was to apply only to the agents of companies chartered by states that taxed the agents of companies chartered by New Jersey.[27] The tax was further reduced to 2 per cent in 1850, and all taxes levied on fire insurance premiums collected in cities or towns where there was a fire department or fire company were to be turned over to the "charitable fund" of the fire department or company.[28]

Beginning in 1860, out-of-state fire insurance companies operating in New Jersey were required to file annual statements to show their "pecuniary condition." The companies were to pay $20 for each annual statement they filed and $5 for each "certificate of authority" to open an agency in New Jersey for one year.[29] The law relative to taxes on foreign insurance companies was further amended in 1865 to require a fee of $5 from agents for filing the annual statements of the financial condition of their companies and a $20 fee for a license to act as agent for one year. The license fee was to replace all other taxes on agents of companies chartered by states that did not impose a heavier tax on the agents of New Jersey insurance companies.

[24] *N. J. Laws,* 52 sess., 2 sit. (1828), p. 176; 62 sess., 2 sit. (1838), p. 167; 63 sess., 2 sit. (1839), p. 25.

[25] *N. J. Laws,* 51 sess., 1 sit. (1826), p. 67.

[26] *N. J. Laws,* 1846, p. 4.

[27] *N. J. Laws,* 1848, p. 46. This provision was repealed in 1860. *Ibid.,* 1860, Ch. 23, p. 54.

[28] *N. J. Laws,* 1850, p. 183.

[29] *N. J. Laws,* 1860, Ch. 151, p. 411.

The agents of companies incorporated in states that imposed larger taxes on the agents of New Jersey companies were to continue to pay the tax of 2 per cent on the premiums they collected.[30] In 1867, the law was altered so that each out-of-state company doing business in New Jersey was to pay a $50 license fee and the 2 per cent tax, but life insurance companies from states that did not charge more than $20 for each agent of New Jersey companies could pay a fee of $20 for each agent in lieu of the 2 per cent tax.[31] According to two 1872 amendments to the law, if other states or nations imposed any taxes, fines, penalties, or fees on life or fire insurance companies of New Jersey doing business within their borders, equivalent treatment was to be given the companies of those states or nations doing business in New Jersey.[32]

The reports of the state treasurer show that, beginning in 1867, the taxes on out-of-state insurance companies yielded a modest revenue to the state. The amounts collected in selected years were as follows:

1867	$ 1,991.25
1870	10,818.94
1873	14,232.46
1875	15,540.42

The New Jersey lawmakers also sought a convenient source of revenue in the companies they chartered to construct the transportation facilities of the state, and it was here that they achieved their greatest success. During the early years of the nineteenth century, it was sometimes suggested that turnpike companies should pay some form of tax on their capital stock. When one such proposal was before the assembly in 1811, the committee appointed to investigate the matter reported that

[30] *N. J. Laws,* 1865, Ch. 420, p. 767. The preamble stated that the law relative to taxes on the insurance companies of other states needed clarification and that New Jersey companies should "be entitled in other states to the benefits of reciprocal laws . . ."

[31] *N. J. Laws,* 1867, Ch. 337, p. 776.

[32] *N. J. Laws,* 1872, Ch. 10, p. 8, Ch. 133, p. 25. These acts did not repeal the fees and taxes regularly required by New Jersey of all "foreign" insurance companies.

"taking into view the unproductive nature of said stock at this time, they deem it inexpedient to report a bill for levying a tax." [33] Since money invested in turnpikes seldom yielded a large return, turnpike companies were never made the objects of special taxation in New Jersey. The 1820 charter of the unsuccessful New-Jersey Delaware and Raritan Canal Company exempted the corporation from all state or local taxes on the property actually used for canal purposes. At the same time, however, the charter provided that if, after twenty-one years from the date of incorporation, the net proceeds at any time exceeded 15 per cent a year on the capital stock the company should pay the state an annual tax equal to one-fifteenth of its profit.[34] The Orange and Sussex Canal Company of 1823 and the Morris Canal and Banking Company and the Delaware and Raritan Canal Company of 1824 enjoyed unconditional immunity from taxes on their canal property.[35] In view of the value of its franchise, however, the Delaware and Raritan company was to pay the state a "bonus" of $100,000 as partial consideration for the grant. It was also to reserve for the state the right to subscribe to one-fourth of its capital stock until a certain time after Pennsylvania should agree to the company's using water from the Delaware River. Although the large "bonus" was paid to New Jersey's treasurer, the company failed to secure the necessary water privileges from Pennsylvania, and they petitioned the New Jersey legislature to refund the $100,000. In 1826, the legislature agreed to return $90,000 to the company,[36] and later the remaining $10,000 was refunded.[37]

The Delaware and Raritan Canal Company and the Camden and Amboy Rail Road and Transportation Company, the companies that finally succeeded in constructing the major transportation arteries across the state on the New York to Philadelphia route, were chartered by the New Jersey legislature in

[33] *Votes and Proceedings of the General Assembly,* 35 sess., 2 sit. (1811), p. 553.

[34] *N. J. Laws,* 44 sess., 2 sit. (1820, public), p. 55.

[35] *N. J. Laws,* 48 sess., 1 sit. (1823, private), p. 166; 49 sess., 1 sit. (1824), pp. 158, 175.

[36] *N. J. Laws,* 51 sess., 1 sit. (1826), p. 87.

[37] *N. J. Laws,* 52 sess., 2 sit. (1828), p. 178.

1830.[38] The legislators were fully aware of the value of the franchises they bestowed on these two companies, and they wrote into the charters certain provisions designed to provide the state with revenue in return for the rights granted. Both charters reserved to the state the right to subscribe for one-quarter of the capital stock of the companies. More important, however, were the "transit duties" that the companies were to pay the state in lieu of any other "tax or impost." The canal company was to remit eight cents for every ton of merchandise, except certain low-priced articles on which the tax was two cents per ton, and eight cents for every passenger transported across the state. The railroad company was taxed ten cents per passenger and fifteen cents for each ton of merchandise.

Shortly after the two companies had been chartered, the lawmakers began to grant them increased privileges in return for assurances of greater financial rewards to the state.[39] In 1831, in return for a gift to the state of one thousand shares of stock, the Camden and Amboy received a guarantee that no other railroad would be authorized to transport goods and passengers between New York and Philadelphia unless the state surrendered this stock.[40] In the same year, the canal and railroad companies were united to form the Joint Companies, and in 1832 they received an absolute guarantee of monopoly in the New York to Philadelphia business. The price of the monopoly privilege was the gift of an additional thousand shares of stock to the state and a guarantee that if the state's revenue from dividends and transit duties did not equal at least $30,000 a year, the deficiency would be paid before any dividends went to ordinary stockholders. The express purpose of the legislature was "to secure to the state the aforesaid sum of thirty thousand dollars, at least in each and every year during said charter." [41]

[38] *N. J. Laws,* 54 sess., 2 sit. (1830), pp. 73, 83.

[39] The story of the relationship between the state and the Joint Companies has been told in some detail in Part I of the present study (cf. *supra,* pp. 52–59), and only the significant facts concerning the financial arrangements between them need be mentioned here.

[40] *N. J. Laws,* 55 sess., 2 sit. (1831), p. 74.

[41] *N. J. Laws,* 56 sess., 2 sit. (1832), p. 79.

The tax provisions in other railroad charters did not follow a consistent pattern. The principle of taxing a company according to the amount of traffic on its road was employed in several instances after 1830. Thus, for example, transit duties were to be paid by the West-Jersey Rail Road and Transportation Company of 1831, the Paterson and Ramapo Railroad Company of 1841, and the Hudson and Ramapo Railroad Company of 1844.[42] The 1832 charter of the New Jersey Rail Road and Transportation Company, authorizing construction of a road between New Brunswick and Jersey City, required the payment of transit duties whenever the road should become part of a continuous line across the state.[43] After this road was connected with the Camden and Amboy's Trenton to New Brunswick line in 1839, it became one of the principal payers of transit duties.

A few railroad companies were required to pay annual taxes to the state of one-quarter or one-half of 1 per cent on their paid-in capital stock after designated periods of time. Examples of these were the Paterson and Hudson River Rail Road Company of 1831 and the New Jersey Rail Road and Transportation Company of 1832.[44] The charters of the Paterson and Ramapo Railroad Company and the Hudson and Ramapo Railroad Company that had required the payment of transit duties were amended in 1845 by the substitution of definite taxes on the capital stock for the transit duties.[45]

The great majority of the New Jersey railroads, however, were subject merely to a contingent tax liability that amounted in most cases to virtual immunity from taxation. The actual charter provisions regulating the tax liabilities of the companies in this group varied widely as a few examples will demonstrate. Many companies were to pay to the state annual taxes of one-half of 1 per cent on the "cost" of their roads when the "net proceeds" or "net income" equalled 7 per cent of the cost.[46]

[42] *N. J. Laws,* 55 sess., 2 sit. (1831), p. 95; 65 sess., 2 sit. (1841), p. 97; 68 sess., 2 sit. (1844), p. 97.

[43] *N. J. Laws,* 56 sess., 2 sit. (1832), p. 96.

[44] *N. J. Laws,* 55 sess., 2 sit. (1831), p. 24; 56 sess., 2 sit. (1832), p. 96.

[45] *N. J. Laws,* 1845, pp. 189, 194.

[46] E.g., *N. J. Laws,* 55 sess., 2 sit. (1831), pp. 66, 80; 1851, pp. 78, 201.

In numerous cases, the one-half per cent tax was to be paid when the net proceeds were equal to 6 per cent of the cost.[47] The tax was based in a few instances on the amount of the capital stock rather than upon the cost of the roads.[48] Another variation that was employed in a few railroad charters made the payment of the tax contingent upon the declaration of dividends of a designated amount.[49]

A significant fact concerning the railroads chartered in New Jersey before the eighteen sixties was that most of them were by the terms of their charters exempted from taxes other than those of the types mentioned in the preceding paragraphs. Some charters made it perfectly clear that "no other tax or impost shall be levied or assessed" upon the companies.[50] Other charters were less explicit and provided, for example, that "no other tax or impost for the support of the government of this state shall be levied or assessed," [51] that "no other state tax or impost shall be levied or assessed," [52] or that "no other tax or impost shall be levied or raised . . . by virtue of any law of this state." [53] The important question soon arose as to whether some of the more ambiguous clauses protected the roads from assessment and taxation by local tax authorities, and in several cases tried during the eighteen forties the issue was decided in favor of the railroads and against the local taxing units.[54]

As early as the eighteen thirties, Jerseymen were optimistic about the anticipated results of their plan to derive sufficient revenue from the transportation agencies of the state to pay the annual cost of running the state government. Governor Seeley declared in his message to the legislature in 1833 that "we may with confidence look forward to no very distant period, when the revenue arising from the several great works of internal improvement in our state . . . will be amply sufficient to defray

[47] E.g., *N. J. Laws,* 60 sess., 2 sit. (1836), pp. 60, 86.

[48] E.g., *N. J. Laws,* 1847, p. 98.

[49] E.g., *N. J. Laws,* 1859, Ch. 81, p. 210, Ch. 109, p. 297.

[50] E.g., *N. J. Laws,* 54 sess., 2 sit. (1830), p. 83; 59 sess., 2 sit. (1835), p. 25.

[51] E.g., *N. J. Laws,* 60 sess., 2 sit. (1836), p. 60. [52] E.g., *ibid.,* p. 119.

[53] E.g., *Laws of New Jersey,* 1856, Ch. 162, p. 340.

[54] Cf. P. M. Tuttle, "History of Railroad Taxation in New Jersey" (Harvard University doctoral thesis, typewritten manuscript in New Jersey State Library), pp. 45–46.

all the expenses of government, and enable the legislature to augment the school fund . . ." [55] Governor Dickerson spoke in a similar vein in 1837. In commenting on the companies engaged in constructing internal improvements in the state, he observed that "it is through their agency, that our treasury is supplied with funds, which under proper legislation, must very soon relieve the people from all taxation for the support of the Government of the state." [56]

This optimism was fully justified so far as the financial returns from the companies in the monopoly group were concerned. By 1836, the Joint Companies were contributing more in dividends and transit duties than the $30,000 a year they had guaranteed to the state, and the annual amounts the state received from these companies steadily increased. By the middle of the nineteenth century, the amount collected in the form of transit duties alone made a very substantial contribution to the public purse. The total amounts of transit duties paid to the state for selected years as shown in the reports of the state treasurer were as follows:

1850	$ 66,298.55
1855	115,347.46
1860	152,307.87
1865	307,374.34

These taxes were contributed principally by the Delaware and Raritan Canal Company, the Camden and Amboy Rail Road and Transportation Company, and the New Jersey Rail Road and Transportation Company.

As might have been expected, the companies whose tax liability was contingent on earnings or dividends of a designated amount generally paid nothing into the state treasury. As late as 1854, Governor Fort declared in a message to the legislature that

The general policy heretofore adopted, of requiring railroad companies to pay a tax on their capital stock whenever their earnings

[55] *Votes and Proceedings of the General Assembly*, 58 sess., 1 sit. (1833), p. 8.
[56] *Ibid.*, 61 sess., 2 sit. (1837), p. 129.

enable them to divide a certain per centum, is perfectly nugatory. These maximum dividends, for obvious reasons, are never reached, and the state consequently fails in obtaining her just rights. Nothing has been, or probably will be received for grants of this character, which should honestly yield a large annual revenue. These charters contain a common *proviso,* "that no other tax or impost shall be levied or assessed upon the said company." They thus escape all taxation, even for municipal purposes.[57]

Other persons also frequently commented in the legislature and in the press on the failure of this group of railroad companies to contribute anything in taxes.[58]

Yet the legislators were well satisfied with the returns from the few companies that did pay state taxes. Very soon it became unnecessary for the state to levy direct taxes on its citizens in certain years, as for example in 1837. Between 1834 and 1850, inclusive, the state received an average of 69 per cent of the amount it expended for ordinary state purposes from dividends and taxes on railroads.[59] In addition, there were the substantial transit duties paid by the Delaware and Raritan Canal Company. No direct state taxes were necessary in any year between 1848 and the Civil War period, and afterwards they were required only to meet the extraordinary expenses arising from the war.

In the eighteen sixties, however, the tax provisions included

[57] *Appendix to the House Journal,* 1854, Message of the Governor, p. 12. At the same time, Fort proposed that no railroad charters should be granted unless the companies were made subject to transit duties or to a tax on their capital stock.

[58] E.g., *Newark Daily Advertiser,* February 7, 1851, and January 26, 1855.

[59] Using the annual reports of the state treasurer, P. M. Tuttle (*op. cit.,* p. 40) constructed the following table to show the percentages of railroad taxes and dividends on railroad stock owned by the state to ordinary expenditures for state purposes:

Year ended		*Year ended*	
Oct. 1834	51%	Oct. 1842	54%
Oct. 1835	95	Oct. 1843	74
Oct. 1836	69	Oct. 1844	62
Oct. 1837	58	Jan. 1846	62
Oct. 1838	46	Jan. 1847	67
Oct. 1839	61	Jan. 1848	64
Oct. 1840	79	Jan. 1849	105
Oct. 1841	65	Jan. 1850	93

in many new railroad charters indicated an awareness on the part of the lawmakers of the increasing financial needs of local governmental units. In a number of instances, the companies were to pay the usual one-half of 1 per cent on the cost of their roads when the earnings were sufficient to sustain dividends of designated amounts, but until the companies could pay "regular and successive" dividends their property was to be taxed in the townships in which it was located.[60] Another form of provision appearing in some railroad charters passed during the eighteen sixties clearly foreshadowed the adoption of a general law to govern railroad taxation. In such cases, provision was made not only for the older type of state tax based on the cost of the road or on the capital stock but also for "such other taxes as may be assessed from time to time by a general law applicable to all railroads over which the legislature shall have power for that purpose . . ."[61]

The need for a uniform system of taxation of railroad companies had become evident by the late eighteen sixties. Beginning in 1866, the annual reports of the comptroller of the treasury made frequent reference to the undesirability of deriving most of the state tax revenue from a handful of railroad companies. The comptroller pointed out that railroads with tax liabilities contingent upon a favorable earnings record usually failed to show sufficient earnings to require them to pay a tax. He also remarked on the fact that the charters of such companies failed to specify the manner in which earnings were to be computed and called attention to the fact that the tax was usually based only on "cost of road" to the exclusion of other forms of railroad property.[62] In 1869, Governor Randolph recommended to the legislature that the system of transit duties be abandoned and a uniform railroad tax law be adopted.[63]

The legislature of 1869 repealed the parts of charters providing for the payment of transit duties, but the companies that had been subject to transit duties were to pay one-half of 1

[60] E.g., *N. J. Laws*, 1863, Ch. 187, p. 339.

[61] E.g., *N. J. Laws*, 1867, Ch. 125, p. 215, Ch. 275, p. 590.

[62] Annual reports of the comptroller of the treasury. *Legislative Documents*, 1866, pp. 195–96; 1869, pp. 449–50; 1871, p. 414; 1873, p. 37.

[63] *Votes and Proceedings of the General Assembly*, 1869, pp. 443–44.

per cent on the cost of all their property not otherwise taxed until a general tax law should be passed. Until that time, none was to pay less than it had paid in all taxes and duties in 1868.[64] A uniform tax law for railroad companies was finally passed in 1873. The law established the "cost, equipment and appendages" of the roads as the basis on which the one-half of 1 per cent state tax was to be computed. Local sub-divisions were annually to tax the real property, excluding the main road bed of not over one hundred feet in width and excluding up to ten acres in one parcel at each terminus, at 1 per cent of the valuation. The act also provided for the appointment of a commissioner of railroad taxation who was to make the assessments on property subject to local taxation.[65]

The earliest telegraph companies constituted a final group of corporations that were subject to special tax provisions. The legislature treated very leniently in the matter of taxation some of the telegraph companies incorporated between 1845 and 1855. New Jersey's first telegraph company, chartered in 1845, was exempted from all taxes.[66] The same sweeping immunity from taxation was granted to three other telegraph companies incorporated between that date and 1855.[67] All of these companies, however, were to pay a form of tribute to the state by transmitting free of charge messages relating to the business of the state government and by assisting the police officers of the state through the "transmission of intelligence." [68] The 1851 charter of another telegraph company required the payment of a tax of one-half of 1 per cent on its capital stock to the

[64] *N. J. Laws,* 1869, Ch. 104, p. 226. If a company had a "contract" with the state on the subject of taxes, the act was not to apply in that case until it had been accepted by the board of directors.

[65] *N. J. Laws,* 1873, Ch. 400, p. 112. Provision was made for railroad companies that claimed exemption from taxation to relinquish their claims and accept the terms of the act on the ground that it would be in their interest to do so and avoid public ill will.

[66] *N. J. Laws,* 1845, p. 119.

[67] *N. J. Laws,* 1851, p. 366; 1853, Ch. 99, p. 247; 1855, Ch. 62, p. 139.

[68] For example: "That it shall be the duty of said company, at all times, without charge, on request of any public officer of this state, to transmit (confidentially, if required,) messages relating to the public business thereof; and also at all times to assist the police officers of the state by the transmission of intelligence; and no other tax or duty shall be imposed on said company."

state treasury when the net earnings exceeded 6 per cent on the capital stock. The charter did not state that this was to be an annual tax nor did it grant any exemption from other taxes. The company was also to transmit without charge messages having to do with the state business.[69] Similar provisions were included in the charter of a company incorporated in 1855 to construct a telegraph line between New York and Philadelphia, except that in this case the tax of one-half of 1 per cent on the capital stock was to be paid to the state as soon as the line across New Jersey had been completed.[70] Later telegraph company charters did not contain special tax provisions, but several companies incorporated after 1855 were required to transmit free of charge the official messages of state officers.[71]

Although certain corporations such as commercial banks, insurance companies, railroads and canals, and telegraph companies were frequently subject to special rules of taxation, nothing about the rules of taxation of corporations in general by the local tax authorities appeared in the various general tax statutes of New Jersey until 1851. In recognition of the increasing importance of intangible wealth, an amendment to the general tax law was passed in 1851 for the purpose of reaching the owners of intangible property.[72] The amending act attacked for the first time the problem of local assessments on the individual owners of corporate securities and on property owned by corporations. According to its terms, all land and personal estate, except that specifically exempted, whether owned by individuals or by corporations, was liable to taxation and was to be assessed at the "actual value thereof." Personal property was defined to include, among other things, "debts due from solvent debtors, whether on contract, note, bond, or mortgage" and "stocks in corporations, whether within or without this state." In an effort to avoid double taxation, the legislators exempted from assessment as much "of the property of incorporated companies, represented by the capital stock thereof, as by virtue of this act is taxed in the hands of the stockholders." Finally, the

[69] *N. J. Laws,* 1851, p. 211. [70] *N. J. Laws,* 1855, Ch. 248, p. 724.
[71] E.g., *N. J. Laws,* 1869, Ch. 120, p. 290. [72] *N. J. Laws,* 1851, p. 271.

law established rules for the determination of what tax districts were to assess and tax the property of any particular corporation. The personal estate of a corporation was to be assessed in the township or ward in which the principal office was located, or if there was no principal office or place for transacting the financial affairs of the company then the assessment was to be made in the place where the company's operations were carried on. The real estate liable to taxation was to be assessed in the township or ward in which it lay, "in the same manner as the real estate of individuals."

In similar amendments passed in 1853 and 1854, it was made clear that in exempting from taxation the property of corporations that was taxed in the hands of stockholders the legislature did not intend "to affect in any way the tax required to be paid by banking or other incorporated companies upon the amount of their capital stock, nor to exempt from taxation their real estate, unless so exempt by their charter." [73] Apparently the legislators did not mean to bring railroads under the general tax system by these amendments, and in a series of court decisions the railroads were declared not to be so taxable.[74]

The system of taxing business corporations was changed in 1862 by another amendment to the general tax law.[75] This amendment provided that all private corporations of New Jersey, except those "which by virtue of any irrepealable contract in their charters, or other contracts with this state, are expressly exempted from taxation," were to be "assessed and taxed at the full amount of their capital stock paid in, and accumulated surplus . . ." [76] Corporations without capital stock were to be assessed for "the full amount of their property and valuable assets, without any deduction for debts or liabilities," but, as an offset, depositors in mutual savings banks and persons holding policies in mutual life insurance companies were not to be assessed on their personal estate for their savings bank deposits or for the value of their life insurance policies.

[73] *N. J. Laws,* 1853, Ch. 129, p. 326; 1854, Ch. 113, p. 296.

[74] Cf. Tuttle, pp. 51–54.

[75] *N. J. Laws,* 1862, Ch. 194, p. 344.

[76] The law provided that "any real estate which such corporations may lawfully own in any other state than this state, shall not be liable to be estimated in such accumulated surplus . . ."

As previously, real estate owned by corporations was to be assessed in the township or ward in which the property was located. The additional provision was made, however, that "the amount of such assessment shall be deducted from the amount of the capital stock and surplus and funded debt, or of the valuable assets of the said corporation."

The amendment of 1862 had the effect of throwing the property of railroads, except in the case of roads that were exempted from taxation by virtue of an "irrepealable contract," into the hands of local assessors. When the tax law was rewritten in 1866, the legislature dropped the word "irrepealable" from the act.[77] This change had the effect of returning the railroads to their pre-1862 status, and most roads once again escaped local taxation.[78]

Although the rule as adopted in 1862 of assessing corporations according to the amount of capital stock paid in and accumulated surplus was retained on the statute books, the legislators granted special tax treatment to fourteen manufacturing companies and four other companies of various types incorporated between 1866 and 1873, inclusive. In these cases, the corporations were to be assessed merely on the value of their real and personal property in the same manner as individual persons were assessed rather than on the value of their capital stock and surplus.[79] The right to claim deductions for debts as though the corporations were natural persons was expressly provided in eight of these cases.[80] Five of the companies were granted a further advantage in that their stocks were not to be taxed in the hands of stockholders.[81] The bill to charter the American Eagle Steam Gauge Company, one of the corporations exempt from the general tax rules, came to Governor Randolph in 1869 for his approval. The governor signed the bill but sent a special message to the legislature in which he pointed out the advantages of adhering to the uniform system of taxation and the in-

[77] *N. J. Laws,* 1866, Ch. 487, p. 1078. [78] Cf. Tuttle, pp. 59–66.

[79] E.g., *N. J. Laws,* 1870, Ch. 527, p. 1309; 1872, Ch. 135, p. 347.

[80] E.g., *N. J. Laws,* 1866, Ch. 249, p. 595; 1870, Ch. 290, p. 650.

[81] E.g., *N. J. Laws,* 1868, Ch. 158, p. 360; 1872, Ch. 165, p. 390. There was one additional manufacturing company that was to be taxed as other corporations but the stock of which was exempt from taxes in the hands of the owners. *Ibid.,* 1873, Ch. 86, p. 971.

justice of favoring certain corporations over others. He also used the occasion to recommend that much of the "confusion and inequality" in the taxation of corporate property would be avoided if the legislature refused to pass special charters in all cases where the legitimate purposes of corporations could be attained under the general incorporation law of 1849.[82]

It should also be noted that manufacturing and other non-banking corporations began in 1864 to seek charter amendments reducing the amount of their capital stock. It is probable that the rule of taxation adopted in 1862 was largely responsible for the desire on the part of such companies to secure reductions in their capital.[83]

At the same time that the New Jersey legislators provided general rules for the assessment by local tax authorities of the property of corporations and corporate securities held by individuals, they also sought to increase the sums paid by corporations directly to the state treasurer. It will be recalled that the only corporations paying taxes directly to the state government were those of the special types mentioned in the first part of the present chapter, and, in fact, most of the taxes collected directly by the state were paid by a very few railroad companies. What was desired was a scheme whereby every company chartered by the state would make a direct contribution to the state revenues.

Persons seeking special acts of incorporation from the New Jersey legislature had always been required to pay the same fees for each reading and engrossing of their proposed charters as were paid by all persons requesting private legislation. At first the fees were paid directly to the speaker of the assembly and to the clerks of the assembly and council, but beginning in 1794 they were paid to the state treasurer for the use of the state government.[84] The fees were nominal, however, being intended merely to defray the cost of passing private legislation.[85]

[82] *Legislative Documents,* 1869, pp. 1275–1277. [83] Cf. *supra,* p. 259.

[84] *N. J. Laws,* 18 sess., 2 sit. (1794), Ch. 473, p. 903.

[85] Samuel Allinson, ed., *Acts of the General Assembly of the Province of New-Jersey* . . . Ch. 210, p. 160 (1747–48); *N. J. Laws,* 23 sess., 2 sit. (1799), Ch. 821, p. 608. In numerous instances, acts of incorporation were declared public acts, and then the incorporators did not have to pay even the small fees. E.g., *N. J. Laws,* 49 sess., 1 sit. (1824), p. 158.

In 1858, the legislature passed "An act to increase the revenues of the State of New Jersey." [86] The purpose of the law was to levy substantially heavier fees for passing special charters and charter supplements on behalf of business concerns. The fees to be paid by banking, canal, railroad, turnpike, and insurance companies for special charters or charter supplements increasing their capital stock were calculated according to the amount of the authorized capital. Banks were to pay at the rate of one dollar per thousand of authorized capital; canal, railroad, and turnpike companies were to pay twenty cents per thousand; and the charge to insurance companies was fifty cents per thousand. Special charters for water and gas companies were assessed at a flat rate of fifty dollars each; charters for manufacturing, mining, steamboat, ferry, express, bridge, and plank road companies were assessed at the rate of thirty dollars each. The fees for supplements other than those increasing the capital of banking, railroad, canal, turnpike, or insurance companies were twenty-five dollars in some cases and twenty dollars in others. Private acts were not to be enrolled in the office of the secretary of state or have the force of law until the required fees had been paid. In the following year, the law was amended to permit the publication of special acts before the fees had been paid, but the acts were to become void if the fees were still unpaid by the first day of the July following their passage.[87]

Although they were on a much more modest scale, the fees charged for special charters and charter supplements after 1858 were reminiscent of the "bonus" taxes that had been levied on several bank charters and one canal company charter during

[86] *N. J. Laws,* 1858, Ch. 95, p. 220.

[87] *N. J. Laws,* 1859, Ch. 167, p. 490. Between 1861 and 1875, thirty-five charters and charter supplements that had become void because of nonpayment of the fees were individually revived by the legislature on the condition that the fees would be paid within a certain time. E.g., *ibid.,* 1861, Ch. 144, p. 439; 1871, Ch. 504, p. 1304. In 1873, the governor issued a proclamation accompanied by a list of the special charters and charter amendments that had been passed between 1860 and 1873 but that were not in force because the required fees had not been paid. *Ibid.,* 1874, pp. 756, 759–791. The legislature passed an act in 1874 reviving any of these charters or supplements on which the assessments, plus an additional $25, were paid by May 1, 1874. *Ibid.,* 1874, Ch. 368, p. 67.

the early years of the nineteenth century. It had been hoped in the early period that a system of "bonus" taxes might be made to yield sufficient revenue to defray all the expenses of the state government; probably no one, however, expected that the revenue derived from the relatively moderate assessments imposed by the act of 1858 would contribute more than a small fraction of the state revenue. In fact, the sums collected under the 1858 act were very small. The annual reports of the state treasurer show that the largest annual amount was the $13,829.10 collected in 1874.[88] The amounts collected in certain other years were as follows:

1860	$2,779.00
1865	4,199.60
1870	9,367.50
1875	6,023.00

The failure of the fees collected under the 1858 revenue act even to compensate the state government for the cost of passing and publishing private laws was commented upon by the comptroller of the treasury in his report of 1867. The comptroller thought that the best solution to the problem might be to require groups desiring to become incorporated to file certificates under the general incorporation laws. He declared, however, that if the legislature was to continue to pass special charters, persons who preferred a special charter should be made to pay for it. He suggested that "the legislature cannot go amiss, if they enact a law raising the rates of assessment from thirty to fifty per cent." [89]

The legislature did not act on the suggestion to increase the fees charged for special acts, but the possibility of increasing the taxes paid by corporations directly to the state government was not forgotten. When Governor Randolph delivered his inaugural address in 1869, he proposed that the state not only impose a tax when a charter was passed but that it also levy an annual tax based on the "profits or dividends" of all the corpora-

[88] This figure includes $3884.10 assessed on acts revived by the law of 1874.

[89] Annual report of the comptroller of the treasury. *Legislative Documents*, 1867, pp. 132–33.

tions chartered by New Jersey. It is significant to note that the governor thought such a scheme would be of particular value in raising revenue from corporations that obtained New Jersey charters in order to carry on business outside the state.[90]

The legislature of 1869 acted promptly on the governor's suggestion by passing "An Act to increase the Revenue of the State."[91] The act provided that every corporation chartered by or doing business in New Jersey, except any that were already paying an annual tax directly to the state treasurer for the use of the state, should report annually to the comptroller the amount of its net income received from all sources during the preceding year.[92] A tax of 2 per cent of the earnings was then to be paid to the state treasurer.

The governor ordered the compilation of a list of all the companies that had been chartered by the state legislature by special acts and of those that had filed certificates of incorporation under the general laws to assist the comptroller in administering the income tax law.[93] In 1870, however, the comptroller reported that although notices had been sent to every company believed subject to the law, only forty-five returns had been received and only $491.00 had been paid. What was even more significant was the fact that the comptroller had observed a considerable amount of resistance to the new tax. Some companies had declared that they were incorporated in other states and paid

[90] The pertinent section of the governor's message read as follows: "The increasing legislation of the State is largely due to the facility with which corporate privileges are obtained by those who scarcely contribute to our material interests. Citizens of other States seek our legislative aid for convenience or economy. Corporations whose capital or labor is wholly employed elsewhere, occupy our legislature and courts to the detriment and cost of our own citizens. The system in practice elsewhere, of requiring a specific tax to be paid the State upon the passage of a charter, and an annual though small assessment upon the profits or dividends arising from the chartered privilege, would circumscribe legislation to needs, and compensate the State for its grants. Many of our corporations now render such assistance to the State, and the imposition should be made general, as it may be made equitable." *Legislative Documents*, 1869, p. 185.

[91] *N. J. Laws*, 1869, Ch. 380, p. 1014.

[92] The act also applied to private bankers and brokers, and all unincorporated banking and savings institutions, and to express companies doing business in New Jersey.

[93] See John Hood, *Index of Titles of Corporations* (1870 ed., and 1871 ed.).

taxes there, some questioned the legality of the tax, some said they could not understand it, and several threatened to leave the state if the tax law was enforced.[94]

In his annual message of 1870, Governor Randolph attempted to justify the principle of imposing heavier taxes on incorporated enterprises than were levied on unincorporated concerns. The arguments he employed in defense of his position are of such significance that they are quoted here in full:

> Some of our most enterprising and liberal citizens, engaged in corporate enterprises, deem the selection of corporations as objects of special taxation a hardship and injustice, and it is asked by them "why corporations should be taxed upon their net income, whilst individuals engaged in the same pursuits, perhaps, are exempted from special assessment."
>
> It is answered that corporations have for their members a privileged class of citizens, who, under sanction of general or special laws, are permitted to do those things which, as ordinary citizens, they could not do.
>
> As bodies corporate they may, for their direct advantage, take and possess lands, not at the owners' valuation, but upon appraisement; they may occupy lines of travel and transportation, not only to their advantage, but to the detriment of existing ones; their capital, unlike that of the individual, has an almost double value, inasmuch as the stock issued to represent it is in itself the basis of a loan for an amount nearly equal to its value. Under corporate protection, capital frequently obtains immunity from full taxation, because of provisions in charters liberally interpreted by the corporate officers, or by complacent assessors.
>
> Lastly: the capital which individuals may propose to invest in a given business, is not the full measure of personal responsibility, for failure or misfortune renders the individual liable for all debts and obligations which the business may have brought about, whilst, in the case of invested values in corporations the liability is in nearly all cases limited to the amount actually invested. Thus the State grants — as only the State can grant — peculiar privileges and ex-

[94] The comptroller also noted that "the great moneyed corporations of the State have wrapped themselves in the mantle of contemptuous silence, not even acknowledging the receipt of the printed forms transmitted to them." Annual report of the comptroller of the treasury. *Legislative Documents,* 1870, pp. 262–63 and 277–78.

emptions to a class of persons — or perhaps more properly stated, to capital — which it does not and should not extend to individual citizens.

I need scarcely add the notorious fact, that nearly the whole of the legislative time, with its heavy attendant cost to the people of the State, is taken up by the wants or demands of private corporations; and it is perfectly safe to say that one half of the time of all the higher courts, with the cost incidental thereto — to say naught of the delay to individual litigation — is made up by contests between corporations, or where corporations are a party thereto; the results of which are rarely of importance, as touching the rights of the great body of the people.

That corporations are most useful, properly guarded in their powers, and that to the capital aggregated under their special privileges — nowise else to be obtained, perhaps — the greatest advantage to the State and to its people have been had, no sensible person will dispute.

It is claimed, however, that for the reasons assigned, and others equally obvious, under the pressing necessities of the State for larger revenues, these objects of its creation and continued fostering care should be required to pay of their ascertained profits a small percentage to the State.

Little hardship accrues, for if they make nothing they pay nothing; and in this respect, as in most others, the revenue law of New Jersey is in marked and favorable contrast with similar laws in other States. I question if any State places as light an imposition of taxes upon its general corporations as New Jersey.

It may be asserted that the tendency of the law will be to drive capital from this to other States. I assert, without fear of intelligent contradiction, that the States of New York and Pennsylvania, which, by proximity to the great centres of trade, are our chief competitors for capital seeking investment in the business done under the corporation effected, place a heavier impost on their corporations, by one process or another, than New Jersey has ever done, or will ever desire to do.

We possess peculiar advantages in every respect for corporate enterprise, and it is the right, as it is the duty of the State, to avail itself reasonably of its advantages.

A large number of corporations, seeking to avail themselves of our liberal grant, or desiring the confessed protection of our Courts, or purposing, perhaps, the evasion of imposts elsewhere, have their capital, labor and interests entirely beyond our limits. Surely they might justly be reminded of the power that created and protects them, without trespass upon their rights.

When the returns from the various corporations of the State are fully had, it is not improbable they will be found so large in the aggregate, as to enable the Legislature to fix a rate of taxation that none can fairly complain of.[95]

As the editor of the *Newark Daily Advertiser* expressed it, New Jersey was "all afloat" on the subject of the taxation of corporations,[96] and in March, 1870, Governor Randolph sent a special message to the legislature to reinforce the views he had expressed in his earlier message of that year. Much of what he had said before was repeated in the special message, but he added further remarks to the effect that capital employed in corporate enterprise had ready "divisibility" that was useful in the event of the death of an owner or of dissatisfaction of stockholders with the business, and he noted that a lower standard of "moral" responsibility was expected of corporations than of individual entrepreneurs. Some of the governor's comments on the latter point were as follows:

Capital obtains the power coming from accretion with greater ease and rapidity, under corporate existence, than in any other way, and as we have ample evidence, can use that power with less of moral or legal responsibility than private capital dare do.

Thus the State seems to give a *quasi* immunity to action that would disgrace the incorporators as private citizens; and yet it is practiced by corporations.

Whatever may be thought of the *morale* of the existence of this conditions of affairs, the fact still remains of such a power had and used.[97]

[95] *Legislative Documents,* 1870, pp. 12–13.

[96] Leading editorial entitled "Taxes on Corporations," *Newark Daily Advertiser,* February 18, 1870. The editor reported that the speaker of the assembly was in agreement with the governor that the tax burden should be made more equal but that he wanted the levy made as light as possible, "openly avowing his wish to bestow special favors on capital invested in corporate enterprise, on the ground that New Jersey, lying between two great commonwealths and having herself a magnificent commercial position, should offer every inducement for capital to come here for investment."

[97] *Votes and Proceedings of the General Assembly,* 1870, pp. 882–884.

In spite of the support the governor gave to the principle of imposing a special state tax on corporations, the income tax law of 1869 was a complete failure. As early as March 1870, the *Newark Daily Advertiser* prophesied that no attempt to enforce the law would be made.[98] The reports of the state treasurer show that in 1869 only two companies paid taxes totalling $33.24. Only twelve companies paid in 1870, and the sum collected from them was only $640.85.[99] In 1871, the total amount collected was only $81.21.[100] Faced with the fact that the law was unenforceable, the legislature repealed it in 1872,[101] and in the following year the treasurer was directed to return all the money that had been collected.[102]

In 1871, when it was clear to all that the income tax would produce no revenue for the state government, Governor Randolph made a new appeal for a reform of the state tax system. Randolph once again pointed out the undesirability of deriving almost the entire revenue of the state government from a few railroad companies, and he warned the legislature that state expenditures were rapidly increasing:

> It will occur . . . to reflecting minds, that this condition of affairs, relieving though it may, the greater portion of our citizens and corporations from state taxation, has manifest disadvantages — not the least of which is, the implied obligations such relations create. The rapidly increasing expenditures of the state will permit legislation to seek a wider and safer scope, for objects from which to obtain revenue.[103]

[98] *Newark Daily Advertiser,* March 19, 1870.

[99] In addition, one private broker paid $15.

[100] Reports of the state treasurer. *Legislative Documents,* 1870, 1871, 1872.

[101] *N. J. Laws,* 1872, Ch. 490, p. 65.

[102] *N. J. Laws,* 1873, Ch. 363, p. 64. It was stated that the provisions of the income tax law had been "practically inoperative, and could not be carried out according to the intent thereof . . . and as grave doubts were entertained of the constitutionality of said law, the same was repealed . . ." Apparently the constitutionality of the income tax law had been questioned because it had originated in the senate. Cf. *Newark Daily Advertiser,* January 12, 1870.

[103] *Legislative Documents,* 1871, p. 6. It is interesting that the governor attributed a large part of the increasing cost of government to "our changed view of what constitutes the duty of the state." For example: "Our prisons are now institutions of reform as well as punishment . . ." *Ibid.,* 1871, p. 7.

In his report of 1873, the comptroller recommended an increase in the assessments levied on private acts under the law of 1858 and also that some method be found to increase the revenue obtained from taxes on the capital stock of railroads and other corporations.[104]

It is important to note that as the period under investigation drew to a close and sources of increased revenue for the state treasury were being sought, the minds of Jerseymen turned almost instinctively to the notion of securing additional revenue from the business corporations chartered by their state. This was the natural result of the state's previous financial history. It has been shown in the present chapter that the idea of deriving a substantial part of the state revenues from corporations had its beginnings in the early years of the nineteenth century. Banks, some insurance companies, and certain canal and railroad corporations had been the special targets of the legislature, and the tax policy was so successful that before the middle of the nineteenth century the revenue obtained from a few railroad companies was nearly sufficient to cover the entire cost of the state government.

The New Jersey legislators did not succeed in their attempts to extend the system of direct state taxes to all corporations during the period under study. Nor did they accomplish this aim for a number of years afterward. The goal, however, was not forgotten, and in 1883 Governor Ludlow in his message to the legislature reiterated the views that had frequently been expressed in earlier years:

We have a large number of corporations formed under our laws; receiving from them privileges and immunities peculiar to themselves; claiming and receiving peculiar protection from our courts, and which, under our present system of assessing and collecting, escape much of the local taxation. A law which should provide for a small State tax on the capital invested in them, levied either upon the capital itself or the product thereof, would produce a large amount in the

[104] Annual report of the comptroller of the treasury. *Legislative Documents*, 1873, pp. 18, 37.

aggregate, without making the burden of any one large, or being unfair to the corporations themselves. That these corporations should be taxed, has long been recognized in principle, and its application in this State has been deferred only through fear that capital thus taxed would avoid this State and seek investment in others. That danger has been removed by the adoption, in both New York and Pennsylvania, of systems of taxing corporations. These laws are found to work well in those States, and should do equally well here.[105]

The denouement of the story of New Jersey's financial policy became a matter of national concern. Before the end of the century, the state had set upon a course of providing for the public purse by means of incorporation fees and annual franchise taxes levied on corporations that were encouraged through attractively "liberal" general incorporation laws to secure New Jersey charters. The part that New Jersey was to play in aiding and abetting the "trust" movement in the United States during the eighteen nineties and the early twentieth century was the direct result of that course.

[105] *Legislative Documents,* 1883, p. 12.

PART III

Conclusion

CHAPTER XIV

Summary and Concluding Observations

BETWEEN 1791 and 1875, the various legislatures of the state of New Jersey produced the impressive total of 2318 special acts of incorporation, over 1800 special acts supplementary to corporate charters, numerous regulatory acts referring to corporate practices and procedures, and twenty general incorporation laws for business purposes under which 494 groups had filed certificates of incorporation by 1875. It is out of this mass of legislation, supplemented wherever possible by evidence gathered from the records of the legislature and from representative newspapers of the state, that the foregoing account of the business corporation in New Jersey has been formulated. The broad lines of the evolution of the state's policy toward the corporation emerge quite clearly from the raw material out of which the study has been made, and it is the purpose of the present chapter to summarize the most significant aspects of that policy as it developed.

The whole period up to 1875 might well be called the age of the special charter in New Jersey. With the minor exception of the rather narrow general incorporation law for manufacturing companies that stood on the statute books from 1816 to 1819, all groups seeking to become incorporated before 1846 had no alternative but to approach the legislature for special acts of incorporation. Even after 1846, when a variety of general incorporation laws were available, the special charter dominated the scene so completely as almost to eclipse the general laws.

To say that the period was the age of the special charter, however, is not to suggest that corporate privileges were hard to obtain. Speaking broadly and of the period as a whole, the legislators were surprisingly openhanded about granting charters to the groups who requested them. This statement must be qualified with respect to commercial bank charters which were granted only sparingly during most of the period and with respect to proposed railroad enterprises that threatened to compete with the state-fostered monopoly of the Joint Companies. It must also be qualified with respect to a few years around 1850 when the lawmakers were distinctly niggardly about chartering by special act manufacturing and mining companies that had the alternative of filing certificates under the general incorporation laws. Otherwise few petitioners for special charters seem to have been refused.

To speak broadly again, the special charters granted were rather generous in their terms. The two constitutions under which New Jersey was governed during these years left the legislators virtually a free hand as to the terms of the charters they dispensed. It is also indicative that no general regulating acts were passed in New Jersey except for the sketchy "act concerning corporations" of 1846. Early in the nineteenth century, several other states had enacted general regulating laws for the principal types of companies they incorporated, and charters passed subsequently were thus made to conform to a standard and sometimes illiberal pattern. The lack of such regulating acts in New Jersey is responsible for the fact that the special charters fail in most cases to show any consistency in their provisions. Since each special charter was a unique production and not cast in a standard mold, the way was always open for petitioners to present for the legislators' consideration a charter bill in which they had written powers and privileges considered advantageous to their enterprise and in which they had drafted the expected restrictive clauses in a form deemed least onerous. The bewildering array of different privileges and powers, regulations and restrictions found in New Jersey's special charters are primarily the result of this circumstance. It should not be supposed, of course, that the lawmakers were completely passive in the chartering process, merely accepting charter bills as they were drafted by would-be corporators or their counsel. As will appear below, legislators were from time to time disposed to insist on particular restrictions and safeguards in various types of charters.

The most significant facts about the business corporation in New Jersey as they appear in the detailed material of the two principal sections of this study are summarized in the following paragraphs. For the purpose of the summary, the years between 1791 and 1875 have been divided into six periods. The division is in part arbitrary, but each period represents a more or less distinct stage in the history of the New Jersey corporation and in the development of public policy with respect to that institution.

1791–1811

Up to the year which witnessed the outbreak of the second war with England, the corporate device was employed in relatively few spheres of business in New Jersey, not, however, because of any discernible policy on the part of the lawmakers but because charters were not sought by enterprisers in other fields. Bridges, canal and canalization projects, and, after 1800, turnpikes were deemed appropriate undertakings for corporate enterprise, and it was here the corporation found its principal employment during the early years. Incorporated enterprise also appeared before 1812 in the business of supplying water to residents of towns and in commercial banking. Although New Jersey's first business corporation — the S. U. M. — had been organized to conduct a manufacturing business, no one attempted to secure another charter for manufacturing purposes until 1809. In that year, a second manufacturing company was incorporated, followed by a third in 1811. There were also two mining companies chartered before 1812.

The basic policy of New Jersey in the matter of "highway" construction was established during this period with the chartering of companies to build major transportation facilities that might otherwise have been reserved for governmental enterprise. In spite of reluctance on the part of some Democrats to turn road building over to private enterprise, most Jerseymen were satisfied to see bridges, canals, and roads constructed without financial obligation or risk to the government. Some charters provided for state participation in stock subscriptions should the legislators wish to invest government funds in enterprises that promised to be financially successful, but in no case was the state obligated to give financial assistance. A number of the incorporating acts also reserved to the state the right to purchase the facilities after a designated time in case the legislators ultimately decided that the government should own and operate them.

Although many years were to pass before New Jersey became notorious for making its corporations the principal source of state revenues, it took the first steps along that road at the beginning of the nineteenth century. The start was made in early bank charters in which the state invariably reserved the right of subscribing to a substantial portion of the stock. Such reservations indicated an early recognition of the fact that subscription rights in banks had a high monetary value rather than any notion that state contributions were necessary to the financial success of the institutions, for in all cases the legislators promptly sold the rights for large sums. Revenues from banks were put on a continuing basis in 1810 with the imposition of an annual capital stock tax.

One further feature of the early charters should be mentioned. Eighteenth century charters were mostly perpetual, but beginning in 1801 incorporation was usually granted only for definite periods of time. Banking privileges were given for but a limited time in every case. The manufacturing companies of 1809 and 1811 were likewise chartered for a definite number of years. All early turnpike companies were of limited duration although they were allowed longer lives than other types of corporations.

1812–1824

The period from 1812 to 1824 witnessed a number of events that are noteworthy in the history of incorporation in New Jersey. Outstanding in the general picture was the relatively large number of manufacturing concerns chartered during the War of 1812 when America's foreign trade was cut off. The industrial depression following the war was apparently responsible for the enactment of a general incorporation law for certain types of manufacturing companies in 1816. The law, closely similar to New York's act of 1811, had been under consideration in Trenton since 1812. It is probable that the Jersey lawmakers' intention in finally passing it was to encourage manufacturing in the midst of depression as the New York legislators had seemingly hoped to encourage it in anticipation of war. New Jersey's effort, however, was a failure, for there is no evidence of any incorporations having occurred under the 1816 law, and it was summarily repealed in 1819.

In the field of banking, the period was marked by the passage in 1812 of an act incorporating six so-called "state" banks. One-half of the stock of each bank was reserved for the state, and whether the legislators decided to exercise the right to subscribe or not they were to control the banks through appointments to the boards of directors. The "state" bank scheme had been sponsored by the Democrats and was heartily condemned by the Federalists. When the autumn elections returned a Federalist majority to the legislature, no time was lost in ordering the sale of the state's subscription rights and in relinquishing the government's power to appoint directors. One aspect of New Jersey's policy on banking was thus settled, and no further attempts were made to set up state-managed or state-owned banks. Another permanent feature of bank policy was established in 1815 with the passage of an act prohibiting unincorporated institutions from engaging in the banking business.

Companies chartered to construct and operate transportation facilities continued to hold the place of first importance among new incorporations. There were many additions to the ranks of incorporated turnpike, canal, and bridge companies, corporations were created for the first time to conduct steamboat and ferry services, and the initial railroad charter was granted. Beginning in 1819, there was much agitation for state construction and operation of canals along the two most important travel arteries, but the legislators adhered to their former policy and chartered companies to pursue the work.

A significant development occurring during this period was the imposition of double liability on certain stockholders. A double liability clause patterned after that in New York's general law of 1811 appeared in the charter of a textile firm incorporated in New Jersey in 1813, was repeated in every manufacturing company charter granted between that date and 1824, and was put into the charter of the one company incorporated during the period to operate a steamboat line. The 1816 general incorporation law for manufacturing companies also contained a double liability clause. In thus imposing a measure of personal liability on stockholders in corporations chartered for ordinary business purposes, the New Jersey lawmakers were participating in a movement occurring in a number of states during the early nineteenth century to put the owners of incorporated concerns in a position more nearly equal to their unincorporated competitors in the matter of responsibility for business debts.

Most of the charters of the period were limited in duration, but the Dartmouth College decision of 1819 made it increasingly clear that a closer and more continuous control over corporations was desirable. The right to alter charters or charter supplements once they were granted had been reserved by the New Jersey legislators on a few occasions before 1819 but in only a very restricted form. After the Dartmouth case was decided, much support was found for the idea that charters should be made subject to alteration and repeal at the discretion of the legislature, but the principle was not applied to any New Jersey charter until 1823 and it was some years after that before the lawmakers saw fit to make all charters revocable.

The notion that the incorporating power could be used to return substantial financial rewards to the state, recognized from the first in connection with bank charters, took even firmer root in New Jersey during these years. The legislators continued to make all new banks subject to the annual capital stock tax and reserved subscription rights in a few, but beginning in 1815 they tried in addition the scheme of demanding "bonuses" for bank charters. Thus most of the banks chartered between 1815 and 1824 were required to pay the state sizable "bonuses" either in the form of cash or shares of stock. The incorporation act of the ill-fated Delaware and Raritan Canal Company of 1824 also called for the payment of what was at that time the enormous sum of $100,000. The year 1824 marked the end of the "bonus" system in connection with new charters.

1825–1834

During the decade from 1825 to 1834, there was a sharp increase in the number of manufacturing companies chartered in New Jersey that can be accounted for by the gathering momentum of the American industrial revolution. Mining companies also appeared on the scene in significant numbers for the first time, several being launched optimistically for the purpose of exploring for and mining coal in New Jersey. New banks were chartered at about the same rate as before, but charters for insurance companies were much more numerous than previously. The decade also witnessed the extension of the corporate device into new fields such as the fishing, peat cutting, and dairy industries although the beginning was modest with each type of business accounting for but one or two charters. Companies continued to be incorporated to build and operate all kinds of transportation facilities, but there was a marked decline in the number of new turnpike companies. The year 1830 ushered in the railroad building era, and thenceforth railroad charters appeared regularly among the session laws. It is significant, however, that between 1825 and 1829 the transportation group slipped into a place of secondary importance for the first time, having been outdistanced by manufacturing and mining companies both in the number of charters granted and in the amount of capital stock authorized.

The last years of the eighteen twenties saw the final struggle between the group advocating state construction of a canal across New Jersey to carry the traffic between New York City and Philadelphia and those who favored chartering another company to do the job that three former ones had failed to accomplish. The outcome hung in the balance for two successive years while bills providing for state prosecution of the work passed the assembly only to be defeated in the legislative council. The issue was finally resolved in 1830 when in the course of the same day charters were granted to the Delaware and

Raritan Canal Company and to the Camden and Amboy Rail Road and Transportation Company authorizing them to occupy the important New York to Philadelphia route. New Jersey thus reaffirmed its stand against governmental enterprise or financial involvement in the construction of major public works and avoided the vast expenditures for such purposes that caused embarrassment to its neighbors a few years later.[1]

The practice of making corporations subject to the continuing control of the legislature was not firmly established until the end of this decade. Having made a start in that direction in 1823, the legislators subsequently followed a vacillating policy and granted charters that were immune from legislative interference to about half the companies incorporated between 1824 and 1833. Thereafter, however, the lawmakers were more cautious in this respect, and after 1833 charters that could be neither altered nor repealed were extremely rare.

The double liability that had been imposed on stockholders in manufacturing companies chartered during the previous decade was seldom repeated in manufacturing company charters after 1824. The stockholders in slightly over one-half the mining firms incorporated in the ten years before 1835, however, were subject to double liability provisions. The legislators espoused a new banking principle in 1828 according to which bank presidents and directors were made personally liable for the circulating notes of their institutions, and for many years thereafter this particular safeguard for the redemption of notes was written into special bank charters in New Jersey.

Another interesting feature of the period is that it brought the earliest authorizations for departures from the former simple capital structures consisting exclusively of common stock. Altogether there were two issues of mortgage bonds and four issues of preferred stock authorized during these years. The privilege of issuing the new types of securities was bestowed

[1] New Jersey stands in sharp contrast to Pennsylvania, for example, which poured millions of dollars into state-constructed public works and into "mixed corporations" in which the state invested along with individuals. See Louis Hartz, *Economic Policy and Democratic Thought: Pennsylvania, 1776–1860*, pp. 82–180.

on turnpike and canal companies that had encountered financial difficulties.

Owing to the increased number of insurance companies and to the rising importance of the insurance business, the legislators singled out insurance companies for special taxation during the eighteen twenties. The first step in this direction was to make several companies subject to annual capital stock taxes. The taxes, however, met with immediate opposition, and some of the companies that had been liable to the levies were granted relief by supplementary acts. Recognizing the failure of their effort to extend the principle of the special bank tax to insurance companies, the legislators soon retreated and did not attempt to make newly chartered insurance firms subject to special taxation. In 1826, a tax based on the amount of business they did in New Jersey was levied on "foreign" insurance companies. This tax was continued in one form or another and eventually became a source of modest but continuing income to the state treasury.

Through a series of enactments of the early eighteen thirties, the New Jersey lawmakers achieved the long-sought goal of deriving a really substantial revenue for the state from the business corporations they chartered. The 1830 charters of both the Delaware and Raritan Canal Company and the Camden and Amboy Rail Road and Transportation Company provided for "transit duties" to be paid to the state for each passenger and each ton of merchandise transported across the state. The "transit duties" were levied in lieu of other taxes. The gratifying financial rewards provided by this novel tax were augmented by dividends from two large blocks of stock turned over to the state government by the companies in 1831 and 1832 in return for a guaranteed monopoly of the transportation business on the New York to Philadelphia route. The canal and railroad companies, united in 1832 as the Joint Companies, contracted to make up the deficiency in case the "transit duties" and dividends did not yield a stated minimum income to the government, but the revenues exceeded the minimum figure as early as 1836 and increased rapidly to the point of providing a major share of the total sum going annually into the state treasury.

The treatment accorded other early railroad companies in

the matter of taxation was not uniform. The principle of the "transit duty" was employed again in a few instances, and some companies were required to pay annual taxes based on the amount of their paid-in capital. Most of the early railroad building projects, however, were so risky and so unpromising financially that the lawmakers favored their promoters with tax immunity until such time as the net income should equal a designated percentage of the cost of the road. Companies with contingent tax liabilities of this sort seldom if ever admittedly fulfilled the conditions requiring them to pay taxes.

The net result of the tax policies adopted by the New Jersey legislature in the early eighteen thirties was that very few railroad companies made direct contributions to the state treasury, but the few that did provided the bulk of the state revenues. The situation was so satisfactory from a financial point of view that for many years preceding the Civil War the state government did not have to levy direct taxes on its citizens. It was only the extraordinary expenses resulting from the conflict which made direct taxes again necessary and spurred the legislators to seek a broader base on which to erect a system of corporate taxation.

1835–1844

The speculative fever of the mid-eighteen thirties occasioned a great increase in the number of incorporations in the fields of railroading and manufacturing during the legislative sessions of 1835–36 and 1836–37. A large percentage of the newly chartered manufacturing companies were authorized to enter the business of producing and fabricating silk, a reflection of the rosy future for sericulture envisioned by many Americans of that day. The depression that set in after the panic of 1837 was responsible for a severe reduction in the number of firms incorporated in every field of enterprise with the exception of insurance, and the demand for charters did not revive until 1844 and 1845.

The most significant feature of the decade was that it brought the beginning of the protracted anti-corporation campaign of the Democratic party in New Jersey. It was true that from the earliest years of the nineteenth century the Democrats had made unsuccessful thrusts against turnpike and banking companies, but during the last half of the eighteen thirties, infused with the new spirit of locofocoism, they opened a broader and more sustained attack against business corporations. Although the precise form that the Democratic argument took varied from time to time and was variously interpreted by different persons, the basic ideas can be summarized as follows: a general hostility to the corporate device in business because it represented "special privilege"; a particular enmity toward banks of issue and manufacturing companies operating in fields occupied by individual enterprises; an insistence that all charters be made subject to repeal; the notion that charters granted to firms operating in the same general field should be uniform in their terms; and the attitude that charters for banks and manufacturing companies should be more strictly drawn than in the past.

Although the anti-corporation Democrats failed in their numerous efforts to secure the passage of stringent general regulating laws for manufacturing corporations, they made their influence felt in the charters passed during the decade. The legislature of 1835–36 was the first to make every charter subject to alteration or repeal, an example that was followed during the next ten years except for one minor defection. Half of the manufacturing companies chartered between 1836 and 1844 were limited as to the amount of land they might hold although such a restriction had rarely been applied to manufacturing companies previously and was imposed only sparingly thereafter. The Democrats' concern for the protection of creditors of corporations was reflected in charter clauses limiting corporate debt, imposing penalties for exceeding the debt limits or for paying out capital as dividends, requiring companies to cease operations unless their capital was paid in within a designated time, and expressly demanding that the corporate capital be paid in in cash. Although such provisions by no means found their way into all charters, they appeared with significant frequency around 1840 in the charters of manufacturing companies.

The constitutional convention of 1844 provided a sounding board for a variety of opinions on the corporation question. The Democratic delegates hoped to dignify their ideas on the subject by making them the basic law of the state, and they endeavored to secure the adoption of constitutional clauses requiring a two-thirds vote of both houses of the legislature for charter bills, making all charters repealable, and subjecting stockholders to a degree of personal liability for corporate debts. All they were able to achieve, however, was a clause necessitating a three-fifths vote for bank charters and limiting the duration of such charters to twenty years. The Democratic advocates of stricter constitutional control over the process of incorporation had to contend all through the convention with their opponents' argument that to tie the hands of the lawmakers in any way would make them unable to grant the generous charters useful in attracting industry into the state and in preventing the flight of capital into other jurisdictions. The argument was a persuasive one, and the Democrats were unable to defend their position against it.

1845–1857

The average number of companies incorporated annually between 1845 and 1857 was considerably larger than it had been during the previous decade. The increase can be accounted for by the revival of business after the post-1837 depression, the natural growth of the economy, and the adoption of the corporate device by industries that had made little or no use of it before. Manufacturing companies continued to hold an important place in the whole picture of new incorporations. Among the enterprises making more frequent use of the corporate form of organization than previously were mining firms, land development companies, mutual savings institutions, companies constructing public halls, gas works, and transportation companies. Among those making their first appearance in the ranks of incorporated business were hotels, plank roads, and telegraph companies. Turnpike charters became numerous once again after an interval of over thirty years during which few had been requested, but most of the new turnpike enterprises were intended merely to construct short "feeders" to the rapidly developing railroads and were capitalized at a low figure.

Since the first attempt to institute a comprehensive system of general incorporation laws was made between 1845 and 1857, the period represents one of the most interesting and significant stages in the development of the business corporation in New Jersey. Although many aspects of the corporation question had been thoroughly discussed in the 1844 constitutional convention, no suggestion had been made on that occasion to outlaw special acts of incorporation and establish a general-law system. The principle of the general incorporation law was well known in the state since general laws for the organization of certain nonprofit corporations had been on the statute books since the eighteenth century and one for benevolent societies had just been enacted in the spring of 1844. Furthermore, for several years the Democrats had shown an interest in such laws for business purposes because the equality of treatment implicit in their operation avoided the "special privilege" which was in the Democratic argument the most objectionable feature of special charters. No other state had as yet, however, taken the drastic step of making special acts of incorporation unconstitutional, and perhaps the members of the New Jersey convention were unable to envision a situation in which companies of every description would be accommodated under a set of general enabling acts. At any rate, they failed to prohibit incorporation by special act and left the legislators free to choose the method by which they would charter corporations. The consequence was a dual system of incorporation that endured for three decades.

As soon as the first legislature under the new constitution convened in 1845, the Democratic members began a campaign for the adoption of general incorporation laws. Having shown particular antipathy during the previous decade to manufacturing corporations, it was natural that they should give those institutions first attention in their drive for reform. Thus a general incorporation law for manufacturing companies made its appearance in the statute books in 1846. It was extended to include mining companies in 1848 and was replaced in 1849 by a law of broader coverage. Although the laws of 1846 and 1849 extended to all the privilege of becoming incorporated for manufacturing and certain other purposes, they were hedged about with safeguards designed to protect creditors and the general public and hence were less attractive to prospective corporators than the more "liberal" special charters. In view of the antibank sentiments expressed by the Democrats during the preceding ten-year period, it is not surprising that the other major project to which they turned their attention was a revamping of the entire banking system. The general banking law enacted under their sponsorship in 1850 provided for the free incorporation of commercial banks, but banks organized under the law were at a disadvantage compared with the old specially chartered institutions since their circulating notes had to be fully protected by securities deposited with public authorities. In an effort to make the general-law system as comprehensive as possible, ten additional general laws were passed by 1857 providing for a variety of enterprises such as plank road, insurance, navigation, and telegraph companies. The only glaring defect in the whole scheme was the absence of a general railroad law. Several had been presented in the legislature around 1850 and two were actually approved by the assembly, but the political influence of the Camden and Amboy group, wielded largely through the Democratic party, was strong enough at that time to prevent any general railroad law from going through to final passage.

Shortly after the first general laws were on the books, certain Democratic legislators made it clear that they expected incorporating groups to make use of the new laws whenever possible, leaving special acts of incorporation to be employed only when no appropriate general law was available. The members of the business community, however, regarded general-law incorporation merely as an alternative if for one reason or another they did not wish to apply for special charters. The two points of view first came into conflict in 1848 when an unsuccessful attempt was made in the legislature to defeat a certain charter bill on the grounds that the applicants could file a certificate of incorporation under a general law. In 1849 and 1850, the friends of the general-law system succeeded in defeating all but one of the applications for special charters for manufacturing purposes, but during the following few years a number of mining and manufacturing companies were incorporated by special act in spite of several vigorous vetoes by the Democratic governor.

The major contest, however, was fought over the banking law of 1850. In spite of the persistence of groups seeking special charters, the legislators refused to create a single new bank by special act for five years after the general law was in force, and several existing institutions whose charters expired were compelled to become general-law banks. The pressure put on the lawmakers for special bank charters had become so strong by 1855 that their resistance finally crumbled and they created a number of new banks and extended the charters of some existing ones. The governor, attempting to salvage the general-law system that had for so long been supported in the platforms, press, and political speeches of the Democrats, vetoed five bank charter bills, but his vetoes were overridden in every instance.

The resumption of the practice of granting special bank charters in 1855 presaged the final collapse of the faltering general-law movement of this period. Although the Democrats again controlled the legislature in 1856, the members generally disregarded the official Democratic position on the corporation question, and by 1857 the general laws were no longer a live issue. The supporters of the movement had achieved the passage of an impressive list of general incorporation laws within a decade, but they had failed to secure general acceptance of the laws and hence were unable to bring about the revolution in the system of incorporation for which they had labored.

It would seem that by the middle of the nineteenth century with the number of applications for charters steadily increasing the time was ripe to abandon the cumbersome system of chartering by special act and thus eliminate the lobbying, logrolling, and temptation to bribery that inevitably accompanied it. Had the Democrats been interested in establishing a "liberal" corporation policy they might have won the support of the commercial community. The fact was, however, that their general-law system offered incorporation on terms that were far less attractive than those formerly obtained under most special charters. Their general manufacturing laws contained provisions designed to assure the payment and maintenance of a definite capital for the protection of creditors, over-all debt limitations, and other regulatory clauses of the type Democratic legislators had endeavored to put into special charters during the late eighteen thirties. The same general laws also failed to grant authority to do such things as mortgage property, float bonds, issue stock in exchange for property, or hold stock in other corporations. The discrepancies between special and general-law charters were even greater in the case of banking since the general law required banks to deposit full security for all the notes they issued. Nor did the Democrats show any disposition to amend the general laws so as to make them more palatable to businessmen, and with special charters continually offering more and more generous powers and privileges the general laws became increasingly less attractive.

The special charters granted between 1845 and 1857 afford ample evidence why entrepreneurs manifested such a decided preference for them over the general laws. In the first place, special charters were tending to become less restrictive than in earlier years. It was typical of the trend that over-all debt limitations which had been imposed on many manufacturing and other corporations chartered during the eighteen forties were seldom inserted in special charters after 1850, and when they did appear they were no longer accompanied by severe penalties for exceeding the limits. Clauses limiting the real estate to be held by manufacturing companies, found in many charters passed during the decade before 1845, were little used after that date. Also there were relatively few instances in which any form of stockholder liability appeared in the charters of non-banking corporations after 1850. The decreasing number of cases in which residence qualifications were imposed on corporate directors and officers is a further example of how special-charter standards were relaxed during these years.

In the second place, the special charters of the period allowed an increasing number of new departures in corporation finance.

Beginning at the end of the eighteen forties, many charters expressly legalized intercorporate stockholding, a privilege that had been granted in only a few instances in earlier years. Also for the first time there were numerous charters and supplementary acts allowing corporations to mortgage their property, issue bonds and preferred stock, and issue stock in exchange for property. Authorizations for issuing convertible bonds and guaranteed bonds made their initial appearance in the early eighteen fifties. Thus well before the Civil War many specially chartered companies were permitted at least an approach to the complex capital structures and intercorporate relationships that are characteristic of many of our present-day business organizations.

There were other reasons for the failure of the first general-law movement. The fact that even Democratic-controlled legislatures persisted in passing special charters greatly weakened the party's ability to convince the public of the sincerity of its official stand against such legislation. Democratic legislators inevitably found themselves in a contradictory position, however, since nearly all had to sponsor charter bills on behalf of constituents, and the temptation to trade votes was irresistible. The Democratic governors, representing a state-wide constituency and not having to pay such close attention to local interests, were in a stronger position to uphold the official party doctrine, but their frequent exhortations in messages to the legislature and even their numerous vetoes of charter bills were insufficient to stem the tide. In their failure to pass a general railroad law the Democratic reformers further weakened the force of their case. Their argument that they favored general laws because specially chartered companies were "monopolies" and hence undesirable was unconvincing when they had left a loophole in their system of general laws to protect the Joint Companies, the one truly full-fledged monopoly in the state.

1858–1875

During the early years of the Civil War, the number of charters granted annually in New Jersey declined somewhat from the levels that had been attained in most years of the eighteen fifties. The lull was brief, however, and as soon as the war was over the state's chartering activity reached an unprecedentedly high level which was maintained until the crisis of 1873 brought a halt to the business boom. The types of corporations that were chartered during this period were for the most part the same as in the previous decade, yet some changes in the general pattern can be detected. A new element was introduced in the field of transportation with the incorporation of many horse-operated street and interurban railways, and after the Civil War there was a sharp upturn in the number of charters for steam railroads and for companies in the express business. Land development, hotel, hall, market, and ice companies appeared in greatly increased numbers, and the corporate device was used frequently in the organization of coöperative stores. During the years between the end of the war and 1875, charters were granted for large numbers of savings banks, trust companies, and a variety of other financial institutions, but the establishment of a national banking system was responsible for a decline in the number of applications for commercial bank charters. It should also be noted, in view of later developments in the state's corporation policy, that a large share of the many mining companies created between 1865 and 1875 were chartered to operate in the western territories rather than in New Jersey itself.

The voices of the proponents of a system of general incorporation laws were virtually silent between 1858 and 1864, and no new general laws were enacted during that time. A renewal of interest in the subject, however, resulted in the broadening of the manufacturing law in 1865 to provide for the incorporation of companies engaging in "any lawful business whatever" and in the enactment of six additional general laws between 1865 and 1875. In spite of these measures, the number of companies receiving special charters continued to run far ahead of the number that were organized under general laws. The reasons are clear. On the one hand, businessmen sought special charters in order to avoid the restrictive provisions of certain of the general laws and at the same time obtain express authorization to use financial devices that the general laws did not permit. With a special charter they could also hope to secure more favorable terms than their competitors enjoyed, or perhaps they expected merely to realize the additional prestige attaching to a special act. On the other hand, the legislators, ever anxious to please their constituents who sought special charters, did little to stem the flood of private bills. The new general laws were passed it would seem merely with the hope that people would voluntarily choose to use them, since, except in the case of railroads after 1873, few attempts were made to force applicants for special charters to resort to the general laws.

The need of more drastic action to bring an end to the annual spectacle of a legislative session almost monopolized by scores of private bills became generally recognized by the end of the eighteen sixties. Once again the governors urged the increased use of general laws, reviving the venerable argument that they guaranteed equality of treatment. The burden that special legislation put upon the legislature, however, provided the most telling case for a general-law system. Overcrowding the sessions with private bills, it could readily be shown, resulted not only in the passage of private legislation that had received merely cursory examination but in the neglect of public legislation as well. Furthermore, the opportunities for lobbying, logrolling, and bribery multiplied as the volume of special legislation increased. Finally, the state comptrollers and others made much of the point that the expense of prolonged legislative sessions and of publishing hundreds of special laws was an unwarranted drain on the public purse, and this argument alone was enough to convince many persons of the wisdom of doing away with private acts.

In spite of the fact that alternative solutions to the chartering problem were suggested from time to time, it was apparent that the only adequate measure was a constitutional prohibition of special acts of incorporation. New Jersey had been slower than many states in taking this step. In 1873, however, the passage of a general railroad law, a measure previously opposed by the Camden and Amboy interests, removed the last serious obstacle to the adoption of a full-fledged general-law system. Accordingly, a constitutional commission appointed in that year recommended the prohibition of all special and private legislation, and upon the ratification in 1875 of the commission's recommendations the era of special charters came to an end in New Jersey.

Between 1858 and 1875, there had been no striking changes in the terms upon which special charters were granted. It is significant, nevertheless, to note the acceleration of certain trends that had had their origin in the preceding period. We find, for instance, the more frequent appearance in special charters of authority to issue mortgage bonds, to make bonds convertible into stock, to guarantee the bonds of other corporations, and to sell bonds on terms that yielded to the purchasers a higher rate of return than was allowed by the usury laws. The privilege of intercorporate stockholding was granted more often, as was the right to issue stock in exchange for property and to create preferred stocks. At the same time, some of the older types of restrictive clauses that had already begun to wane in importance before 1858 were used less and less often until by the eighteen seventies they were almost forgotten. The terms of the various general laws, on the other hand, were not changed in any important particular and thus failed completely to keep abreast of the swiftly changing fashions of corporation finance.

Final mention should be made of two revenue measures adopted in New Jersey during this period because they represent early experiments in the search for a scheme of taxation under which the state would be more adequately compensated for its grants of corporate charters. It has already been pointed out that although by the middle of the nineteenth century business corporations were the principal source of the revenues going into New Jersey's treasury, the burden was very unequally distributed. Most of the payments were made by a handful of railroad companies in the form of "transit duties," capital stock taxes, and dividends on stock that had been given to the state, with smaller sums derived from the capital stock tax on banks. The great majority of the state's corporations paid no direct tribute to the government. It was inevitable, under such circumstances, that the legislators should be attracted to the notion of broadening the base of corporate taxation.

The first step they took in this direction was to substitute rather substantial fees for the nominal charges formerly made for special charters and charter supplements. Although the plan was put into operation in 1858, on the very threshold of an era during which more and more special charter legislation was passed, the fees proved too low to yield more than a modest return. A further difficulty developed because frequently charters or supplements were passed and published among the laws only to become void when no one came forward to pay the required assessments. The net result was that the income from such fees did not increase the state revenues to the extent the legislators had anticipated and, in fact, probably did not even cover the cost to the state of private legislation passed for the benefit of business corporations.

The other step was the enactment of a corporation income tax in 1869. It was primarily the increased cost of operating the state government after the Civil War that set the legislators once again on the search for convenient sources of increased revenue. The governor suggested in 1869 that a larger proportion of the state's corporations, including those chartered in New Jersey to conduct business elsewhere, should contribute annually to the public treasury, and the lawmakers hastened to pass an income tax based on the net earnings of corporations either chartered by or doing business in the state. It was almost immediately evident that the new tax law was doomed to failure. Most of the companies subject to the income tax either openly challenged, resisted, or ignored the measure, and only a negligible amount of money was collected. Although the governor in two messages delivered the following year attempted to defend the principle of making corporations pay higher taxes than unincorporated concerns paid, enforcement of the income tax proved impossible, and its repeal followed in 1872.

By 1875, the date at which the present study ends, New Jersey had not appeared upon the national scene as the leading incorporating jurisdiction that it was to become before the nineteenth century had run its course. Yet it should be noted here that New Jersey's pre-1875 policies with respect to the business corporation were in a very real sense a prologue to later developments and help to explain why the state became a leader in the interstate competition for the business of chartering corporations.

As we have seen, the notion that corporations chartered by the state could be made to pay a large share of the expenses of government had very early been put to good purpose in New Jersey. Even before the middle of the nineteenth century the revenues from certain business corporations were so substantial that no direct state taxes had to be levied on individuals. This happy state of affairs came to an end in the post-Civil War period when the cost of government ran far ahead of corporate contributions, and the lawmakers endeavored to remedy the condition by devising a scheme of taxation whereby payments would be made to the state by all its corporations rather than merely by the relative few on which the treasury then relied. Although all efforts made before 1875 to broaden the base of corporate taxation failed, the idea did not die and by the end of the century was made to yield handsome financial rewards.

The leadership that New Jersey assumed in the developments of the late nineteenth century also finds an explanation in the well-grounded tradition that the legislators at Trenton were not averse to accommodating entrepreneurs who were unable to secure elsewhere the generous charter terms they desired. The practice of granting charters designed to attract industry into New Jersey went far back into the nineteenth century and resulted quite naturally from the paucity of capital in the state and the proximity of the great financial centers of New York City and Philadelphia. The argument that New Jersey's peculiar situation dictated a "liberal" corporation policy had long been used successfully against reformers who sought from time to time to tighten the standards of the charters granted by the legislators. Even companies that neither had nor intended any real affiliation with New Jersey were accommodated with special charters on several occasions before 1875. Although special charters could not be granted after that date, there was nothing in the constitution to hinder the lawmakers from enacting the most "liberal" general incorporation law in the land and thus invite everyone to make use of the state's incorporating facilities.

The Civil War left a legacy of financial burdens that strained New Jersey's fiscal resources in the final quarter of the nineteenth century at the very time when several periods of serious depression caused a decline in revenues. State officials, searching eagerly for new sources of revenue, were presented with the ready-made solution of making New Jersey's corporation laws so attractive that large numbers of companies would come to the state for charters. This was the program they adopted, combining it, of course, with a plan to collect tribute in return for the valuable favors they were prepared to dispense. The financial success of New Jersey's venture was highly gratifying. Since it was launched in an era that witnessed the emergence of many large corporations in the American economy and that was marked by a tendency toward concentration of control in industry, businessmen from all over the country availed themselves of the friendly and coöperative treatment they could expect in Trenton. New Jersey was able to maintain its preeminence as an incorporating jurisdiction until the early years of the twentieth century when other states, coveting a portion of the fees and franchise taxes, began actively to bid for an increased share of the lucrative business of chartering corporations.

APPENDIX I

A. Business Corporations Chartered by Special Act in New Jersey, Maryland, and Pennsylvania,[a] 1782–1844

Year	N. J.	Md.	Pa.	Year	N. J.	Md.	Pa.
1782	..	..	1	1815	13	10	15
1783	..	1	..	1816	10	23	22
1784	..	..	..	1817	2	10	23
1785	..	1	..	1818	3	12	11
1786	..	..	1	1819	3	10	24
1787	..	1	1	1820	2	2	9
1788	..	..	..	1821	1	1	4
1789	..	..	..	1822	4	3	5
1790	..	1	..	1823	5	8	11
1791	1	2	1	1824	13	4	4
1792	1	1	2	1825	10	5	12
1793	..	1	5	1826	5	7	30
1794	..	1	3	1827	..	6	16
1795	2	4	1	1828	24	16	22
1796	1	3	2	1829	5	21	18
1797	2	..	1	1830	9	6	22
1798	1	3	4	1831	14	5	37
1799	2	2	..	1832	11	22	39
1800	2	..	..	1833	14	27	38
1801	3	2	2	1834	14	13	35
1802	3	..	..	1835	12	9	30
1803	..	..	6	1836	36	36	70
1804	11	1	14	1837	45	12	31
1805	..	10	4	1838	12	13	64
1806	9	2	6	1839	15	35	43
1807	4	..	9	1840	8	10	33
1808	5	5	2	1841	8	7	31
1809	5	..	13	1842	7	4	23
1810	..	11	15	1843	1	5	31
1811	12	..	17	1844	11	11	40
1812	10	9	12		—	—	—
1813	4	..	11	*Totals*	403	425	995
1814	8	11	69				

[a] The Maryland figures are from J. G. Blandi, *Maryland Business Corporations: 1783–1852*, p. 14. The Pennsylvania figures are from J. S. Davis, *Essays in the Earlier History of American Corporations*, II, Figure I, pp. 22–23, and from William Miller, "A Note on the History of Business Corporations in Pennsylvania, 1800–1860," *Quarterly Journal of Economics*, LV (November 1940), Table II, p. 155.

APPENDIX I (Continued)

B. Types of Business Corporations Chartered by Special Act in New Jersey, Maryland, and Pennsylvania,[a] 1782–1844

(Expressed as percentages of the total number of business corporations chartered in each state)

	New Jersey	Maryland	Pennsylvania
Manufacturing and mining	32.8%	27.9%	7.1%
Bank and savings institution	11.1	17.2	9.2
Insurance	7.5	8.0	10.7
Turnpike	12.7	18.1	33.6
Railroad	8.7	4.2	12.6
Bridge and ferry	9.5	4.9	15.5
Steamboat	3.8	2.8	.9
Canal and waterway	5.0	4.9	6.0
Other	8.9	12.0	4.4
	100.0%	100.0%	100.0%

[a] The figures for Maryland have been taken from Blandi, table on page 14 and list on pages 93–111. Those for Pennsylvania have been taken from Davis, II, Figure I, pp. 22–23, and from William Miller, Tables II, IV, and V, pp. 155–159. Since the figures for Pennsylvania are less detailed than the others, it has been necessary to group certain types of companies together. The author has regrouped his own figures for New Jersey and those of Dr. Blandi for Maryland to obtain comparable data.

APPENDIX II

New Jersey General Incorporation Laws: 1786–1875

Nonbusiness Corporations

An act to incorporate certain persons as trustees in every religious society or congregation in this state, for transacting the temporal concerns thereof. (March 16, 1786). *N. J. Laws,* 10 sess., 2 sit. (1786), Ch. 129, p. 255

An act to incorporate societies for the promotion of learning. (November 27, 1794). *N. J. Laws,* 19 sess., 1 sit. (1794), Ch. 499, p. 950.

An act to incorporate trustees of religious societies. (June 13, 1799). *N. J. Laws,* 23 sess., 3 sit. (1799), Ch. 816, p. 572.

An act to incorporate benevolent and charitable associations. (March 12, 1844). *N. J. Laws,* 68 sess., 2 sit. (1844), p. 197.

An act to authorize the formation of societies for the protection of property. (March 13, 1851). *N. J. Laws,* 1851, p. 243.

An act authorizing the incorporation of rural cemetery associations. (March 14, 1851). *N. J. Laws,* 1851, p. 254.

An act to incorporate benevolent and charitable associations. (March 9, 1853). *N. J. Laws,* 1853, Ch. 134, p. 355.

An act to incorporate companies to erect buildings for the use of lyceums, public libraries, scientific, charitable, and benevolent associations. (March 17, 1854). *N. J. Laws,* 1854, Ch. 186, p. 448.

Business Corporations

An act relative to incorporations for manufacturing purposes. (February 9, 1816). *N. J. Laws,* 40 sess., 2 sit. (1816, public), p. 17.

An act to authorize the establishment, and to prescribe the duties of manufacturing companies. (February 25, 1846). *N. J. Laws,* 1846, p. 64.

An act to encourage the establishment of mutual savings associations. (March 4, 1847). *N. J. Laws,* 1847, p. 172.

An act to encourage the establishment of mutual loan and building associations. (February 28, 1849). *N. J. Laws,* 1849, p. 227.

An act to authorize the establishment, and to prescribe the duties of companies for manufacturing and other purposes. (March 2, 1849). *N. J. Laws,* 1849, p. 300.

An act to authorize the business of banking. (February 27, 1850). *N. J. Laws,* 1850, p. 140.

An act incorporating homestead and building companies. (February 25, 1852). *N. J. Laws,* 1852, Ch. 41, p. 83.

An act authorizing the incorporation of plank road companies. (February 26, 1852). *N. J. Laws,* 1852, Ch. 51, p. 95.

An act to provide for the incorporation of insurance companies. (March 10, 1852). *N. J. Laws,* 1852, Ch. 74, p. 159.

An act to incorporate telegraph companies. (March 5, 1853). *N. J. Laws,* 1853, Ch. 122, p. 304.

An act for the incorporation of companies to navigate lakes, ocean, and inland waters. (March 17, 1854). *N. J Laws,* 1854, Ch. 201, p. 470.

An act incorporating vessel building associations. (April 5, 1855). *N. J. Laws,* 1855, Ch. 245, p. 706

An act to encourage the agricultural developments of the state, and enable persons of moderate means to become land holders, &c. (April 10, 1855). *N. J. Laws,* 1855, Ch. 256, p. 754.

An act to authorize the formation of associations to aid those who may wish to establish and carry on useful branches of industry in either of the counties of Mercer, Hunterdon, or Gloucester. (March 20, 1857). *N. J. Laws,* 1857, Ch. 130, p. 373.

An act to encourage and facilitate the improvement of lands in this state. (March 30, 1865). *N. J. Laws,* 1865, Ch. 379, p. 707.

An act to authorize and encourage the improvement of property in this state. (April 9, 1867). *N. J. Laws,* 1867, Ch. 378, p. 855.

An act to facilitate the formation of companies to dig and cut peat, stone and other articles. (March 31, 1869). *N. J. Laws,* 1869, Ch. 374, p. 1001.

An act to authorize the formation of railroad corporations and regulate the same. (April 2, 1873). *N. J. Laws,* 1873, Ch. 413, p. 88.

An act to authorize the establishment and to prescribe the duties of corporations for manufacturing and selling gas in any of the cities and towns of this state. (March 27, 1874). *N. J. Laws,* 1874, Ch. 509, p. 124.

An act to incorporate building companies. (April 9, 1875). *N. J. Laws,* 1875, Ch. 379, p. 85.

Bibliography

OFFICIAL PUBLICATIONS

Massachusetts. *Official Report of the Debates and Proceedings in the State Convention, Assembled May 4th, 1853, to Revise and Amend the Constitution of the Commonwealth of Massachusetts,* 3 vols. Boston, 1853.

New Jersey. *Acts of the —th General Assembly of the State of New Jersey . . .* 1776–1876. [Titles vary.] (Cited as *N. J. Laws.*)

In referring to any New Jersey law passed between 1776 and 1844, inclusive, it has been necessary for complete identification to indicate the legislative session, the sitting, and the year during which the law was passed. The reason is that, previous to the adoption of the 1844 constitution, the acts of the legislature were published as session laws and not as annual laws. Each session of the legislature commenced its work at a first sitting held in October and usually reconvened at a second sitting in January of the following year.

Beginning in 1845, each session of the legislature met for the first time in January, and the work of the session was completed by March or April of the same year.

From the 36th Session (1811–1812) to the 48th Session (1823), inclusive, and in 1875, a distinction was made in the statute books between Public Acts and Private Acts, each group having a separate pagination. In citations of laws passed during those years, the group in which they are to be found has been indicated.

Laws passed between 1776 and 1809, inclusive, and between 1852 and 1876, inclusive, were assigned chapter numbers when they were published. The chapter numbers have been given in the footnote references, and, since the chapters were not always arranged in the statute books in strict numerical order, page references have also been given to aid in locating the laws. Acts passed between 1810 and 1851, inclusive, were not given chapter numbers in the statute books

The page numbers given in all references to the New Jersey laws indicate where the titles of the laws referred to are to be found.

New Jersey. Samuel Allinson, editor, *Acts of the General Assembly of the Province of New-Jersey . . .*

New Jersey. *Appendix to the House Journal.* 1852–1861. [Titles vary.]

New Jersey. *Documents of the —th Legislature of the State of New Jersey . . .* 1862–1876 and 1883. [Titles vary.] (Cited as *Legislative Documents.*)

New Jersey. *Journal of the Proceedings of the Convention to Form a Constitution for the Government of the State of New Jersey . . .* Trenton, 1844. (Cited as *Journal of the Proceedings.*)

New Jersey. *Journal of the Proceedings of the Legislative Council of the State of New Jersey . . .* 1776–1844. (Cited as *Journal of the Legislative Council.*)

New Jersey. *Journal of the Proceedings of the —th Senate of the State of New Jersey . . .* 1845–1875. [Titles vary.] (Cited as *Journal of the Senate.*)

New Jersey. *Report of the Committee of Council, on the Proposed Alteration of the Constitution of the State of New Jersey.* Trenton, 1841.

New Jersey. *Reports of a Majority and Minority of Committee, appointed to investigate into the Charge of attempting to bribe one of the members of the House of Assembly, to vote for the Re-Charter of Certain Banks.* Trenton, 1855.

New Jersey. *Revised Statutes of the State of New Jersey.* 1875.

New Jersey. *Votes and Proceedings of the —th General Assembly of the State of New Jersey . . .* 1776–1875. [Titles vary.] (Cited as *Votes and Proceedings of the General Assembly.*)

New Jersey: Secretary of State. *Corporations of New Jersey: List of Certificates Filed in the Department of State from 1846 to 1891, inclusive.* Trenton, 1892.

New Jersey: State Revenue Department. John Hood, compiler, *Index of Titles of Corporations Chartered under General and Special Laws by the Legislature of New Jersey, between the Years 1693 and 1869, inclusive . . .* Trenton, 1st ed., 1870; 2nd ed., 1871. (Cited as *Index of Titles of Corporations.*)

New York. N. H. Carter, W. L. Stone, reporters, and M. T. C. Gould, stenographer, *Reports of the Proceedings and Debates of the Convention of 1821, Assembled for the Purpose of Amending the Constitution of the State of New-York . . .* Albany, 1821.

New York. S. Croswell and R. Sutton, reporters, *Debates and Proceedings in the New-York State Convention, for the Revision of the Constitution.* Albany, 1846.

New York. *Laws of the State of New York . . .* 1801–1875. [Titles vary.] (Cited as *N. Y. Laws.*)

New York. C. Z. Lincoln, editor, *Messages from the Governors . . .*, 11 vols. Albany, 1909.

New York. *Revised Statutes of the State of New-York.* 1827.

New York. E. F. Underhill, reporter, *Proceedings and Debates of the Constitutional Convention of the State of New York, Held in 1867 and 1868, in the City of Albany,* 5 vols., paged continuously. Albany, 1868.

United States. B. P. Poore, editor, *The Federal and State Constitutions, Colonial Charters, and other Organic Laws of the United States,* 2 vols., paged continuously. 2nd ed., Washington, 1878.

OTHER PUBLICATIONS

Abbott, C. C., "Corporations," in *Dictionary of American History.* New York, 1940.

—— *The Rise of the Business Corporation.* Ann Arbor (lithoprinted), 1936.

Angell, J. K., and Samuel Ames. *A Treatise on the Law of Private Corporations Aggregate.* 1st ed., Boston, 1832.

Blandi, J. G., *Maryland Business Corporations: 1783–1852.* The Johns Hopkins University Studies in Historical and Political Science, Series LII, No. 3. Baltimore, 1934.

Byrdsall, F., *The History of the Loco-Foco or Equal Rights Party, Its Movements, Conventions and Proceedings, with Short Characteristic Sketches of Its Prominent Men.* New York, 1842.

Callender, G. S., "The Early Transportation and Banking Enterprises of the States in Relation to the Growth of Corporations," *Quarterly Journal of Economics,* XVII (November 1902), 111–162.

Clokie, H. M., "New Jersey and the Confederation," in I. S. Kull, editor, *New Jersey: A History,* II, 537–556. New York, 1930.

Cole, A. H., editor. *Industrial and Commercial Correspondence of Alexander Hamilton.* Chicago, 1928.

Davis, J. S., *Essays in the Earlier History of American Corporations,* 2 vols., Harvard Economic Studies, No. 16. Cambridge, Mass., 1917.

Day, Clive. "The Early Development of the American Cotton Manufacture," *Quarterly Journal of Economics,* XXXIX (May 1925), 450–468.

Dewey, D. R., *State Banking Before the Civil War.* Washington, 1910.

Dodd, E. M., Jr., "The Evolution of Limited Liability in American Industry: Massachusetts," *Harvard Law Review*, LXI (September 1948), 1351–1379.

—— "The First Half Century of Statutory Regulation of Business Corporations in Massachusetts," *Harvard Legal Essays*. Cambridge, Mass., 1934.

Dougherty, J. H., *Constitutional History of the State of New York*. 2nd ed., New York, 1915.

Durrenberger, J. A., *Turnpikes: A Study of the Toll Road Movement in the Middle Atlantic States and Maryland*. Valdosta, Ga., 1931.

An Enquiry into the Propriety of Granting Charters of Incorporation for Manufacturing and Other Purposes, in South-Carolina: By One of the People. Charleston, 1845.

Evans, C. J., "Private Turnpikes and Bridges," *American Law Review*, L (July–August 1916), 527–535.

Evans, G. H., Jr., *Business Incorporations in the United States: 1800–1943*. National Bureau of Economic Research, No. 49. New York, 1948.

—— "The Early History of Preferred Stock in the United States," *American Economic Review*, XIX (March 1929), 43–58.

—— "Early Industrial Preferred Stocks in the United States," *Journal of Political Economy*, XL (April 1932), 227–243.

—— "Preferred Stock in the United States, 1850–1878," *American Economic Review*, XXI (March 1931), 56–62.

Fee, W. R., *The Transition from Aristocracy to Democracy in New Jersey: 1789–1829*. Somerville, N. J., 1933.

Griffith, William. *Eumenes: Being a collection of papers, written for the purpose of exhibiting some of the more prominent errors and omissions of the Constitution of New Jersey*. Trenton, 1799.

Gronert, T. G., "The Corporation in the State Constitutional Conventions of 1835–1860," *Proceedings of the Fifth Annual Convention of the Southwestern Political and Social Science Association*, 1924, pp. 78–96.

Hammond, Bray. "Free Banks and Corporations: The New York Free Banking Act of 1838," *Journal of Political Economy*, XLIV (April 1936), 184–209.

Handlin, Oscar, and Mary F. Handlin. *Commonwealth, A Study of the Role of Government in the American Economy: Massachusetts, 1774–1861*. New York, 1947.

—— "Origins of the American Business Corporation," *Journal of Economic History*, V (May 1945), 1–23.

Hartz, Louis. *Economic Policy and Democratic Thought: Pennsylvania, 1776–1860*. Cambridge, Mass., 1948.

Howard, S. E., "The Limited Partnership in New Jersey," *Journal of Business*, VII (October 1934), 296–317.

—— "Stockholders' Liability Under the New York Act of March 22, 1811," *Journal of Political Economy*, XLVI (August 1938), 499–514.

Kehl, Donald. "The Origin and Early Development of American Dividend Law," *Harvard Law Review*, LIII (November 1939), 36–67.

Kemmerer, D. L., "Banking," in *Dictionary of American History*. New York, 1940.

Kessler, W. C., "Incorporation in New England: A Statistical Study, 1800–1875," *Journal of Economic History*, VIII (May 1948), 43–62.

—— "A Statistical Study of the New York General Incorporation Act of 1811," *Journal of Political Economy*, XLVIII (December 1940), 877–882.

Knox, J. J., *A History of Banking in the United States*. New York, 1903.

Lane, W. J., *From Indian Trail to Iron Horse: Travel and Transportation in New Jersey, 1620–1860*. Princeton, 1939.

Larcom, R. C., *The Delaware Corporation*. Baltimore, 1937.

Livermore, Shaw. *Early American Land Companies: Their Influence on Corporate Development*. New York, 1939.

—— "Unlimited Liability in Early American Corporations," *Journal of Political Economy*, XLIII (October 1935), 674–687.

Memorial of the Convention of Delegates assembled at Trenton on the 22d of August 1827, on the subject of revising and amending the Constitution of New-Jersey. n.p., n.d.

Miller, William. "A Note on the History of Business Corporations in Pennsylvania, 1800–1860," *Quarterly Journal of Economics*, LV (November 1940), 150–160.

Mulford, I. S., *Civil and Political History of New Jersey*. Camden, 1848.

Muscalus, J. A., *The Use of Banking Enterprises in the Financing of Public Education, 1796–1866*. Philadelphia, 1945.

Sackett, W. E., *Modern Battles of Trenton*. Trenton, 1895.

Schlesinger, A. M., Jr. *The Age of Jackson*. Boston, 1945.

Smith, J. G., *The Development of Trust Companies in the United States*. New York, 1927.

Steffens, Lincoln. "New Jersey: A Traitor State," *McClure's Maga-*

zine, XXIV (April 1905), 649–664; XXV (May 1905), 41–55.

Stoke, H. W., "Economic Influences Upon the Corporation Laws of New Jersey," *Journal of Political Economy*, XXXVIII (October 1930), 551–579.

NEWSPAPERS AND PERIODICALS

(Dates indicate the issues examined in the preparation of the study.)

Emporium and True American (Trenton). 1829–1843.

The Federalist; New-Jersey Gazette (Trenton). 1798–1800.

The Federalist and New-Jersey State Gazette (Trenton). 1800–1802.

Hazard's United States Commercial and Statistical Register . . . (Philadelphia). Edited by Samuel Hazard. 1839–1842.

The Merchants' Magazine and Commercial Review (New York). Edited by Freeman Hunt. 1839–1868.

New-Jersey State Gazette (Trenton). 1799–1800.

State Gazette (Trenton). 1846–1849.

Trenton Emporium. 1827–1829.

Trenton Federalist. 1802–1818.

True American (Trenton). 1815–1828.

True American: Tri-Weekly Campaign Series (Trenton). August 28, 1838, to October 8, 1838.

Newark Daily Advertiser. 1844–1875.

Sentinel of Freedom [Titles vary] (Newark). 1816–1819 and 1846–1849.

MANUSCRIPTS

Tuttle, P. M., "History of Railroad Taxation in New Jersey," 1920. Harvard University Doctoral Thesis. Typewritten Manuscript in New Jersey State Library.

Petitions Submitted to the New Jersey Legislature. Filed by date in the Manuscript Collection of the New Jersey State Library:

1 dated March 15, 1796
2 dated October 26, 1810
2 dated November 1, 1810
2 dated 1811 [no day]
2 dated January 13, 1812.

LEGAL CASES

Black v. *The Delaware and Raritan Canal Company,* 24 New Jersey Equity, 455 (1873).
Leggett v. *The New Jersey Manufacturing and Banking Company,* 1 New Jersey Equity, 541 (1832).
Lucas v. *Pitney,* 27 New Jersey Law, 221 (1858).
President, Managers, and Company for Erecting a Bridge over the River Delaware at or near Trenton v. *Trenton City Bridge Company,* 13 New Jersey Equity, 46 (1860).
Scudder v. *Trenton Delaware Falls Company,* 1 New Jersey Equity, 694 (1832).
State, The Morris and Essex Railroad Company v. *Commissioner of Railroad Taxation,* 37 New Jersey Law, 228 (1874).
State, The Warren Railroad Company v. *Person,* 32 New Jersey Law, 134 (1866).
Story v. *Jersey City and Bergen Point Plank Road Company,* 16 New Jersey Equity, 13 (1863).
Stratton v. *Allen,* 16 New Jersey Equity, 229 (1863).
Taylor v. *Griswold,* 14 New Jersey Law, 224 (1834).
Zabriskie v. *The Hackensack and New York Railroad Company,* 18 New Jersey Equity, 178 (1867).

INDEX

Bei Fragen zur Produktsicherheit wenden Sie sich bitte an:
If you have any questions regarding product safety,
please contact:

Walter de Gruyter GmbH
Genthiner Straße 13
10785 Berlin
productsafety@degruyterbrill.com